Life and Death in the Balkans

For Madge, Una and Stella

Bato Tomašević

Life and Death in the Balkans

A Family Saga in a Century of Conflict

Hurst and Company, London

First published in the United Kingdom by
HURST Publishers Ltd,
41 Great Russell Street, London, WC1B 3PL
© Bato Tomašević, 2008
All rights reserved.
Printed in Serbia by Publicum, Belgrade

The right of Bato Tomašević to be
identified as the author of this volume
has been asserted by him in accordance with
the Copyright, Designs and Patents Act, 1988.

A catalogue data record for this volume is available
from the British Library.

ISBN 978-1-85065-913-6

www.hurstpub.co.uk

Contents

Acknowledgements

I should like to express my gratitude to those who have generously given their help and encouragement in the writing and publication of this book: my wife Madge Phillips Tomašević, who translated the manuscript from Serbo-Croatian into English and served as my long-suffering secretary in connection with the publication of the various language editions; Dr Dejan Djokić, Lecturer in Modern and Contemporary History, Goldsmiths College, University of London, who reviewed the manuscript and gave his professional opinion; the Hon. Anthony Monckton, who kindly read the manuscript and with his expert knowledge of the Balkans made many useful suggestions; my erudite publisher friend Martin Heller, who likewise read the manuscript and set me straight on a number of points; Mira Grujičić Popović, long-time editor-in-chief of Vuk Karadžić Publishing House, Belgrade, for her invaluable editorial assistance on Montenegrin matters; Gane Aleksić, who has been a much valued collaborator involved in the production of this and many other books.

My thanks are also due to my publisher, Michael Dwyer, for his wonderful encouragement and advice, to Maria Petalidou for her editorial work and the designer Fatima Jamadar.

Exeter, March 2008   BATO TOMAŠEVIĆ

Pronunciation Guide

The language known as Serbo-Croatian (now Bosnian, Croatian, Montenegrin, Serbian) is a phonetic, 'read-as-you-write' language, in which each of the 30 letters corresponds to only one sound. Two scripts are in use: Latin and Cyrillic.

Vowels are 'pure':

A   as in 'mat'; E as in 'egg'; I as 'ee' in 'see'; O as in 'on'; U as 'oo' in 'shoot'.

The following letters differ from English:

C   as 'ts' in 'fits'

Č   as 'ch' in 'church', very close to Ć

Ć   as 'tch' in 'witch'

Dž   as 'dg' in 'judge', very close to Đ

Đ   or Dj as G in George

J   as 'y' in 'yes'

Lj   as 'lli' in 'million'

Nj   as 'ni' in 'onion'

R   is rolled as in Scottish 'kirk'

Š   as in 'sugar'

Ž   'zh' like the 's' in 'pleasure

Map

AUSTRIA

ITALY

Ljubljana

SLOVENIA

Trieste

Rijeka

Zadar

Split

Adriatic

Sea

N

0   200
       km

Danube (Duna) R.

Drava R.

HUNGARY

Zagreb

CROATIA

Sava R.

Osijek

Bihać

Banja Luka

BOSNIA-
HERCEGOVINA

Sarajevo

Mostar

Dubrovnik

VOJVODINA

Novi Sad

Belgrade

Danube R.

SERBIA

Niš

Pljevlja

MONTENEGRO

Nikšić

Kotor

Cetinje

Podgorica

Bar

Shkodra
(Skadar)

Tirana

ALBANIA

ROMANIA

BULGARIA

Priština

KOSOVO

Prizren

Skopje

MACEDONIA

Ohrid

GREECE

Map   ix

They rose to where their sovran eagle sails,
They kept their faith, their freedom, on the height,
Chaste, frugal, savage, armed by day and night
Against the Turk; whose inroad nowhere scales
Their headlong passes, but his footstep fails,
And red with blood the Crescent reels from fight
Before their dauntless hundreds, in prone flight
By thousands down the crags and through the vales.
O smallest among peoples! rough rock-throne
Of Freedom! warriors beating back the swarm
Of Turkish Islam for five hundred years,
Great Tsernagora! never since thine own
Black ridges drew the cloud and brake the storm
Has breathed a race of mightier mountaineers.

Montenegro by Alfred, Lord Tennyson

Preface

In some fortunate parts of the world, a hundred years may pass without their inhabitants experiencing war. The Balkans is not one of these. Between us, my grandfather, father and I lived through seven wars, at the last count – there may be more to come. This narrative records the story of my Montenegrin family from the latter part of the nineteenth century, when my grandfather fought the Turks, down to the bombing of Belgrade in 1999 and the fall of Milošević and his delivery to The Hague in 2002. Though these events may appear quite unrelated, by delving into the history of the ever-turbulent Balkans it is not hard to find a connection: the conflict between East and West, which has so often erupted on this territory where Europe meets Asia. Over the past two millennia this conflict has taken various forms: Roman Catholicism against Eastern Orthodoxy; Christianity against Islam; western-style democracy against Soviet-style communism.

The land that was Yugoslavia, occupying the central area of the Balkans, was always on the front line: for five centuries the Turkish frontier ran through it, shifting with the rise and decline of the Ottoman Empire. Even little Montenegro (Crna Gora, 'Black Mountain'), tucked away in the mountains, was never at peace. At Yalta in 1945, the Allies agreed to split Yugoslavia fifty-fifty.

By recounting the destinies of relatives, friends and chance acquaintances who were participants in or witnesses of the many wars and political upheavals, I have tried to show how people, regardless of nationality, behave in different situations in which they find themselves, often involuntarily. My aim was not to write history, though historical events are, I believe, accurately presented, but to indicate how all that has happened in former Yugoslavia in the past decade or so has its roots in the past. This family saga of life in the Balkans, it is hoped, may give readers a deeper insight into the historical background and mentality of its peoples, perhaps even help to clarify the tragic events that marred the end of the second millennium.

The greater part of the book deals, naturally enough, with my own life, which has not been devoid of dramatic incident: living in the Balkans is rarely dull. Perhaps influenced by the Montenegrin tradition of oral history and story-telling, at which my father was so gifted, I have presented many events through dialogue, remembered or, occasionally, recreated from hearsay, but though there are episodes that may read like fiction, nothing is invented or exaggerated. There was no need.

The problem, rather, has been the abundance of material and deciding what to leave out, for my family, in one way or another, played an active role in the stormy history of Montenegro, Kosovo, and what was Yugoslavia under King Alexander and President Tito. If there is an over-emphasis on warfare, invasions, flights of refugees and human suffering, it is because history repeats itself, and in the Balkans always as tragedy.

Tales of Warriors

My earliest memory is connected with a dramatic event in 1934. In my mind's eye I can still see the big, muddy yard of our house in Mitrovica in the province of Kosovo. All around it is a tall wooden fence of sharp-pointed stakes, to stop any Albanian getting in.

My mother rushes out of the house, waving her arms and calling to the neighbours in a terrified voice: "They've killed the King! They've killed the King!"

Frightened by the tone rather than the actual meaning of the words, which I don't understand, I run to my mother, who stands there weeping and beating her breast with crossed arms. Other women, followed by children, come running out of nearby houses, calling to one another in panic. I don't know what's going on, but I feel threatened by something terrible that's about to happen.

Above our heads there's a strange noise. In the sky over Mitrovica a biplane appears, circles around dropping pieces of paper that flutter slowly to the ground, and vanishes. Indelibly fixed for all time is the memory of my mother's face, tears streaming down her cheeks, and the feeling of utter amazement at my first sight of an airplane…

The assassination of King Alexander of Yugoslavia in Marseille on 9 October 1934, during a state visit to France, was mostly mourned by the Serbs and Montenegrins. Alexander was the son of Peter I Karadjordjević of Serbia and Zorka, a princess of the Montenegrin Petrović dynasty. To achieve the unification of the South Slavs under the crown of Serbia, the largest nation, King Nikola of Montenegro, Alexander's maternal grandfather, had been compelled in November 1918 to abdicate in favour of his son-in-law.

The dream of a united South Slav state (Yugoslavia) was cherished not only by Serbs and Montenegrins, who already had their own independent kingdoms, but by the South Slav Croats and Slovenes, who had lived for centuries within the Austro-Hungarian Empire. The new state, at first called the Kingdom of Serbs, Croats and Slovenes, was proclaimed in Belgrade in December 1918.

The victors in the First World War whose leaders gathered at Versailles to redraw the map of Europe gave their approval, believing that a strong and populous state in the ever-turbulent Balkans, the proverbial 'powder keg', would foster peace and stability in the region. What is more, it could usefully serve as a buffer against Lenin's Bolshevik Russia and the westward spread of communist revolution: it had already reached neighbouring Hungary, where Bela Kun proclaimed the 'Hungarian Soviet Republic'.

The new state was also expected to reconcile the three religions on its territory: Orthodox, Catholic and Moslem, whose adherents spoke the same language in several variants, or similar languages, but who differed in many ways because of their diverse historical, cultural and economic backgrounds. In addition, the boundaries confirmed at Versailles included within the state sizeable populations of some non-Slav nations: Albanians, Hungarians and Germans.

Problems soon beset the new state created under the wing of Serbia, which had played a heroic role in the First World War. The Serbs, by far the most numerous of the South Slavs, regarded their wartime sacrifices and contribution to victory as their mandate to govern the other nations. Not surprisingly, Serbian rule, headed by King Alexander, who soon succeeded his father, Peter, was not popular among the Croats and Slovenes, nor, indeed, among the Macedonians. Following the defeat of Turkey in the First Balkan War (1912), Serbia had simply proclaimed these last to be Southern Serbs and its part of Macedonia to be Southern Serbia.

Alexander's death in Marseille struck the first blow at South Slav unity. The assassination was prepared by the Ustashas, a Croatian emigrant organisation, with the support of Italy and Hungary, both with territorial aspirations towards Yugoslavia.

My father was a fervent Yugoslav patriot and royalist, ever ready, if need be, to die for king and country. In our house in Kosovska Mitrovica, the only picture on the wall, apart from the family icon of the Holy Archangel Michael, was a portrait of King Alexander with Queen Maria, a Romanian princess, and their three sons, Petar, Tomislav and Andrej. Their names symbolised the union of the three eponymous nations of the new kingdom: Petar (Peter) is a common name in Serbia and Montenegro, Tomislav in Croatia and Andrej in Slovenia.

Because of his support for the new state, my father was at odds with many of his fellow countrymen who were strongly opposed to little Montenegro losing its statehood for the sake of some higher South Slav ideal. They wanted to preserve the freedom and independence for which their ancestors had fought continuously for centuries, while the Serbs, Greeks, Bulgarians, Romanians and other Balkan peoples had been subjects of the Ottoman Empire. Montenegro saw itself as a bastion of Christianity, an island in the sea of Mohammedanism which had twice threatened even mighty Vienna, metropolis of the Austro-Hungarian Empire. Many Montenegrins therefore mourned for their last ruler, the aged King Nikola, known as 'the father-in-law of Europe', since he had succeeded in marrying most of his nine tall, slim and beautiful daughters to European rulers, princes and grand dukes. (Jelena became Queen of Italy, Zorka married the future King Peter I of Serbia; Milica and Anastasia were married to two Romanov Grand Dukes, brothers of the Russian Tsar; Anna married Prince Franz Joseph of Battenburg…).

Assassination of King Alexander Karadjordjević in Marseille, 1934

After his departure into exile, Nikola's modest little palace in his capital, Cetinje, was turned into a museum of the Petrović dynasty. Its furnishings, paintings, collection of arms and other exhibits show that by the end of the nineteenth century, pastoral, tribal Montenegro had already taken its first tentative steps into modern Europe.

Together with its statehood, Montenegro lost its military and political significance and soon began to decay and fracture. Many young men left to seek work in other parts of the new state or abroad.

Some sixty thousand Serbs and Montenegrins, my parents among them, responded to the patriotic appeals from Belgrade for the 'reconquest' of Kosovo, lost by the Serbian Empire after the famous battle of Kosovo Polje in 1389, in which most of the Serbian nobility were killed.

When my father and mother arrived in Kosovo in 1920, Mitrovica was a wild, backward little place of muddy streets with no drainage or sewage system, rife with disease and often ravaged by epidemics. In those early years in Mitrovica, these carried off my elder brothers Milan and Branko. Because of its location, the little town was chosen as the first stop and foothold for further penetration into Kosovo and the regaining of 'sacred Serbian land', now mainly inhabited by ethnic Albanians. The Montenegrin 'colonists', as they were called, also encountered a smaller Turkish population, families who had remained after the Turkish withdrawal. They regarded both Albanians and Turks, 'people of an alien faith', as their enemies.

The Orthodox Christian newcomers were much heartened to find a small number of their fellow Orthodox Serbs, the 'old inhabitants' of Kosovo, who had managed throughout five hundred years of Ottoman rule to maintain their language, faith and customs. They had also kept alive the memory of Serbia's medieval power and glory, the legends of bygone heroes and victories, and of the greatest defeat in Serbia's long history – the battle of Kosovo Polje, fought on St Vitus' Day (Vidovdan), 28 June 1389. It was not by chance that five centuries later, in 1914, a group of Bosnian Serbs chose this day to assassinate Archduke Franz Ferdinand of Austria in the city of Sarajevo. It was this act that triggered the First World War, the disintegration of the Austro-Hungarian Empire and the creation of new states in Europe, among them the Kingdom of Serbs, Croats and Slovenes.

Life in Kosovo at that time was far from easy and by no means safe. For this reason, soon after their arrival my father and mother brought from Montenegro their parents, brothers and sisters and other relatives, so that at the time of my birth, in 1929, there were twenty-three adult members of the two families, Tomašević and Rajković, living in Kosovo. This meant, as they used to say, 'twenty-three rifles, and three times as many pistols'.

Tomašević family portrait taken in 1936. Bato stands next to his father; in the back row (l. to r.) Duško, Ljuba, cousin Gina, Stana; in front: Nada with the dog and Aco

My father, like all the colonists, firmly believed that all the land in Kosovo should be taken from the Albanians and given to the Serbs and Montenegrins, justifying this on the grounds of the 'sacred Serbian right' to this territory. He threw himself wholeheartedly into the campaign to resettle the province, writing letters to all parts of Montenegro urging relatives and friends to "come down from the wild mountains, leave behind your goats and miserable life, and join in the reconquest of Serbian Kosovo". In his letters Father mentioned how much arable land each family could get and other benefits: favourable bank loans for building a house and buying livestock, horses, tools… What he did not dwell on in his letters was the fact that this land was in the hands of Albanians, from whom it had to be taken, sometimes by force. The arrival in Kosovo of the Montenegrin highlanders with their military traditions was announced by rifle fire and, sometimes, by massacres of the Albanian inhabitants whose land they were seizing.

In the eyes of the Montenegrins and Serbs, the Albanians were a remnant of the defeated enemy, Turkey, so they felt morally justified in treating them as they would the Turks. After all, they used to say, the Albanians were brought here by the Turks, after the downfall of the Serbian Empire, to settle on Serbian land, and adopted the Turkish faith and customs.

The Albanians, however, believe that they lived in Kosovo many centuries before the Serbs arrived. They consider themselves to be descendants of the Illyrians, an ancient people who once inhabited the entire eastern Adriatic region from the Alps to present-day Albania. For several centuries the Illyrian tribes successfully resisted Roman penetration of the eastern Adriatic seaboard, until the famous battle near Nesactium (just north of present-day Pula) in 177 B.C., when the defeated Illyrian king and his nobles committed collective suicide. As there is no decisive historical evidence as to who first settled in Kosovo, Serbs or Albanians, the dispute is insoluble and has remained a permanent source of ill-feeling between these two nations, not dissimilar in character or customs.

The conflict over land in Mitrovica and throughout Kosovo led to frequent bloodshed. The Montenegrins and Serbs had to travel in groups and take care not to wander alone into an Albanian village. Even an ordinary trip to market called for the utmost caution. After the war, a Mitrovica neighbour of ours recalled those days:

"I remember your mother, Milica, in her long black dress wearing a leather belt with two revolvers, one on either side. You young ones always kept close beside her. Our Montenegrin women could shoot two-handed, and heaven help anyone who tried to touch their children."

Before darkness fell, the men of the family would secure all the doors and windows, check all approaches to the house, and at bedtime hand out weapons to the able-bodied members of the household. In the morning these were collected and stashed away until nightfall. Every father considered it his duty to teach all his children, boys and girls alike, how to handle weapons. I remember how the crack of rifle shots echoed from all the courtyards as families practised their marksmanship. Even before I started school, Father had taught me how to shoot straight: "The day may come when your life will depend on it," he used to say.

In our courtyard there was an old pear tree which was always full of twittering birds, a favourite target of us children: we would compete as to who could shoot the most. They would all fly off when the firing began, but soon returned as there was a dung heap under the tree.

܀

The evenings when the members of our large family gathered together have stayed in my memory as the happiest times of my early childhood in Kosovo. After supper, our elders would sit around the long wooden table in the main room, while we young ones squatted down wherever we found floor space. Then the menfolk – my two grandfathers, my uncles and my father – would take it in turn to tell stories late into the night, until the children, one by one, fell asleep on the floor. The first, in order of seniority, was Grandpa Filip Tomašević. He often told us about the famous battle against the Turks at Grahovo, on the border of Montenegro and Herzegovina, in 1858. He would clear his throat, smooth his long white moustaches, and wait for his audience to quieten down before starting this oft-repeated tale.

"I had just turned fifteen when thirty thousand Turks under the command of the infamous Omer Pasha Latas attacked poor little Montenegro, which could hardly muster five thousand men. With my father and two brothers, only a bit older than myself, I set out for the rallying place from where we would march against the Turks. Mother, in tears, wrapped up some bread and dripping for each of us.

"Our forces were commanded by Prince Danilo. Knowing that with his hungry soldiers he could not withstand the mighty Turkish army, well fed and well armed, he resorted to cunning. He had us march back and forth on the hills around Grahovo dressed in various costumes and caps five or six times in the day. The Turks, observing us through their telescopes, were taken in and thought there were many different units numbering perhaps thirty thousand, like themselves.

"Knowing from earlier battles how brave and dangerous Montenegrins are, especially when they bring out their daggers, the Turks hesitated and kept their distance. That's why Prince Danilo decided to attack at night, so the enemy couldn't see how few of us there really were. Shouting at the tops of our voices, we rushed upon the sleeping Turks. They fought back for a while, and then turned and fled to save their lives, throwing away all their equipment as they ran. But we caught up with them and slaughtered several thousand of them. We captured several hundred alive. At dawn, when the battle ended, we cut off their ears and noses, saying: 'If ever you come back to Montenegro, we'll recognize you by this, and then we'll cut off your heads as well.'

"So these Turks, their heads wrapped up in bloody rags, went off to join the others who had got away. But the Turks were not bad fighters either: they cut down a lot of us, my father and my two brothers among them. Some relatives helped me to bury them and we said a prayer for their souls, as was the custom. Our victory at Grahovo was celebrated by all Christian peoples throughout Europe."

We children enjoyed hearing about the Montengrin victory, but not Grandpa Filip's graphic description of the long columns of Turks without ears and noses. Seeing our expressions of distaste, Grandpa Aleksa, my mother's father, would start his story in defence of the Montenegrins' cruel behaviour.

"Well, children, they did worse to us! One of my relatives who had become an outlaw was captured alive one day by a trick. The punishment for outlaws was either impaling or burning alive. The bloodthirsty Turkish commander, Haji Beg, decided he was to die by impaling on a stake, an even more painful death than Jesus suffered on the Cross. These stakes were smooth, covered with sheep's fat, fifteen centimetres wide and two metres long, with a sharp point at one end. The Turks were skilled at pushing this point up through the back passage to come out at the neck without piercing the stomach or the liver. They then fixed the stake in the ground and the man was left hanging there. According to a witness, it took three days for our relative to die. Ravens and other carrion birds flew down and attacked him, tearing off pieces of his living flesh and pecking out his eyes. So you see, children, they used to impale us alive on stakes, and we, as a rule, just cut them down with the sword in a Christian fashion so they didn't suffer."

But the most interesting stories for us were those about the battle of Kosovo, fought at the place known as Gazimestan only a few kilometres from our house. These recounted the heroic deeds of the Serbian nobles and knights, above all Miloš Obilić, who sacrificed himself for the Serbian cause. We heard about Miloš as often as other children hear about Little Red Riding Hood.

According to the legend, which every child knew by heart, the Serbian nobleman, seeing that the bigger Turkish army was beginning to get the upper hand, made his way with several companions to the tent of mighty Sultan Murat. His followers shouted to the Turks that Miloš wanted to kneel before Murat and bring his men over to the Turkish side. Permitted to enter the tent, Miloš, young and strong, bent low before Murat, as if to kiss his slipper in submission, then quick as a flash drew his dragger and slit the Sultan, as the folk song says, 'from his girdle to his white throat'. Miloš tried to escape in the confusion, but the Turks cut him down, together with his companions.

The news of Murat's death gave renewed strength to the tired Serbs and threw the Turks into disarray, but not for long. Murat's son, Bayezit, known as Lightning, arrived on the scene with a huge fresh army and took over command. Thirty thousand Serbs were left dead on the field. The Serbian leader, Tsar Lazar, was slain in the battle, and the once mighty Serbian Empire sank into darkness. That, at least, was the version of events passed down through the centuries and immortalised in folk songs and legends.

※

It was the custom among the Serbs and Montenegrins in Kosovo to make an annual pilgrimage to the battlefield to honour the shades of their ancestors. The Tomašević and Rajković families always took part in this national ritual. On Vidovdan, 28 June, families would gather at Gazimestan and light candles for the souls of the dead, vowing to avenge the Kosovo heroes and martyrs and restore the lost Kosovo to Serbia for ever. As the Turkish rulers were no longer there, this vow was now directed against the Moslem Albanians.

Before this annual pilgrimage, excitement in the family ran high. "To walk on the sacred ground, soaked in Serbian blood, is to be at the very centre of Serbian history, where our great empire vanished," my father used to declare.

The days before were filled with busy preparation. My mother would boil a large ham, bake cakes, wash and iron our best clothes, so that we would all be clean and tidy for the great occasion.

From a heavy wooden chest, Grandpa and Grandma would bring out their formal Montenegrin dress, worn only on special occasions: christenings, weddings, funerals, *slavas* (family saint's days) and, after moving to Kosovo, Vidovdan. Father would don his police dress uniform with gold braid and epaulets, and buckle on his short sword with a gilt sheath. Compared with Father's attire, Mother's clothes, a combination of traditional Montenegrin and city dress, seemed very modest. Tall and thin, with a black ankle-length skirt and a long black kerchief falling down her back and covering her hair, which was wound in braids round her head, she resembled the nuns of the nearby medieval convent of Gračanica.

It was still early morning when we all lined up in our big yard, waiting impatiently for the arrival of the cabs our father had ordered for the occasion. One of these, with two sleek black horses, he himself owned. On ordinary days the cabs carried passengers from the railway station to the army barracks or the town, since there were still no automobiles in Mitrovica at that time. The crowd awaiting the cabs included Mother's brothers Jovan and Marko, and Father's brothers Luka and Djuro, with their families, all dressed in their best.

Eventually, through clouds of dust raised by the horses' hooves, the shiny black cabs would appear. Father would usher each family into a cab together, warning the parents: "Don't let those children out of your sight. And watch out! You never know what's round the bend!"

What he had in mind, of course, was the possibility of an Albanian attack or ambush. When we were all seated, the cabs set off with the cracking of whips, drivers' curses and clatter of hooves for the two-hour drive along winding unpaved roads. We could scarcely see for the clouds of dust, but that didn't bother us. Eventually Father would give the signal to stop and suddenly an immense vista opened up before us: the gently rolling hills of the endless Kosovo plain (Kosovo Polje).

"Wait for us here and don't budge, is that clear?" Father would order the drivers in a stern voice. He then called upon the members of the two related families, by now numbering forty or so, to follow him on foot. From then on everything followed as if according to some tribal ritual. Father walked proudly, his head held high, a few metres in front of the rest of us, occasionally pausing to say or explain something, like a guide with a well-planned itinerary. His voice solemn and reverent, he would point to the great plain covered with large crimson peonies:

"Our people believe that the red peonies sprang up from the blood of the Serbian martyrs who fell on the field of Kosovo."

We children believed it too as we gazed at the vast crimson carpet of blooms.

"It is a well-known fact," he would add, "that this flower grows nowhere in the world except here on Kosovo Polje."

This assertion further impressed upon us the unique importance of the place and the events connected with it.

Father would go on to quote the great Montenegrin poet Njegoš, whose works he knew almost all by heart.

"*Neka bude borba neprestana…*" ("Let the struggle never cease…")

And when we came upon a flock of ravens, which were to be found in large numbers on this plain, Father used to stop, take from his shoulder the military rifle that he carried at all times, motion us to stand still, and fire in the direction of the birds. When their squawking had died down, he would turn towards us and explain, as if apologising for disturbing the silence of that sacred place:

"The ravens that fly over Kosovo Polje, our people say, are the souls of the Serbian traitors who are eternally damned for their treachery. If it hadn't been for the traitor Vuk Branković, who delayed his arrival on the battlefield, the Serbian Empire would today be bigger than the British."

Walking on Kosovo Polje was a solemn and moving experience, like attending the funeral of a much-loved member of the family.

The most dramatic event Father left for later:

"Here on this spot, mark it well, children, was Murat's tent, and from over there, from that direction, came the valiant Miloš Obilić with his knights, and after killing Sultan Murat he fled, cutting down all before him, in the direction of Tsar Lazar's tent over there."

After a short pause to allow our impressions to sink in, he continued:

"It was here that the Turks, accursed unbelievers, struck down Tsar Lazar, and further off the nine Jugović brothers fell, one by one, to the eternal sorrow of their grieving mother."

Then Father, like some Shakespearean player, would recite at length from the national epic ballads so much admired by Goethe, Byron and Pushkin, which brought the Serbs and their oral literature to the attention of Europe in the nineteenth century. These poems, the romanticised creation of a subjugated and humiliated people, gave a lengthy and detailed description of the battle and of the death of every prominent Serbian nobleman.

Father would end his moving account of these fateful events by recapitulating the history of the Serbs from their arrival in the Balkans in the seventh century down to the present day, addressing the grown-ups as well as the children:

"In the time of Tsar Dušan the Mighty, the Serbian Empire stretched from Belgrade to the Aegean Sea. Besides Serbian lands, it included Albania, Epirus and Thessaly, Macedonia and the coasts of the Adriatic and Ionian Seas, from the mouth of the Neretva river to the Gulf of Corinth. The Serbs were only a step away from capturing Constantinople and Dušan taking its throne. In mortal fear of this, the Byzantine emperor, Cantacuzene, called the Turks to help him against the Serbs, and by this treachery to the Holy Cross brought the Turks for the first time into Christian Europe. Not long after, on this sacred ground, we lost everything."

Scattered all around the area were other family groups led by fathers or grandfathers, all recounting the same stories.

After this discourse, rough army blankets would be spread out in a suitable spot and we would seat ourselves expectantly, while Mother and the aunts unpacked wicker baskets and handed round the food prepared for our picnic.

On the journey home, tired out from all the exertion and excitement of the day, we young ones, sitting on someone's lap, soon fell asleep. By the time we reached Mitrovica we were all wide awake again and as soon as we entered the house begged Father to go on with his story-telling:

"You didn't tell us about the Kosovo maiden who went around the battlefield comforting the wounded..."

This story was a particular favourite because of the maiden's great beauty, her large dark eyes and pearly teeth, as well as her goodness. How lucky the young knights were, we thought, that she was the one to come to their aid after the battle, bringing them wine to quench their thirst and holding their heads in her lovely white arms as they lay dying…

Father was a wonderful story-teller, in the tradition of his forebears, who lived in a society without books, except for the Bible, which few but the priests could read. As a boy he had listened to the tales of his father and other male relatives, who between them had lived through many battles and adventures. The cult of the battle of Kosovo had a profound influence on the behaviour and spiritual life of the Serbs and Montenegrins. Courage, pride and integrity were measured by the standard of the Kosovo heroes. For centuries the *guslars*, the bards who chanted the epic ballads, sawing away on the one-string fiddle (*gusle*), incited the Serbs and Montenegrins to revenge themselves on their conquerors. To slay Turks – in battle, in ambush, or wherever one encountered them – was the sworn aim and sacred duty of all generations from the battle of Kosovo down to the battle of Kumanovo (1912) and the expulsion of the Turks five hundred years later.

Another concept deeply rooted in the minds of Montenegrins was 'a life for a life'. The greatest misfortune was not to die fighting but to lose one's life without killing at least one adversary.

King Nikola
reviewing veterans of
the Russo-Turkish War
(1878) in which Bato's
grandfather fought,
Cetinje, 1910

"The more heads you take defending yourself in battle," people used to say, "the quieter you'll rest in your grave. He who fails to take a life for a life has died in vain."

Mount Lovćen was another object of veneration among the highlanders in Kosovo. Though Durmitor, rising to 2,552 metres, is the highest mountain in Montenegro, and there are many other peaks over 2,000 metres, Lovćen, only 1,750 metres, is specially revered as the burial place of Montenegro's prince-bishop (*vladika*) and greatest poet, Petar Petrović Njegoš. Eagles forever circled around his small mausoleum chapel perched on the very summit. Its peak visible from afar when approached from the Gulf of Kotor and the sea, Lovćen is the subject of countless songs, poems and stories, and served throughout history as a symbol of the people's free life and independence.

In 1482, Ivan Crnojević, ruler of Zeta, as Montenegro was then called, moved his seat from Žabljak on the fertile shores of Lake Skadar to the barren wilderness below Mount Lovćen, rather than surrender to the might of Ottoman Turkey. Here he founded the fortified settlement

14   Life and Death in the Balkans

he named Cetinje. For more than three centuries it was the seat of the ruling prince-bishops, who united religious and secular power and led the Montenegrins in their endless battles against the Ottoman Turks.

On the Kosovo plain, in dusty Mitrovica, the colonists cherished the memory of this high, clean mountain and celebrated it in song at every festive gathering. My father and his fellow countrymen in Kosovo had a kind of dual historical allegiance: to Kosovo and Serb nationalism on the one hand, but equally, if not more strongly, to Montenegro and its history.

"Remember, children," Father often said with pride, "that right down to 1878, the only free Slavs, apart from the Russians, were the Montenegrins. All the others – the Poles, Czechs, Slovaks, Bulgars, Serbs, Croats, Slovenes – were under Austria or Turkey. Only brave little Montenegro and great Russia carried the torch of freedom."

He would often recite passages from Njegoš – he knew nearly the whole of the epic 'Mountain Wreath' by heart – and translations of poems by Tennyson, Pushkin, Goethe and others praising the Montenegrins. Extolling the great qualities of his fellow-countrymen, he would quote the words of famous statesmen:

"The great Gladstone compared Montenegro to glorious Sparta and us to the heroes of Thermopylae. And he had good reason to do so. In the Russo-Turkish War of 1878, for instance, six thousand of our men died on the battlefield. The Turks managed to capture only one Montenegrin – and he was wounded. Our history is full of similar examples of heroism, like those of which great Homer sang."

"We Montenegrins," he would remind us, "are the tallest people in Europe." And since he himself could hardly be regarded as a good example, he added at once, "I'm a bit shorter than the others because I take after my mother's Italian side."

Cowardice had no place in stories about Montenegrins. If anyone took flight, it was always the enemy. A man who betrayed his fear in public would bring shame not only on himself but on all the members of his clan, who would never forgive this. He would have to move away, change his name and live out his life in an alien land.

Besides Lovćen and Montenegro, my father loved to talk about his native village, Bukovik, in the district known as Crmnica, up in the mountains above Lake Skadar, about his childhood and his wartime experiences. Through his stories we learnt about great historical events in the Balkans, battles and suffering, heroism and death. It was less important to survive than to die with honour, so that your name would be respected and your deeds recounted by posterity. "It's a pity to die in bed," people used to say.

Father always began stories about his childhood and youth in the same way. This repetition, which we never found tedious, was intended to teach us about his native region and make us feel close to our roots. He wanted us to form an abiding picture of the way of life our fore-fathers had led for centuries in that part of Montenegro which he and Mother had left to settle in Mitrovica.

"The story of my childhood," he would begin, "is almost no different from the one I heard from my father when I was a boy – the same story told by many earlier generations who lived and often, sad to say, died young in Montenegro. We lived in Crmnica and belong to the Crmnički clan. Crmnica is made up of a string of villages, rising one above the other, from Lake Skadar to the top of Mount Rasatovac. For centuries it stood on the border with Turkey. Whenever the Turks attacked, we were the first in their path. We're from Bukovik, the highest village: our house stands alone at the very top of it. From our terrace you can see the whole of Crmnica stretching down to Lake Skadar, and as far as the Albanian mountains. The Tomaševićs have lived there from time immemorial with just a few other families. The village never grew in size because most of the young men did not live long enough to marry and have children – they were cut down in battles and skirmishes."

After this introduction, he would launch into one of the exciting tales that we never tired of, perhaps about Taraboš, a battle between the Montenegrins and Turks in the First Balkan War, in which Father, then a lad of sixteen, was seriously wounded. He was left with a sizeable hole in his forehead as a lifelong reminder of his first experience of warfare.

"Taraboš, children, is a hill in Albania, west of Skadar, between the Bojana river and Lake Skadar. It had a strong Turkish fortification, at a height of 600 metres. The Coastal Regiment, which I belonged to, had been fighting to capture it for a full seven months. Montenegro entered this war in 1912 with 30,000 soldiers, and lost one in three – over 10,000 of her finest men, the flower of her manhood, none better in the whole wide world…

"Our Crmnica Battalion with a unit from each village kept attacking the Turkish trenches, which were protected by rows of barbed wire. We Montenegrins began this great war against Turkey, called the First Balkan War. Then Serbia, Greece and Bulgaria joined in on our side.

"The Turks were much better armed than we were, so that all our assaults were checked in front of the barbed wire and many of our relatives and friends were killed. The Montenegrin High Command had ordered that Taraboš must be captured at whatever cost. King Nikola personally came to the front with his guards to encourage us. Taraboš was also of great importance to Turkey, so it was defended by elite troops. They had to prevent the Montenegrins from taking it and so penetrating behind their lines and weakening the Turkish position in relation to the Serbian army. Spurred on by patriotic zeal, the Serbs were at that time sweeping all before them. One by one they took Macedonia, Kosovo, Metohija and the greater part of the Sandžak.

"We few lads of my own age from Bukovik kept together and waited for our turn to attack. Our commander, named Nikola like the king, had not yet sent us into battle, as if he wanted to save us for a few more days to gain a little strength before our weak arms had to wield a sabre. My friend Pero Popović spent every free moment practising sabre cuts. 'It's too heavy for us, Petar. A cudgel is more our style!' he used to lament.

"Sergeant Nikola at first used us for carrying messages during the fighting. We covered the distance between the units as fast as we could and dashed back with the replies.

"It was the close of day, I remember. The last rays of the sun were catching the Turkish trenches on the hill a hundred metres away from our position. We could clearly see their soldiers running forward and back, changing position, bring up more guns and ammunition. Several attempts to rush the trenches that day had ended in catastrophe. The no-man's-land between the Turkish and Montenegrin lines was covered with bodies of fighters from Crmnica. The wounded were dying without a murmur in our trenches. Now it was our unit's turn! I knew all the men well – several generations together, as there has always been, in all battles. We got into formation, thirty men in each line. In the front row, as a rule, were the strong young men in their twenties. They could run fast and had stamina, so that when they jumped into the enemy trench they would have enough strength left to struggle with and stab the young Turks who were waiting for them. Mitar Lukin, tall and powerful, heaved the machine-gun on to his shoulder. Now we were all quiet, looking at Sergeant Nikola. He, too, was silent, knowing that the fateful moment was near, before speaking the words customary at such times. 'Let us bid farewell, brothers!' he said in a solemn voice. 'Forgive each other for any wrong-doing and embrace. He who survives will have something to tell his children.'

"Then Nikola drew himself up and thundered in a quite different, military voice: 'Follow me, my heroes, brave Obilićes, for holy Kosovo…!'

"We set off at a run towards the Turkish trenches. Our neighbour, Ilija Radača, who happened to be beside me, shouted: 'Keep with me, Petar. We'll sink or swim together!'

"Paying no heed to those who fell around us, we reached the first line of barbed wire. There were several gaps in it from shells fired by our artillery during the day, and the strongest and most eager had already jumped through them. Shouting curses and insults, the rest of us followed and began attacking the Turks with our knives. Soon the survivors began scrambling out of the first trench and retreating to the one behind. Our men followed them, stabbing them in the back as they ran. Those that fell were slaughtered like sheep.

'Keep going, lads! Drive them out of the other trenches!' shouted Nikola.

"Elated by our success, by the fact that it was our unit that had made the breakthrough, we regrouped, drew our sabres and charged towards the next trench. Suddenly a terrible fusillade burst upon us, probably according to a plan prepared for such a contingency, and the Turks began jumping out of the trench and rushing at us. I kept running beside Radača, with Pero Popović on the other side. In a kind of daze I saw him raise his sabre to strike a Turk, but this one, older and more experienced, sidestepped and brought his sabre down on Pero's arm, sending the hand and sabre flying. With his hand cut off, Pero went on running with us. Then I saw our commander, Nikola, fall, and other people I knew in our unit. Just before the next barbed wire, our machine-gunner, Mitar Lukin, was cut down.

"Without our machine-gun and our commander, exhausted by all the running and fighting, the unit began spontaneously retreating to the trench we had just taken. The roll was called and survivors counted. A new commander was chosen: Ilija Radača. In our army, when a commander is killed in battle, he is replaced at once by another, as soon as a member of the unit calls out his name. Anyone can become the commander because all fighters in the unit are equal; we don't recognise that anyone is a better or braver soldier than the rest. Each man considers himself as good as those who lead him.

"Commander Radača was now obviously in need of the machine-gun left lying in front of the Turkish trench, beside the body of Mitar Lukin. He stood up, as if an idea had just struck him, and in a penetrating voice, so that all in the trench could hear, shouted: 'Whose mother bore the hero who will get that machine-gun by the wire? Without it there's no new attack, nor victory!'

" 'Here's my chance!' I said to myself, and before anyone else could move, I leapt to my feet and set off towards the Turkish trench. Hardly able to believe my luck, I reached the wire without a single bullet being fired. Was it possible they hadn't noticed me? I picked up the heavy machine-gun and was about to turn round and run back when I saw a Turk with his rifle raised taking aim at me. We couldn't have been more than twenty metres apart. Rooted to the spot, I could only stare at the barrel of the gun. I never heard the shot…

"In a fresh attack at dusk, the Crmnica unit captured the second Turkish trench. When Radača picked me up, he was certain I was dead: the Turk had shot me right in the forehead. Where the bullet passed and how I survived was never established because no doctor treated me or examined me later on. This hole in the middle of my forehead has stayed with me as a souvenir of my first battle.

"Oh, yes, one more thing," Father would add, seemingly as an afterthought. "I was awarded the Miloš Obilić Star with crossed swords. It was presented to me personally by King Nikola at a ceremonial parade in Cetinje, for bravery in action at Taraboš."

۶

The youngest of seven children, Petar was the only one who attended and completed elementary school. He was the only literate member of the family, and virtually the whole village. As such, he was in great demand for writing and reading letters, mostly for the relatives of peasants who had left home to seek work in America.

At the turn of the century, many young men from the Crmnica villages, the most capable and ambitious, set sail for the promised land, eager not just to make money but to see something of the world, to escape the monotonous life herding goats in the mountains and tilling the patches of land dug out of the rock or cut out of the hillsides, which were good only for potatoes and the Crmnica vines that gave the renowned purple Vranac wine.

One day in 1908, my father's five older brothers – the only sister had already died in early childhood – came to tell their parents that in a few days' time they would be sailing from the nearby port of Bar for Trieste and there find a cargo boat to America. Having no savings, they expected that, like many others before them, they would be able to work their passage.

In the weeks before their departure, there had been a lot of talk about America, about people from Crmnica who within a year or two had become their own masters and were now living a life of luxury with their American wives, about gold that was as plentiful as poppies in a cornfield, how newcomers found great nuggets of it and got rich overnight. There was no end to such stories, embroidered by a fertile Mediterranean imagination. In the long warm summer nights, the young men of Bukovik sat around at the threshing ground beside the little church, sometimes until dawn, discussing who was going to leave, when and with whom, which girl to propose to and marry before setting off. They all firmly promised and believed that they would send for their brides as soon as they managed to make a home and save enough money for the ticket.

Two months passed after the brothers announced they were leaving in a few days. Nothing more had been said, and the parents were hoping they had abandoned the idea, when one day they suddenly all appeared together, Luka, Vaso, Djuro, Savo and Jovo, to say goodbye. Each carried a knapsack on his shoulder with a change of clothing for when they arrived in America, a few tobacco leaves they had grown themselves and a little food. Tall and lean, they stood there before their parents bareheaded, as if in church.

"We shall all travel and keep together, look after one another, so there's no need to worry," Luka assured them.

Grandpa Filip, himself tall and thin, fair-haired, and tiny Grandma Stana had no choice but to accept the fact that their five fine sons, now of an age to get married and settle down, were suddenly setting off for far-away America and might never return. Their sole consolation must have been the hope that they would have a better life than in Bukovik, where no amount of labour could turn rocks into fertile soil.

Three years later a letter arrived with a photograph, reproduced in this book, showing four of the brothers. Jovo, the youngest of the five, was missing: perhaps sick or working in another place. They are seated in a row, all with neatly trimmed moustaches and smartly dressed in the kind of dark suits photographers used to hire out to their customers, with gold pens in their breast-pockets and gold watch-chains. The photo gives the impression of prosperous young men who have made good in the New World. The brief letter reported that they were working in a gold mine in Alaska and were all well, but there was no mention of sending money to their parents or returning home.

Stana used to spend long hours peering closely at the picture, trying to detect something in the faces that had previously escaped her notice.

She showed it around the village, eager to hear compliments on how handsome and prosperous her sons looked. At the same time she would ask those with sons in America for every scrap of news they had about life over there and whether, by any chance, there had been any mention of her own sons in the letters.

乀

Uncles of Bato Tomašević photographed in America, where they worked as miners, c. 1910

My grandmother, born Francesca Papani, came from a family of Italian origin. When she married, she left the mild coastal region where she had grown up and the peaceful, well-regulated life of her Catholic family for the hardships and hazards of life in the wild, rocky Montenegrin highlands with their clan traditions and Orthodox faith. As the first and only Catholic in Bukovik, she was always regarded as an outsider. In order to be accepted, she agreed to change her name from Francesca to Stana, a very common name which the Crmnica peasants usually gave to the second daughter born in a family, in the hope that the next child would be a boy, since 'Stana' meant 'stop'!

She had to forget her Italian, which anyway she had no opportunity to use in Crmnica, and adopt her husband's religion. In short, by marrying Filip she was deprived of her name, her faith and her mother tongue. How and why she came to marry him always remained a mystery.

I can still picture Grandma Stana, tiny, thin, dark-eyed, and the tidy room in which she and Grandpa Filip lived in our house in Mitrovica. In memory, it was always pervaded with the scent of the ripe quinces she kept on an old cupboard, together with jars of compote and honey biscuits. As a small child I loved to go into this warm, sweet-smelling room, sure that Grandma would always welcome me with open arms, cuddle me, sing me songs in Italian and give me something sweet. My father was the only son who took after her in face and stature; all the others were more like Grandpa.

※

Neither my father nor Pero Popović fought in the Second Balkan War of 1913, waged by Serbia, Greece and Montenegro against their former ally, Bulgaria, over the division of Macedonia: Pero had lost his hand and my father was still recovering from his head wound. They therefore missed the triumphant entry into Skadar (Shkodra) by troops of the victorious Serbian and Montenegrin armies.

Both countries emerged from the Balkan wars considerably enlarged. Elated by its victories, Serbia had visions of regaining or even surpassing its medieval glory in the reign of Dušan the Mighty. Its hope of gaining control over Bosnia and Herzegovina, which besides Orthodox Serbs was populated by Catholic Croats and Moslems, had been dashed in 1908 by Austria's annexation of these territories. On the other hand, a strong Serbia represented a major obstacle to Austria and Germany, ambitious of extending their influence eastward. Germany's dream of building a Baghdad-Berlin railway and gaining direct access to the Middle Eastern oil fields would never be feasible while Serbia controlled the central Balkans. Austria, moreover, was alarmed that the Serbs' victories in the Balkan wars would unsettle the Slav nations within its rambling multi-national empire, turn them towards Serbia and intensify their separatist aspirations. This applied, above all, to the Serbs who for several centuries had been living in the Lika, Banija and Kordun regions of what is now Croatia. These formed the Vojna krajina (*Cordon militaire*), which had been Austria's main bulwark against Turkish attacks and the westward spread of Islam. The train of events that would eventually, at horrendous cost to mankind, resolve this conflict of interests was set in motion in Sarajevo.

In this cosmopolitan Bosnian city on the Miljacka river, people of different faiths and nationalities had lived together harmoniously for centuries. Unwisely and provocatively, in view of the tense state of Austro-Serbian relations, an official visit to Sarajevo by Archduke Franz Ferdinand, heir to the Austro-Hungarian throne, was arranged for 28 June 1914 – Vidovdan, the anniversary of the battle of Kosovo, with all its patriotic associations for the Serbs. The rest is history. The Archduke and his wife were shot dead in the street by a young Bosnian Serb nationalist, Gavrilo Princip. Austria accused the Serbian Government of complicity and issued an unacceptable ultimatum which Serbia, though still recovering from the Balkan wars, had no option but to reject. Austria declared war on Serbia. Germany, Turkey and Bulgaria took Austria's side, while Serbia was backed by France, Britain, Russia and Montenegro, later to be joined by Italy and the United States. The Great War had begun.

༄

Life in Bukovik, in the meantime, had resumed its usual uneventful course. Now recovered from his war wound, Petar, more interested in books than in tilling the soil, divided his time between helping his father and working in the office of the Crmnica Commune in Virpazar, a picturesque little place on the shore of Lake Skadar. Before dawn he would set off to walk the dozen kilometres downhill to the commune office. For a restless young man eager to learn and improve himself, the journey to and from Virpazar, though strenuous, was far preferable to working the land, cutting firewood and tending the livestock. Grandma Stana, in particular, encouraged Petar's ambitions, hoping that her youngest son would escape the hard life of the Crmnica peasant and become a government official. Petar was volatile and quick-tempered, ever ready to get into an argument or quarrel. In this respect, too, he was more like her Mediterranean kin than his father's family – quiet, self-sufficient people. Petar, on the contrary, constantly felt the need to prove himself to his family and neighbours, to take the lead. Grandma Stana, afraid that his temperament would get him into trouble in the village, perhaps even cost him his life, often urged him to leave: "If you stay here, you'll become one of those goatherds who spend their lives searching for lost kids in the wilderness, rescuing them from wolves."

Under her influence, he began to think of leaving Bukovik, family and friends and abandoning the life his ancestors had led for countless generations.

View of Lake Skadar. In the background, the Crmnica district, home of the Tomašević family

Love and War

When news reached Bukovik of the assassination of Franz Ferdinand by a Bosnian Serb, it was greeted with spontaneous celebration. The men took out their rifles, always kept clean, oiled and ready for action, and started firing into the air, as they always did on some joyful or momentous occasion. And while Europe anxiously followed the development of events in the hope that war might be averted, in the towns and villages of Serbia and Montenegro units of all the able-bodied men were being formed. The veterans of the two Balkan wars were preparing for a third, this time against a different enemy: the Austro-Hungarian Empire.

The border with Austria was only a few kilometres from Bukovik, on the seaward side of Mount Rasatovac. For several centuries most of the eastern Adriatic coast had been under the rule of the Venetian Republic, until its abolition by Napoleon. In 1815, at the Congress of Vienna, it was given to Austria. The only exception was the small town of Bar and a short stretch of coast down to Albania, which the Montenegrins had wrested from the Turks in 1878 following a famous siege. The massive fortress of Stari Bar with its Turkish garrison under Selim Beg held out for several months against the Montenegrin forces led by Prince (later King) Nikola. By the time they captured it, the great citadel, dating back to the early Middle Ages, had been reduced to ruins, but Montenegro had at last gained access to the Adriatic. Now the Montenegrins saw their chance to seize the rest of their natural coastline from Austria.

Awaiting developments, all the Bukovik men spent the next few days in front of the church, with the women coming from time to time to bring them bread and cheese before hurrying home to do the chores. This gathering gave every adult male a chance to have his say in public, declare himself, and once consensus was reached it would be binding for all. One by one the villagers rose to speak with patriotic fervour, citing examples of the heroic deeds of Montenegrins in earlier wars, the courage and sacrifices of members of his own family. As a rule, the speaker ended by calling upon those present to say whether anyone from the family of Radača, Bokan, Živković, Tomašević…had ever flinched in battle, yielded to the Turks, failed to acquit himself with the valour that had distinguished the family for centuries. "Well, then, do you think I'm any worse than my forefathers, that I'm not a branch of our proud family tree?"

With these rousing discourses stressing their warrior traditions they passed the time while waiting for news from Cetinje. It was brought by a military messenger who, after a roll on his drum, read the announcement that Montenegro, in support of Serbia, had declared war on Austria.

When the messenger finished reading and the meaning of the proclamation had sunk in, all the assembled peasants, as one man, reached for the pistols they always wore at their belt and began firing into the air. The mountains of Crmnica roared that day, and it was hard to tell whether it was the echoes of their own guns or the firing from other villages which had simultaneously received the news of Montenegro's entry into yet another war.

With around three hundred thousand inhabitants, the little kingdom could at best mobilise some thirty thousand men. This number may not have been of much military importance, but Montenegro's support gave a great boost to Serbia's morale: the news was greeted in Belgrade by the firing of cannon as well as the usual celebratory discharging of pistols and rifles by delighted soldiers and civilians.

By tradition, at such times all males fit to bear arms would get ready to set off with their unit without waiting to be conscripted. Drawn up in line in front of the church, they would listen to the rousing, patriotic sermons of the parish priests, who were generally themselves active combatants.

Among the mothers who came to see off their sons in front of the Bukovik church was Stana, clutching some food wrapped in a napkin so that her Petar would at least not die hungry, if die he must. Dressed like all the other Crmnica mothers in an ankle-length black skirt, a white silk blouse embroidered with gold thread under a black sleeveless bodice and a long black kerchief on her head, she stood motionless, her unwavering gaze on her youngest child. Since the departure of her older sons, her hopes and dreams had been centred on Petar, who might now be destined to fall in the first battle. All the mothers stood silent, as if turned to stone – an oft-repeated scene under those southern skies, where passions were quickly roused and blood spilt, where life was governed by harsh tribal laws, and women wore black for most of their lives, forever in mourning for a relative killed in some battle or dispute. A Montenegrin woman dressed in white only once in her life: on her wedding day.

Assassination of Archduke Franz Ferdinand of Austria and his wife Sophia by a Bosnian Serb nationalist, Gavrilo Princip (far right) in Sarajevo in 1914

The Bukovik unit, standing to attention, the mothers, wives and other assembled villagers were addressed by young Father Dobrković. In a thunderous voice he reminded all the fighters of their sacred duty to preserve the glory and heroic name the men of Crmnica had earned in past battles and wars:

"Anyone who dishonours our blood that has been shed, our good name and this holy cross from our church cannot be buried in this graveyard of ours by this church of ours, beside the bones of his ancestors. But he who dies with his head held high, not bending low to escape bullets or hiding from the blade of the sabre and bayonet, will be given a worthy funeral in this holy place, as befits the eagles of Crmnica, and his name will be spoken with pride by his descendants for all time!"

Dobrković then said a prayer in the Old Slavonic language used only by the Church, removed his epitrachelion, raised his rifle for all to see and, still in his cassock, joined the other soldiers in line.

The news that Serbia and Montenegro were at war quickly circled the globe. From America volunteers set out for home, eager to play their part in the fateful struggle for survival of these two small nations. They left behind the promised land, many abandoning good jobs and earnings, to make the long journey to the Balkan battlefields.

Six months had passed since the outbreak of war. With Petar somewhere at the front, Filip and Stana waited anxiously for any news, spending much of their time sitting on the terrace in front of the house, from where they could see all the Crmnica villages, Lake Skadar and as far as the snow-covered peaks of the Prokletije Mountains in Albania. As if expecting their long-lost sons to appear, day after day they scanned the immense panorama below them. They had begun to lose hope of ever seeing any of them again when one night, as they were getting ready for bed, Luka and Djuro burst into the house.

News of the war had reached the two of them working in a silver mine in Arizona. Other Montenegrin miners had set off at the same time, travelling in small groups and spending on the journey what money they had saved labouring long hours in the mines in the most arduous and hazardous conditions. Some succumbed on the way to sickness and various mishaps. In December 1915 some four hundred volunteers drowned when their boat was sunk by a mine off the Albanian harbour of Medes (San Giovanni di Medua), almost within sight of Montenegro.

Though their journey had taken three months, Luka and Djuro spent only one night at home. Next morning they set off in their thick miner's shirts to enrol at the military command post at Virpazar. From there they were sent straight to the front, where Luka suffered a serious head wound in his first action against the Austrians, which put an end to his part in the war.

A month later, Vaso, the handsomest of all the brothers, arrived at Bukovik. His parents begged him to spend a few days at home with them, to rest after his long journey. To their surprise, he readily agreed, though it seems, as my father later recounted, that this was less to please his parents than to see a girl he had left behind in a neighbouring village. She had waited patiently for him to send the promised ticket to America, but when time passed and there was no word from him, she had eventually married another young man. Now she was living with her parents-in-law, as was considered proper when a husband was away fighting.

The day after Vaso's return, some friends came to invite him to be the standard-bearer at a wedding, an unusual event in wartime. For this occasion Filip saddled up his horse, which he rarely rode, and when the young man mounted, "You couldn't imagine a finer sight," the villagers would recall long afterwards. "Vaso was as bonny as a golden apple, in his fine clothes on the prancing horse, holding high the proud flag of Montenegro."

Late that evening, friends brought home his body with a bullet hole in the head… What exactly happened at the wedding during the customary celebratory shooting into the air remained a mystery. When some guest raised his weapon, did his hand tremble or his horse stumble, so that the bullet took a lower trajectory? Or did someone take advantage of the general noise and commotion of the wedding celebration and the bursts of firing to settle an old, or new, score? When he died, whether by accident or design, Vaso was twenty-four.

About a month after Vaso's death, Stana was returning home from her daily visit to the graveyard as the sun was dropping behind Mount Rasatovac, bathing Bukovik's dozen or so scattered stone dwellings in crimson light. Climbing the winding path leading to her house, she came to a sudden stop: a man was sitting hunched up on the doorstep, his hands covering his face. At first she didn't recognise him, but she quickened her pace. Could it be…? Hearing her steps, the man raised his head and she cried out like a wounded creature:

"Savo, my son, my sorrow, what have they done to you in America?"

One glance at his sunken, feverish eyes and emaciated figure told her he was dying of tuberculosis.

"Wait here for your mother to bring you some warm milk. It's not long since I milked the cow. There's nothing better than milk for any illness. You must drink it every day to get your strength back. Any moment now your father will be back from the mountain with the flock. Get up, son, and come into the house. I'll bank up the fire so you'll be warm and comfortable."

At his mother's bidding Savo tried to stand, but his strength failed him. On the journey from America to the threshold of the family home he had used up the last ounce. Realising her son's desperate condition and seized by panic, Stana shouted to the neighbours for help. A few women and elderly men came hurrying over and together they carried Savo indoors. Stana spread out a blanket in front of the fire and they placed him on it. All night he lay there shaking, in a state of delirium, uttering only disconnected words. Next morning, as the sun rose, he breathed his last.

And so, within the space of a month, Stana and Filip buried two of their sons. Stana continued her daily visits to the graveyard, now carrying two candles with her. When she returned, she would again sit on the terrace until nightfall, hoping to discern in the distance the figure of her last missing son. But Jovo never returned home to fight, nor after the war. No news of his fate ever reached the family. There was speculation that he might have been robbed and murdered in some port on the journey from America to Montenegro. Perhaps he had been among the four hundred volunteers drowned when their vessel sank off the Albanian coast in December 1915…

Two years went by. The Great War had turned into a general slaughter of armies facing each other from their trenches along static fronts. Senseless attacks cost the lives of millions in the mud of Flanders and at Verdun. Few any longer saw the purpose of this mayhem except in Serbia and Montenegro, where the entire nations were united in defence of their invaded countries. In the first months of the war the Serbian army won two famous victories over the Austro-Hungarian forces, at Mount Cer and on the Kolubara river.

At dawn on 12 August 1914 the Second and Fifth Armies invaded Serbia, but the planned great military sweep was checked at Cer, with disastrous losses for the enemy. Austria-Hungary threw 200,000 men into this battle, against 180,000 Serbian troops. The Serbs had drawn up a tactical plan of operations which they now abruptly abandoned, and the whole army moved into a frontal attack. The enemy was driven back across the border in disarray, with 25,000 casualties and 5,000 taken prisoner. The Serbs lost 16,500 men in this battle.

The Austrian High Command, shocked by this debacle, made preparations for a fresh invasion with much larger forces. In mid December, five months after the battle of Cer, Serbia, which this time could deploy only 120,000 men, came up against an Austrian army of 300,000. The battle raged for a month along a front 200 kilometres, so that the numerically inferior Serbian army was fairly thinly stretched. The Serbian High Command again decided on a frontal assault on the Austro-Hungarian troops, choosing the section of the front along the Kolubara river and bringing up the elite Serbian cavalry. This fierce counter-attack completely broke the Austrian forces, driving them into rapid retreat before the determined Serbs and compelling them to withdraw once more from Serbian soil.

These two victories were greeted by Serbia's allies as a major contribution to the cause of the Entente.

When it declared war on Serbia after the assassination of Franz Ferdinand, Austria-Hungary expected to inflict swift punishment on its southern neighbour and, more important, eliminate the main obstacle to its Balkan ambitions. As events quickly proved, it had miscalculated by not taking into account the strong surge of patriotism among the Serbs following their military victories in the recent Balkan wars and their stubborn resistance when faced by the threat of invasion.

❦

With Germany's inclusion in the Balkan theatre of war and the Bulgarian attack 'from the rear' on the already exhausted and depleted Serbian army, the High Command decided to withdraw all its forces from Serbia and, with French and British help, cross to the Greek island of

Corfu, to rest, regroup and, above all, recover from the typhus epidemic that had struck not only the troops but the rest of the country.

The retreat of the Serbian army, accompanied by thousands of fleeing women and children, in the bitter winter weather of early 1915 has been called the 'Serbian Golgotha'. Besides blizzards, harsh terrain, hunger and disease, the retreating army was hampered by daily attacks from Albanians, who saw Serbia's growing might as a threat to national plans for a greater Albania. But the biggest obstacle was the concentration in Montenegro of Austrian forces preparing to cut off the Serbs' retreat.

The Montenegrin High Command undertook to secure the withdrawal and hold the Austrians, thus enabling the Serbs to pass through Albania to the Adriatic coast, where allied transport vessels were waiting for them. A major battle was fought between the Austrian and Montenegrin forces at Mojkovac, a small place at the entrance to the canyon of the Morača river. On hearing that the Serbian army would get through only with their help, the Montenegrin regular army and even the elderly, men and women alike, anyone who could be of any use, all made for Mojkovac.

Among the soldiers were Stana's sons, Petar and Djuro. With fixed bayonets, the Montenegrins checked the Austrians' attacks in desperate hand-to-hand fighting. For them this was still clan warfare, in which the fighters recognised and called out to one another, giving advice and encouragement. From one such attack Petar brought out his brother with a bayonet wound.

The great victory at Mojkovac which allowed the Serbian army to carry out its plan of withdrawal was greeted with exultation all over the country, but when the Serbs had gone the Montenegrins realised that they were left to fight alone.

From then on there was little cause for celebration. There was a growing awareness that times had changed and that the old saying: "The battle is won not by weapons but by the heart of a hero" was no longer true. A brave heart was not enough. The Austrian soldiers were out of sight, protected by their long-range guns, and the Montenegrins had no means of responding. The age of heroic feats and Homeric battles had gone forever. Now what counted was military technology, in which they had no skill and which anyway they did not possess.

For the first time in their five-hundred-year history, the Montenegrins signed an act of capitulation. Their soldiers, among them my father and other men from Bukovik, were taken into captivity.

❧

The Montenegrins could not passively resign themselves to the occupation. Resistance took the form of attacks on enemy check-points, patrols and soldiers, to which the Austrians responded by 'wiping out the rebels': villages were put to the torch, women and children marched off to camps, while men who were captured were publicly hanged.

One such camp was set up in Stari Bar, that same citadel which King Nikola had wrested from the Turks to gain an outlet on the Adriatic. Within its damaged but still mighty walls the Austrians incarcerated women and children from the mountain villages of Kuči, a wild, rocky region bordering on northern Albania. Its inhabitants, the Kuči clan, were famous even among the Montenegrins as intrepid warriors who had honed their fighting skills in frequent clashes with the Turks. For this reason, Austrian repressive measures were particularly severe in Kuči, where groups of guerrilla fighters (*komiti*) had formed immediately after the occupation. All the villages were depopulated so that the rebels would be deprived of any support in the form of food and weapons.

In one of the columns of women and children forced to walk for several days from Kuči to Stari Bar were my grandmother Jovana, my mother Milica, not yet sixteen, her three younger sisters and one brother. Amidst the ruins of the citadel, uninhabited since the siege of 1878, exposed to the biting winds sweeping down from Mount Rumija in the winter months, they spent the first year half-starved and without adequate clothing. They had no news of Grandpa Aleksa, who had fled into the hills with his two elder sons, Jovan and Marko, to fight the invader in the age-old guerrilla tradition of his ancestors.

In the Stari Bar camp the first to die were the old and weak. My mother's family somehow managed to survive the cold and hunger of that first year of internment. Then, suddenly, a fresh threat appeared: 'Spanish fever', a particularly virulent form of influenza.

"People began dying like flies," my mother recalled. "The Austrians sealed off the camp so that no one from outside could enter, and left us to our fate. When the number of dead grew, some strange-looking men appeared, wrapped up so you couldn't see their faces or their hands. They collected the bodies into heaps, poured quick lime on them and set them alight. You couldn't see the sky for the smoke from the burning corpses. The Spanish fever lasted for several weeks and hardly one third of the prisoners survived."

One day, when the epidemic appeared to be on the wane and it seemed to Jovana that her family had mercifully escaped the scourge, the dreaded symptoms appeared. Two of her daughters and her youngest son developed a high fever. Though Jovana knew full well that whoever was stricken in the camp was doomed, she still hoped against hope that God would spare her children, as He had preserved the righteous Noah during the Flood. Day and night she sought in vain for help, calling out in desperation for someone to save her dying children. But there was no response, let alone help, for all the inmates of the crowded houses and barracks had their own tragedies; many other mothers, like her, were calling for help, praying, and cursing their fate.

And so, one evening at twilight the bodies of three of her children were consumed by flames on one of the many pyres within the camp.

᷍

The Austrian authorities eventually decided to repair some of the ruined buildings in which the inmates lived by mending roofs and boarding up gaps in the walls to keep out the wind and rain. To carry out this work, one day they brought prisoners-of-war from a nearby camp. That day, as my father and mother often recalled, was when they first met. Father, then twenty-two years of age, happened to be assigned to repair the little house in which the surviving members of the Rajković family were living: Jovana, my mother Milica and her sister Mileva. Petar immediately took a liking to Milica, a tall, thin girl of eighteen. She, however, was not impressed by the young man, scarcely taller than herself – lack of height was regarded as serious defect in a Montenegrin – with a hole in his forehead, half-starved and dressed in a ragged uniform. But what did attract her from the very first was his animated and interesting way of talking, his eloquence and power of expression – a characteristic of 'Crmnica gentlefolk'.

The house repairs took several days, giving Milica and Petar time to get better acquainted. On the last day, on his insistence, they both vowed that, if they survived, on the very day the war ended they would meet in Novi Bar, only five kilometres away from Stari Bar and their camps. The meeting place was to be the home of Pero Popović, Petar's friend wounded at Taraboš, who had spent the war in a house close to Bar harbour.

⁊⁊

Half a year later, the great Austro-Hungarian Empire collapsed like a house of cards. In the first week of November 1918, all the camp ad-ministrators and guards vanished overnight, along with all the Austrian battalions and brigades in Montenegro, eager to get home as quickly as possible, to escape from the war, in which many had fought against their will, and perhaps most of all from the vengeance of the Montenegrins.

My mother and father reached Pero's home at almost the same time. Pero was overjoyed to see his friend alive and well. When they were all seated around the table for a meal, Petar took advantage of the presence of Pero, newly-married, and his bride to propose. In the warm, cheer-ful room in the company of the friendly young couple, enjoying her first hours of freedom after two years in the camp, Milica felt safe and happy. Without hesitation she accepted his proposal and the wedding was fixed for a few days later.

Petar and Milica moved in for a while with Pero, who had been their best-man (*kum*) and witness at the brief civil ceremony, so that the bond of friendship between the two young men was further strengthened.

Pero had managed to find occasional work in Bar harbour, where ships of the Allies, France and Britain, were now arriving daily, bringing aid for devastated Montenegro. Soon Petar joined him there, so the two were together all day and not only over supper, which the young wives prepared for them. My mother, who had never done any cooking before, did her best to learn from watching and copying her new friend without admitting her total ignorance.

Montenegro was free once more, but now found itself torn between two political options: independence or union with Serbia. The nation was split on whether the Kingdom of Montenegro, enlarged by the territory conquered in the Balkan wars, should be preserved and King Nikola recalled from exile to his palace in Cetinje, or whether the country should unite with Serbia under King Peter. As part of this enlarged kingdom, Montenegro would then enter into a new state created by unification with the South Slav lands, notably Croatia and Slovenia, that had been under Austria-Hungary. Prior to this, the South Slav leaders in these lands had expressed the desire of their people to join such a state, a decision welcomed by most of the Entente powers, anxious to see a strong, stable country in the heart of the turbulent Balkans.

It was natural that the leading role in the new state should go to Serbia, by far the largest of the South Slav nations, which had fought heroically in the war. After a period of recuperation on the island of Corfu, the Serbian army, with its French and British allies, had broken through on the Salonika front and fought its way back into Serbia. But the price of victory was appallingly high: the loss of over half its male population. Turkish power in the Balkans had now been replaced by the considerably enlarged Serbian state with its battle-hardened army.

On the hotly debated question of Montenegro's future, Pero and Petar were of one mind, favouring the creation of a single South Slav kingdom. There were many, however, particularly in the capital, Cetinje, and the surrounding region known as Old Montenegro, who wanted to preserve the country's sovereignty and the Petrović dynasty. They could not accept that five hundred years of history filled with battles, suffering and sacrifice, glorified in legends and folk poetry, should be swallowed up in a common state of the South Slavs, which, as they perceived, would suit the Serbian military and nationalist circles, intent on expanding Serbian territory with a share of the spoils of the defeated

Nicholas, King of
Montenegro

Austro-Hungarian monarchy. King Nikola's supporters claimed that the Montenegrin victory at Mojkovac had saved the Serbian Army from destruction. Had it not been for this battle, Serbia would have lost its army and shared the fate of Montenegro. The latter would, in fact, have been in a better position: thanks to its mountains it could have waged a guerrilla war, awaited the victory of the Allies as an armed force and independent state, and continued to exist as a kingdom.

The population was thus divided into the so-called Whites and Greens, the former in favour of the union, and the latter opposed to it. The Whites argued that the Montenegrins were Serbs, descended from those who had fled to the mountains after the defeat at Kosovo and later, to escape oppressive Turkish rule. They recalled that over the past few centuries Montenegrins had played a decisive role among the Serbs, instigating and fighting in many rebellions against the Turks in Serbia. The major insurrection in 1804, which encouraged other Balkan nations to rise against the Turkish occupiers, was led by Karadjordje ('Black George') Petrović, who was from Montenegro.

The aged King Nikola, who had gone into exile in Italy after the capitulation of his country in 1916, awaited the triumph of the Greens and his return to Cetinje. On the eve of the war, the tiny capital had been enlivened by the presence of twelve foreign legations, whose European life-style, manner of dress and behaviour served as a model for the better-off citizens. As early as 1888 Cetinje had its theatre, where the works of Shakespeare and other world classics were staged, as well as plays written by the Montenegrin ruler himself. The town had its high school (*gimnazija*), teacher-training school, music school… There were well-kept parks, tennis courts, clean and tidy streets. All this was now threatened, the Greens declared, for Cetinje's growing prosperity would be blighted if it were no longer the Montenegrin capital.

Kosovo: The Dream that Faded

Among those who celebrated the proclamation of the new Kingdom of Serbs, Croats and Slovenes (the Montenegrins and Macedonians were counted as Serbs) were the two inseparable friends, Pero and my father. They talked incessantly about the unification, for the first time in history, of the great family of South Slavs from the Alps to Albania, and rejoiced in the belief that these brotherly nations would never again be separated or conquered.

But their euphoria over the formation of the new state was soon to be dampened by the realities of everyday life and the need to earn a living. As the number of vessels docking at Bar diminished, there was no longer work in the port for Pero and Petar. For days they discussed their future prospects, what to do and where to go, without reaching any conclusion: to stay in Bar, where my eldest sister, Ljuba, had already been born, in the hope of finding other work, or return to the village – Petar had not been to Bukovik since the day his mother had seen him off to war for the second time.

One day, when he returned from Bar market, where he had met several men from Bukovik, Petar told Milica to pack their few belongings, for next morning some friends would be coming with horses to take them to the village.

At Bukovik word had already got round that Petar was returning and bringing his wife and daughter, so when they arrived the whole village had turned out to greet them. There were few men of my father's age, for during the last three wars many had fallen on the battlefield or, having left home, had then settled down elsewhere. The older men one by one raised their glasses of strong Crmnica *loza* in a welcoming toast, urging him to stay in Bukovik: "There's no better place than at home, among your own folk." Worried that only old people would be left, they hoped that Petar's return might bring back others who had survived the wars and were now roaming round the world.

In the evening, when the family was alone at last, the men seated themselves around the big hearth with a fire that was never allowed to go out. Grandfather Filip sat down first, then Luka, Djuro and finally Petar, in order of age, as was the custom. Grandma Stana and her daughters-in-law – Luka's wife, Maša, and my mother – stood to one side, against the wall, ready to serve the menfolk when they wanted something to eat or drink.

Filip then told his sons that there was no longer any reason to postpone the division of the house and land, since three of them were now at home, and when Jovo came back from America, the brothers could each give him a part. He and Stana needed only a small corner of the house; everything else should be shared among them in a brotherly fashion. While Filip was holding forth, his sons expressed their full agreement and the women kept silent. They were expected not to interfere in men's talk; they would hear what they needed to know from their husband, father or brother.

"That very first evening, I decided to change all that," my mother later recalled. "In Kuči, the women always sat as equals of the men. I made up my mind to do what was right and proper for myself and my children, not to respect and accept ways that didn't suit me. Straight away I told Maša, who was five years older, what I thought, and then Stana. Then, one evening, when the family was alone, I went over to the hearth and said to Petar: 'Move over, I want to sit down.' Nobody budged, but my brother-in-law Luka said: 'Just now we're discussing men's work.'

"'Men's or women's, it's all the same and affects all of us. If we women could push your cannon, carry ammunition and food, bandage your wounds, spend years, because of you, in Austrian camps, there should be no more separation into men's and women's business. Mark my words: if what I say doesn't suit you, tomorrow I'll take Ljuba and go straight back to my people in Kuči.'

"There was a deathly hush while everyone waited for Filip to speak. He was silent for a minute or two, thinking it over, and then to their amazement he said: 'Child, I think you're talking sense. We can't let you go back to Kuči alone with your little girl. From now on, sit where you want and say what you like, seeing as how times have changed.' "

From that time on, as Mother recalled, the women had an equal say in all discussions and decisions concerning the household, land and children.

Not long after, my parents' second daughter was born and named Stana after her grandmother, and probably also in the hope that this would put a stop to the birth of girls. Though the safe delivery of the child was a matter for rejoicing, there was a certain disappointment that the new baby was not the male heir every Montenegrin father longed for. Grandma Stana consoled her young daughter-in-law, assuring her that the third child was bound to be a boy, who should be named Dušan after the great ruler of the Serbian Empire.

Life in Bukovik followed its quiet, slow pace. Luka and Djuro, much better suited to farming than my father, did most of the field work to spare their physically weaker brother.

But after his wartime experiences and stay in Bar, Petar could not settle down in Bukovik to a life of tending livestock and tilling the land. It seemed to him that he had outgrown this, that his future lay elsewhere, though in which direction was not yet clear. The answer came in the form of a challenge that the restless and ambitious young man of twenty-four could not resist.

Faced with religious and national problems, difficulties in organising the new state, high unemployment and dissatisfaction among demobilised soldiers, in 1920 the Belgrade Government issued a patriotic call to these young men: "Forward to Serbian Kosovo!"

As the Government expected, it evoked the biggest response in Serbia and Montenegro, where veterans like my father saw this as the solution of their existential problems so often promised them during the war.

An act on the settlement of the newly conquered territory in Kosovo, Metohija and Macedonia had been passed by the Serbian Government back in 1914, at the end of the Balkan wars, but the outbreak of the First World War soon after had stopped its implementation. This act was intended to end feudal relations on the land, most of which was in the hands of Turkish and Albanian landowners (begs). The majority of Serbs had left Kosovo, led northwards by their Patriarchs in two large-scale migrations, in order to escape Ottoman reprisals for Serbian support of Austria in the Austro-Turkish wars of the 17th and 18th centuries. By carrying out an agrarian reform in these regions – in fact, appropriating the estates of the feudal landlords – the Belgrade Government now had large areas of fertile farmland at its disposal to distribute among colonists. These were given full ownership of the land, thereby strengthening the Serbian and Montenegrin presence in Kosovo, with its predominantly ethnic Albanian population.

In the course of this resettlement, various abuses and ill-considered measures by the Belgrade and local authorities triggered a rapid worsening of relations between the Serbs and Montenegrins, on the one hand, and the Albanians, who under Turkish rule had lived in relative harmony with the 'old' Slav inhabitants. The newcomers enjoyed the full support of the authorities, who confiscated and distributed not only large estates but the land of ordinary Albanian peasants. The Kosovo question was to be solved not by fostering co-existence but by creating conditions that would encourage the Albanian and other Moslem inhabitants to emigrate to Albania and Turkey.

❧

Among the twelve thousand families, some sixty thousand people, who set out for Kosovo from various parts of Serbia and Montenegro were my parents and sisters Ljuba and Stana

When the day fixed for their departure dawned, all the villagers, with Father Bokan at their head, gathered in front of the church, where the women of Bukovik had laid out a table with various sweetmeats, brandy and wine. Young Father Bokan, who had replaced Father Dobrković, killed in the battle of Mojkovac, raised his glass:

"Well, Petar Tomašević," said the priest, "never forget that if you ever return to your hearth, we shall all rejoice. In Bukovik you are a tree with deep roots, like the olive trees in front of our houses that were planted who knows when and will last another thousand years, but out there, in the wide world, you will be only 'a straw tossed by the winds', as the great Njegoš says."

It was a gloomy gathering. All of them felt that the war had taken away not only husbands and sons left on the battlefield, but the old order, contentment and certainty, when life had followed a steady and familiar course from the cradle to the grave, governed by the unwritten laws of the Crmnica clan. Everyone had taken part in every event of importance in the lives of their fellow villagers: baptisms, weddings, family feast days, funerals… Before they had felt part of one strong community, but now families were beginning to go their own way, take decisions by themselves, not caring about others or the good of the clan.

When the horses were loaded, Petar turned to his eldest brother, Luka: "If all goes well and I send word for you to join us, sell up everything, the house, land and livestock, and bring all the family with you. You and Djuro have been in America and in the war, seen something of the world. Can you now spend the rest of your lives looking after goats in these mountains? That's not for you any longer. Most of our generation have been killed, and we who survived our wounds are half crippled and not fit for much. Kosovo can be our salvation, the new life we dreamed about, our America. The Serbs will rise from the ashes there and become greater and stronger than in the time of Tsar Dušan. I see a future for us in Kosovo. That's where history is being made now, while this place belongs to the past. And as for the Albanians there, it won't do them any good to cause trouble. Kosovo has been Serbian since ancient times, the cradle of Serbia, and so it will remain, as long as there are mothers to bear Serbian heroes like Miloš Obilić."

Then he set off, accompanied by his brothers and several neighbours, for Virpazar, the assembly place for families from the area, from where they would be driven to Mitrovica in army trucks. In each vehicle there were several armed soldiers, for the convoy had to cross the high pass on Mount Čakor, through which the Serbian army had retreated in 1915. This wild and rough terrain where the trucks could only crawl was now full of Albanian rebels, lying in wait to attack the convoys in an attempt to stop the Serbian and Montenegrin colonisation of Kosovo.

Next day at noon they arrived in Mitrovica, a dusty or muddy little town, depending on the weather, with a hundred or so houses. This was the reception centre for all the newcomers to Kosovo. Here, at the military headquarters, the settlers were given the deeds to a house and land before leaving to take possession of their new property with an army escort, since in some cases this meant coming into direct conflict with the Albanians. Mitrovica was a scene of indescribable confusion, with crowds of people hurrying in all directions, some trying to buy milk for their children, bread or any other food that was available, others searching for somewhere to spend the night.

Most, though, had come well prepared, arriving in their farm carts, drawn by oxen or horses, with a sufficient supply of food to tide them over for a month or two. Waiting for an armed escort, whole families might have to spend several days in their carts, from which projected the barrels of military rifles: their owners had failed to hand them in after the war and now, more than ever, refused to be separated from them.

The very first day Petar managed to find a friend who agreed to put up Milica and the little girls for a few days in his already overcrowded house. This freed Petar to look around the town and see how best to proceed, rather than accept the first thing that was offered him. First of all he made his way to army headquarters to register his arrival and enter his name on the list of men liable for military duty, should the need arise. The place was crowded with newcomers waiting to be allocated land and houses. Petar decided to try the local government office instead. Here there was no-one around except a couple of soldiers on guard, from which he concluded that this, too, was run by the military. The man in charge, a Major Golubović, received him in person. As soon as he heard that Petar had only just arrived in Mitrovica, he interrupted him to say he had come to the wrong place and should go at once to the army headquarters, where land was allocated.

"I don't mind waiting a bit for the land," Petar replied. "I'd rather work for a salary in Mitrovica."

He then told the officer, whose curiosity was aroused, that he had fought in two wars and won a medal for bravery, that he had been employed in the local government office in Virpazar as a clerk because of his good hand-writing, and everything else in his favour he thought might interest the Major. Finally he added that he had been a supporter of Montenegro's union with Serbia, and now he would like to work to strengthen the new state in Kosovo.

Major Golubović must have been impressed by the young man's determination not to be just another colonist tilling the land, but to help the military authorities establish civilian government in Kosovo. As luck would have it, at that moment he was in need of someone to assist with correspondence with Belgrade and the military authorities throughout Kosovo, so Petar was offered temporary employment.

The very next day, after Petar had submitted for signature several well-composed letters in good hand-writing, the Major sent for him:

"Well, Petar, it looks as if you were born under a lucky star. It seems to me that the two of us will be working together for a good while to come. Let's see where we can fit you in until something better turns up. As you know, there are disputes, fights and murders enough in Kosovo, but nobody in authority is settling or punishing them. Up till now, the Albanians have dealt with such things among themselves, when their own people were in question, and the Serbs have done the same. That's the way it's always been and neither side wants any outside interference. What we have here, Petar, is complete lawlessness and anarchy. You can kill anyone you like, and if you have relatives and friends to protect you, nobody can touch you. It's useless to try to take someone into custody, examine the scene of the crime or question witnesses unless you have an armed squad with you. Only the military can do anything here; without the army, it's hopeless."

In the hard-working and ambitious young man, Major Golubović had found just the colleague he needed, and he no longer started any new undertaking without consulting him. For this reason he went out of his way to help Petar solve his housing problem, arranging for him to get a bank loan to build a house. This modest, single-storey dwelling, completed in less than two months, had a spacious, grassy yard backing on to a large stretch of common land where the Albanians grazed their water buffalo. For greater security, my father chose a site on the north bank of the Ibar river, very close to a dozen houses, clustered together, belonging to other Montenegrin colonists.

One morning a month or two later, Major Golubović told him they had been called to Belgrade in connection with the plans to establish a proper civilian administration and police force in Mitrovica. For Petar, not long arrived from Montenegro, a summons to the capital, the centre of power where the strongest state in the Balkans was now being shaped, was far and away the biggest challenge to date in his brief career in government service.

When Petar arrived with Golubović at Belgrade railway station early one morning, expecting that everything in the capital would be orderly and well-regulated, he was astonished by all the noise and confusion. Families with numerous children in tow hurried forward and back between the waiting trains and, as the carriages were unmarked, kept stopping to ask others before getting into what often proved to be the wrong train. On discovering their mistake, in a panic they would start throwing baggage out of the carriage window on to the platform, where rival porters, shoving and cursing one another, were waiting to grab it.

Many of the porters were Serbs from the barren, rocky Lika region of Croatia, whose ancestors had mostly fled from Kosovo centuries before. Having found themselves unemployed after the break-up of the Austrian Empire, they now wandered around Serbian towns looking for work. For centuries these strong, healthy highlanders had served in the Austrian army, not a few of them becoming famous generals. Now that there was no longer any demand for their military skills, being untrained for any other profession and having no fertile land to till, all they could do was sell their strength. Followed by one such porter loaded with bags full of official files, Major Golubović and Petar arrived at Police Headquarters.

In 1921 Belgrade had some one hundred thousand inhabitants, many of them recently arrived from the interior of the country, Montenegro and the newly liberated regions. Apart from the main street, named after Prince Mihailo (Michael) Obrenović and adjacent area, the character and architecture of the town still bore the strong imprint of more than three centuries of Turkish rule. It was, in fact, less than fifty years since Turkey had finally withdrawn its garrison from the great Belgrade fortress of Kalemegdan ('field of duels') rising above the confluence of the rivers Sava and Danube and overlooking the vast Pannonian plain to the north. In and around the walls of the fortress, the nucleus of the city that had survived some forty wars since its origins in pre-Roman times, there was still in those days a small 'Turkish' quarter with a mixed population of Turks, Serbs, Greeks and Jews.

At Police Headquarters, senior police officers asked Petar to outline his views on the new civilian police force. Seizing this chance to put forward his ideas and plans, he told them what he had observed during his brief period of work in Mitrovica, what he thought needed to be done and what could realistically be achieved in the early days of the service and before the coming general election. Obviously satisfied with his response, they promptly invited him to head the new service.

"How old are you, Petar Tomašević?" one of them asked.

"Twenty-four."

"You'll succeed in Kosovo, Petar, no doubt about that, unless you stop a bullet first!"

The following day he was issued with the uniform of a police official, complete with gold epaulets, a peaked cap with a badge, similar to a French kepi, and a short gilt sword. On his return to Mitrovica, my mother, immensely proud of his appearance as well as his unexpected and rapid success, used to spend the evenings, after the children were in bed, painstakingly polishing all the buttons and other metal ornaments of this resplendent uniform.

With his small squad of policemen, selected for their height and power-ful physique, Petar was determined to establish law and order in the Mitrovica district. Following Major Golubović's advice, he had two trusted friends among the five policemen who made up the local force at that time. The Major continued to supervise police activities, for the army remained in complete control of Kosovo and the colonisation campaign.

At that time a number of disillusioned colonists were trickling back into the town, having sold the land allocated them to Albanians, often the very ones from whom it had been taken. They hung around the cafés and bars that had sprung up overnight in Mitrovica, together with their singers, women of dubious reputation who were prepared, after performing their 'artistic programme', to cater for other needs of the exclusively male customers. When these men had had too much to drink, they would take out their revolvers, fire at the ceiling and make open threats against those who wanted to send them back on the land or to the places they had come from. Sometimes they would publicly curse Petar Tomašević, challenging him to come in person and try to drive them out of either the café or Mitrovica.

Petar, who had promised meetings of settlers that he would make the town safe for all its inhabitants, set about this task with ruthless determination, arresting and charging all who wanted to turn it into a violent, lawless place of gambling and drinking dens. With his dedi-cated and fearless policemen, all of them veterans like himself, he would burst into these bars and arrest the troublemakers, shooting it out if they resisted. Very soon his group was the talk of the whole district, gaining support and respect among the peaceable Serbian and Mon-tenegrin population, but also enemies among some of the colonists and Albanian leaders.

One day Petar set out with two policemen to investigate an army re-port that shooting had been heard in an Albanian village and might have resulted in fatalities. Since this was an 'internal' matter involving only Albanians, according to age-old custom they would have settled it among themselves, with the heads of families acting as arbitrators. These obliged the quarrelling parties to make peace, decided what apology or compensation was required, or, if there had been a killing, arranged for a family tie that would prevent any future blood feud. But now, for the first time in Kosovo, the law required all violent incidents to be investigated by the civil authorities, more precisely, the police. On this occasion, Major Golubović offered to accompany Petar, together with an army escort, in case there was trouble, but my father declined his help:

"We can't resort to military force all over Kosovo for every minor incident. We'll try to settle the matter by ourselves following the normal procedure."

He was well aware of how the army had been dealing with similar cases: the many burnt-out Albanian houses and whole villages were evidence of this rough military justice.

Petar was determined to try to change completely the manner in which disputes among the Albanians were resolved. He wanted to get to know their leaders and talk with them amicably, without the threat of guns. This, he hoped, would make it easier for the Albanians and colonists to live together in peace.

Having rejected the Major's offer, he ordered a horse and carriage for the journey as the police had no car. Since there were no paved roads in Kosovo, a car would not have been of much use in any case. With two policeman, one of them a relative, Petar drove along the winding, rutted dust road for a couple of hours until they reached the turning for the village. Just beyond the crossroads they stopped at a group of newly built houses belonging to Montenegrin colonists. These were delighted to see the police, the women immediately bringing out compote and water, as was the custom when guests appeared, and offering them brandy and coffee.

"Do you mix at all with those others in the village? Do you know anything about some quarrel and killing there?" Petar enquired. Amongst themselves the Montenegrins rarely mentioned the word 'Albanians', but usually referred to them as 'the others', as though they were some alien race.

"Yes, we heard some shooting yesterday," one replied. "I hope to God they kill each other off, then it'll be safer for us and our children. Let them fight among themselves, better than turning on us. But if they get any ideas of that kind, they'll have it coming to them. All of us in these houses take it in turn to keep a look out, day and night. But what are you doing here risking your lives without the army? Do you want some of our young men to go along with you for protection?"

To their surprise, Petar turned down their offer with thanks. For some time he had been firmly convinced that they had to find a common language with the Albanians, come to some understanding. For him it was important that the law should apply equally to all, regardless of whether the wrong-doer was 'one of us' or 'one of the others'. When the Albanians saw that there was one law for everyone, he reasoned, they would be prepared to accept it. For as long as rough justice was administered by the military, accompanied by armed colonists, there would be no peace in Kosovo. And so, with a wave to the small crowd that had gathered, he drove off towards the Albanian village.

They had not gone more than two hundred metres when they heard rifle shots coming from a hill close by and the horse staggered and dropped dead.

"Ambush!" all three shouted in one voice, jumping out of the gig and throwing themselves flat on the ground. In no time the colonists they had just been talking to appeared with their rifles and bandoleers. But the unseen Albanian attackers had already made off.

When he heard about the ambush, Major Golubović reprimanded Petar:

"Didn't I tell you to take the military? Those people are wild animals, and only cannon fire will teach them sense. I've ordered a squad commander to go with you tomorrow and flatten the whole village if anyone gets in your way, or even gives you a nasty look. You have a wife and children, Petar, so don't gamble with your life."

"I don't want any soldiers with me, Golubović," Petar replied. "We have to find some other way to talk with them, not always over the barrel of a gun."

"If you don't care about yourself, think about your men. Are you going to let them kill the few policemen we have? In your place, I'd take better care of myself and my men. It'll be a long time before we and the Albanians sit down at table together, so don't try showing off your courage by going without the army."

But Petar was adamant: "I'm sticking to my decision. I won't take any soldiers with me. I don't need them."

After this first serious disagreement between the two men, their friendship gradually cooled. They held radically different views on how to pacify the Albanians and ensure a secure and peaceful life for all in Kosovo. Petar was for keeping the lines of communication open, talking with their leaders, listening to their requests and agreeing to those that were justified. This, he believed, would eventually improve relations and create a situation in which Serbian, Montenegrin and Albanian children could go to school together, not grow up apart, their minds poisoned by their parents' hatred.

"Don't you understand," he would often say to Golubović, "that the army can't protect my children if the others find a reason to kill them? Your army families are all safe back home in Serbia, and ours are here."

Despite these arguments, the two men still appeared to everyone to be the best of friends, often working together until late at night.

The day after the ambush, Petar summoned the office odd-job man, an Albanian:

"Listen, Šukrija. I want you to go to the village of Vaganica, where we were all nearly killed yesterday, and find the headman, Riza Beg. Tell him that tomorrow Petar Tomašević will be coming alone to have a friendly talk with him. Say that I have faith in Albanian honour that no-one will shoot an unarmed man. Otherwise, I'd come with the army."

The man returned late that evening:

"Riza Beg sends word that he'll be waiting for you. While you're in the village and with him, no one will harm a hair on your head. He'll send two young men to meet you near the village."

Before setting out next day, Petar dropped in to say goodbye to the Major:

"Let me finish this in my own way, Golubović. If anything happens to me, I count on you to arrange for my family to return to Bukovik. Life will be easier for them there than it would be here."

"Petar, my friend, you're out of your mind," replied the Major. "Do you really believe they'll let you change their customs, go into their houses and see their women, judge them according to our laws, when they have been their own judge for time out of mind? I wouldn't give a tinker's cuss for their word of honour, let alone trust my life to it. They can promise you anything, and shoot you down like a mangy cur. Go, if you must. You'll be the first colonist to give himself up to them without firing a shot. I wish you luck and, if need be, I'll look after your family."

When Petar reached the cluster of colonists' houses, he left his gig and weapons with them and walked towards the village, his jacket undone, without his belt and sword. By the hillock from where the shots had come on his previous visit, two armed Albanians were standing in wait.

"Take me to Riza Beg," he ordered in the voice he used for issuing commands.

Entering the village, he noted that every house was surrounded by a high brick wall with a number of loopholes for rifles, so that each was like a small fortress. Since Moslem women were confined to their own courtyard, these slits also served the purpose of allowing them to see outside without being seen. The village looked empty, deserted. Not a living soul in sight. Riza Beg had probably told them to stay indoors and wait, in case Petar had some trick up his sleeve and soldiers were following him.

The beg's house, standing a little apart on higher ground, was bigger and more imposing than the rest, with a higher and thicker outer wall. In the middle of the spacious courtyard stood Riza Beg, a lean, wiry man in his forties, wearing the traditional small round white cap and white home-spun costume of his people.

"Have you come in good faith, Petar?" he asked.

"Certainly, Riza Beg. Otherwise I surely would not have come alone. Will you invite me into your home, as I would do if you called on me?"

Without a word, Riza Beg turned and led the way indoors to the men's part of the house, where he spent much of the day seated on a divan receiving male relatives and villagers. Like all traditional Moslem dwellings, it had separate men's and women's quarters, laid out so that there was no chance of the womenfolk meeting a male visitor.

In the main room the beg seated himself on his divan and offered Petar a three-legged stool with a sheepskin seat. Between them stood a large engraved brass tray resting on a three-legged wooden stand, set with a coffee pot and small porcelain cups – a sign of high social status. The room had no other furniture except a large chest, in which the beg would have kept his weapons and his clothing for festive occasions.

"I hear you come to the market in Mitrovica," Petar remarked, to break the awkward silence. Then, employing his few words of Albanian, he invited the beg and his companions to visit him in his home as his guests.

"You know our language?" said the beg in astonishment; he had never before met a Serb or Montenegrin who spoke Albanian. Even if they had picked some up, the colonists thought it beneath their dignity to speak the language and insisted the Albanians address them only in Serbian.

"I'm trying to learn it, Riza Beg. It would be easier for me to communicate with Albanians who don't know Serbian."

This was, in fact, the vast majority of the ethnic Albanian population in Kosovo. The beg was silent for a while before replying:

"What happened the day before yesterday was not my doing. Believe me, if I had known about it, I would have prevented it. There are some wild young men who don't consult me but do as they like. As soon as I heard about it, I called the heads of families to discuss what to do, since there are some of our people with no sense in their heads. They don't think what trouble they could bring upon us."

"That's true, Riza Beg. It would have been a disaster for all of us if any of our people had been killed. We must live in peace, not be forever ambushing and shooting at one another – and for what reason?"

"There can be no peace," the beg broke in, "for as long as you kill our sons and take our land, burn down our houses and force your laws upon us, when we have our own. We are now foreigners in our own country and nobody asks us about anything. You decide everything and we must do as you say if we want to survive. Your soldiers open fire for the least thing, shooting and killing on the spot. Don't drive us to rebellion, Petar, for when we are pushed too far there will be rivers of blood."

"The more we get together to talk and reach agreement, the less need there'll be for the military. The army, like every army, relies on force and uses it. I'm for civil government, for the soldiers to stay in their barracks and let us administer the same justice for all, Albanians and our people. I shall ask for prominent Albanians like yourself to be included in the council where they can have their say, put forward their complaints, so that good relations can be established." Little by little, as they talked Riza Beg became more relaxed and called for a servant to bring more coffee, a signal that he would like the guest to stay on. Before him sat a man who didn't mind speaking Albanian, who did not rely on the army, like all the other colonists, who had risked his life to enter an Albanian house and offer friendship. Petar's words must have struck him as convincing and sincere, so he asked why he had previously come to the village with his policemen.

"I was informed, Riza Beg, that there was some shooting here, and perhaps bloodshed. I know you'll say this is a matter for Albanians, but while I am in authority, Albanian and Serbian blood is the same. If innocent blood was spilt, the person responsible must be brought before a court, judged according to the law, and either freed, if he was not to blame, or kept in prison if guilty. It would be best if those involved in the shooting were called to say what happened."

The beg listened carefully, and simply said:

"Luckily, nobody was killed, only two of the villagers were slightly wounded."

House of a well-to-do Albanian family in Kosovo

Petar then proposed that the beg bring them to him in Mitrovica, where a report could be written and filed. After that, he promised, the two would be free to go home or wherever they liked.

"As for that ambush, I won't press charges now, in the hope that it won't occur again. You know very well, Riza Beg, that I could have come here with soldiers, but I didn't. I came trusting your word, as I hope you will come to my house with those two young men after the report has been written, so we can eat together and drink a toast to our new friendship. I offer to be godfather to your children or blood brother to you or whatever you wish. But however you decide, remember that it depends on you and me, and others like us, whether our people, our children, will live in peace or in eternal fear of bloodshed."

To his great satisfaction, Riza Beg agreed to bring the two men with him to Mitrovica on the next market day and, after the business of the report had been finished, come with them to lunch.

On the appointed day, Petar asked a number of the most respected colonists to join them for the meal. When Riza Beg and the two young men entered, they all stood up and shook hands with the visitors.

"Welcome to our home, Riza Beg," Petar greeted him. "From this day on, my friends are your friends, so it would be good to get to know them."

When they were seated, a dozen of them in all, Milica offered the guests food and drink with the help of neighbours' wives who had come to give a hand, one serving cakes, another making coffee. The Albanians had never before been guests in a Montenegrin home or engaged in normal conversation with so many colonists, let alone had an opportunity to get a close look at their wives.

After this lunch, Riza Beg and Petar often visited each other and after some time became blood brothers, the closest relationship outside the family both among the Orthodox colonists and among the Moslems in Kosovo.

In 1924, Grandma Stana's prophecy was fulfilled: my mother gave birth to her first son, named Dušan after the mighty ruler of the medieval Serbian Empire, but always called Duško. All the relatives and Father's friends in Mitrovica gathered in the house to celebrate this great event with gunfire, feasting and drinking that went on all night. My father, bursting with pride and joy, declared:

"This one is mine. I'll raise him, and let Milica look after the girls!"

In the next three years there were two further celebrations for the birth of two more sons, Milan and Branko. Father chose as their godfathers his friends and wartime comrades with whom he wanted to strengthen family ties, for to be chosen as a *kum*, whether godfather to a child or best-man at a wedding, created a special relationship between the families concerned. To the great sorrow of my parents, both boys died before the age of three, during two of the epidemics that periodically swept through Kosovo.

At the end of 1927 my sister Nada ('Hope') was born. Still suffering from the death, one after the other, of his two sons, my father is reported to have commented: "It looks like God has turned his back on us."

❧

That same year he was summoned to Belgrade for ten days to familiarise himself with the work of the 'modern police' in the capital. While there, he heard about a "minor Albanian riot" in Mitrovica and the surroundings connected with the upcoming elections. "Thanks to the military, this was quickly suppressed and order restored," he was told at Police Headquarters.

The army's way of restoring order was what Petar feared most, so he tried to find out the scale of the rioting and its consequences. But the police knew nothing more, this being an army matter, and at Army Headquarters he was told that the information was classified as a military secret. There was nothing left to do but hurry back to Mitrovica and find out on the spot what had happened. Apart from others, Mother gave him her account of the events:

"The trouble started when there were separate election meetings, the Serbs and Montenegrins on the one side, and the Albanians on the other. The Albanians had come here from villages around. Our people wanted to break up their meeting, fighting started, and one of our colonists was killed. Then our people took their guns and went after them to the villages. Major Golubović sent the army with them, and a real slaughter followed: about thirty of their young men were killed. Their bodies were brought here on ox carts to the marketplace and left lying there, for everyone to see. Their wives and mothers were not allowed to come near. It was two days before they let them take away the dead for burial.

"When the hunt started, Petar, a young lad managed to escape into our yard. He wasn't more than fifteen, if that. Whether he knew whose house it was I can't say, but when he saw me he started begging for help:

'They'll kill me if they get hold of me, if you hand me over to them!'

'Don't be afraid, son,' I said. 'No harm will come to you in our house. They won't dare touch you except over my dead body.'

"Then I took him into a room, locked the door and took my revolver, just as the group that was chasing him arrived at the gate. All kids, no older than him, apart from a couple who were the ringleaders. I stood on the doorstep and barred the way.

'We want that Albanian bastard hiding in your house,' they shouted.

I drew my revolver and waved it at them:

'Do you know, you miserable lot, whose house this is?' I asked. 'It's the house of Petar Tomašević, who's well-known to you all, so force your way in if you dare.'

'We won't if you hand him over,' one of them said.

'Listen, you scum,' I answered. 'If you, or anyone else, crosses this threshold, it'll be over my dead body and those of my children. And if you kill us all, you'll be able to boast that you murdered the family of Petar Tomašević, a hero of Taraboš and other battles.'

"Luckily, at that moment some of our neighbours appeared with their guns and took my side. And so, grumbling, they went off, and when the coast was clear the young lad crept out and hurried home to his village."

❧

Next day in the Major's office the soldier and the policeman had another serious quarrel which finally ended their friendship. Petar could not contain his rage and frustration:

"You, Golubović, sent the army into Albanian villages to burn and kill. Everything we've been working towards, everything we've achieved, so that people can live more or less normally, has been destroyed. We've broken our promises, our word of honour. After this, no-one will ever trust us again."

"Let me give you a word of advice," responded the Major. "Don't set yourself up as their defender; look after you own people. They need your protection. All Mitrovica is already saying that Petar Tomašević is more for the Albanians than his own folk, and that's not good for you, your career or your family, who you have to feed and give a start in life. As for your Milica not handing over that fellow who took refuge in your house, do you know what they're saying? 'Where else would he go but to the house of his blood brother, Petar?' Do you think people don't notice these things and gossip about them when they get together at some *slava*, funeral or wedding?"

After this, Petar began writing letters to Belgrade without consulting Golubović about the contents, as he had always done previously. He asked for the civil authorities to be strengthened and for greater protection and justice for the Albanians when they were in the right. At the same time he encouraged the colonists to make friends with them, invite them to their homes, let their children mix... He himself invited Albanian elders and neighbours for his *slava* and on holidays, and encouraged his daughters Ljuba and Stana to learn Albanian and make Albanian friends.

All of this represented an open challenge not only to Major Golubović and the army, but to all the Serbian and Montenegrin national extremists, so that my father's position was seriously jeopardised. He then resorted to the age-old strategy of summoning one's relatives, ever ready to protect their own even at the cost of their lives. From Bukovik he brought his brothers Luka and Djuro and their families. Grandma Stana came with them, but Grandpa Filip refused to leave the house where he had been born and lived for eighty years.

"He mourns for Bukovik, which everyone is leaving, and lives almost like a hermit, spending more and more time at the graveyard," a neighbour reported. My father then set out for Bukovik, and under pressure from him Filip agreed to come to Mitrovica 'just temporarily'. Then he would return home, he insisted, to be buried together with his forebears and his sons, Vaso and Savo.

"Petar," he said, when the moment came to leave his home, "bring me back to Bukovik soon, I beg you. Don't leave me in that place where we had no need to go, for we lacked for nothing here. It is a great sin and shame to let the fire die out in the ancestral hearth, sacred to our family."

❧

And so one wet winter day Filip arrived in Mitrovica. He gazed around at the shabby, Turkish-style houses, leaning this way and that, raised in no kind of order on this plain, the like of which he had never seen before, and crossed himself in wonderment:

"Was it for this muddy place, my poor Petar, that you left our beautiful mountain and clear air?"

Grandpa Filip and Grandma Stana were now reunited, though neither gave any sign of being especially pleased about this. Most of the time they spent in their small room in our stone house: she, quiet and serene, content to be near her youngest son; he, like a wild creature in captivity, pacing up and down the narrow room, glancing out of the window every now and then as though hoping, by some miracle, to catch sight of his native mountains. As time passed, he became more and more subdued and melancholy, as though the light within was dying. He realised that his return home was as remote as ever, perhaps would only happen after his soul had journeyed to eternity.

Next, Petar managed to persuade all Milica's family to move to Mitrovica: her father Aleksa, mother Jovana, brothers Marko and Jovan, and sister Mileva. They left behind their houses and land in the Kuči region, where the Rajković family had lived, they claimed, ever since their ancestor had escaped from Kosovo after the battle in 1389. Their decision to come was to some extent prompted by the belief that after five centuries they would be returning in a sense to their original homeland.

When my mother's family arrived, instead of sending them off to settle on some Albanian land, my father kept them in Mitrovica, where they lived in one of our newly built houses. He employed her brothers, two rough-and-ready, quick-tempered young men, as policemen, so strengthening his own position.

Then Petar brought to Mitrovica other friends and relatives from Crmnica and Kuči. The family circle also included the husbands of his nieces; two of them were married to tall, tough Herzegovinians, very similar in appearance and temperament to their Montenegrin neighbours. Now the Tomašević and Rajković families in Mitrovica formed a strong clan linked by ties of blood and marriage, ready, if necessary, to die for one another without a moment's hesitation.

৵

In November 1929 I was born and given the name Nebojša, meaning 'fearless', after the hero of a Slav folk tale. Doubtless my father considered this an essential characteristic for any boy growing up in Kosovo. But my brother and sisters called me 'Bato' ('little brother'), and the name stuck.

As my mother recalled, before the age of three I was twice at death's door during the epidemics of virulent diseases that periodically swept through the town and which had already carried off my elder brothers, Branko and Milan. On one occasion, when the doctor explained to the anxious parents that there was no hope, in accordance with custom they summoned the Orthodox priest to say a prayer for the soul of little Nebojša.

One bitterly cold winter morning, with a blizzard howling outside, family and friends gathered to be at hand to comfort the parents when the worst happened.

They sat there all day, talking in hushed voices about their own children lost in similar ways, to ease the pain they all shared, the candle by my head slowly burning down. Suddenly, my mother recounted, I opened my eyes and declared I was hungry. The priest jumped to his feet, crossed himself, and thanked God for another miracle.

৵

Life was full of dangers and uncertainty, not only in Mitrovica and Kosovo, but on the broader political canvas. Trouble between Serbs and ethnic Albanians drew less public attention than the clashes and mutual accusations of Serbs and Croats in the Belgrade Parliament. During one heated debate in 1928, a Montenegrin deputy pulled out a revolver and shot dead the Croatian leader Stjepan Radić. Soon after, King Alexander, endeavouring to preserve the kingdom and the leading role of the Serbs within it, dissolved Parliament and instituted a monarchic dictatorship – a move that only heightened the discontent of the Croats, Slovenes, Macedonians and other non-Serb sections of the population.

The Kingdom of Yugoslavia, as it was called from 1929 on, was beset by socio-economic conflicts as well as national antagonisms. The outlawed Communist Party stepped up its clandestine activities and agitated against the royal dictatorship. The police had their hands full hunting down Party members. Many of their leaders were arrested and sentenced to long terms in gaol; some were liquidated without trial. The Yugoslav Party's future general secretary, the metalworker Josip Broz, who had taken part in the October Revolution in Russia, was brought before a Zagreb court charged with anti-state activities. When asked to make his plea, he declared:

"I do not recognise the judgement of the bourgeois court, only the judgement of the Communist Party to which I belong." He was then given a five-year prison sentence, which he served in full. On his release, he escaped to Moscow. Several leading communists, among them the Yugoslav Party Secretary, were seized, taken to the border and murdered there. The press was then shown their bodies as evidence that the communist leaders were engaged in anti-state activities and illegally crossing the frontier.

The impact of the world-wide economic crisis, the high level of unemployment, national and religious tensions – all these contributed to general unrest and disaffection in the state which had existed for little more than a decade.

❧

In 1933 Petar and Milica had their eighth child, a son named Aleksandar after King Alexander 'the Unifier', who a year later was to be assassinated in Marseille. His death gave encouragement to all nationalists, at home and abroad, who were opposed to the unified kingdom. Among these were the Kosovo Albanians who, emboldened by the new course of events in the country and Europe, waited and readied themselves for their chance.

The murder of King Alexander profoundly grieved and horrified our family. For several days a deathly silence reigned in the house, as though it had been struck by some cataclysm.

"Nothing will be the same again," Father kept repeating. "Without the king, the country will split up. Everything created by generations will fall apart, as it did after the death of Tsar Dušan. It will be as Njegoš said: 'The great lords, curse their souls, will tear the empire to pieces'."

From a personal viewpoint, I think it was at this time that I became a conscious being. I remember my mother, with all the neighbouring women, weeping over the king for days. A dark cloud, like the end of the world, seemed to have descended on the Montenegrin colony in Mitrovica. As a child I sensed the fear that had taken hold of my family. More and more often I sought the reassuring comfort of the quince-scented room of Grandpa Filip and Grandma Stana.

Of the six surviving children in the family, it seems that I was Grandma's pet, perhaps because I was sickly and most resembled her youngest and favourite son, Petar, when small.

I can still see her room with a row of quinces ripening on top of the cupboard. She used to brush her long hair that had never been cut in front of the mirror and wind it in a plait around her head, like a coronet. Over this she would throw a long black-lace veil, completely covering the hair and secured with a gold pin. Apart from her wedding ring, this was the only piece of jewellery she possessed. Every morning I would sit in the corner of the room watching her slow preparations for her appearance – dignified, head erect – before the numerous Tomašević family. More than Grandpa Filip, who was less formal, she was the centre of attention. In exchange for her name, religion and language, renounced for the sake of her marriage, she had gained the place of highest respect at the head of the large table, where never fewer than ten persons sat down for a meal, under the icon of our family saint, the Holy Archangel Michael.

Filip spent much of his time with Duško, the eldest boy, as grandfathers do in Montenegro. Perhaps he saw in my brother, a tall strong lad for his age, the means of returning to Crmnica, to the family hearth of which he dreamed.

"This is his grandfather's great hope," Filip would say. "He'll be the guiding star for all of us, leading us in the way of our forefathers, like Moses led the Israelites." Then, turning to Duško, he would continue: "Don't follow your father's path. He's a real Papani, takes after his mother, not us Tomaševićs. Mark my words! No one knows what life has in store. If trouble befalls you, make straight for Montenegro. There you'll be safer."

But my father, to show how confident he was he had done right in coming to Kosovo, went ahead putting all the money he could spare into building new houses. His ambition was to give each of his six surviving children their own home one day, and have one for himself and my mother. So Filip and Petar, father and son, each stubborn and strong-willed in his own way, worked to achieve their opposing goals.

&❧

That same year yet more relatives were persuaded by Petar to come to Mitrovica: my mother's first cousin, Mihajlo Rajković, his Macedonian wife Vasilija and their son and daughter, Dragan and Dragica, a few years older than myself. Mihajlo, our first relative to graduate from university, had been working as a magistrate in the small Macedonian town of Strumica near the Greek border. On settling in Mitrovica he was promoted to district judge, so that my father's influence now extended also to the judiciary. Though Mihajlo was a university graduate while Petar had completed only four years of primary schooling, he made no attempt to 'take over', as might have been expected. On the contrary, not only was there never any hint of rivalry, but Mihajlo wholeheartedly supported Petar in his ambition to hold the reins of power in Mitrovica. To bind him more closely to the family, Petar gave him the rent-free use of one of our houses. Now, when all the relatives met in our home, there were some twenty children dashing around our spacious yard. Dragica immediately made friends with the girls – she was around the same age as my sister Stana – while Dragan, a little younger than Duško, joined the boys' camp.

❧

A few months later Mihajlo's brother, also named Dušan, a young man of twenty-five, arrived in Mitrovica from Slovenia, where he had been undergoing treatment for tuberculosis in a sanatorium on Mount Golnik.

"If you'll let me, I've come here to die. I wouldn't be a trouble to you for very long, just a few months, the doctors say."

My mother, who remembered him from Kuči as a handsome, cheerful boy, was much moved by his sickly appearance and sad fate, and so immediately proposed to Father that he should stay in the small empty outhouse at the far end of our yard. Even so, his arrival caused considerable alarm in the household.

Tuberculosis, or *jektika* as it was popularly called, was at that time common in Mitrovica, and the family was aware of the possible danger of Dušan's presence for the children. Grandpa Filip took this opportunity to warn:

"You see what happens when highlanders come down to the plain, to the mud and the dust. If we stay here, none of the children will live to old age."

The very first day Petar gathered all the children and threatened them with dire consequences if they went anywhere near the little house where Dušan was living. It was agreed that his brother Mihajlo and my mother, as his closest relatives, should look after him. Mihajlo, afraid of contracting the disease, avoided taking Dušan his meals whenever he could, so that my mother, besides attending to her own large family, bore the main burden of caring for the young man in the last weeks of his life. She would take him warm milk, chicken soup and other food she thought he could or should eat, washing and leaving all his dishes there so as not to mix them with those used for family meals. Day and night Dušan's coughing echoed around the yard.

One day, when no one was about, I couldn't resist peeping into the sick man's room. I had seen him when he arrived, tall, thin, with large, sunken eyes, and was attracted to this gentle, fragile, sad figure. He had smiled at us children and in a weak voice asked us not to come near. Now, when I dared to open the door of the little house and stepped into the room, I was shocked to see he was holding a wash basin in front of him and throwing up clotted blood. There was blood on his face and his big dark eyes bulged from the bout of coughing that was choking him. When he caught sight of me, he managed to stop for a moment to wave me out of the room. Horrified at the sight, I instantly fled. But when I got half way across the yard, I stopped and turned back. Again he motioned me to leave, begged me with his eyes, but I stood stock still against the wall, in a state of shock, and gazed at him. After a while, making sure I was unobserved, I returned to the house.

From then on I felt it was my duty to see him regularly. When no one was around I would slip into his room and watch over him. As the days passed he grew weaker and could no longer speak. We would look at one another for a while, then he would signal me to leave. I would stay a minute or two longer, and then be off. When this pattern was established, Dušan stopped sending me away, perhaps because he was too weak or perhaps because my visits were some small comfort, the human companionship he needed as he lay on his death bed. Between bouts of coughing he smiled at me, as though thanking me for this belated friendship between relatives twenty years apart in age. One day when I slipped into his room he did not greet me with his sunken gaze. I realised that something terrible had happened to Dušan and fled. No one ever knew our secret.

※

In 1936, I started school when not yet seven, the prescribed age. I was the smallest and feeblest child in the class, having suffered every infectious disease around, from scarlet fever to influenza, in the preceding year. Thin as I was, nothing but skin and bone, I would certainly not have been admitted several months early but for my father's influence.

Before my first day at school, I remember, I spent half the night awake, sick with excitement and anxiety. Early in the morning Father handed me my new satchel, a whistle, a slate, some chalk and a sponge, further increasing my agitation. As Father and I set off down the main street in the direction of the school, Mother threw a glassful of water after me for luck.

"We'll stop at Izidor Levi's on the way, to see whether he has anything nice for our Bato," said Father. The small, bearded, Jewish grocer, dressed in black, greeted me like an old friend. As previously arranged with my father, he handed me a small green notebook. Several Jews who kept small shops in the main street – the grocer, tailor, watchmaker and others – had introduced the custom of giving credit for goods and services to reliable customers. They would enter the amounts owed in indelible pencil in small notebooks and get paid at the end of each month, when government employees received their salaries. Father explained to me that every morning on my way to school I should call at Izidor's and take what I felt like eating, and he would settle the bill at the end of the month. There was only one condition: I must eat what I bought on the way to school. He obviously hoped that in this way his puny son would gain a little weight and strength. The result, however, was that I stopped eating anything at home and became very popular among my classmates, who soon learnt of my privilege and helped me make lavish use of it. After only a couple of months Father decided to do away with the little green notebook.

Schooling in Kosovo was not compulsory but it was free for those who wished to attend. In my class, besides a score of children from colonist families, there were six or seven pupils of Turkish or Albanian origin. On this first day, brought along by their fathers they stood all together at one end of the corridor, apart from us and our parents. Impatient, excited, yet apprehensive, we all waited to be summoned one by one. When at last I heard my name called, I was so paralysed with fright my father had to give me a push from behind in the direction of the classroom. We approached a table at which the teacher was sitting and making a note of something. He turned towards me and said in an intimidating voice:

"So you're that Nebojša!"

Handing me over to the teacher's care, Father said, as was customary:

"If he misbehaves, don't spare the cane!"

Our parents departed and we were left to the mercy of this stern-faced man with his menacing stare and slender cane, which he flicked around as he talked:

"Take a good look at this! Now I'll give you your places and each of you must sit where I put you. Woe betide anyone who moves his seat!"

To emphasise the severity of his threat, he raised the cane above his head and brought it down with a whiplike crack. He then directed the Albanian and Turkish boys to sit at the back and put the rest of us in front of them, leaving a couple of empty rows between the Orthodox and Moslem pupils.

"Here we shall learn Serbian and speak only Serbian," the teacher declared. "Those who want to speak Albanian, let them do so at home, out of my hearing, or they'll be in trouble!"

In the days and months that followed the Moslem boys tried to learn Serbian as quickly as they could, inevitably making mistakes in grammar and pronunciation, which the rest greeted with ridicule. With the tacit approval of the teacher, who made no attempt to check them, the majority of the Orthodox pupils openly insulted and humiliated their classmates, repeating opinions they had heard at home. In these circumstances there was no question of making friends: the class was split into two hostile camps.

Towards the end of my first year there was an incident, the culmination of all that had gone before, which could have had fatal consequences. Though I was always in the group of Serbian pupils, I was not a ringleader in inventing 'jokes' at the Moslem boys' expense. One day during a break between lessons, several of the bigger and stronger boys in my class, their pockets filled with pork scratchings, cornered a number of Albanian boys standing together at the far end of the school-yard, grabbed hold of them and began stuffing the pork fat into their mouths. I can still see the looks of horror and disgust on their faces as they struggled to free themselves and spit out the pork, which their religion forbade them to touch with their hands, let alone their lips. This was the last straw for my Albanian classmates, who pulled out the concealed knives they carried with them and rushed after their retreating tormentors.

Though I had not taken part in this defilement, I took to my heels before the enraged Moslem boys. But, perhaps because I didn't feel guilty, I didn't run as hard as the others so I was the last to reach the schoolyard wall. They had all managed to get over as I was still climbing up. Suddenly I felt a piercing pain in the back of my leg. One of the pursuers had stabbed me, inflicting a deep wound from just below the knee to half way down my calf. The injury was quite serious and kept me hobbling around for several weeks.

One consequence of this incident was that the teachers carried out periodic spot checks, searching the Albanian pupils and their bags for knives. The colonists' children were never searched.

At this time when I was starting school, a British company, Trepča Silver Mine Limited, was operating in the Mitrovica area, having obtained the concession to exploit the lead and silver mine not far from the town. There must have been several hundred British (or 'English', as we invariably called them) – engineers, supervisors, technicians, clerical staff and their families – living in specially built bungalows on the lower slopes of Mount Zvečan. Above them, on its summit, stood the ruins of one of the largest and most famous Serbian castles, dating from the ninth or tenth century, the scene of many historical events and testimony of Serbia's erstwhile power and glory. After a lengthy siege, it eventually fell to the Turks seven years after the battle of Kosovo.

On the slopes of Zvečan, which descend quite steeply to the swift-flowing Ibar river, the English lived in their own fashion. Soon after their arrival they had started their own model livestock farm, so they would have a regular meat supply and not be dependent on the Mitrovica market. The more prominent Serbs, Montenegrins and even Albanians could visit this farm and see for themselves, for the first time, various breeds of pedigree cattle and pigs – quite unlike the half-wild types of livestock to be found in Kosovo. The English also kept horses to ride for pleasure and had a well-organised social life, in which a number of Serbs and Montenegrins and their families were sometimes included: several doctors, teachers, priests, Jewish shopkeepers, my father representing the police and Uncle Mihajlo the judiciary.

જ

At the end of 1936 the English sent out invitations to Kosovo's first ball, to be held in the little Hotel Božur (Peony), and brought a band from Belgrade for this momentous occasion. Father, invited with a partner, took my eldest sister, Ljuba, who was just seventeen. In the course of the evening the Yugoslav guests mostly sat around eating and drinking, while the dancing was mainly done by the English among themselves. Until then, the idea of embracing someone else's wife or daughter, even when dancing, had been inconceivable in Kosovo. Among the handful of adventurous local people who tried to learn the dances was my sister.

At one point the English master of ceremonies, who had welcomed the guests at the start, announced that cards would be distributed to all the gentlemen to choose the belle of the ball. The young lady who received the most cards would receive as a prize a new gramophone, donated by a British company which hoped to sell its products in Kosovo. At the same time, all the Yugoslav guests were invited to visit Zvečan the following Sunday to tour the farm and stables, where horses would be ready-saddled if anyone wanted to go riding.

When the cards were counted up at the end of the evening, my sister Ljuba was proclaimed the belle of the ball. Father was very proud of his daughter's beauty, though slightly worried that socialising with the English might turn her head and perhaps harm her chances when the time came to marry. Ljuba was presented with the promised gramophone and a few records, so for the first time we listened to music in the house. Until then the only musical instrument had been grandfather's *gusle*, and its harsh strains that accompanied the chanting of epic ballads could hardly be classed as music.

Next day, the whole household gathered around this astonishing machine, which was wound up by hand. Listening to the songs emanating from the depths of its loudspeaker, we could scarcely believe our eyes and ears that such a thing was possible.

⁂

The following Sunday, my parents and we six children set out for Zvečan with Uncle Mihajlo and his family in two horse-drawn cabs. Father had given instructions for these vehicles to be properly cleaned and oiled, so we should not feel ashamed in front of foreigners. What I remember most clearly about that visit was the terrifying bellowing of the huge bulls with rings through their noses. Ljuba and Stana, who was just sixteen, were most attracted by the stables and the riders. All the way home the two of them pleaded with Father to let them learn to ride. Very soon riding became their great passion and Father, who adored his daughters and found it hard to refuse them anything within his power, bought two fine riding horses for them.

Neither Filip nor Aleksa could understand why their grand-daughters should want to sit on a horse unless they had to, or go galloping around Mitrovica bringing shame on the Tomašević and Rajković families.

"No good will come of this, mark my words," Filip would warn. My mother, on the other hand, was delighted to see her daughters on horseback and always defended them:

"Never mind, Filip. Times have changed and girls nowadays want all the same as boys. They want to do things their way, not ours."

One day, when my sisters were out riding in the meadow that stretched from our house right down to the Ibar river, Ljuba's mount was startled by something and bolted back towards the house. As she struggled to rein in the horse, she failed to notice the lintel above the big gateway into the yard. At full gallop she struck her head against it and was left lying unconscious on the ground. She spent the next week in bed recovering from severe concussion: Grandpa Filip's forebodings had not been far from the mark.

Now, more and more often, instead of our Sunday family excursion to Kosovo Polje in fine weather, we made for Zvečan. This change of destination upset our grandparents, but it was Ljuba and Stana who dictated to Father where we should go. They had outgrown the tales of Serbian chivalry and were more interested in the horses and entertainment provided by the British. Making their acquaintance was a completely new experience for Father, but with his volatile Mediterranean temperament he found them too reserved and restrained. He never warmed to them much, whereas Mihajlo talked of nothing else but the 'English' and his admiration for their democracy and social order. He quickly learnt a few dozen words and phrases of English and so could communicate with them more easily than Father could. His children, Dragan and Dragica, took lessons from the British wives, who had nothing much to occupy their time.

At about this time Father acquired a dozen hectares of land in the village of Pirče, half an hour's drive by cab from Mitrovica. He had a house built on this land, and we started to go there for week-ends and holidays. But when everything seemed to be going smoothly according to Father's plan, our life filled with happy, noisy family gatherings and everyone doing well, as often happens in life there occurred an event which changed everything.

❧

At dusk on a frosty December day in 1936 a funeral cortège of some thirty men accompanying a coffin alighted at Mitrovica railway station and started looking for somewhere to spend the night: no easy task in view of the number of people and the coffin. Father was immediately informed of their arrival and who they were. Hearing that they were people from Crmnica, he invited them all to his home.

I remember that we younger children were still dashing around the yard in the twilight as all these unfamiliar men started coming in. At their head was a tall priest in his long black robe with a large silver cross on his breast. As soon as he saw us, he raised this crucifix in our direction and uttered a blessing. Several hefty youths carried in the coffin on their shoulders, followed by a long line of mourners. The coffin was placed on a table in our guest room, as custom and respect for the dead required. Enough chairs were somehow found – mostly borrowed from neighbours – for all those accompanying the deceased. Mother served them all with *loza*, cheese and ham: the family always kept reserves in store for just such occasions when unexpected guests appeared, which was not unusual in our home. Father sat with them for a while, conversing mostly with the priest, who was the brother of the dead man, and then went off on night duty. At dawn they again thanked our family for their hospitality, and left in procession, as they had come.

All this would have been a normal and customary courtesy towards a family from the same area of Montenegro had the deceased not been a well-known communist leader who had been tortured and beaten to death by the police in a Belgrade prison. Some of the escort were also members of the banned Party. Father, a dedicated and active anti-communist, had offered them shelter in his house, fully aware that he was contravening the law of the land and duty of a senior police officer, in obedience to a much stronger and more ancient tribal law.

The following day an order arrived from Belgrade headquarters, whose spies had been following the journey of the funeral cortège, that Petar Tomašević was to be immediately suspended from duty while awaiting a final decision on his future. A commission was formed, headed by Major Golubović and including a senior police inspector from Belgrade.

"What's to be done with you now, Petar?" Golubović greeted him. "You have a family of six children, yet you gamble with their future. It's not enough that you've turned your house into a meeting place for Albanians; now you've decided to welcome communists as well. And there is talk, Petar, that at the last elections you voted for the opposition party, though we have no firm proof of this."

"I did not allow the dead Vukmanović and his funeral party to pass the night in my house, among my children, because I agreed with his ideas, but because there was nowhere else for them to go. To refuse to receive them and not to offer them a glass of brandy would have brought eternal shame on us."

Major Golubović and the other members of the commission questioned Father some more and then sent him home to wait until Belgrade decided his future on the basis of their report. That day Father came home much earlier than usual and spent all afternoon shut up with Uncle Mihajlo, studying the relevant laws and possible consequences.

"Just as long as they don't discharge you," Uncle kept saying. "Everything else – a fine or punitive transfer – will soon pass, and things will go on as before."

A couple of days later Major Golubović summoned my father and spoke on behalf of the commission:

"You're luckier than you might have been, Petar. I begged them not to discharge you, as they meant to do. Instead, as a punishment you will be transferred immediately to Plav."

"For how long?" Petar asked. "Should I leave the children in school here, since there are no secondary schools in Plav, as far as I know?"

Major Golubović, choosing his words carefully, explained in the fatherly tone he had used when they first met that the transfer was permanent: "It has been decided that you can no longer serve in Kosovo."

It did not take Father long to grasp the disastrous consequences of his transfer to a tiny mountain town in Montenegro close to the border with Albania. He had persuaded his brothers, his own and his wife's parents, and many other relatives and friends to leave their homes and build a new life in Serbian Kosovo! What could he now say to all those people who looked to him for leadership and protection? His great ambition was wiped out by a single bureaucratic decision from Belgrade. Realising it would be useless to argue or protest, Father rose and without a word made for the door.

"Petar, stop for a minute," Major Golubović called. "I want to say a few words to you. Don't think badly of me. We've had some good times working together over the years. Both of us have failed. We haven't made friends and allies of the Albanians, as you wanted, and military force hasn't worked. They're the devil's own people. They keep together, collect arms, and wait to attack. What more can I say? Two religions, two languages and two peoples cannot live together as equals in Kosovo. One must rule. And if the Albanians don't like it, let them get the hell out of Kosovo to wherever they like – Turkey or Albania – and leave us alone. And you wanted to make friends of them!"

While Father was having his fateful interview, all our relatives gathered in our house – about twenty-five adults and as many children. The grown-ups wandered around our yard in small groups, talking quietly as they waited anxiously for Father to appear. After leaving headquarters, for a long time Petar wandered the streets of Mitrovica alone, trying to find some kind of excuse or justification to ease his conscience a little. What was he to say to those waiting at home? When they finally caught sight of him slowly approaching, his head bowed, they had no need to ask: they knew that their fate was sealed.

"What shall we do, Petar?" Luka asked, speaking for all the assembled relatives.

"What about us all going to Belgrade and begging them, on our knees if we have to, to let you stay in Kosovo with us?"

"It's no use, brother. I have to go where they send me. From Plav I'll do everything I can to get back. I'll write to friends in Belgrade asking them to help. I'll be back again in a few months, you'll see. It won't be long, and in the meantime, let Mihajlo Rajković, a clever and educated man, lead and advise you. He's a judge and he'll do it better than I can. I shall leave everything here, houses and land. I won't sell anything. Only Milica and the children will go with me."

While Petar was speaking, some of the women began to weep and pull their children closer, as if an unseen danger was suddenly hovering over them. The men, grim-faced, remained silent, without a word of reproach, but wondering what was to be done. Their anger was directed against Belgrade and those who had unjustly accused and punished Petar – and all of them with him. In their eyes it was perfectly natural to offer shelter at night to fellow clansmen. Each one of them would have done the same in his place. As the Montenegrin saying goes: "First ask your own folk in, then ask them why they've come."

Next day Petar had recovered his composure and calmly gave instructions on who was to do what. He invited Mother's brother, Jovan, to move with his wife and two sons into our house, which was stone-built and larger and more comfortable than his, and asked him to look after Filip and Stana, who would remain there. He sold the cab and horse to the brother of Šukrija, the messenger at police headquarters. His two hunting dogs, of which he was extremely fond, he took outside the town and shot, since there was no way he could take them with him.

The biggest problem was what to do with the older children, who could not continue their schooling in Plav. Ljuba had just graduated from a kind of secondary school for girls which taught practical domestic skills more than academic subjects, to which she was not inclined. It was decided therefore that she should go to Plav with the family. At eighteen she was the best looking of us six children. Tall and slender, with luxuriant curly chestnut hair, large dark eyes and an alabaster complexion, she was a refined, gentle, kind-hearted girl. "She can pick any husband she wants," everyone said.

But what about Stana, generally thought to be the cleverest of the children? High-spirited, stubborn, independent, she was the great joy and worry of our father.

On the recommendation of the headmaster of Mitrovica secondary school, after an interview she was accepted as a boarder at the highly regarded French teacher-training school for girls in the Serbian town of Kragujevac.

Father, believing there would always be jobs for teachers, wanted Duško also to train for this respected profession. He was told that there was a good teacher-training school for boys in Sarajevo, so thirteen-year-old Duško was enrolled and dispatched to that city.

"The lad's determined, hard-working and brave. He'll succeed in whatever he does," Father used to say.

For their tuition and keep Father had to set aside a large part of his salary. As for us younger children, it was generally agreed that our education would not suffer much in Plav. And so, a few days later, the six of us – my parents, Ljuba, Nada, Aleksandar (always known as Aco) and myself – set out from Mitrovica.

The only person who was not upset by this sudden downturn in Petar's career was Filip, for it revived his hope that he, and perhaps all the Tomaševićs, would return to Bukovik.

⁊≁

On the appointed day a large black motorcar, which Father had ordered from Belgrade for our move, roared and rattled into the yard in a cloud of dust. It transpired that this was a large taxi bought in England, one of the great fleet of London taxis in the early thirties.

Countless bundles of bed-linen, clothing, pots and pans and other portable household goods were stowed away in this capacious vehicle or tied to its roof.

Ljuba carefully packed separately the gramophone and records, our greatest treasure. As we carried everything out, our relatives, friends and neighbours stood by, silently watching, as if at a funeral. Our relatives were aware that from now on things would be different. Their dreams of a powerful and influential Tomašević-Rajković clan in a great Serbian Kosovo now seemed distant and unattainable.

Then Father came out of the house dressed in uniform, immaculately pressed and brushed, with gold epaulettes and braiding, his sword and revolver at his belt, wearing his peaked cap…Without a word to anyone, he jumped on to the running board and sat beside the driver. Mother and Ljuba arranged themselves in the back seat with Nada between them, Aco, the youngest, on mother's lap and me on Ljuba's.

At that moment the tall Rikalović from Herzegovina, married to my cousin, stepped out from the group of relatives, rifle in hand, and ran towards the car.

"Let me stand on the running board to Plav, to see you off in a fitting way and protect you against the bandits on Mount Čakor. It's dangerous for you to travel alone with the children."

"No, Rikalović," Father answered. "I don't need an escort. But God be with you, and may we all meet again soon, safe and well."

He told the driver to start and waving goodbye we left behind our relatives and friends in our Mitrovica yard…

Ethnic Albanian shepherd
near the border between
Kosovo and Macedonia.
The powerful sheepdogs
protect the communal
flocks from wolves

Wanderings in the Wilderness

The journey to Plav was the first of several such moves in the next three years. For hours on end we bounced and swayed as the sturdy London taxi made its way upwards on the rough, winding and dusty road to the top of the high Čakor pass. By the wayside children offered the rare passers-by berries or medlars in little baskets made of bark. Father asked the driver to stop near one such group of boys so we could all have a short rest and stretch our legs. He bought a dozen of these little baskets and the scent of the fruit filled the car all the way to Plav.

On the journey we passed occasional rough-stone cottages. In front of them stood their Albanian owners, rugged highlanders with moustaches and menacing expressions, in white, homespun traditional dress.

This journey would have remained in my memory as an enjoyable family outing had we not suddenly run into a calf on a bend in the road just below the summit of Čakor. The unfortunate animal had been at the back of a small herd of cattle which a couple of fairly elderly Albanians were driving along the road. Seeing that the calf was fatally injured, they raised the axes they were carrying and made towards us. Father, always prepared for some sudden turn of events, jumped out of the car and fired twice into the air. Taken by surprise, they stopped and dropped their axes. At the same moment, Mother, clutching Aco with one arm, drew out her own revolver and thrust it through the open window.

Terrified at what might happen, my gaze turned now to Father, now to Mother. With his free hand, Father pulled some money out of his pocket and offered it to the two Albanians.

"I leave you the calf and pay you this as compensation," he said in Albanian, so they would be sure to understand.

Seeing two revolvers pointing at them, they took the money without a word, and moved the animals, dead and alive, off the road so we could pass.

Our driver, a Bosnian, who had sat petrified and speechless throughout this confrontation, having satisfied himself that the taxi was unscathed, drove off at top speed to put as much distance as possible between us and the nearby Albanian dwellings. Immensely relieved that all this had ended without the shedding of any blood, apart from the calf's, he burst into a popular Bosnian song: 'A red fez, mother, have I on my head!' I couldn't help laughing as our driver was indeed wearing a red fez, the mark of Bosnian Moslems, the majority of whom were South Slavs converted to Islam during the five hundred years of Turkish rule.

⅏

At that time Plav had only fifty or so houses, of typical Turkish style, rectangular with wooden roofs. Even in such a small community, the Albanian and Montenegrin inhabitants lived separately. Only a few kilometres from the Albanian border, on the lower slopes of the wild Prokletije (Accursed) Mountains, Plav had been the scene of much fighting between the Turks and Montenegrins for control of this region. After the 1878 war between Montenegro and Turkey, at the Congress of Berlin the Plav district was given to the former. Turkey, however, did not respect this decision, and a combined Turkish-Albanian force managed to repulse attempts by the Montenegrin army to take possession of the little town in 1879 and 1880. It was not until the First Balkan War of 1912 that the Montenegrins finally added it to their kingdom.

When we arrived in the place, the heads of Montenegrin families came out to welcome us; the Albanians stayed at home. Father had become the 'supreme authority' for Plav and neighbouring Gusinje, which was even smaller. Both places were reliant on the military garrison located between them. Here, too, the senior officer advised Father not to trust the Albanians, but to look to his own people for support and protection.

"There's a state of emergency here," he was told. "Everyday there's some skirmish or other on the frontier. People get killed, just like under the Turks."

Here, Father usually went out to investigate a crime with an army escort, since two untrained constables made up his entire force. But in those scattered villages in the wilderness it had always been hard to apprehend wanted men, who were as a rule protected by their kin and their neighbours. If that wasn't safe enough, they would take refuge in the mountains, where it was impossible to track them down. These well-armed outlaws would return at night for food and to visit their families, vanishing again with the dawn. On the way they often committed further crimes, attacking and robbing passers-by. If they ran into soldiers and government officials, they wouldn't hesitate to open fire: somehow they were never short of ammunition. This was why every time Father went out of town to investigate a crime we awaited his return with a feeling of dread. Even so, feeling safe with our forceful and determined mother, we enjoyed our life in this wild and remote area, where wolves were common and sometimes came right into the town.

One day Father brought home a tiny wolf cub as a pet for us:

"Look after it till it gets stronger and dangerous, then I'll take care of it."

Our ownership of a real live wolf cub, while other children had only dogs, was a source of great excitement in the family and neighbourhood. Ljuba found a baby's bottle and we eagerly took turns feeding it. The cub sucked greedily, downing large quantities of milk and growing rapidly in size and strength. The neighbouring children would gather round to watch, and dash off screaming if it made a move towards them. After they got used to it, they brought their own small dogs or puppies, and we had hours of fun watching them play and wrestle together. When our cub had finally had enough or got carried away in the game, it would suddenly show its wolfish nature by biting its playmates.

Before long we had to chain it up. This was not at all to its liking and it would howl all night. We brought it food and water by day, but we no longer picked it up to pet it, afraid that it might bite us. The creature no longer trusted us either, greeting us with its tail between its legs, tossing its head and showing its sharp teeth. Mother kept urging Father to get rid of it:

"Its howling will attract other wolves here, or it will do some harm to the children, pass on some disease…"

"Let them grow up with wolves, get to know the wolf's nature – it may come in handy some day," Father joked.

One morning it was no longer attached to its chain. We searched for it all around without success. When Father came home in the evening, we all attacked him:

"What have you done with him? You've killed him for certain. You're always telling us how many wolves you've shot out hunting…"

"You let him go," Ljuba and Nada suggested, preferring this explanation of the wolf's disappearance. Father at once agreed:

"Yes, I let him free to join the pack he came from, to be with his brothers and sisters, mother and father. He wouldn't be happy here, children."

We never found out the truth…

⚜

At Easter, Duško and Stana came to Plav for their school vacation. Now the house was full again. Mother boiled, dyed and decorated a huge bowl of eggs, so that we could crack eggs with one another and with the neighbouring children to our heart's content.

"Give eggs to the Albanian children," Mother urged, "so they can see our fine customs."

On Easter Sunday we had guests. One of them was the mysterious Dr Zorati, an Austrian from Vienna who spoke excellent Serbian. His fine features were somewhat marred by scarring from gunpowder burns on one cheek and he had a couple of fingers missing on one hand. He spent much of his time hiking and mountaineering, for the clean sharp highland air, he often said, was good for his damaged lungs. Few evenings passed when he did not drop by our house for a chat with Father. They often spoke about the last war, in which they had fought, on opposite sides.

We children, especially Ljuba, liked to listen to him, for unlike Father, whose conversation was mainly about Balkan history, wars and the hard life of the highlander, Dr Zorati spoke of another, previously unknown world: Vienna, Berlin, Goethe, Beethoven, German history and culture.

"You see, I left all that behind to come here. I love your mountains and the unspoilt life of the Montenegrins and Albanians more than our high civilisation."

As a mark of gratitude and appreciation, he drew up a plan for a small park in Plav, and paid for it to be laid out, with several stone benches where the elderly could sit and rest. This being the first park in this part of Montenegro, his philanthropy gave rise to various comments.

At the Easter Sunday lunch, the priest blessed the house, the family and guests, as was the custom. At the end of the meal, Father proposed a toast which ended with the words: "May there be no more war, so that Dr Zorati and I will never again have to fire on one another."

Later, Ljuba brought out the treasured gramophone and played our limited collection of records, starting with the popular song 'Oh, Dona Clara, most beautiful of women!' This was followed by 'city songs', tuneful ballads with a slight Turkish rhythm that were popular in Belgrade and other Serbian towns. A crowd of local children, peering into the room through the open window, gathered to listen in amazement and wonder at the source of this music.

I spent much of the Easter holiday with Duško who, after Father, was the greatest authority for me. Tall and powerful for his age, he seemed to me even more impressive on his return from distant Sarajevo. He took me everywhere with him as he explored Plav and Gusinje – or, to be more precise, I tagged along, trying to keep up with his long strides. In his company I felt completely safe.

Late in the evening, when everyone else was in bed and there was finally peace and quiet from the commotion created by the children as well as neighbours and others who were constantly dropping in, Father would begin writing letters, asking friends and acquaintances to intervene on his behalf for a transfer. He wanted to return to Mitrovica, to his parents, his relatives and all his property: the seven houses and land he and Milica had acquired through hard work and self-denial over more than fifteen years in order to secure their children's future. But if that were not possible, then he begged them to help him get transferred to

Cetinje, to be closer to Crmnica, to which his parents and brothers might return.

Through his nephew Jovan, Luka's son, and Mother's cousin Mihajlo, the only fully literate members of the Tomašević and Rajković families in Mitrovica, he still exerted a decisive influence upon his many relatives there on all important matters. In his letters to them he begged them to ensure that his own and Milica's parents were short of nothing, and asked them to help his brother Djuro find a new wife so he wouldn't live alone, like a hermit. Djuro had in fact been married to a good-looking woman called Višnja, whom Father and Uncle Luka had persuaded him to cast off, after some time, on the grounds of her 'dubious morality', though more probably because she was childless. Although he eventually submitted to his brothers' pressure, Djuro steadfastly refused to look at another woman for years. Father's family letters ended with the hope that his request for a return to Mitrovica would soon be met, and in the meantime they should all keep together and help one another. They looked on him as their undisputed leader, temporarily banished, but soon to return even more powerful and successful than before.

Then, one day, the transfer arrived: not for Mitrovica, or Cetinje, but for Kolašin, a small highland town in central Montenegro near the entrance to the canyon of the Morača river. Close by was the famous Morača Monastery, founded in the thirteenth century by one of the Nemanjić family, rulers of medieval Serbia. Another swift mountain river, the Tara, also flows through the commune before cutting a deep gorge through the Platija massif and entering Serbia. Lying as it did on communication lines important for the whole region, Kolašin had been of military strategic significance in the past and was certainly a livelier and more congenial place to live than on the remote and dangerous border with Albania. For Father this move marked a partial rehabilitation and for the rest of us a great improvement on godforsaken Plav and Gusinje, which we left without much regret.

According to Father's transfer order, he was to take up the post of Kolašin's chief of police within seven days. There was no time to lose for one of his first duties would be to maintain law and order in the commune before and during the upcoming general elections for members of the National Assembly in Belgrade. The campaign was already well underway, with candidates busy making speeches promising what they would do for that particular area, village or town if they and their party were elected. As proof of this, some would go so far as to engage local builders and labourers to begin work on a rural road, school, hospital or whatever else was lacking in the area. If they were not elected, they wouldn't have to spend money on completing the project. In fact, everyone knew that from previous elections Montenegro was left with dozens of unfinished schools, roads, bridges, mills…

There were many parties in Montenegro, among them the Communist Party, which enjoyed considerable clandestine support but had no candidates since it was banned. Its members, predominantly young people, were hunted down by the police and mercilessly persecuted as enemies of the state. "Wasn't Yugoslavia created as a barrier against the spread of Bolshevism?" Father would ask, in justification. Even so, the tide of communism was rising in the Balkans.

On the evening before the elections, Father took us from our rented house to the home of a new friend.

"Don't let anyone see you or know you're here. Don't leave the house or draw back the curtains," he warned us.

Now we were no longer threatened by Albanians, for virtually all the two thousand inhabitants of Kolašin were Montenegrins. But political passions among them ran so high as to be no less dangerous than religious and ethnic animosities.

On election day, voters started arriving at dawn from the scattered villages of the large but sparsely populated Kolašin constituency. They came on rough-coated mountain ponies which shied and reared at all the commotion. A strong police contingent led by Father, reinforced with soldiers from the nearby garrison, controlled the entrances to the town and searched the incoming voters, relieving them of the rifles, revolvers and knives they had brought to have at hand, if need be, when casting their votes. After being given receipts to reclaim their weapons on leaving town, they made for the centre of Kolašin and immediately started congregating in groups according to party allegiance and coming to blows with staves, in the absence of firearms.

All day we hid behind the curtains and watched with fearful excitement as these highlanders, inflamed by party passions, some with bloody heads, chased one another up and down the street, shouting threats and exchanging blows, while the police and soldiers did their best to arrest the most aggressive and drag them off to the local gaol. Luckily, they were fully occupied fighting among themselves and did not attempt to enter any houses.

It was already dusk on that short winter day, with darkness rapidly descending like a shadow from the mountains around the town, when down at the far end of Kolašin's main street we noticed the bright flickering light of flames.

"They've set a house on fire!" we shouted in chorus. Our host, the elderly Rakočević, aware from long experience of the possible danger, told us to get ready to leave at short notice. If they failed to put out the fire, it could quickly spread along the street and we might find ourselves spending a cold night out of doors: "In my lifetime I've seen the whole of Kolašin burn down!"

This was perhaps not surprising since the houses, like those in Plav and Gusinje, were built half of stone and half of pine and fir timber, and cooking was often done on open hearths.

Though the house blazed for a long time, luckily there was no wind and the flames did not spread.

Late in the evening, exhausted by the dramatic events of the day, we all fell asleep where we happened to be – on the floor or the bed – fully dressed, so that we could escape quickly if necessary. Only Mother stayed awake all night, watching over us and anxiously waiting for Father to appear. When he finally arrived at dawn, we learnt that there had been a number of injuries, mostly from fists and clubs, but also a few from bullet wounds. Luckily there were no fatalities, which had made it easier to calm the hotheads and the voters enraged by the fact that the polling booths had been closed and the election called off in Kolašin because of the fighting. As for the fire, no-one knew how it had started, but when there was a danger that the whole town might go up in flames, all the political opponents at once forgot their differences and joined forces, pumping water and passing chains of buckets until it was under control. Then they brought out their brandy flasks from their knapsacks and the former enemies cheerfully began drinking to one another's health and congratulating one and all that by their combined efforts they had managed to save the town.

One winter day, a message arrived from Mitrovica. Grandpa Filip, patriarch of the Tomašević clan, had died, after a brief illness, at the age of ninety-four. So ended the life of a proud highlander, veteran of many battles against the Turks, in which he was twice wounded and lost his father and two brothers on the battlefield. Now he had ended his long life in muddy, lowland Mitrovica, where he had least wished to close his tired eyes. It seems that Filip finally realised that he would never return to Bukovik and, having lost hope of seeing his native Crmnica and the family hearth again, he lost any desire to live. Towards the end, he refused all food and fell silent, as though fixing his mind on his youth and those mountain tracks he had wandered throughout his long and blameless life.

Less than a month after his journey to Mitrovica to attend the funeral, Father received notification of yet another transfer, this time to the small town of Nova Varoš in the Sandžak region. When, in 1929, the Kingdom of Yugoslavia was divided into new administrative districts (*banovine*), the area known as the Sandžak (a Turkish word for 'region') formed part of the Zeta *banovina*, which incorporated present-day Montenegro. At the time, the Sandžak was considered, after Kosovo, the most backward part of the country. It had only half a dozen small towns of oriental appearance, among them Nova Varoš ('New Town'), close to the source of the Bistrica river. Well-known in the nineteenth century for its cattle market that served the whole Zlatibor region, it was liberated from the Turks by the Serbian Army in 1912.

All the small towns and villages in the Sandžak had an ethnically mixed population of Moslems, Serbs, Montenegrins and Gypsies. There was a large number of the last: every place had its Gypsy quarter, usually on the outskirts and on the least fertile land, beside some ditch or brook, out of sight of the other villagers. Here, as in Bosnia, the Moslems were mostly of Serbian origin.

Nova Varoš, with about one thousand inhabitants, lay in the foothills of the Zlatibor massif. It had only one proper street, flanked with Turkish-style houses with overhanging upper storeys and shop fronts with counters where goods, mainly imported from Turkey, were displayed. The houses were mostly clad with coniferous timber, found in abundance in the forests surrounding the little town. In the absence of mains water or sewage, epidemics were frequent and child mortality was high.

At the top of the main street stood a square stone house with a red-tiled roof, built by a certain Burić, a settler from Montenegro. Above the baker's shop on the ground floor there were two bedrooms and a large living room that served at the same time as kitchen, dining room and guest room. There was no bathroom; the well and WC were in the yard behind the house. Its most attractive feature was its large balcony, the only one in Nova Varoš, which commanded a splendid view of the whole length of the main street and the surrounding hills. Father quickly reached an agreement with Burić, a fellow Montenegrin, for us to rent the upper floor of this house.

In Nova Varoš father was again in charge of the police, but this time with the new task of rooting out the clandestine Communist Party cells in the little place and nearby villages. The growing anti-fascist movement in Europe had given a fresh boost to the communists in Yugoslavia and encouraged their ever more overt activities against the royal regime. The Party had already organised a campaign in aid of the Spanish Republic, dispatching numerous volunteers, many of them communists, to fight in the international brigades. The rising tide of fascism, the territorial aspirations of Germany and Italy towards Yugoslavia, the government's failure to resolve the country's internal problems, such as economic backwardness and the national question – all this worked in the Party's favour. In the past two years its ranks had been much strengthened by the return to the country of senior Party members from the Soviet Union, where they had spent several years working in the Comintern organisation. Among these was the Party's newly elected secretary-general, a Croatian-born metal worker named Josip Broz. After serving five years in gaol for his political activities, he had escaped abroad and spent some time in Moscow, where he managed to survive Stalin's purges and all the Comintern intrigues and in-fighting. As Party Secretary, he travelled around the country and abroad in various disguises and under assumed names, always one step ahead of the police.

In this multi-national state, all the legal political parties represented the interests of a particular nation – the Croatian Peasant Party, for instance, or the Serbian Radical Party. Only the Communist Party, still banned, had a programme that called for social, national and religious equality. As such, it attracted many idealistic young people, more and more of them willing to risk police persecution and join its ranks.

Many a time Father would come back home at dawn, muddy and tired out, and recount to Mother how during the night they had surrounded and arrested another group of communists in some remote village. He was totally convinced that what he was doing was for the good of his family and the country. To check the spread of Bolshevism was, as he said, "the sacred duty of all normal, respectable people and patriots". In all his letters to Stana and Duško, he would warn them at length against falling into some kind of communist trap, against swallowing the Party's propaganda and so ruining their lives.

"I know they'll never take to drink or any kind of vice, but the communist poison attacks the young and innocent, and they could easily fall prey to those devils," he would often repeat to Mother, giving voice to his greatest worry.

❧

Nova Varoš, on the border between Serbia and Montenegro, had long been of strategic significance, located as it was at the junction of routes along which many armies and rebel bands had passed in the nine-teenth century. Every day we were able to observe from our balcony the life of the little town and the arrival of peasants on their sturdy ponies. They would tether their animals in our street, shake the dust from their home-spun garments, wind their long white woollen scarves more tightly around their heads, throw their cloth saddlebags over their shoulders. Like spectators in a theatre of life, we would watch these bony, moustachioed farmers set out for town from below our balcony, shouting greetings to one another. Sometimes there were arguments, even fights, to hold our attention.

Around midday, the whole street was redolent with the smell of freshly-baked bread coming from our landlord's bakery downstairs. Then the café owners would carry their grills with red-hot charcoal out on to the street and arrange pieces of freshly-slaughtered lamb on these. Previously whole animals would have been roasting for several hours on their spits, turned and basted by the wife and children of the *kafedžija*, until the skin was crisp and brown. When the irresistible smell of hot bread began to mingle with that of roast lamb, we would start feeling hungry and looking down the street to see if Father was coming home for the customary family lunch. Quite often he would arrive with half a roast lamb, some salted clotted cream (*kajmak*) and young cheese bought from a peasant on the way home. This he would place on the table together with several bunches of spring onions and two large loaves, still steaming hot from the oven. Mother would then hand around plates and we would help ourselves to the feast spread out before us.

❦

Most days we used to go to the home of the three Musić brothers, sons of the Gypsy blacksmith. The youngest, Hajro, a well-built boy with blue eyes, unlike his darker brothers, was in my class at school and several times defended me and Aco in various children's fights. Helping his father shoe horses had developed his muscles, so he was good to have as an ally. Aco and I were the first to pay regular visits to the smithy, and later we were joined by Duško when he was home on vacation from

Sarajevo. We loved to hang around there in the warmth, supposedly making ourselves useful by pressing the footpad to pump the bellows, holding the horse's head as a shoe was fitted, or playing with a foal while its mother was being shod. Sometimes old Musić allowed us to hammer the red-hot horseshoes. We never tired of watching the sparks fly and the steam rise as the sizzling iron was plunged in water.

Duško spent more and more time chatting with the elder brothers, Musa and Ramo. One evening our landlord, Burić, who usually dropped in when his bakery closed to sit for a while over a cup of Turkish coffee and a glass of *loza* and to hear the latest news from Father, suddenly turned the conversation to the Musić family.

"I've been wanting to mention something to you for some time, Petar. What call have your children got to visit those Gypsies at the smithy? All kinds of scoundrels gather there, attacking the government, spreading unrest, speaking against the King and country. No good can come of that."

Father, strict and firm when dealing with grown-ups, was gentle and indulgent towards us children, always careful not to hurt our feelings. Still, Burić's remark that dubious characters, perhaps even communists, met at the smithy impelled him to issue a stern warning to Duško and myself not to go there again and to find different company. Turning to me he added:

"If you want to bring Hajro home now and again, you can do so, but don't go to his place any more."

Despite Father's ban, Aco and I still went secretly to the smithy from time to time. Musa, the eldest of the brothers, a young man of about twenty, used to ask after Duško, who had returned to Sarajevo, and always welcomed us warmly, offering us food and drink, pleased that his youngest brother was friendly with the police chief's sons.

In April 1939, the Government ordered a general mobilisation of the armed forces following Italy's sudden attack on Albania, until then considered as falling within the sphere of interest of Yugoslavia, which had helped King Zog come to power. From our balcony we could see, moving along the main street, lines of trucks packed with soldiers and hauling field guns, soldiers in horse-drawn carts and columns of infantrymen. Crowds of people lined the street, cheering them on, offering fruit, water, small gifts… Veterans of the Balkan wars foretold that the Serbs would again take Skadar and march across Albania to the sea.

All these troops were making their way through Nova Varoš and Kolašin to Plav and Gusinje on the frontier.

"Good job we got out of there in time!" was Mother's comment.

War, which Father believed would never come again, was at the door. Now it seemed that he realised for the first time the great mistake he had made in life, his personal failure.

"How could I have been so naive?" he confided in Mother, something he rarely did except in times of great trouble. "If it really does come to war, we must make for Crmnica, for the family land and hearth. Filip was right, but I wouldn't listen to him. I must go to Mitrovica – they're still waiting for me there. I must tell them to leave everything, all they've worked for and scraped together, and go back where they came from. This is the end of our Kosovo dream."

Then Father again began writing letters to various friends and connections, asking for help to get a transfer to Cetinje, the nearest town to Crmnica. For the first time he never mentioned Mitrovica. He decided to go to Cetinje himself for a few days, to push his transfer request in person. He managed to get a meeting with the Governor of Zeta Province, which had its seat in Cetinje. To my father's great satisfaction, he promised to arrange the transfer, but days passed into weeks and there was still no news. Then a police inspector from Cetinje passing through Nova Varoš told Father that he had personally seen the transfer order, so now we all lived in a state of high expectation, awaiting the fateful message.

※

Finally the long-awaited transfer to Cetinje arrived. Now Father was returning to his native region, which he had left nearly twenty years earlier, taking most of his family with him. He was returning older and wiser, already grey-haired at the age of forty-two, with his wife and six children.

Once again a large taxi drew up in front of our house and was loaded with bundles of household goods, some strapped to the roof. A crowd of neighbours, mostly indifferent, gathered to watch the six of us leave (Stana and Duško were away at college). We said an affectionate farewell to Burić, our landlord, and I expected Hajro to appear, as he had promised, but surprisingly there was no sign of him. The car slipped slowly down the steep street. At the bottom of the hill, near the smithy, as chance would have it we saw several policemen leading Musa Musić in chains. He stopped when he caught sight of our car, seemed to want to say something, but a policeman pushed him forward with the butt of his rifle.

"You had him arrested!" we all shouted at Father.

As we drove towards Cetinje, Father did his best to convince us that it was not he who was to blame but his successor, who had arrived with lists of suspects compiled in Cetinje. Though we believed him, for he had never been known to lie to us, this event cast a shadow over the journey.

Again we passed through Kolašin. The first snowflakes, heralding winter, began to swirl around the car. All day we made our way, on the edge of the abyss, along the terrifying winding road through the Morača canyon towards Podgorica. When we reached the level of Kuči, my mother asked the driver to make a break. She rarely spoke of herself and her family, but now, moved by the closeness of her native place, she began to talk about her home:

"Over there, in a cave in that snowy mountain, the flower of our family died, a dozen young men between sixteen and twenty years of age. It was about a year before the Balkan wars. Wanting to show they were grown men and ready for anything, some untried lads set out to plunder the Turks – in fact, they were Albanians, but because of their religion we always called them Turks. With their rifles on their backs and a bit of food in their bags, they walked through the snow for several days to raid some 'Turkish' village on the other side of the mountains.

"When they got there and started firing, the 'Turks' ran off, leaving their houses and livestock. Then my crazy relatives went through the houses and took whatever valuables they could find, drove the sheep and cattle out of their pens, and set off back the way they came. But the 'Turks' soon came to their senses and followed them. If it hadn't been for the animals, which slowed them down, they would have got away, but the pursuers caught up with them on the very border, just as they were about to cross into Montenegro.

"Surrounded on all sides, they left their plunder and livestock and took refuge in a cave. The 'Turks' kept them bottled up there for a week, and when they were almost out of ammunition, they turned their guns on themselves, so as not to fall into enemy hands, and so ended their young lives.

"And over there is Medun," Mother went on, pointing to a distant fortification. Not usually very talkative, now no-one could stem the flow of memories. "That fortress was held by the Turks, but our relative, Marko Miljanov, a famous hero and commander, the chief of the Kuči region, kept attacking them and gave them no peace until Podgorica and the whole of Kuči was freed from the Turks in 1879, if I'm not mistaken."

At dusk we arrived at Podgorica, which lies, as its name says, 'below the mountains', at the confluence of the Morača and Ribnica in a broad valley. For centuries Podgorica was a market town and crafts centre. On one river bank stood a typical oriental-style quarter with Moslem inhabitants, and on the other, long rows of one-storey stone dwellings where the Orthodox Montenegrins lived.

It was already dark by the time we reached the house of Slavka Perović, a relative of my mother, and knocked on her door. She was delighted to see us and not at all put out by the unannounced arrival of six people to spend the night. Straw mattresses and extra blankets were borrowed from neighbours and soon there were beds for all of us in various parts of the house, which was far from large. At that time it was customary when travelling to put up at the home of relatives or friends, and considered perfectly natural to descend on them without giving any advance notice: few people wrote letters and there were no telephones for private use. Slavka then hurried off with Ljuba across the bridge to the Turkish quarter, where there were shops selling delicious meatballs (*ćevapčiće*) sizzling hot from charcoal grills. Made of minced lamb and beef, with lots of chopped onion, they were an unforgettable feast for us children, tired and hungry after our long, cramped drive.

"I'm so glad you're going to Cetinje," said Slavka to my parents as we sat down to supper. "That's a real town. Podgorica and Kolašin, Plav and Nova Varoš, not to mention Mitrovica – all of them put together aren't worth a tenth of Cetinje. The people there are true 'noble' Montenegrins. All the rest are wild and uncouth. I'll be able to visit you now and again, when I go to stay with my sister Kitka. Her husband, Sasha Martinenko, a Russian émigré, works in the government offices, so I expect he and Petar will become friends."

Slavka herself had never married and made a living, very unusual for a woman at that time, as a portrait photographer – the only one in Podgorica.

Early next morning we were all on our feet, eager to leave and get to Cetinje as soon as possible. Most impatient of all, perhaps, was Father, who appeared attired in his dress uniform and in the best of spirits: his lifelong dream was about to be fulfilled. Before we left, Slavka grouped us together in her studio and took a family photograph.

꙱

Not long after setting out for Cetinje, we caught sight of the summit of Mount Lovćen. The taxi started to climb, groaning under the heavy load and steep ascent. Then we descended to the picturesque small place of Rijeka Crnojevića: two rows of colourfully painted Turkish-style houses with overhanging upper storeys. A crowd of Moslems and Montenegrins thronged around concrete tables where fish was laid out for sale – mostly carp caught in Lake Skadar. Flat-bottomed wooden boats, like country cousins of Venetian gondolas, slowly made their way to or from the quay, propelled by tall highlanders standing upright and thrusting their long poles into the bed of the shallow lake.

In the past, this tiny place, which takes its name from the little river Crnojevića, had been the main Montenegrin trading link with the town of Shkodra on the Albanian side of the lake and with Turkey. From this period a few Moslem inhabitants had remained there.

When Father appeared in the smart uniform of a senior police officer, all the people from Crmnica who had come down to buy or sell at Rijeka Crnojevića's market immediately noticed him. A couple of men from Bukovik hurried over to greet him:

"Is it really you, Petar Tomašević? Well, bless us, we never thought we'd set eyes on you again!"

After enquiring about people in Bukovik, Father asked them to tell the villagers that he was now taking up a post in Cetinje, and that, all being well, he would soon come to see them. What pride must have gone into those words "taking up a post in Cetinje"! He, the smallest in stature of all the Tomašević brothers, and perhaps of all the men of Bukovik, was the only one to achieve such success. Now he was to be deputy chief of police not just of King Nikola's Cetinje, but of the Zeta *banovina*, which covered the whole of Montenegro, Metohija and the Sandžak, and all the places except Mitrovica in which he had previously served. Bursting with pride, boosted by his encounter with the Bukovik villagers, and happy to be near both his native place and Cetinje, Father could not contain his satisfaction – further increased by the prospect of the return of Duško from Sarajevo and Stana from Kragujevac:

"Finally, Milica, we shall all be together. We shan't have to divide our income among Duško, Stana, Grandma, and ourselves. I'll bring Mother from Mitrovica, and we shall all be able to live quite comfortably on my salary."

❧

From Rijeka Crnojevića to Cetinje is only sixteen kilometres as the crow flies, but along the dangerous, narrow, unpaved road climbing steeply upwards with many sharp bends and potholes, it took several hours to reach the former Montenegrin capital. Every few kilometres the driver had to stop to let the engine cool down, pour in some water and check whether a sharp stone had punctured a tyre. We took advantage of these halts to get out and gaze down at the hamlets far below. This dizzying view of the abyss filled me with fright as I imagined what might happen if we suddenly met another vehicle on a bend or our brakes failed.

At one of our stops, Father showed us the place where, a few months earlier, the only son of Rakočević, our landlord in Kolašin, had swerved off the road to his death. He had been found, Father recounted, in the battered remains of his car at the bottom of a ravine several hundred metres below the road. As he was the last male in the family, a black flag now permanently fluttered from his house in Cetinje, as a sign that the male line had died out, that "the house was buried". This was considered the worst tragedy that could befall a Montenegrin family, even if half a dozen sisters remained alive and well.

And while we gazed down, looking for the wreckage of the car and envisaging the dramatic accident, Father said, as if to himself:

"When we reach Cetinje, we could move into that house, which is standing empty. Later on, with a bit of luck, we can find something else to rent or buy."

Before leaving the serpentines on the Rijeka Crnojevića side, we stopped for the last time on a slight widening, from where we could see the entire meandering stony road we had climbed from Lake Skadar. Below us lay the cascading villages and the lake: the most beautiful sight I had ever seen.

Vladika Petar II
Petrović Njegoš
(1813-1851)

Cetinje: The Promised City

In the late afternoon, as the sun slipped slowly behind Mount Lovćen, we arrived in Cetinje. What most interested me was whether there would be a black flag flying on the house where we were going to live, for I had been much impressed by Father's story of the last son of the Rakočević family. And sure enough, there it was, a little faded by the weather but still fluttering in the breeze that begins to blow down from Lovćen in the evenings.

The first few nights we spent in that house after we had rented it I had terrible nightmares of cars crashing into ravines and the mutilated body of the young Rakočević. In my dreams he had become confused with the figure of my brother Duško, whose arrival from Sarajevo I was impatiently awaiting. He, too, would take that road, drive around that fatal bend… But very soon I got accustomed to the flag of mourning, and when children at my new school asked where I lived, I would say: "In the Rakočević house, where the black flag flies."

Soon after, Duško and Stana arrived.

"Now we're all together again, children, like we used to be in Mitrovica, when you were young," said Father with obvious satisfaction when we sat down to the special dinner Mother had prepared for the occasion. "Now no-one can separate us. Let's have no quarrels. Love and care for one another. In a year's time Stana will qualify as a teacher, and the year after, Duško. The two of you will then be able to stand on your own feet, and perhaps help Nada, Bato and Aco to complete their education. Then Milica and I can be proud of having raised you all healthy and in one piece, without any serious accidents or injuries, and of setting you on the right path…"

After spending our lives in a variety of backward little places, Cetinje, with some five thousand inhabitants in 1939, seemed to us a city of great size and beauty. Father, at the peak of his career, had brought us to the former capital of King Nikola, the very heart of Montenegro. Its main street, in which we lived, was named after Prince-Bishop Petar Petrović Njegoš. His epic poem 'Mountain Wreath' tells of an historical event when the Montenegrins decided to destroy all their fellow countrymen who had converted to Islam. This powerful work glorified a Montenegro purified of all traitors to Christendom and called for heroic resistance to the mighty Ottoman Empire, which like a black cloud covered most of the Balkans at that time. Now Njegoš lay at rest on the summit of Lovćen, in a small chapel which we could see from our windows. I was filled with joy and pride that I was privileged to live so close to the great Njegoš, in the historic city of the Montenegrin people to which my family belonged.

On fine days, as the sun slid slowly down behind the chapel on Lovćen, its last rays bathed in a warm rosy glow all the harsh grey rocky hills that encircled Cetinje and reached down to touch the tin roofs of the little houses. These stood in several straight rows, like columns of soldiers drawn up before one of the many battles which the Montenegrins, led by their prince-bishops, fought against the eternal enemy, the Turks.

After the Congress of Berlin in 1878, where the international powers, including Turkey, formally recognised Montenegro's independence, emissaries of a number of nations began arriving in the little capital and setting up their 'legations', as the Cetinje people called them, at first in rented and adapted buildings. In the first decade of the twentieth century, they raised purpose-built legations that served as both offices and residences. Among the more impressive were the French, Russian, Austrian, Italian and British. These buildings were mostly in architectural styles typical of the country whose diplomatic representative would live there. The exception was the French legation, which was in an exotic style and larger than all the rest. It was generally believed that officials of the Quai d'Orsay had got two sets of plans mixed up and sent the one meant for Cairo to Cetinje, and vice versa. Be that as it may, within a few years the capital of the little principality, tucked away in the mountains, had acquired a dozen more handsome buildings to add to those raised by the Montenegrins in the spate of construction that followed the recognition of their sovereignty.

Prince Nikola was proclaimed king in 1910 in Cetinje. His coronation was attended by many members of European royal families, led by

his son-in-law, King Victor Emmanuel III of Italy. Nikola had an excellent command of French, which was the language spoken by foreigners at his court. The exception was the representative of the Romanovs, who had an almost daily royal audience that was conducted in Russian. Because of its similarity to Serbian, most Montenegrin diplomats preferred speaking Russian whenever possible.

Besides building their legations, in the thirty or so years they lived in Cetinje the diplomats and other foreigners laid out tennis courts, small parks and gardens, and brought a cosmopolitan air into the life of the little town. Their tastes, habits and dress were copied by those local families who socialised with them, the 'Cetinje gentry' as they were called.

The Montenegrin royal family with their spouses photographed in Cetinje in 1910 on the occasion of the golden jubilee of King Nikola and Queen Milena

✾

When we arrived in Cetinje, though more than twenty years had passed since its glory days as Montenegro's capital, these influences could still be felt. There were still families who spoke French, Italian or English, followed European dress fashions, and slept on imported 'French beds' instead of the rough wooden beds of local construction. On special occasions, meals were served on fine china left behind by the foreigners or brought from abroad by Cetinje people who had themselves been diplomats in various countries.

I remember pre-war Cetinje as a clean, tidy town of some five thousand inhabitants, with flower beds down the middle of the main street – something unknown in any other Montenegrin place at that time. You weren't allowed to play ball in the street, only in your own or a friend's yard. Smartly uniformed police constables patrolled the streets making sure that no child was disturbing the peace.

In addition to the 'legations', the town had other buildings of some size that were quite different in style and function. To me they all seemed enormous and extremely grand. Besides the ancient Cetinje Monastery where the prince-bishops had lived, there was the royal palace built for Nikola; the former residence of Crown Prince Danilo, where I went to high school; the Danilo I Hospital; and the Zetski Dom Theatre, opened in 1888 with a performance of the verse drama *Balkan Empress* by King Nikola, who wanted to emulate the literary achievements of his uncle, Njegoš. Though he signally failed to do so, the play was still on the repertoire, along with other historical works, in 1939. To celebrate our arrival, Father took the whole family to see this play – the first time any of us had been to the theatre. Then there was the Banovina, the office building housing the administration of Zeta Province; the army barracks with a large courtyard, enclosed by a high wall, from which the sound of rifle practice was often heard; the impressive Vladin Dom (Government Building), built for Nikola's coronation, where the King and his ministers used to meet; and two apartment blocks, the only ones in Cetinje, built not long before to house senior officials of Zeta Province.

❧

Besides Montenegrins, Cetinje's population at that time included a sizeable group of Russian émigré families. Fleeing from Bolshevism, it was natural that many sought refuge with their Serbian and Montenegrin brethren, who shared the same Orthodox religion, spoke a similar language, and had close cultural and historical ties with them. Russian émigrés were to be found all over Yugoslavia, in all towns of any size, and were very welcome, for the newly created state was in dire need of educated specialists of all kinds, especially teachers for secondary and higher schools. And so it happened that many of my teachers in Cetinje were Russians. They all spoke Serbian with a soft Russian accent that was immediately recognisable. The town's physicians, engineers and architects were also mainly Russians. My father got to know many of them, but was on the closest terms with the family paediatrician, Dr Gerasimović.

During our first winter in Cetinje, perhaps because we were not yet adapted to the climate and new environment, one or other of us six children was always ill. Dr Gerasimović would visit us bringing aspirin, cough mixture and advice to Mother on what each child needed. He lived at the lower end of town with his wife and sixteen-year-old son Dima, proud possessor of the only motorcycle in Cetinje.

Dressed in a leather pilot's suit, with a flying cap, dark goggles and leather gloves, he would roar through the streets, the envy of his contemporaries. He didn't seem to have any friends and led a solitary kind of life. His mother was said to have been a famous ballerina who had suffered terrible things at the hands of the Bolsheviks that had left her a little crazed. When she walked down the main street, her outlandish style of dress, sometimes reminiscent of a ballet costume, and broad-brimmed, flower-trimmed hats aroused a good deal of amusement.

One day, when I was going home after school with a group of classmates and passing by their house, which was near our school, Mrs Gerasimović came out to meet us and invited us in. Curious to find out the reason for this, we followed her indoors. In the spacious living room a dozen or more chairs were set out as in a theatre and a curtain partitioned off the back part of the room. We sat down on the chairs, as Mrs Gerasimović instructed, and she disappeared behind the curtain. This was soon drawn back, a gramophone started to play and Mrs Gerasimović appeared in tutu and tights. Our reaction to this unusual sight was to burst out laughing. Nothing daunted, our hostess began to dance, waving her arms and taking leaps across the 'stage'. As we had never heard of ballet, let alone seen a performance, we were soon doubled up with mirth. But when we started copying her movements, waving our arms and legs about, Mrs Gerasimović, a look of shocked surprise on her face, finally halted the performance and started scolding us:

"You're all a lot of common peasant children. Your place is with the goats. I've gone to the trouble of arranging a programme for you, to bring you a little culture, and all you can do is laugh like the stinking Bolsheviks. Get out! All of you out of my house, you ungrateful brats!"

Mrs Gerasimović then seized a walking stick and starting laying into the boys in the front row. Terrified, we all dashed for the door to escape from the enraged ballerina, only to find Dima, also brandishing a stick, waiting for us in the yard in his aviator's kit. He now chased us around, striking out left and right at those nearest to him, until we finally managed to dodge past and make our getaway. I guessed that he had known his mother was to give a performance for us children, had anticipated the outcome, and had planned this in advance as his contribution to the 'entertainment'. Anyway, after this experience we all steered clear of the young Russian, whom we now called Crazy Dima, and went out of our way not to pass the Gerasimović house.

To our house with the black flag Duško, now fifteen, brought various friends: some of the same age, but others who were older. These were not from the Cetinje teacher-training school he now attended but apprentices and workers employed in the town's craft and service trades: tailoring, repairing shoes or household goods, and the like. I particularly remember a young man of seventeen whom everyone called Lame Talaja as one of his legs was shorter than the other. He worked in his father's bicycle shop, where the fortunate owners of such machines could have their punctured tyres repaired. There were very few bicycles in Cetinje, so Talaja kept a dozen battered ones he hired out to us children, almost his only customers, who wanted to show off riding through the streets of Cetinje to the envy of our peers.

Because of Talaja's friendship with Duško, I enjoyed a privileged position. Bicycles were hired by the hour, and while other children had to return them on time, I would often come back half an hour late, knowing that Talaja would tolerate this from Duško's brother. Quite often he even let me go for a ride when I had no money:

"Off you go, Bato! You'll pay me when you grow up. Then you'll have pots of money, so don't forget me!"

Lame Talaja not only hired out bicycles by the hour but for the same fee also taught children to ride, counting on their becoming future regular customers. As he had only full-sized men's bicycles, it was not that easy to learn, but he was a very patient teacher, holding the cycle and running lamely alongside. Almost all the children in Cetinje, myself included, were taught to cycle by him.

"Why do you invite that Talaja home?" Father reproached Duško. "Apprentices are no fit company for you."

All the same, Duško continued to divide his free time between schoolmates and young people employed in the town's few workshops.

Father was even more worried by Stana's behaviour. She was then in the final year of the teacher-training school, but instead of devoting herself entirely to her studies, as Father urged, she seemed increasingly occupied by matters quite unconnected with her future teaching vocation. She often visited villages around Cetinje, sometimes stayed overnight, and like Duško was friendly with workers and their wives.

"I know," Father would say, "that Stana won't do anything wrong in those villages where she spends the night, that there's no harm in her being friendly with workers, but I can't understand the change in her since the last time we talked like father and daughter, when she was home on vacation in Nova Varoš. She's altered since then, become secretive. She no longer talks openly to me, like she used to do.

"Perhaps that's the way it is when children grow up," he mused, "when they become independent and no longer need their parents' advice. They think they can solve their problems better on their own.

That's how it was with me and my late father. I grew apart from him. And now he's no more, I wish I could bring him back for at least an hour or two, to tell him he was right about everything, but I didn't want to heed his words."

༉

Wednesday has always been market day in Cetinje. On the neatly set out concrete slabs that served as stalls, women from the surrounding villages would offer eggs, a few vegetables, figs, milk and other dairy produce, oil, lard… From early morning the streets would echo with the braying of laden donkeys, which the women would lead while their menfolk, dressed in black and carrying a stick or umbrella, strode several yards ahead, upright and dignified. The men came to Cetinje not to sell – that was women's work – but to hear the latest news, buy a newspaper and some tobacco, and talk amongst themselves.

We children would wait at the market for the donkeys to arrive, help unload them, and for a small sum lead them off and tether them away from the market-place, near Cetinje Monastery or in the open space by the little chapel at Čipur. Our reward was not so much the few coins which the thrifty peasant women grudgingly gave us but the chance to ride the donkeys to the place where we tethered them and back again in the afternoon, when the market closed.

One event at the market-place made a deep impression on me. One morning, at the time when the crowd was at its thickest, a man in his twenties named Vlado Dapčević climbed on to an empty table, made a clenched-fist salute, and began addressing the peasants and buyers in a strong, penetrating voice, calling on them to join the clandestine Communist Party of Yugoslavia, in which all people were equal, regardless of religion, language and nationality…

"Our movement will bring prosperity, like in Russia since the great October Revolution!"

"Long live Stalin!" shouted someone from the crowd.

He had not got very far with his harangue when the police appeared, led by my father, pushed their way through the crowd and dragged Vlado Dapčević from his 'rostrum'. All the time he was being led away to the gaol, not a hundred metres from the market-place, he kept on shouting against the King and the police, and calling on people to protect him. Vlado's family and ours were on good terms, so that evening his sister came to our house looking for Father. Stana met her at the door and the two of them talked for a long time. Next day Vlado was released from gaol.

There was a lot of talk in Cetinje about Vlado's outburst, especially among the young people:

"That's the way to tell them, straight out, like Vlado did. What can they do to him? They've already beaten him up so many times he's got used to it, and they daren't kill him because of his family."

࿐

One day a telegram arrived for Father from Uncle Luka in Mitrovica:

"Dear Petar, This morning at five o'clock our mother Stana died. A few days ago it was her eighty-eighth birthday. God rest her soul."

This brief message struck Father like a thunderbolt out of the blue.

"Oh, Mother," he lamented, "why did you hurry when I was just getting ready to bring you to Cetinje, to take you to Bukovik to see your children's graves and light candles for them? I was going to take you to the coast, to see the house where you were born, your relatives, the shining sea…"

This was the first time I saw my father shed tears. It must have been his Italian side coming out, for Montenegrin men didn't weep.

In Kosovska Mitrovica the brothers Luka, Djuro and Petar, with bowed heads, followed their mother's coffin to the grave. Next came her grandchildren: Luka's son, Jovan, and four daughters with their families, and after them my mother's family: Grandpa Aleksa and Grandma Jovana, Mother's brothers Jovan and Marko with their families, and her sister Mileva. Also in the procession were my mother's first cousin, Uncle Mihajlo, with Aunt Vasilija and Dragica and Dragan. At the graveside the members of the two families stood together for the last time, a final gathering of the fifty or so people whom my father, in one way or another, had brought to Kosovo. For a long time they stood silent and downcast, as though conscious that this funeral foreshadowed the end of all their hopes and dreams, the outdated patriotic romanticism that had brought them to Kosovo from their highland homes.

Before Father's return to Cetinje, anxious relatives questioned him:

"Is there going to be a war, Petar? Are the Germans going to turn against us?"

Others answered for him:

"They'll come to get their own back for the last war when we brought down their empire, without rhyme or reason. There's no help for us if another one starts. These Albanians will slaughter all our children."

Again the black taxi drew up in our yard in Mitrovica. Again the giant Rikalović from Herzegovina, married to Father's niece, leaning on his army rifle addressed him as had done when we left Mitrovica:

"Well, Petar Tomašević, we all believed in you and looked to you as our greatest hope. Don't leave us now in Kosovo, but take us back to where we came from. For us grown-ups it doesn't matter, but it'll be a great sin on your conscience if anything happens to these children."

The last person to say goodbye was Uncle Mihajlo:

"I'll be coming after you to Cetinje, Petar, and bringing Vasilija and the children with me. I count on you finding me some job in the court. Perhaps we could live together again: our families have always got on well and been close."

❧

Ten days later Uncle Mihajlo and his family arrived in Cetinje. Now there were a dozen of us packed like sardines into the house with the black flag, so Father and Mihaljlo started looking round for a larger place where the two families could live together in greater comfort. They didn't want to split up for, as they joked, the police and judiciary always hung together. As Mihajlo had hoped, Father had managed to find him a post in Cetinje's law court.

They soon found what they were looking for: a fairly large detached stone house in which we occupied the upper storey and the Rajkovićs the ground floor. It stood by itself on the outskirts of the town beside the road to Rijeka Crnojevića, the way we had come to Cetinje. From our windows and from the terrace, reached by a steep flight of steps, we could see the whole of Cetinje spread out below and, even more important, the peak of Lovćen with the chapel of Vladika Njegoš.

"To live in Cetinje and not have a view of our Montenegrin shrine is like being a prisoner languishing in gaol without sight of the sun," Father used to say.

Our house was new, not even completely finished, and had no address, so we called it the House by Black Rock – the name of a huge boulder by the roadside only a hundred metres or so from our house.

∂₹

Our arrival at once attracted the attention of the children living in that part of town. The boys of my age, ten or thereabouts, naturally interested me most. I soon realised that the leader in all their scrapes and dangerous games was a strong, stocky lad called Tomo. Before long I was joining them on expeditions to catch snakes. In the rocky terrain around Cetinje there were plenty of vipers, the cause of many deaths among livestock, and even people, throughout Montenegro. We all set out carrying stout forked sticks, scanning the ground for snakes as we walked. When we saw one, each of us tried to be the first to capture it by pressing its neck to the ground with his stick. Then, while the successful 'hunter' held it down, the rest of us would beat it to death with thin branches. It was our belief that a snake could be killed only by a thin stick, though why this should be so nobody ever attempted to explain.

This and other received wisdom shared by all the children prompted us to carry out ritual cremation of the snakes we caught and then bury the charred remains under a heap of stones. Otherwise, the snake would come back to life and crawl at night into the bed of the boy who had trapped it.

Tomo was the only one among us who dared to take hold of a live snake, picking it up by the neck with finger and thumb while it was pinned to the ground.

Around this time workers were widening the road from our house near Black Rock towards Rijeka Crnojevića. The only way to do this was by blasting. After drilling holes for the sticks of dynamite, the men would cover them with piles of branches and shout warnings to any passers-by. All day long we could hear the cries of "Mines! Mines!" followed by the sound of explosions that long after echoed around the hills encircling Cetinje.

On Sundays we had a respite from this noise. And it was on a Sunday that Tomo hit upon the idea of trying to find where the road-builders hid their explosives. With several boys from his gang he searched the nearby caves and found the boxes of dynamite. When news of this discovery got around, we all hurried to join him, curious to see what it looked like, the source of the immense power that shook the ground and made a noise like thunder. Full of self-importance he arranged several sticks of dynamite in a row on the ground, picked up one, struck a match and lit the wick. When it had caught and started to burn, he hurled it far in front of him in the direction of the road.

"Everyone get down!" he shouted.

Taking cover behind a rock, we waited with bated breath. A deafening explosion roared around the hills. Tomo lit another stick and then another. In a short time he had exploded half a dozen. Down below us on the road some people had collected and were looking up in our direction, shouting and cursing and shaking their fists. We quickly made off, scared they would call the police.

Tomo next decided to open up a stick and shake out the powder. First of all he poured it on to the ground, but then he noticed my school cap:

"Give us your cap, Bato. Or you can hold it with both hands while I'll shake the powder in."

"Here's my cap," I replied, "but hold it yourself!"

I backed away a bit and the other boys followed my example so that we formed a wide circle around Tomo. He pulled the wick out of another stick of dynamite and poured the powder into my cap.

"Have I got to do everything by myself?" he sneered. "You're all a lot of sissies! What are you waiting for, Tomašević? Come and help me if you dare!"

We all edged a little closer to take a look at the black grainy powder that glittered in the sunshine. There then followed a dispute as to what should be done with the stuff. One boy from Tomo's group struck a match and offered to set it off. Another said it wouldn't explode, only smoke and stink. Others had different theories. It was clear that Tomo was enjoying this argument and being the centre of attention.

Then the boy who had previously struck a match lit another unnoticed, darted forward and dropped it into the cap just as Tomo was bending over it. With a loud bang the powder exploded right in his face. A ball of fire seemed in a flash to bounce off his head and vanish in the acrid smoke it left behind. Luckily for the rest of us, at that moment we had been standing well back from Tomo, who was now lying on the ground screaming horribly, his face, hair and whole head still smoking. I ran over to him.

"Kids, run for help!" I shouted, but when I looked round they had all taken to their heels. I tried to comfort him, then dashed off down the steep hillside. In no time I was at home, where luckily I found Duško and Ljuba. She hurried into town to fetch a doctor while Duško and I climbed the hill as fast as we could. The boy was unconscious, his burnt face, blackened by the gunpowder, a horrible sight. My strong brother easily picked him up and carried him down to our house. A doctor soon arrived in an ambulance: though there were no private telephones in Cetinje, the ambulance service functioned remarkably well.

Tomo spent a long time in hospital. I don't think the doctors managed to save his sight. When I visited him there once with my father, his whole head was swathed in bandages.

"I've brought you some oranges to eat," I mumbled, but after that could think of nothing more to say or ask. I sat there silently for some time and then left.

I never saw Tomo again, nor did I go wandering with the boys around the rocky hillsides.

❧

This was the last of my childhood games. Other things occupied my mind and time. In a few months I would have to sit the high-school entrance examination.

"There's to be no more games or fooling around until you pass that exam," Father warned.

He engaged Professor Grabovski, a Russian émigré who taught mathematics at the *gimnazija*, to coach me in this subject (all our high-school teachers were addressed as 'professor'). The fact that, contrary to the school regulations, he gave private maths lessons to children who would later be his pupils was overlooked since there were very few in Cetinje who were competent to do so. He was said to have been a great landowner in Russia who had lost everything in the Revolution and had arrived in Cetinje without a penny to his name. Grabovski came to our house twice a week, and just before the exam received from my father not only his usual hourly fee but an extra 'tip'. Taking the money, he explained apologetically:

"I have to save up, sir, to get my own home again. My wife and I can't spend the rest of our days in rented rooms."

In return for this, I presume, the day before the entrance exam Grabovski, a member of the examining board, passed on to Father the questions he would ask me.

And so I became a first-former at Cetinje *gimnazija*. The school was housed in an imposing and beautiful building known as the Blue Palace, which had been the residence of Crown Prince Danilo, King Nikola's eldest son. With its air of grandeur, its clean, spacious classrooms, it instilled a sense of awe and pride.

One event at this time disrupted the peace of our family life. The police were informed that a number of students of the teacher-training school were spreading communist propaganda and causing trouble for the school authorities. Several ringleaders had been promptly expelled so as to eradicate this 'disease' before it infected more students: all the Russian émigré teachers had voted for this and most of their Montenegrin colleagues, who shared their fear of communism.

When the expulsions were announced, the students threatened to strike unless their fellows were reinstated forthwith. The protest soon assumed such a scale that the principal called in the police to intervene.

However, the appearance of policemen in the school yard only inflamed passions further: the students announced a deadline for the return of their fellows, after which they would carry out their threat of a general strike and march through the streets of Cetinje to demonstrate their dissatisfaction with the School Board and the police.

To his horror and mortification, Father learnt from the principal that Stana was one of the students most active in urging the rest to stick to their demand, even though it would inevitably lead to a direct conflict. Extremely upset, he at once went to look for her.

"Is it possible, Stana," he asked angrily, "that this is how you repay all the sacrifices Milica and I have made to educate you, to prepare you for life? Can you understand what it means for a deputy chief of police to have a daughter mixed up in communist activities? If you can't, I'll tell you: disaster for all of us, my dismissal from the force, the end of schooling for your brothers and sister. Do you think that now, when we are all together again, when things have finally started looking up after so much trouble and sacrifice, you have the right to ruin everything?"

"I'm sorry, dad," Stana replied, "I'm truly sorry because of you and the family, but I can't do anything else. I gave my word, and now I can't betray my friends."

"But don't you realise they want to make use of you, drag you into all this, just because you're my daughter? They push you to the fore in order to shield themselves, sacrifice you and ruin me. Isn't that obvious to you?"

On the eve of the day fixed for the student demonstration, Father spent a long time with Uncle Mihajlo, discussing its possible consequences from the police and judicial aspects. Stana spent the evening at home with Mother and Duško talking over the same subject. One thing was clear to all of them: Stana, having given her word, could not now break it, for in Montenegro a commitment made publicly had to be honoured. Only death could excuse an unfulfilled promise. At bedtime, Father went over and said in a mild voice:

"Well, Stana, so be it. Tomorrow you'll do your duty and I'll do mine."

Next day the whole of the teacher-training school turned out, about three hundred students, who were not only from Cetinje but came from all parts of Montenegro. Not a single student was left in the classroom. As the broad column of strikers reached the middle of Njegoš Street, Father was waiting with about thirty policemen. In the front row of students marched Stana, while Father stood in the front row of his men. At a certain moment he raised his arm towards the strikers, and in a loud, firm voice commanded:

"Ready! Advance!"

The police were carrying truncheons, the students their schoolbags. When the two advancing columns met, Father raised his truncheon and struck his daughter. This was the signal for the rest of the police to lay into the students.

Then he seized Stana by the arm and handed her over to the policeman who always accompanied him when there was trouble, to be handcuffed and led off to prison. The strike at the teacher-training school ended with many of the students nursing bruises from police truncheons and some twenty of them, members of the strike committee, spending several nights in Cetinje gaol.

Father came home in a state of nervous collapse.

"This is the end of us!" he lamented loudly as he came in. "The beginning of the end. I had to beat and arrest my own daughter. There she is now, in prison."

Turning to Mother, he added, almost weeping:

"Stana will never forgive me for this. And how much I wanted us to be a happy, harmonious family."

Duško, as a younger student, had been at the tail-end of the column and had returned home unscathed when the march was broken up. Now he watched Father calmly and asked with a hint of a smile:

"And why do you think, dad, that we shan't go on being a happy family?"

A few days later Stana and the other students were released from prison. At home she found Mother, who at once told her how miserable Father was that he had hit and arrested her, that he was afraid she would never forgive him.

When Father came home that evening, Stana went over and hugged him warmly, which she rarely did, saying:

"Don't worry, dad. I'm not angry with you. Both of us did our duty, like you said."

The following day the School Board unanimously voted to exclude all twenty members of the strike committee from further attendance at the Cetinje teacher-training school. Now Father had to run around to help Stana enrol somewhere else, so she wouldn't lose a year's schooling. Through some contacts he managed to get her accepted by the teacher-training school in Sarajevo, and ten days later she set out for that city. Again Father had to put aside a considerable portion of his salary for her living expenses and tuition.

Father's determined action against the student strike before it could have serious political repercussions, coupled with the fact that he had arrested his own daughter, were taken as extenuating circumstances and, somewhat surprisingly, he did not lose his job, nor was he punished by a transfer to some small place, as he had expected. But times were now different from when he was in Mitrovica.

Somehow, dignified and well-ordered Cetinje was never quite the same after this event. Law and order was no longer as secure. The police kept uncovering new communist groups in the *banovina* and arresting their members. The relatives of these then turned against the authorities and the police, for in Montenegro you always supported and defended your kith and kin, regardless of their political views. War threatened to engulf Yugoslavia and the whole country was in a state of tense expectation. The communists and their sympathisers stepped up their political activities and agitation, and the police seemed less and less capable of controlling the situation.

The stage was now set for the appearance in Cetinje of a gang of young men with criminal inclinations – scum, people called them – of the type that always surfaces in troubled times. Under the pretext of fighting communism, they attacked and beat up known or suspected communists, at the same time robbing them of any valuables they might have. This group, led by a certain Vlado, nicknamed Kokotan, did their best to ingratiate themselves with the police as anti-communists, so they would be allowed to carry on their criminal activities unchecked. Father refused their help and arrested them from time to time, declaring that communists at least had some principles and many were from decent families (probably thinking of his own!), while Vlado Kokotan and his band were without any moral scruples, the dregs of society:

"They're ready for anything when they get the chance: burglary, theft, fraud and worse crimes…"

❧

That Christmas, Father arranged for Duško and me to go to Bukovik, to spend ten days with our 'relatives' in his native village, so that we could get to know them and celebrate Christmas Eve. We were given the honour of bringing the *badnjak* (oak branches) into the house at midnight to throw on the open-hearth fire. When these dried branches began to crackle and flared up to the roof, everyone, flushed with wine and the fire-light, stood up and embraced, saying 'Christ is born!' and responding 'Truly, He is born!' After ten days of being feasted in every house, we returned to Cetinje, as we had come, crossing Lake Skadar by the old paddle steamer *Skenderbeg*.

Arriving home, we found the house full of neighbours. Our first thought was that something terrible had happened in the family, but Nada, seeing our alarmed expressions, at once calmed us down:

"Don't worry! It's just that Father's bought a wireless so as to listen to the news, so now all the neighbours come here and stay until all hours."

At that time radio sets were a rarity in Montenegro. I had heard there was some invention like a gramophone that also talked, but I had never before actually seen a radio. Duško and I were thrilled by Father's purchase. Till then we had only occasionally played the gramophone, in order not to wear out the records, but now, I thought, we would be able to listen to music on the radio every day. I soon realised, however, that for my father and the neighbours this technological marvel had a different kind of attraction. Leaning towards the set so they could hear better, they drank in every word that came out of the wooden box, but they were not in the least interested in music. I also saw that the arrival of the radio would completely change our lives. While it was turned on, there was to be no noise or distracting movement in the room. And when the radio crackled or the sound faded, they all hissed in chorus: "Silence! Shush!" Those long evenings when the family sat around listening to Father's stories were a thing of the past. This was not exactly the fault of that wooden box but of the news that it transmitted. Radio Belgrade broadcast frequent reports from the battlefields. For the first time I realised that elsewhere in Europe a war was raging. The news got worse day by day. England had been fighting alone for more than six months now. Czechoslovakia, Poland, Belgium, Holland, Denmark and Norway had fallen one after another to Hitler's panzer divisions. Even France, Serbia's great ally in the last war, the country on which Yugoslavia relied most for protection, had succumbed. Our neighbours Romania, Hungary and Bulgaria had turned their backs on us and joined the Axis powers. Only our oldest friend, Greece, was heroically resisting Italian forces and even scoring some victories.

In those first weeks of 1941 the situation was changing from day to day. Black clouds were gathering over Yugoslavia, the noose was tightening around it. My parents, Uncle Mihajlo and the neighbours seemed every day more worried and gloomy. Was Hitler going to attack Yugoslavia? This was the main question of everyone who came into the house, expecting my father and uncle, as important men in the police and judiciary, to have the answer. They ought to know what was going on behind the scenes in Belgrade, whether Hitler had given the Government an ultimatum: join the Axis pact or be treated as an enemy. And both Serbia and Montenegro had had bitter experience of what that was like in the First World War.

❧

Father and Uncle Mihajlo were both fervently anti-German, but Mihajlo expected help to come from Britain and America, whereas Father put his trust in Russia. Because of their shared Orthodox faith, similarity of language and customs, and historical ties, Father, like most

Montenegrins, was for renewing friendship with Russia, regardless of its present Bolshevik government and the Molotov-Ribbentrop Pact, signed in August 1939, which he and most people in Montenegro understood as a tactical ploy on the part of Stalin to gain time for a military build-up. Prepared for the time being to forget the danger of communism, he would declare:

"Now that France has collapsed, only mighty Russia can save us. Better to make a pact with the devil than with Hitler. Serbs and Montenegrins can never be friends with the Austrians and Germans. The Austrians will never forget that we brought down their empire, and the Germans that we blocked their route across the Balkans to the Middle East and the rich oil wells."

When our anxious neighbours finally dispersed to their homes, Father and Uncle would stay up long after, still arguing about England and Russia. This was the first time that Mihajlo had a serious disagreement with Father:

"What Russia! It's a communist dictatorship and rotten to the core. I say: 'Thanks very much for your Russian aid!' The English and Americans are stronger than any Germany. The English rule half the world, and if you add on the American fleet and airforce? You and I, Petar, can never join up with the reds. Our salvation is the West, not the East."

While conceding the threat of Bolshevism, Father would cling to his main argument:

"But the Russians are our people, and the English are foreign to us…"

Uncle Mihajlo expounded his views ever more often and vehemently, but found himself increasingly isolated in his conviction that help would come from the West. Not only Father but all the neighbours found it hard to accept that, if war broke out again, they would not have brotherly Russia for an ally.

During those long evenings of foreboding, waiting for news broadcasts, someone would occasionally relieve the tension with a joke, often at the expense of Montenegrins. It was then that I first heard the oft repeated anecdote connected with the battle of Grahovo in 1858, in which tiny Montenegro inflicted a defeat on the mighty Ottoman Empire. On the eve of the battle, the Turks asked scornfully:

"And how many of you Montenegrins are there, that for centuries you keep trying to fight great Turkey?"

To which one of them replied:

"We and the Russians are two hundred million."

The Montenegrins had, in fact, fought without the Russians at Grahovo, but they always had the feeling that 'mighty Russia' was not far away and would come to the aid of fraternal Montenegro whenever needed. In point of historical fact, this was not exactly the case: the Russians fought on the side of Montenegro only when it suited their own interests, and there were those who claimed that the Montenegrins had joined in to help Russia more often than the other way round. But Father liked this anecdote, which every Montenegrin heard a hundred times in his lifetime, and added:

"And that was just little Montenegro, with scarcely three hundred thousand souls, but now we are big Yugoslavia with fifteen millions, stretching from the Alps to Albania. We can fight the whole world and not lose the war," he would assert, getting more and more carried away by patriotic fervour. From my bed I could hear them discussing late into the night, sometimes till dawn.

One day the family friend and physician from Plav, Dr Filotić, arrived in our house with his wife and two young sons.

"What good news have you brought from Plav?" Father asked, when everyone was seated round the table.

The short, stocky doctor, whom we remembered as always affable, smiling, and telling jokes, now looked grave and depressed:

"Bad news, Petar. The Italians are building up their forces on the Albanian side and we're doing the same on ours. The local Albanians are now making open threats against the Montenegrins, who are busy grouping and arming themselves. They put their trust in our army, but that army, Petar, is reaching the frontier with guns pulled by ox-carts, like in the Balkan wars. And on the other side, they say, the Italians are bringing up more and more tanks and armoured cars. Their whole army is motorised. Not a single Italian solider goes on foot. What's our infantryman with his rifle going to do against that?"

"Don't talk nonsense!" Father broke in angrily. "If anyone hears you, you'll end up in gaol as a fifth-columnist."

"I wish it were not so, Petar," Dr Filotić replied, "but I'm telling you the honest truth. That's why we're all on our way to my wife's parents in Budva. If war comes, life will be easier and safer down on the coast, I hope."

The Doctor's words set Father thinking aloud:

"They're coming in ox-carts you say, Doctor? Perhaps that's what the army happened to have at hand and, since this frontier isn't important, they sent them to Plav. But then again it may be some kind of military trick to lead the Italians on, and when they cross the frontier, our army will bring out the tanks hidden in the forest nearby."

"Believe what you like, Petar. All I know is that this won't end happily. But you realised that yourself earlier on, and moved your family to Cetinje and safety in good time. But what'll happen to those left in Kosovo, I wonder?"

Father also wondered. What would become of his two brothers and their families – Luka's children and grandchildren? And what about Milica's people, and his own houses and land? He had been trying to keep his mind off Mitrovica, avoiding that painful subject.

"I'll have to think up something quickly," he responded, speaking half to himself. "We can't leave them there, but where can they go, poor folk, when there are fifty of them now?"

"What about Dr Zorati?" Ljuba asked. "Is he still in Plav?"

"Zorati? Like any spy, when his work was done he vanished, went over the border to the Italians. One day the police caught him taking photos of the army with their field guns. They took away his camera and said they would have a talk with him next day. But next day he was nowhere to be found. When they developed the film, all the pictures were of armed troops. And as for that park he had laid out in Plav, it turned out that from the air the paths show up in the shape of a swastika, which no-one had noticed on the ground."

As Dr Filotić spoke, I could picture Zorati's smooth, refined face with the scarring left by a gunpowder burn on one cheek, and hear his pleasant voice discoursing in fluent Serbo-Croatian on Beethoven, Goethe and Schiller. Those were the most interesting talks we had ever heard, and our introduction to German culture.

Hoping to avert war and bloodshed, on 25 March 1941 the Belgrade Government, headed by Prince Regent Paul, signed the so-called Tripartite Non-aggression Pact, whereby Yugoslavia would allow free passage of German troops across the country, in exchange for which Germany and Italy would refrain from attacking it.

The signing of the Axis pact was the last desperate attempt by Prince Paul Karadjordjević, personally considered to be an Anglophile, to save the country from destruction. Some months earlier, he had been invited to pay an official visit to Berlin with his wife, Olga, a Greek princess of German extraction, sister of Marina, Duchess of Kent, sister-in-law of King George VI of England. Hitler, it was said, was captivated by Princess Olga's beauty and insisted on the Yugoslav royal couple dining with him every evening. During the visit, an impressive military parade was staged in their honour. As hundreds of tanks, columns of armoured cars and dozens of motorised units roared past, while Stukas and other fighter planes zoomed overhead, it must have been clear to Paul, and any other observer, that if it came to war, his country would have no chance. This was the message Hitler wanted to convey, as he had done successfully with previous guests from some other countries. The Prince Regent was thoroughly alarmed. Seeing no alternative, he and the Government tried to negotiate an agreement with the Axis powers on the least humiliating terms. The Prince's main objective was the preservation of Yugoslavia as a state, so that the various nations that had acceded to it were not tempted to break away.

"If Yugoslavia goes to war," Uncle Mihajlo kept repeating, "you can't count on the Croats to offer any serious resistance to the Axis forces because of their Catholic faith and the Vatican."

Around noon on 27 March, in our house by Black Rock I heard what sounded like a crowd of people shouting. Father was in his office, and only Mother, Aco and I were at home. The noise seemed to be getting louder all the time.

"What on earth can it be, in God's name?" Mother asked, visibly alarmed.

Without waiting, I dashed off towards the centre of town to investigate. From all sides, people were hurrying in the direction of Njegoš Street, where the noise seemed to be coming from. When I reached there, it was impassable because of the crowd, so I dodged down some side streets until I came out at the head of the procession, which had stopped for a moment. Then I could hear clearly what people were shouting: "Better war than the Pact!" Being up-to-date with events, thanks to our radio, I realised at once that they were protesting against the signing of the pact with Hitler and the Axis powers.

"No pact with Hitler!" the crowd roared. "We want a pact with Russia!"

Then I caught sight of Father. With several of his policeman he was at the front of the crowd, as always when he had to calm people down, but to my utter amazement I realised that he was shouting with the rest, and his policemen too. Throughout all those years spent in the police force, Father had tried to keep law and order, but now something of overwhelming importance must have happened to make him behave in this way.

One surprise followed another: marching and shouting near Father was none other than Vlado Dapčević, the communist agitator he had arrested in Cetinje market. Now they were all marching together: students and staff of the teacher-training school, communists with policemen, people of all walks of life.

I caught sight of Duško with Lame Talaja, a bit later Ljuba and Nada. Only Stana was missing, still in Sarajevo, where she had been taking her final exams to become a primary school teacher. I ran to join Duško, naturally, for I always felt safe beside him. For the past year he had been practising judo and other martial arts with the police, so if things got rough I could count on his protection!

All day long the citizens of Cetinje demonstrated by marching through the streets. Whenever the procession stopped for a moment, there were spontaneous speeches, all on the same theme: Yugoslavia would never bow to Hitler.

Late that evening a large group of neighbours squeezed into our house, sitting or standing wherever they could find space in the rooms and hall and on the balcony. Everyone was waiting in suspense to hear Belgrade's reaction to the demonstrations. From the news broadcast they learnt to their surprise that Cetinje was only one of the cities throughout the country where there had been mass protests. The news gave a lengthy report on the biggest demonstrations in Belgrade, where over one hundred thousand people had taken to the streets, demanding that the Government renounce the humiliating pact. Simultaneous demonstrations had occurred throughout 27 March in smaller towns like Cetinje, where people were unaware that they were part of a nation-wide outburst of revulsion.

In our house nobody got much sleep that night, and lights remained burning all over town. Everyone realised this was a fateful moment in their lives and wondered what the morrow would bring.

❧

Next morning Pero Popović, my parents' best-man, arrived from Bar. I realised at once that the lean, grey-haired man with his right hand missing was my father's old friend – how many times we had listened to the story of Taraboš and how fifteen-year-old Pero had kept running forward after a Turkish sabre had severed his hand. When I met him now, I could visualise the scene with painful clarity. After Father was shot in the same battle, they had become lifelong friends, linked by the bond of *kumstvo*. Alarmed by recent events and fearing the worst, he had come to urge my parents to move with the family to his house in Bar, where they would be safer, he said.

During the day, Duško was visited by his friends. Besides Lame Talaja, who arrived on a bike and immediately gave it to me 'to look after', there was Mošo, with black curly hair, large dark eyes and a strikingly pale complexion, and Gojko Kruška, small in comparison with the others, with straight brown hair and hazel eyes. They were none of them classmates: their friendship had a different basis.

With regard to the question, hotly debated throughout the country, of what should be done in the present critical situation, Duško and his friends had very definite views. Tired of riding the bicycle, I went into the room to tell Talaja I had brought it back. Completely engrossed in their discussion, they didn't notice me open the door and squat down quietly in a corner: I didn't want Duško to send me away, as he often did when I tried to listen in. In a moment or two I was thunderstruck, unable believe my ears. My brother was saying how they ought to steal and hide any weapons and ammunition they could lay their hands on, anything the soldiers left lying around. Just then Duško happened to look in my direction and our eyes met. I wanted to get up and run away, but he just waved me down, saying calmly:

"Sit down, it doesn't matter now if you listen."

I realised that my brother and his friends were engaging in something completely forbidden and highly dangerous. Shocked and frightened, I could hardly wait for Father to come home to tell him everything I'd heard. It would be the first time I'd ever told on Duško, but I was certain it was for my brother's good. To my surprise, Father listened to my story without uttering a word. I had expected him to react at once, show astonishment or rage, go to Duško and try to stop him doing anything stupid. Instead, all he said, in a quiet, almost resigned voice, was: "Don't you worry, Bato, I'll have a talk with Duško."

In the evening our house was again packed with people. Besides our two families, there were Duško's friends, who had stayed on to hear the news, father's friend Pero, and the usual crowd of neighbours. When Father walked over to turn on the radio at the appointed hour, you could have heard a pin drop. As he fiddled with the buttons, tuning in, the set let out an ear-shattering crackle. He adjusted the volume, and everyone waited in a state of suppressed excitement for the News to start. The tense, strained expressions on the faces of my parents and every other grown-up in the room filled me with a terrible dread. For the first time in my life something was happening that was beyond my father's control.

Suddenly the national anthem ('God Save the King') boomed out from the radio. Everyone rose and stood motionless. Then, in a voice trembling with emotion, the announcer broadcast the momentous news: there had been a coup d'état in Belgrade, the young King Peter had been proclaimed of age, a new Government had been formed, headed by General Simović). He ended with the words: "Long live invincible Yugoslavia!"

Suddenly everyone leapt up again, repeating these words and hugging one another. So the demonstrations had succeeded! I felt a kind of pride since I had been part of them. Father pulled out his big police revolver and fired through the window, and soon gunfire could be heard all over town.

"We've saved Yugoslavia," Father shouted joyfully, "saved it from a shameful fate!"

After some military music, the radio announced that the whole country had greeted this turn of events with enthusiasm and was celebrating the formation of the new Government.

More music of a solemn kind followed and then again the news of the coup, which had been warmly welcomed by the Allies. Prime Minister Winston Churchill had announced: "Early this morning the Yugoslav nation found its soul! A revolution has taken place in Belgrade, and the Ministers who but yesterday signed away the freedom and honour of the country are reported to be under arrest."

That evening there was no more news, only martial music, but nobody showed the least intention of going home. They talked for hours on end, discussing the best strategy for defeating the Germans in the imminent war.

"It's high time someone stood in their way, and who better than the Montenegrins?" an elderly neighbour declared. "In the past we've beaten the Turks, the Bulgars, the Austrians and Germans, the Hungarians and the Venetians; we beat Napoleon Bonaparte when no-one else could, and we'll beat Hitler."

⁊℆

Cetinje: The Promised City 127

During the Easter vacation, Cetinje was full of young people who were away for much of the year studying in Belgrade, Zagreb, Ljubljana, Prague… Now they were waiting to see how events would develop. If all turned out well, when the vacation was over they would return to their studies. Their parents were happy and relieved to have them back, believing that if it came to war again, the young people would be safer here than in some distant bigger city. The young people of Cetinje all knew one another, had grown up and gone to school together, so when they came home there was an easy familiarity among them. In the evenings they met at dances in the Students Club.

Among the students there were a few who played a musical instrument – not that common among Montenegrins, whose reputation as an unmusical people was based on their fondness for the *gusle*. But the traditional one-stringed fiddle was no good for dancing to, so young people turned instead to the more romantic and melodious violin. Savo Popović studied the instrument in Prague, where he had met and married a pretty Czech fellow-student named Elsa, and often played at the club when at home in Cetinje. Quite often I used to stand around outside with other children of my age, peeping through the doorway or with my nose pressed against a window to see what they were getting up to in that stuffy, crowded hall.

One evening, while I was hanging around near the entrance, Ljuba and Stana turned up with some friends. Catching sight of me, Ljuba came over with one of the young men:

"This is my brother Bato."

"And I'm Vicko," he said, holding out his hand to shake mine, a gesture I always regarded favourably, as a sign of respect for younger people. "Come inside with us and see what's going on," Vicko added, leading me into the hall, which was entered directly from the street.

After a while Ljuba, Vicko and I, standing together and watching the dancers, were joined by Savo Popović, who was Vicko's brother. They were both very dark young men with neatly trimmed moustaches, and powerfully built. Vicko disappeared for a moment and returned carrying three bottles of *klaker*, a soft drink that had a round glass ball as a stopper.

I noticed that Ljuba kept glancing at me, eager for me to finish my drink so that she and Vicko could join the couples on the dance-floor.

"Now you've seen what it's like inside, met Vicko and Savo, so it's time you went straight home, little brother," she said with all the authority of a sister ten years my senior.

I left as she instructed, but instead of going home made for the *korzo*. The lower part of Njegoš Street towards King Nikola's palace was the scene of this nightly promenade. From as early as five o'clock it began to fill up with people, young and old, who came out for a walk, to meet friends and have a chat. Following an unwritten rule, the strollers were divided into those who walked on the right-hand side towards the palace and those who went on the left-hand side towards the French Legation. When you saw a person you wanted to speak to, you would simply cross over, if necessary, and start walking in the opposite direction.

Now both sides of the street were crowded with people neatly dressed and well-groomed. Looking at them, I felt proud to belong to Cetinje, to the 'Cetinje gentry'. After some time, the senior citizens, many of them government pensioners, for the town had been an administrative centre ever since King Nikola's time, bade one another good-night, shaking hands at length, and set off home. On the way, they would raise their wide-brimmed, plush-felt, black hats to greet acquaintances and swing their canes or umbrellas – sudden violent rainstorms were quite common in Cetinje. That evening I hung around at the *korzo* until ten o'clock, kept there by the feeling that this wonderful night might never be repeated.

When I reached the house it was full of people, as usual. Father came over to ask me where I had been until so late. I began trying to justify this, but he interrupted:

"Don't give me any explanations, but I want your solemn promise that for the next few days you won't go anywhere without telling me or your mother. It's important we all keep together. I must know where you children are at any given moment."

Instead of scolding me, as I'd expected, he had only asked me to do as he said, in a voice that was not as firm and decisive as before.

Duško Tomašević
(right) with a friend
in Cetinje shortly
before his arrest
and internment
in Italy in 1942

"Yugoslavia Must Be Destroyed"

When Hitler was informed of the massive demonstrations, the over-throw of the Yugoslav Government and rejection of the pact, he summoned his generals in a fury and ordered that Yugoslavia, which had refused the hand of friendship, be destroyed, mercilessly punished, as an example to the whole world.

※

The morning of 6 April 1941 dawned gloomy and overcast. We had just sat down to a late breakfast when Father, who had been on duty half the night at Police Headquarters, appeared in the doorway, deathly pale and clearly distraught. We all jumped up, realising something terrible must have happened. It was some time before he managed to pull himself together and speak:

"This morning, this morning at six o'clock, while people were sleeping in their beds, the Germans destroyed Belgrade. Thousands of women and children are buried under the ruins, crying for help."

The silence that followed his words seemed to last an eternity. It was broken by the roar of motorcycles below our windows. We dashed downstairs and saw a long column of perhaps fifty army trucks slowly groaning their way uphill, packed with young recruits armed with rifles, bayonets at the ready. From a young officer Father learnt that this was part of the Montenegrin Iron Regiment which was leaving Cetinje barracks to join the troops of the Zeta Division. These, the officer said, had already entered Albania, after scattering the Italian forces massed on the frontier. The news that our Montenegrin troops had already scored a victory over the Italians somehow made the bombing of Belgrade a little easier to bear.

"If they keep advancing like that, they'll get as far as Tirana," said Father, "and the Montenegrins will finally rule all the lake and the rich city of Skadar, as we've always wanted to."

Father went on talking in an agitated way about the Albanian theatre of war, which had played a part in shaping his life and the lives of all the family for generations back. War on this front had always been *their* war. The other fronts towards Germany, Italy, Hungary, were distant and unreal.

�

About ten o'clock in the morning, Father returned to Police Headquarters. Before leaving, he warned us once again not to go far from the house. If there should be a bombing raid, he reasoned, we would be safer there than in the town centre.

A little later, Duško and I went over to a neighbouring house, about fifty metres away across the road, where the three Nikolić girls lived. Anka, the eldest, was Stana's good friend and former classmate, the middle one was in Duško's class and the youngest, Stanka, was in Nada's class. We met Stanka in the yard and I stopped to talk to her while my brother went inside. A plump, jolly girl of thirteen, Stanka began telling me of some pranks they'd got up to at school, what one cheeky pupil had said to a teacher, and such like. She asked where Nada was. I said she was just helping Mother in the house and would be over right away: in recent days, with no school, we had spent a lot of time in their pleasant, tidy yard. After about ten minutes we heard the drone of aircraft.

"That's our pilots going to Skadar to back up the Iron Regiment," I said with a knowledgeable air.

It was a cloudless day and we could clearly see the aircraft gleaming silver in the sunshine. I had been fascinated by planes ever since my first sight of one in Mitrovica in 1934, dropping leaflets when the King was killed. Like most boys, I admired pilots and dreamed of becoming one, so I could soar like an eagle high above the peaks of Montenegro. Now I was thrilled to see so many planes and how they were regrouping, getting into formation as they came closer.

The noise brought Duško running out of the house to get a better look at this truly beautiful sight. As the three of us stood there gazing upwards, heads tilted back, some small black spots starting falling from the aircraft and growing in size at lightning speed.

"Bombs! Bombs!" Duško shouted, grabbed my arm and pulled me a dozen metres away from the open space in the centre of the yard. He just managed to push me down and fall on top of me before there was a terrible explosion nearby, then a second and a third. As when a thunderbolt strikes Lovćen in a summer storm, the roar echoed and re-echoed around the Cetinje hillsides.

The planes passed over and everything went quiet. Shakily we got up and at the same instant looked towards the spot where Stanka had been standing. There was no sign of her. I sighed with relief: so she, too, had escaped. But where had she gone? Then we both froze as we saw her lying on the opposite side of the yard beside the fence, her body all twisted and drenched in blood.

Horrified at the sight of death, I was unable to move or speak, but Duško ran over and tried to pick her up. In a kind of daze I heard the shrieks of her sisters, the voice of my panic-stricken mother shouting for us and for Nada, who had started out to join us only moments before the bombs began falling. She had had the presence of mind to dive for shelter behind a boulder, and this had saved her life, for one of the bombs had fallen on the other side of it. Contrary to Father's reasoning, the Italian planes had dropped their bombs around our house by Black Rock, killing several people, and not one had fallen on the centre of town.

※

Soon after Father appeared, out of breath, and almost fainted with relief when he saw that we were all unharmed.

"Those planes will be back," he said, so he and Duško at once set about digging a shelter a short distance from the house. In a few hours it was finished and well camouflaged.

"As soon as you hear the sound of aircraft, everyone make straight for the shelter," Father instructed.

As a kind of dress rehearsal, all of us, together with Uncle Mihajlo, Aunt Vasilija, Dragica and Dragan, crowded into the shelter, which was quite spacious and protected by rocks on two sides. That day Father did not return to work but stayed with us, in case the planes came back. As a precaution, we spent most of the day sitting outside at the bottom of the steps.

Towards evening we heard firing in the distance. In the direction of the coast, above Kotor, the sky was clear and sunlit. Behind Njegoš's chapel on Lovćen we could make out aircraft of the same silvery colour we'd seen that morning. Shrapnel was exploding under their wings.

"That's our defences at Kotor protecting the port and ships," Uncle said.

"Good luck to them," Mother commented. "I hope they kill the monsters who murder innocent children…"

For a whole hour Italian planes criss-crossed the sky beyond the chapel on Lovćen as the anti-aircraft guns resounded, battling to defend our coast.

In the evening, still in a state of shock from what we had lived through that day, we listened to the news. Stanka's twisted, blood-drenched body kept appearing before my eyes. The announcer started speaking in a trembling, almost tearful voice, the words sticking in his throat. Then the radio began crackling and we couldn't make out the words, though we could sense that he was speaking of terrible events. Bit by bit, his words started to make sense, like pieces of a jigsaw coming together:

"It is estimated that at least ten thousand people in Belgrade alone were killed in the early morning while asleep in their beds. Some four hundred German bombers, accompanied by two hundred fighter planes, flew over the capital several times releasing their deadly load of bombs. People are still pulling the survivors and dead from the ruins, while at the same time extinguishing dozens of fires that have broken out in the city. Today," the announcer says, "Belgrade has suffered its thirty-ninth destruction in its history. Kalemegdan, the heart of the old city, is on fire."

The newsreader went on to give a long list of other towns bombed that day: Sarajevo, Mostar, Cetinje, Skoplje, Niš, Split, Knin… Fourteen towns throughout Yugoslavia had suffered air attack in the space of a few hours.

"Wait a moment," said Uncle Mihajlo. "I don't hear that Zagreb was attacked. In all the towns mentioned there are a lot of Serbs living. Does this mean that only Serbs and Montenegrins are Hitler's targets?"

"This is not the moment for such discussions," Father broke in. "The fact that Zagreb wasn't attacked today doesn't mean it won't be tomorrow."

The announcer then went on to speak of the victories of our troops against the million-odd soldiers from four states – Germany, Italy, Hungary and Bulgaria – that had simultaneously attacked Yugoslavia.

"The enemy has failed to capture one square metre of our territory!" the announcer ended.

❧

Early next day, Mošo and Gojko came to the house to see Duško. After conferring for a long time shut up in his room, they finally emerged and Duško announced that the three of them had decided to go together to the military headquarters and enlist to fight on the front – any front, but preferably against the Germans.

"If a million troops are invading us, it is the duty of all who are capable of bearing arms to stand against them."

Mother, totally shocked, was unable to utter a word. Father was not at home, so Uncle Mihajlo responded in his place.

"How old are you, Duško?" he asked.

"Sixteen," Duško replied.

"And you, Mošo?"

"Eighteen."

"And you, Gojko Kruška?"

"Almost sixteen."

"And you boys are ready to fight with rifles against German tanks?" Mihajlo asked with a sarcastic smile.

"Not with rifles but with grenades. If each of us stops one German tank, it will be some help to our men at the front."

Without another word, the three of them went straight to the Command Headquarters, which was busy carrying out mobilisation and, in the time-honoured army tradition, was not much concerned whether volunteers were of military age.

When they left, Mihajlo turned to Mother:

"Well, Milica, why did we ever go to the trouble of raising a family? I can see the misery and suffering of the Austrian camps happening all over again. The flames of a new war could easily swallow up all we have, including our children."

While Uncle spoke, Mother wept silently, wiping away the tears with the back of her hand. Perhaps she was thinking of the happy times when her children were small, or maybe the mention of the Austrian camps had brought back memories of her own youth, pictures of the long column of internees trudging from Kuči to Bar, in which the figure of her mother became identified with herself, and those of her brother and sisters, consumed in the camp fires of 1917, with her own children, now perhaps facing the same terrible fate.

Several days passed. I found Duško's absence very hard to bear. Was it possible, I kept thinking, that something dreadful could happen to him, as it had to Stanka? That very day her funeral procession passed our house: four strong male relatives carrying the coffin with her parents, sisters and other family and friends following. As it moved slowly by, the thought struck me that Duško and I had been the last to see her alive, talk with her and hear her laughter.

Towards evening, we watched again as Italian planes tried to attack the Adriatic fleet based in the Gulf of Kotor. Our defences, well placed on mountain tops surrounding the Gulf, kept firing at the planes as they came over. Shrapnel seemed to be exploding just under their wings, but we never saw any aircraft falling out of the sky. Then the light faded rapidly behind Lovćen as night fell, the planes vanished and the noise of firing and explosions ceased. All was peace and quiet again until the uncertain morrow.

But nothing happened next day, or the day after. It was on the morning of 12 April that Duško came rushing home from the barracks, his face flushed dark red, his eyes wild. In a voice hoarse with despair, he started shouting while still on the steps: "Treason! Treason! The damned generals have betrayed us! Yugoslavia has capitulated!"

Moments later, just behind Duško, Father also came running. He burst into the house, grabbed a revolver from the cupboard where he kept it, and without a word dashed out. He had not got more than about twenty metres from the house when Duško, having grasped in a flash our father's intention, caught up with him just as he was raising the gun to his temple. With a powerful blow he knocked the weapon out of his hand and overpowered him with a judo hold. Father made no attempt to resist, knowing that his son was physically stronger.

Horrified at the thought of what had nearly happened, I just stared at Father in disbelief as he walked quietly and obediently beside Duško. He seemed completely dazed, unaware of what was going on around him. Duško led him into the house, in the way you do a sick person with no strength, and sat him down at the table. Father tried several times to say something, but couldn't utter a word. Then he broke down and wept. The sight of our proud father in tears was proof to us of something indescribably terrible about to happen, something which only he, who had lived through several wars, was capable of understanding and foreseeing. Then all of us, one by one, began to weep, realising for the first time in our lives that Father was unable to help his wife and children or himself, that he had no solution to offer for the present situation.

Hunched over the table, he seemed completely withdrawn into himself. Somehow he looked suddenly smaller and older, and we understood, as he himself did, that his patriarchal role was from that moment over, that authority in the household had passed from father to eldest son, just as it had done in every generation in Bukovik since time out of mind. Duško immediately took over Father's role, and started giving orders and instructions, and the rest of us obeyed, just as we had obeyed Father until a short time before. This changed situation did not alter Duško's attitude to Father, whom he addressed with the greatest respect.

❧

From downstairs we heard Uncle Mihajlo shouting:

"Petar! Duško! Help me!"

Father remained seated at the table while Duško ran out.

"Heavens, has there been an accident?" Mother asked in alarm.

Down below we found Uncle struggling to drag a large sack of flour into the house.

"Down there at the army stores people are carrying off anything they can grab," he recounted breathlessly. "The guards are trying to stop them, firing into the air, but people say: 'If you had any guts, you'd fire at the Germans, not at unarmed civilians.' But you'd better hurry up and grab as much as you can for your family. Tomorrow there'll be nothing left."

Duško rushed back upstairs and from the doorway called Ljuba, Stana, Nada and me to follow him at once. Father and Mother with Aco stayed at home while the rest of us hurried as fast as we could towards the army stores. There we found a great jostling crowd of Cetinje people of all ages intent on securing reserves of flour for the coming lean times. The most successful in this respect were the members of Vlado Kokotan's gang, who had plenty of experience in robbery. They had brought a truck and were loading it up with anything they could later profitably sell. One of them was guarding what they had amassed, while others were wresting sacks from women and older people and heaving them into the truck.

We were already late on the scene, so all we could do was scrape up flour spilt on the ground and push it into a sack. Duško left the rest of us to do this while he went to see if he could find anything better. The flour smelt strongly of moth-balls, since some naphtalene had somehow got scattered on the ground as well and was mixed up with the flour. We just hoped we had managed to scoop up more flour than naphtalene. Then we waited outside for Duško, who turned up after some time with Mošo, Gojko and Lame Talaja. All of them were empty-handed.

"How come none of you managed to get anything?" asked Ljuba.

"We did," Mošo replied, "but we gave it to the mothers of some friends who are out of town, and to some elderly people who couldn't get anything because of Vlado Kokotan and his gang."

We carried the sack of flour home and put it in a corner of the kitchen, but we soon had to move it because the stink of naphtalene made it impossible to sit there.

⅋

For a whole day and night our radio was silent. There was no news to hearten us from anywhere. Total uncertainty. Where were the Germans and Italians? When were they coming and what would happen to us? Our house was no longer filled with neighbours: as worried as we were, they all stayed at home with their families. All the time we were listening, expecting… Was that the sound of tanks? No, just a truck rumbling past.

Before dawn, we sat down together around the table. Mother made tea.

"Forgive me, children," Father began. "Forgive my weakness and cowardice. All my life I believed I'd be able to protect you. Then suddenly I realised that some power much greater than myself held your fate in its hands. I've lived through three terrible wars, all the pain and suffering they brought. The very thought that you, my children, could go through all that, and there was nothing I could do to help you, made my life seem utterly worthless. I see now what a terrible mistake, no, crime, I could have committed. Now is the time when we must all cling together. And if anything forces us apart, we must try to find one another, help one another all we can, so we can all survive. But it may happen, children, that after this coming war we never meet together again. I have only one last word for you, a final message: the most important thing is that those who survive can afterwards walk with their heads held high, their honour unsullied. War brings many temptations. Even the strongest may stumble and fall. We must never do that. We must safeguard our family name and pride. If you should find yourselves alone and have to make your own decisions, remember these words, which my father spoke to me and my brothers on the eve of war. Apart from this message, I have nothing else to give you."

Exhausted, our nerves at breaking point, filled with anxiety and foreboding, we spent the whole morning together in the warm kitchen, as we used to do in Mitrovica on a holiday. Our father's words had disturbed and moved us: we wanted to show him that we loved him and didn't blame him for anything.

❧

Another day passed. Then from the frontier regions of Montenegro, groups of soldiers started entering Cetinje, most of them hurrying through on their way to their homes in surrounding villages. They were returning from Albania, they said, where their units had penetrated deep behind Italian lines before they heard the news that Yugoslavia had capitulated.

Duško and his friends then went into action. They intercepted the soldiers, offering to free them from the burden of their weapons and hand these over to Army Headquarters for them. Some of the soldiers willingly accepted this offer, but others declined:

"No, thanks, we'll be needing them to kill wolves in winter, and perhaps for other targets."

Duško and his friends hid the weapons and ammunition they collected in caves around the town, from where their contacts took them to surrounding villages.

Next day Jovo Radača arrived from Bukovik. He was the youngest son of Ilija Radača, who had saved my father at Taraboš, and about Duško's age. The two had become very friendly during our ten-day stay at Bukovik at Christmas time.

"Ships full of Mussolini's Blackshirt units have docked in Bar," he said as soon as he entered the house. "They're unloading tanks and other heavy weapons, and in a day or two they'll be on their way here."

Father asked what had brought him to Cetinje. Jovo said he had come to help Duško and his friends, and carry 'certain things' to Crmnica, as it would be a pity if the Italians got hold of them: "Anyway, they have plenty of their own, and very soon all this may come in useful again."

It was perfectly clear to Father what Jovo was referring to, so he warned him:

"If you meet any Germans or Italians on the road, they'll shoot you on the spot."

"Don't worry, Petar, we've been preparing for this for a long time. We're going to load up several donkeys and ponies and take the whole load to Crmnica along side tracks where the enemy won't see us. We'll hide some of them above your house, in the caves in the mountainside, and some in other Crmnica villages."

"And who are you, the people that Duško's involved with?" Father questioned.

"We're all communists, Petar. All the rest have betrayed the country, but we haven't, and won't. We're just waiting for the right moment to act. Our time is coming, Petar. Your Government has collapsed and gone. It had the chance to turn Yugoslavia into a just society, but it never made use of that. You thought too much about the Serbs and not enough about the other nationalities. Now you're paying the price for that. We've seen how well all those fat generals defended us when they were needed. And we paid them more than any other country. We have to wash away the shame and disgrace they brought upon us before the world."

Father had long been aware that Stana and Duško had friends who were communist sympathisers, but he could not believe that his own children actually belonged to a banned, clandestine organisation. For years he had been fighting communism, uncovering and breaking up Party cells, while here, under his very nose, Stana and Duško had been engaged in communist activity.

But now it no longer mattered. The young King Peter II and the Government had fled to Cairo, the army had disintegrated, the state he had loved and dedicated his life to no longer existed, and the Germans and Italians could enter Cetinje at any moment. Everything he had worked and fought for was destroyed.

Cetinje did not have to wait long. The next morning we heard a loud rumbling beneath our window. Hidden behind the curtains, we saw about a dozen tanks, the first I had ever set eyes on. They stopped just in front of our house, where there was enough space for them to manoeuvre and get themselves into formation before entering the town. In front they put four or five smaller Italian tanks, painted several colours, and behind them the big German Tiger tanks with a white cross on the side.

"This is just the advance force," Father said. "The troops and armoured vehicles will follow."

With a deafening roar the tanks set off again downhill towards the town, raising clouds of dust behind them.

Less than an hour later, though it seemed an age as we waited, motorised units appeared, just as Father had predicted. Now, for the first time, we saw the faces of German and Italian soldiers. They were quite different from each other in every respect: the shape of their helmets, their uniforms and their vehicles. On Zündapp motorcycles with sidecars sat young blond German soldiers wearing goggles and covered with dust from the journey. They reminded me at once of Dima Gerasimović. The Italians also had motorcycles with sidecars, but both vehicles and riders seemed somehow less military, particularly those with bunches of cockerel feathers on their helmets. Uncle Mihajlo even tried to make a joke at their expense:

"Mind your chickens, Montenegrins!"

That day nobody felt like laughing, and this didn't even raise a smile.

The advance tank unit had surely reported back that entrance to Cetinje was unopposed, so the soldiers got out of their vehicles, gazed down at the town and took photographs of one another as souvenirs, just like the German and Italian tourists before the war.

Contrary to general expectations, the entry of the occupiers was not accompanied by the bombardment, arrests and massacres that had marked the Austrian occupation of Montenegro in the previous war. It seemed that these forces did not intend to carry out any punitive measures against the citizens of Cetinje. Disbelief slowly gave way to the hope that this might turn out to be a peaceful occupation and a more humane war than the last, that none of the evils we feared would come to pass.

Already next day the German units left Cetinje so it was clear we would be under Italian occupation.

"That's much better than being under the Germans," Uncle Mihajlo commented. "We're sort of related to the Italians through Queen Jelena. Perhaps they'll spare Montenegro real slavery, hunger and persecution for her sake."

The first measure taken by the Italian authorities was to summon all males between the ages of fourteen and sixty to report that same day to the *carabinieri* headquarters to give their particulars and get identity papers. Father, Uncle Mihajlo and Duško spent the whole day and following night in the courtyard, waiting in line to report.

Their next step was to order all radio sets to be handed in, under threat of imprisonment for non-compliance. And so, only a few days after the Italians' arrival, we were left without our precious source of information. Luckily, the military authorities were more lenient towards the Russian émigrés in this respect, and our relative by marriage, Sasha Martinenko, was able to keep his. In the daytime he had it tuned in loudly to Rome or Berlin, but at night, behind closed doors and windows, he listened quietly to London and Moscow. It was from him we learnt the fate of other parts of Yugoslavia and their peoples.

The whole of Yugoslavia was split up into occupation zones administered by the various Axis states. Slovenia, bordering on Austria and Italy, had been immediately occupied by the Germans, who also overran Serbia, Bosnia and Herzegovina. Hungary was made the occupying force in Vojvodina; Bulgaria in Macedonia and, together with the Albanians, in Kosovo. Besides Montenegro, Italy held all the eastern Adriatic coast with the islands. The 'Independent State of Croatia' was proclaimed, which also incorporated most of Bosnia and Herzegovina. The defeat and destruction of the Kingdom of Yugoslavia was complete. All those neighbouring states that had joined in the attack were rewarded with territory they had long coveted.

Sasha Martinenko recounted to us what he heard from London, giving us terrible details about the massacre of Serbs in Croatia, in Bosnia and Herzegovina, and in Kosovo. The worst crimes, it seemed, were being committed in Croatia, where, under German auspices, a huge slaughter was underway of the local Serbian population, which had been living in Croatia for centuries. Radio London reported that there were pits and caves full of murdered Serbs, while the bodies of the elderly, women and children who had not managed to flee in time floated down the rivers. In this 'cleansing of Croatian territory', Jews and Gypsies were also being wiped out.

A few refugees who had succeeded in surviving massacres in different parts began trickling into Cetinje at that time, seeking shelter with relatives or friends, and gave their own harrowing first-hand accounts. Terrified and starving groups of Serbs were wandering in the mountains and along the roads of Croatia, they said, hoping they would somehow escape the Ustasha units hounding them down. In Bosnia and Herzegovina, in the first few days alone, Moslems, together with the Ustashas, had killed over thirty thousand Serbs. In Kosovo the picture was similar. Albanians were killing Serbs and Montenegrins, burning houses and taking the land. From many places people were being driven out and forced into Kosovoska Mitrovica, which had become a kind of ghetto for the Serbs and Montenegrins.

⁊

About ten days after the Italians' arrival, an army truck drew up in front of our house and several *carabinieri* jumped out. After unloading picks and shovels, they started digging up the road, narrowing it to the width of one tank or large truck, and erecting a ramp. Then a barrack was rapidly put up at the roadside, large enough to hold a score of men.

"That's what the Austrians did in the last war," Mother commented. "Nobody could enter or leave any place in Montenegro without permission. Now it's happening all over again."

But that was not the end of it. At dusk the same day, several *carabinieri* banged on the house door. With them they had an interpreter, a man named Niko Milošević whom Father knew well. He explained that the Italian military police wanted everyone in this house by Black Rock to move out within two days since it was in the zone of a check point for controlling entry to Cetinje.

"Does that mean that no-one will be able to travel, for example to Podgorica, where my relatives live, when you block entry to the town?" Uncle Mihajlo broke in.

"It means precisely that," their officer replied. "Travel will be permitted only in exceptional circumstances and only with a special permit."

When the *carabinieri* left, all twelve members of the two families gathered together. We were faced with an extremely serious problem, difficult to solve in the short time we had been given to move out.

"Listen first of all, Petar and Milica, and you, children, to what I have to say," Uncle Mihajlo began. "We thought we should always be together in Mitrovica, and then in Cetinje. But now the moment has come when we must decide what to do and where to go. I'd like to head for Podgorica with Vasilija, Dragan and Dragica, so as to be closer to Kuči, where I have relatives and we can take refuge, if need be, just as you can always get to Crmnica from here, Petar. In bad times, when others control your fate, people always turn to their native place, their family roots, their own clan. As the saying goes: 'When guns fire, every bird to its own flock.' Don't take amiss what I'm going to say now, but I plan to leave for Podgorica early tomorrow, if I can, before they close Cetinje, even if we have to leave everything behind. Podgorica is in a more fertile area than Cetinje, and people know me there. It'll be easier to get enough food to survive than here among these barren rocks."

There was a long silence: what else was there to be said when the country had collapsed, when homes were being destroyed and people killed?

"Go, Mihajlo. Take the family. Get out quickly while you can," Father said at last. "Let's hope to God that this war is soon over, that we all survive and meet up together again, at least for a short while, so we can recall the times we've spent together and our children can renew their friendship."

Then we all embraced. Mother and Aunt Vasilija wept.

"What'll become of my people in Macedonia," Vasilja lamented. "Shall I ever see them again?"

Early next morning our *kum*, Mato Mrvaljević, owner of one of the few trucks in Cetinje, arrived to transport Uncle's family to Podgorica.

"I'm taking a risk for your sake, Petar," he said. "Bad times have come. There are guns everywhere, and you can lose your life for a packet of cigarettes, let alone a loaded truck!"

Then we all helped to carry out their small amount of furniture and baggage and with heavy hearts waved goodbye as the truck rounded the bend at Black Rock and was lost to sight. We all stood there silently for a while, picturing the family on their journey and still unable to believe that they had so suddenly vanished from our life in Cetinje.

⁂

Now it was our turn to move house in a hurry, but where to? There was no time to go from house to house making enquiries. Father's only option was to go to the home of a good friend, preferably someone who owed him a big favour, and say: "Here I am! I've come with my family to stay until better times." There were not, of course, that many people he could turn to, but it was an age-old custom that if you did someone a great service, you never asked for anything in return or spoke of it later, but that person remembered it as a debt of honour. Then, if ever you were in need of help, any self-respecting person would gladly repay the service.

"I'm going to see Vukmanović," Father told Mother. "He'll make room for us."

Vukmanović was the priest who had spent the night at our house in Mitrovica with the body of his brother, a communist leader tortured to death in a Belgrade prison, and a large group of friends and relatives who were accompanying the coffin to his native village. This act of solidarity with his Crmnica clansmen had cost my father his post in Mitrovica and set us off on our wanderings from place to place.

He found Father Vukmanović at home. The tall priest with his neatly trimmed greying beard and long black robe, hurried to greet him:

"What good fortune brings you here, Petar?" he asked, embracing him.

"Not good fortune, Father, but dire need. This very day Milica and I and our six children are being thrown into the street. The Italians need the house by Black Rock, they say. Might is right and knows no justice!"

"My home may be a tight fit for a large family, Petar, but when friends are in need, there's always room," the priest at once responded. "I haven't forgotten Mitrovica. Many's the time I've thought about what you did for us, the sacrifice you made, and prayed to Almighty God that the day would come when I could repay at least a small part of that. This opportunity makes me happier than I've been in a long time. Welcome to our home, Petar, together with your family. Stay for as long or short a time as you like."

Until late afternoon we waited, our nerves on edge, for Mate to return from Podgorica and help us move. The impatient *carabinieri* came twice during the day with an interpreter to warn us to vacate the house by evening or they would throw everything out the windows and make a bonfire of it.

The second time, Stana, unable to suppress her anger, burst out:

"What right have you got to drive people out of their homes and burn their property? Who asked you to come here to a foreign country, and force your way into other people's houses?"

One of the *carabinieri* stepped towards her and raised his arm, but the officer checked him:

"No! We Italians are gentlemen. We don't strike a lady, especially if she's young and pretty."

As one could never tell how a 'pretty young lady' might fare if she quarrelled with the occupiers, Father decided we should wait no longer. He told all of us to carry as much as we could and set off on foot for the priest's house in town. Mother, always a practical woman with her wits about her in a crisis, organised this, handing each of us a share of the clothes, bed-linen and other portable essentials.

As dusk fell, loaded down with bags and bundles of all shapes and sizes we started off in a strange procession: Father in his police uniform leading the way, followed by us six children, and Mother bringing up the rear, cursing the Italians who had come to ruin everything just when the whole family was together again.

In the house of Father Vukmanović, which had a large and beautiful courtyard, much of it overspread by the boughs of a huge, ancient linden tree, we occupied two rooms and a kitchen. The priest and my father respected each other and got on well, spending long hours conversing and the evenings playing chess. The fact that both came from Crmnica was another bond.

❧

When the Italians established themselves as the occupation force, they naturally took over the policing, which meant that Father was left without a salary. Since we had no other source of income, we were soon in financial difficulties. Even before, with six dependent children and Stana's schooling expenses in Sarajevo, it had been hard to make ends meet and impossible to put much by for the rainy day that had now come. Still, my parents tried to keep up an appearance of normality and the custom of Sunday lunch, when we all ate together.

One Sunday in May we were sitting around waiting for Ljuba, who had just "popped out for a while" and was late for lunch, which was most unusual. Just as we had decided not to wait any longer, there was a knock on the door and Stana went to see who it could be calling at that odd hour. We heard her burst out laughing, then Stana and Ljuba giggling together. The whole thing became clear, at least to me, when I caught sight of Vicko, whom I had not seen since that night at the dance when he had bought me a *klaker*.

"Mama, welcome your son-in-law," Stana cried. "Bring another plate someone."

Vicko shook hands with Father and Duško and hugged Mother and Nada.

"We were married this morning," said Vicko, beaming with pride and happiness. "That's why Ljuba is late for lunch."

"Everyone please be seated for the wedding banquet," Stana called out in a mock-solemn tone, then added: "We have some delicious beans without meat, but with plenty of onion, just as Ljuba likes them."

"I know it's wartime, but you could have told us in advance," our flustered mother protested. "I might have been able to find something better to eat. Or at least I could have baked a cake – we still have that flour."

"You mean the stuff that smells like moth-balls?" Stana teased.

"We never thought Ljuba would have this kind of wedding," said Father.

"I know I've turned up unannounced and unplanned," Vicko joked, "but I hope you won't hold it against me."

Then we all set about eating our meatless bean soup.

"Well, it's a very pleasant surprise for me," Stana declared. "I don't know how I could have gone on sleeping with my sister in that narrow bed. I sincerely hope, Vicko, that you aren't planning to move in here, but will take Ljuba away with you."

"Your wedding, children, puts me in mind of my own and Petar's wedding in Bar," said Mother. "I do believe we had beans for lunch as well. The only difference is that then the war had just ended, and now another one's just begun. It was easier for us than it will be for you. But that was how my mother got married, and I think my grandmother, too. We were born in wartime, grew up, got married, raised children – always in some war or another. That's how it's been since time out of mind. That's our fate in this accursed world."

After lunch, Ljuba packed up a few clothes and pots of face cream, and without more ado moved to her husband's family home, a large house in the lower part of Cetinje. Stana and I escorted her to her new home and spent the evening there. Vicko's widowed mother, Jelena, greeted Ljuba with open arms, delighted that he had found such a beautiful girl from a good family.

"I'm only sorry now for poor Savo," said Jelena. "He came back for the vacation and left his wife in Prague. Now he can't stop worrying and reproaching himself for leaving her. Who knows when they will be together again. What war does to people!"

Savo did not respond to his mother's words but took his violin from a corner of the room; "I'll play you a piece Elsa loves. I played it at our wedding."

That evening he played with exceptional feeling for his younger brother, for Ljuba, for Elsa in far-off Prague, for the wonderful evenings they had spent in that lovely city.

⊰⊱

As the weeks passed, Father, usually so active, was desperate at having nothing useful to occupy his days and no means of earning anything to support the family. One morning, not long after Ljuba's surprise wedding, we saw a large shiny open limousine drawing up in front of the house. Recognising this as the car of the recently-arrived Italian governor of Montenegro, General Pirzio Birolli, we were all thrown into a state of high excitement. This was compounded when an interpreter with the driver asked for Father.

"His Excellency General Birolli has sent his car and asks Mr Tomašević to come at once to speak with him."

Father quickly got shaved, put on his police uniform, which had been packed away in moth-balls in the belief that he would no longer need it, and buckled on his gold-braided belt and gilt sheath. He left the actual sword at home, as a sign that he was no longer in the King's service. He stood still while Mother brushed him down, as she had done every day before he left for work for the past twenty years. Immaculate in his uniform and freshly shaved, Father was once more the dignified representative of the law. For a moment, it seemed that the war had never happened, that we had stepped back in time and all was well.

With his head held high he walked towards the Governor's limousine, but then paused and called Mother aside:

"I don't know what's going to come out of this, Milica, good or bad, but as Njegoš says: 'Fear for his life oft turns a man coward.' But judging by the car, this smacks more of good than bad."

The unexpected arrival of the well-known limousine in front of our house at once drew a crowd of children and neighbours, who gathered round curiously to examine the vehicle close-up and conjectured aloud on why it was there.

Father's appearance, the magnificent car, the crowd of bystanders – all this filled me once more with the pride I had felt so often in earlier times, in Plav, Kolašin, Nova Varoš. We stood watching as it progressed down Njegoš Street in the direction of the English Legation, now the residence of the Governor of Montenegro.

All day and the following night we waited for Father to return. During the day I kept picturing him arriving home in the same car, loaded with gifts sent to us personally by Pirzio Birolli. I imagined these would include some *torone*, a kind of hard, chewy cake with nuts in it which I had seen Italian soldiers eating and had even tasted myself, when a soldier had thrown me a piece from a passing truck.

When evening came and there was no sign of Father, we got worried. Perhaps he had been taken ill suddenly and was now lying in hospital. But how to find out? Who to ask when it was already dark and the curfew was in force. Where was the interpreter, Niko, who had come to fetch him, though Father in fact had learnt quite a bit of Italian from his mother.

"If he doesn't turn up in the morning, Niko is sure to come as soon as he can to tell us why," Stana consoled Mother. "There must have been some good reason for Father to stay. Otherwise he would certainly have come home by now."

Sure enough, early next morning Niko knocked on our door.

"Forgive me for not coming sooner, as I promised Petar I would, to tell you what has happened. I was kept there on other business and afterwards it was too late because of the curfew."

He then recounted the whole course of events in great detail, repeating the crucial bits at our request, until everything sank in.

"At first all went well. General Birolli greeted Petar in a very friendly way – couldn't have been nicer. He offered him a cigarette and a drink, asked about his wife and children, enquired what you were living off. When he heard that you were in straightened circumstances, he promised that this would be put right at once, that the family of Petar Tomašević would lack for nothing. The General was particularly interested to hear about Petar's mother, where she was from and how she had come to marry into your family.

Cetinje in the 1930s: bottom right, the modest former royal palace, with a porch, now the King Nikola Museum

"Then he told Petar that they wanted to re-establish civilian authorities. 'There's work for both the military and civilians,' he said. 'I will run military affairs and you, civilian matters. We aren't enemies, but friends of Montenegro. We want Montenegro to be free again, as it has been for centuries. Our Queen Elena, beloved by all Italians, is your Montenegrin princess. She is eager to pay a visit to Cetinje, as soon as possible, to see the palace where she grew up, friends and relatives. And King Victor Emmanuel III is coming here very shortly. We need you to take over the police, establish the law and order that all the citizens of Cetinje long for. Peace and calm is what Montenegrins need now.'

"Then General Birolli filled two glasses of *loza* to the brim, handed one to Petar and proposed a toast. 'You are now chief of police, Petar Tomašević, and will take up your duties straight away. Let us drink to the Kingdom of Italy and the Kingdom of Montenegro!'

"The General emptied his glass but Petar only took a token sip. 'We know everything about you, Mr Tomašević,' the General went on, obviously satisfied with how things were going. 'We know you've been fighting the communists, just as I have for many years. We'll work together to free Montenegro from that evil. First thing tomorrow you'll bring me the list of suspects, so we can go over it together and decide what's best to be done. Perhaps some of them should be isolated, so they can't stir up trouble.'

"Petar, white in the face, listened to all the General had to say, and when it was his turn to speak, he said in an agitated voice: 'General, sir, I am a royalist, but I have sworn an oath to serve Yugoslavia, not an independent Montenegro. To separate Montenegro would mean breaking up Yugoslavia. As for the communists, you're quite right: I've spent years trying to halt their activities and influence. But now, General, my country is occupied. You are the victors; we are the defeated. I cannot hand over to the occupier any lists of my fellow-countrymen, even communists. That would be treason, and there has never been a traitor in my family.

'Forgive me, General, for what I'm going to say. It has been my life's ambition to become chief of police, but I cannot accept the post from your hands. I am Italian on my mother's side, and proud of it, but I was born here and serving Yugoslavia has been my greatest ideal all my life. Now, Yugoslavia is no more. It has been destroyed. So let the Tomašević family fall with it, but never let it be said that we were cowards or traitors.'

"Believe me, Milica and children, it was with a heavy heart that I translated all this word for word, as I had to, knowing full well what the consequences could be for Petar and all of you. General Birolli kept silent for a while, certainly surprised by Petar's answer. Then he turned to the officers who were standing there listening, and said: 'Arrest Mr Tomašević!'

"So now Petar's in prison, together with a number of suspected communists. I'll see if you can take some food to him, and he'll need a change of clothing – all he has is his police uniform."

All day long in my mind's eye I kept picturing my father in his fine uniform sitting in gaol with a crowd of Communist Party members.

Next day, the interpreter came, as he had promised, to collect some clothes he would try to pass to Petar. Mother had already prepared a bundle with a civilian suit, underwear, a thick jumper, a blanket and cigarettes.

"I've found out," Niko told us, trying to be as helpful as he could, "that food can be taken to the prison at two o'clock every Wednesday afternoon. The trouble is there are about thirty prisoners, mostly younger men from various parts of Montenegro who have no-one to bring them food, so everything you take for Petar will be divided up among them. He won't have much benefit from it, and it'll be a great expense and trouble for you. Visits aren't allowed, unfortunately, so for while you won't be able to see Petar."

Niko was unable to say how long Father might be kept in prison, but told us that the Italians were now mainly after communists, and as Father didn't fall into that category, perhaps he would be released fairly soon. He promised to use any influence he had to secure his earliest possible return home.

The interpreter came from a respected Montenegrin family. His father had served King Nikola at court and had escaped with the King to Italy, where he had been educated. Now he was back in Cetinje with a group of like-minded Montenegrins who were trying, with Italian help, to restore the country's independence, just as General Birolli had indicated.

An 'independent' Montenegro would make it easier for the Italians to pacify the occupied country and would ensure their post-war influence on the south-eastern Adriatic seaboard. The Greens, supporters of King Nikola and the separation of Montenegro from Yugoslavia, were now collaborating closely with the Italians to achieve their goal – activity that Father had condemned as treason well before his arrest.

The news that Father had refused to collaborate with the occupiers and was in gaol quickly spread through the town. Duško could hardly conceal his pride that his father was in prison and sharing his food with Party members. Now our great problem was what to take him every Wednesday when we had virtually no food in the house except that sack of smelly flour.

Stana had left for a few days to stay with a girlfriend in a nearby village, she said. This friend, Danica Marinović, lived with her widowed mother, an illiterate peasant woman who used to come daily to Cetinje on her donkey bringing milk for sale in order to put her daughter through school. Danica, a bright, pretty girl, had often spent the night at our house and Stana used to go to her home in the village. The two of them had left together a couple of days before the Italians completed the barbed-wire encirclement around the town and controlled all exits, so that we began to worry how she would get back.

Duško, now acting as head of the family, outlined a survival plan:

"We're not going to eat this flour, but the Italians will, and we'll buy some better stuff for ourselves. Mother, you'll make doughnuts from it, and Nada, Bato and Aco, you'll sell them to the Italian soldiers every morning as they're leaving Cetinje. If any of them get poisoned by the flour, it'll be harder to trace the source when they're leaving than when they're arriving."

That very night Mother got busy making doughnuts. Not only was the flour contaminated, but the oil she fried them in, which Duško had managed to get hold of somewhere, was rancid. No matter, at first light the three of us were standing by the side of the road that led from Cetinje across Lovćen to Kotor. The soldiers passing by were pleasantly surprised to see our large baking tray full of doughnuts and in no time the whole lot had vanished. By this means we managed to get rid of the whole sack of dubious flour, buy a fresh sack, and on Wednesdays carry a large pan of thick bean soup to Father and the other inmates, to supplement their meagre prison fare.

In spite of everything, life in Cetinje for a brief period was relatively bearable, and for us children, in fact, more entertaining than usual. The Italians did their best to make it so. Every day their soldiers, in smart, well-pressed uniforms, with brilliantined hair, paraded along Njegoš Street singing tuneful marching songs that echoed the length of the boulevard. As they sang they cast sidelong glances at the local girls, who had been strictly forbidden by fathers and brothers to wear smart clothes, silk stocking and make-up, so as not to attract unwanted attentions from the soldiers.

Every evening a military band played in front of the former royal palace, drawing a crowd of elderly people and children. Cetinje's senior citizens still recalled the time when a military band would play there in the presence of King Nikola, Queen Milena and their nine daughters, seated on the balcony. While listening to the music, they would nod graciously to the various foreign diplomats who promenaded past every evening so as to be noticed by the King. Duško and his friends thoroughly disapproved of this daily musical entertainment by the military and discussed how best to disrupt it, believing that it diverted the Montenegrins from what they considered the paramount task: "the struggle against the occupier".

"You see with what ancient Latin cunning they're trying to exploit the nostalgia of some Cetinje people for the Montenegrin kingdom, so as to divide and rule us," they complained to one another.

Gojko Kruška hit upon the simplest solution.

"All we need," he said, "is a few lemons, Bato, Aco and a couple of their friends."

Next day, each of us with half a lemon in his pocket, we placed ourselves in the very front, as close as we could get to the bandsmen. When they started playing, as arranged we all brought out our lemons and began licking and sucking them, making awful grimaces indicative of their sourness. One after another the wind instrument players dried up and the music stuttered to a stop while the military police started chasing us round in circles to roars of laughter from the crowd of children. We disappeared for a few minutes, waiting for the music to restart, and then repeated our lemon routine, with the same satisfactory results. After three or four times, we went home to report our success and bask in the praise of Duško and his friends.

One day the Italians started a small radio station in Cetinje. On the trees and the electricity and telegraph poles along Njegoš Street they rigged up loudspeakers so that all day long the people of Cetinje could listen to music interspersed by talks on the historical ties between Italy and Montenegro and information on all the projects that the Italians had built and begun since their arrival. Popular Italian and Montenegrin songs were performed by young local singers specially chosen for their talent.

To impress and win over the people of Cetinje, the Italians staged military parades. This was the first time I ever witnessed the *paso Romano*, the march ascribed to the victorious legions of ancient Rome. Holding one another by the belt, the wide, close-packed rows of soldiers progressed with their high stamping action along Njegoš Street, which echoed with the beat of their iron-tipped boots. In front marched the band in colourful uniforms, and at the head of the procession, the bandmaster, keeping time by raising and lowering a multi-coloured baton which he occasionally tossed and caught with a nonchalance that impressed us children more than the marchers and the music.

What I found most thrilling, however, were the new bicycles the Italian officers rode, with their silver mudguards and a bell on the handlebar to warn pedestrians to take care. These were the very latest models, the pinnacle of bicycle engineering – objects I had not even imagined could exist, so far removed were they from the heavy, rusty bikes we had hired by the hour from Lame Talaja.

The Italians' efforts to convince the population that theirs was a friendly army were successful among one section that had mourned the departure of King Nikola. At the beginning they managed to bring some colour into the grey, monotonous life of patriarchal Montenegro, for they organised similar entertainments in all bigger places, not only in Cetinje. Even Duško and his friends were reluctantly obliged to admit this. They still managed, however, to find plenty of reasons to ridicule the occupiers and belittle them as soldiers.

"Just look at them," someone would say, "how small and puny they are! When they do that stupid march of theirs, throwing their short legs in the air, it looks as though a wasp has stung them on the arse. They're good for the circus and nothing else. That's why they dress up in those fancy uniforms and stick feathers on their heads, as though they're going to start crowing any minute."

All this time Stana had not yet come back from the village. Mother grew anxious, but Duško reassured her:

"Don't worry about Stana. Let her stay for a while with Danica. She's better off in the village than here."

ða

At that time there were still a number of sons of Montenegrin emigrants who had stayed in Italy after completing their education, and were now awaiting the right moment to return to the country and enter government service. In Cetinje there was a lot of talk about Prince Mihajlo, grandson of King Nikola, who was living in occupied France, from where he was said to be returning, with Italian help, to ascend the restored Montenegrin throne.

One day we saw furniture and trunks being unloaded from a large army truck drawn up in front of the apartment building just opposite our house. What particularly caught my eye was a shiny black grand piano, which the soldiers handled with particular care. We all wondered who could be the owners of such beautiful and expensive articles, who was moving into one of the bigger apartments, reserved before the war for senior government officials.

The unloading had just been completed when an army limousine drew up and a young couple got out with a girl, obviously their daughter, who looked to be a little younger than myself. The dark-haired little girl turned around, gazing wide-eyed at the low, one-storey houses and the hills rising on all sides of the town. It was only a matter of minutes before the news spread round the neighbourhood that this tall, good-looking man in civilian clothes was a relative of the Italian queen, who had personally supervised his education in Rome. His wife, small, plump and black-haired, was obviously not well pleased with what she saw on arrival and made no attempt to conceal her disdain. While her husband shook hands with curious neighbours who had come out to make their acquaintance, she summoned the little girl in Italian, took her hand and marched into the building without a smile or greeting to anyone.

Next day I discovered that the dark-haired little newcomer was called Olga. As my Italian was already quite fluent, at the first opportunity I started to question her about where they were from and whether they were going to stay long in Cetinje. I often stood at the window to see whether she was in front of her house or was going somewhere with her parents. When her mother saw Olga talking to me, she angrily called her indoors: a bare-footed, scrawny, local boy was certainly no fit company for her neat and well-dressed daughter. I was eleven years old and this pretty little 'foreigner' was the first girl to catch my imagination.

Mausoleum-chapel
of Prince-Bishop
Petar Petrović Njegoš,
Montenegro's greatest
poet, on the summit
of Mount Lovćen above
Cetinje, photographed
in the 1950s

Uprising in Montenegro

One evening Duško got us together to warn us that on no account should we leave the house next day.

"We've found out that the Italian king is coming to Cetinje tomorrow. They have been making secret preparations for this visit for a whole month, but so have we. The king may fare no better than Franz Ferdinand in Sarajevo!"

The next evening he told us that King Victor Emmanuel had indeed come to Cetinje, but less than an hour later had left hurriedly, much to the surprise and disappointment of the hundred or so friends of Italy who were expecting to meet and welcome him, as the visit was supposed to last all day.

⚓

The morning of 13 July 1941 dawned bright and fine. The music from loudspeakers to which we had become accustomed was suddenly interrupted around noon, replaced by the roar of tanks moving in two directions: one column making off at top speed in the direction of Kotor, while the other headed for Black Rock and the road to Rijeka Crnojevića. The tanks were followed by armoured cars and open trucks filled with helmeted soldiers holding rifles with fixed bayonets.

What was all the hurry? Why were the soldiers so serious? Generally relaxed and cheerful, now they just stared grimly ahead, clutching their short Italian rifles, not talking among themselves.

Mother, thoroughly alarmed, started calling for Duško and lamenting that Stana was stuck in the village. Her wailing was cut short by the appearance of a heavy armoured vehicle pulling a huge gun, the biggest I'd ever seen. This stopped just outside the house and the gun was positioned right in front of the yard gate. Father Vukmanović rushed in, extremely upset, and asked me to find out why they'd put the gun just there. I tried to do so, but the soldiers only swore at me and sent me away.

When Duško came back, clearly very agitated. Mother scolded him for not staying quietly at home instead of wandering around "like a mad dog". When she put some food in front of him he refused it, saying:

"Who feels like eating at a time like this?"

"What's happened, Duško? If you know, for heavens' sake tell us," she cried.

Instead of answering, he picked up a spoon and tried to take a mouthful of soup, but his hand trembled so much it spilt and he gave up the attempt.

"It's started, Mother!"

"What's started, son?"

"Our uprising, our fight!"

"Whose fight, son? Not yours, heaven forbid! Your father's in prison. Stana's who knows where in the country. And here we are, left with nothing. Now the most important thing is for us to keep together…"

Mother went on in this vein, threatening, warning, begging.

Duško didn't wait for her to finish but grabbed a hunk of bread, jumped over the back fence of the yard and disappeared.

Not long before curfew, Mara Laković, an acquaintance who lived nearby, called at the house. Self-taught, with no formal education, Mara was a very quick-witted and resourceful young woman. She had come to Cetinje from a village and met her husband Bogdan, a shoemaker, at some workers' gathering. Stana, in particular, was friendly with them both.

After checking that no-one else was around, Mara motioned us into a corner and spoke in a low, confidential tone:

"If anyone asks where Stana is, say she's staying at Crmnica with relatives for a while, and you're not sure when she'll be back."

Mara told us that Bogdan was also away from home.

"But not for long," she said proudly. "The whole of Montenegro is up in arms. For the first time women are fighting side by side with the men, as equals. If I had anyone to look after our little boy – he's only three – I'd join my Bogdan in the woods."

Then we learnt from Mara the reason for all the recent military commotion: in the hills above Rijeka Crnojevića, the Partisans, as our fighters were called, had that day ambushed an Italian battalion of six hundred men. Thirty-six young men and women from the Cetinje area had opened fire on them with machine-guns obtained from the Yugoslav army when it disintegrated, and had taken the entire battalion prisoner.

"Now our people don't know what to do with so many of them," she added. "But never mind, they'll have to put up with it until our brothers arrive from Russia. They say the Red Army is already marching across Romania, making straight for Belgrade, and the Black Sea fleet is on its way to Kotor. All being well, we'll soon link up with the Russians, and our two armies, Russian and Montenegrin, will march side by side under the red flag of Lenin," exulted Mara, getting more and more carried away.

Then she lowered her voice to tell us in the strictest confidence a secret that no-one else must find out at any cost:

"I have been told by our comrades to be your contact, to take care of you and keep you informed on everything you need to know. You mustn't trust anyone else: they might be Italian undercover agents. There are traitors even among Montenegrins."

That evening, as usual, Father Vukmanović dropped in. Tall, dignified, with his neat beard, long black cassock and large silver pectoral cross, he was much liked and respected by the family. Though he wasn't seen ever to conduct services in any church, he carried with him the heady scent of incense, which lingered around the room long after he had left. According to Duško he was a 'religious ideologist' in the Bishop's office, and for this reason had quarrelled with his surviving brother, Svetozar, a leading Montenegrin communist.

"Sit down, Father, while I put on the coffee," Mother said, as was customary. "I've just finished roasting some wheat and only have to grind it."

From the first day of the war, in our household roasted wheat had replaced coffee beans. The priest, however, remained standing, making the excuse that he didn't feel like coffee.

"There's something I must say to you, Milica," he went on. "Petar is dearer to me than my brothers. I'm very sorry he's still being kept in prison. If it weren't for the communists and their uprising, I believe they would have released him by now. We could have come to some agreement with the Italians and got through this terrible war somehow without bloodshed, instead of stirring up hatred, setting brother against brother, which is what's going to happen, it seems.

"Stana, I've just heard, has gone off into the woods, and Duško keeps very bad company. If Petar were here, he wouldn't allow it, but without him everything's gone to pot. I wouldn't like anything illegal, anything that could upset the authorities, to take place in my house, so I must ask you, Milica, to move elsewhere as soon as you can."

Mother, thunderstruck, attempted to find excuses for Stana and Duško, but he refused to listen. As he left, he added:

"Don't misunderstand me, Milica, or hold this against me. For years I've had more than enough trouble with my brothers to want to be implicated in more communist activities. May God Almighty come to your aid. I no longer can."

When Father Vukmanović departed, there was only a short time left before curfew and Duško was still not home. Mother, overwhelmed by everything, began to lament the family's misfortunes and curse our miserable fate at the top of her voice. Soon after the clock struck six, the curfew hour, Duško dashed in, having just escaped a patrol, to be greeted by our distraught mother with threats, curses and pleas to stay quietly home in future.

When she had calmed down, Duško told us the latest news he had gleaned in town:

"They've started rounding up suspects. The Italians got a list of them from Vlado Kokotan, so Pirzio Birolli has made him chief of police instead of Father."

"It's always the same when a country's ruined," said Mother. "When there's a flood, shit floats to the top. Now it's the time of the Koktans, God help us and all decent people! Keep off the streets, children. Only mad dogs roam around there, looking for innocent prey."

❧

It was a warm, clear July night, heady with the powerful scent of the blossoming linden trees that flanked the main streets. A full moon had long risen high above the hills around Cetinje, turning to silver the little chapel on Lovćen, which seemed within arm's reach. In the bright moonlight, almost like day, we could see Italian soldiers moving around the big gun outside the gate.

"What on earth are they doing there at this time of night that they couldn't do better by day?" Mother wondered.

We soon found out. A tremendous explosion rocked the house and cracked all the windows at the front. For minutes after, the roar went on reverberating. Terrified, we ran to see what had happened, thinking there had been some mishap, that a shell had exploded while being carried or the gun was being cleaned. We then saw the soldiers bring up another large shell, load it and carefully adjust the long gun-barrel in the direction of Lovćen. Shortly after we were shaken by another deafening explosion. This was repeated at twenty-minute intervals until dawn.

"They want to demolish the tomb of the great Njegoš," Duško explained. "They want to destroy the symbol of liberty of all Montenegrins, our spirit of resistance."

❧

Next morning Ljuba and Vicko came to tell us that Savo had 'escaped' to join the Partisans.

"On one shoulder he had his rifle and on the other his violin," said Vicko. "He couldn't bear to be parted from it. We agreed that I should stay with Ljuba and Mother here in Cetinje, operating undercover, and Savo would go to fight. His Elsa is relatively safe, far away in Prague, so he's freer than I am."

Vicko then told us that most of their friends had gone into the Partisans, joining the Lovćen Detachment, and that Stana had been chosen as commissar of a battalion:

"She's the first woman commissar in the history of Montenegro, Mother!"

Ljuba and Vicko had only just left when two *carabinieri* strode into the yard accompanied by Niko, the interpreter.

"Where's your daughter Stana?" they demanded.

As instructed by Mara, Mother said she had gone to stay with relatives in Crmnica before the 'trouble' started and would be back in Cetinje as soon as it was safe to travel.

"What are they called, those relatives?"

They wrote her answer down in a notebook.

"We'll check that out and come back," they warned as they were leaving.

Niko let the Italians go out ahead of him and pushed a note into Mother's hand, murmuring: "I saw Petar yesterday. He's well and sends greetings."

The message from Father was brief and addressed to Stana:

"My dear Stana, Whatever happens, stay in the woods, no matter what the consequences may be for me. If you're wounded, don't let them take you alive. Always keep one bullet for yourself.

Your loving father."

Father had already been moved to the part of the prison where the Italians now held as hostages members of the families of those who were suspected of having joined the Partisans. The previous day notices had been nailed on Cetinje's linden trees warning that the occupation forces – the term was used here for the first time – would execute the closest relatives of the bandits who had fled to the woods if a single Italian soldier were killed. Ten hostages would be shot for every soldier.

Bogdanov Kraj, as the prison was called, had served in the time of King Nikola to house a small number of prisoners, most of them held for murder related to a blood feud or in defence of their honour if publicly insulted. Murder for gain was practically unheard of in Montenegro. Now this small, dilapidated building was crowded with prisoners of another kind. Just before the war, my father had asked a policeman to take me around it, to show me what happened to law-breakers. The prison was divided into two by a high wall, on the top of which guards patrolled. The dark, dank chambers had earthen floors and water dripping down the walls. Now my father was himself inside one of those rooms.

❦

Every evening at the same hour the big gun in front of the gate began to roar and shake the house every twenty minutes; the only sleep we got was in the intervals while they were reloading. The night-time cannonade gave way during the day to the drone of airplanes. From the direction of Podgorica, where an Italian military aerodrome was located, waves of bombers flew low over Cetinje and circled above the surrounding villages, dropping their load. We watched them disappear behind the hills, heard a series of explosions, and saw them return in the same formation. And so it went on for the next couple of weeks: shelling by night and bombing by day. All of this was intended to reduce the insurgents' pressure on encircled Cetinje. At the same time the Italians stepped up the arrests, threats and other measures to intimidate the population, but to no avail: the armed uprising spread like wildfire throughout Montenegro. Soon the Partisans controlled all areas except Cetinje and a few smaller towns.

"In the heart of occupied Europe, Montenegro is again free!" Duško declared with pride.

Alarmed that the Montenegrin example could ignite armed resistance in other parts of Yugoslavia, the occupation authorities took drastic steps to check this dangerous conflagration. Punitive expeditions of Blackshirts left burning villages and slaughtered civilians throughout Montenegro. News of these atrocities soon reached Cetinje.

"Whole families, old people, women and children, are locked inside their houses, which are then set on fire," Mara reported. "The families of many of our comrades have been burnt alive. From captured fascists we've found out that before they came to Montenegro a lot of them were serving time in Italian gaols for robbery and murder."

Early one afternoon Duško came rushing in and from the doorway broke the news that Lame Talaja had been arrested, given a summary trial and, being still a minor, sentenced to one hundred and one years' hard labour. At the same time, three Partisans, captured while asleep in the village of Bjeloši, had been sentenced to death by firing squad. The sentence was to be carried out that afternoon in the slightly elevated open space known as the Tablja. In the past, this had been the place where salvoes in honour of distinguished visitors were fired, and where the severed heads of Turks killed in battle were displayed impaled on stakes. It was not until 1850 that this custom, adopted from the Turks themselves, was abolished by order of Njegoš. Duško knew one of the young men condemned to death. By an odd coincidence, he, like Talaja, had a limp.

"It's been agreed that none of us will be at the execution, in case the Italians guess we're their friends and arrest us on the spot. That's why I've rushed home to tell Bato to be at the Tablja at three o'clock, watch carefully what happens and tell me everything this evening. There's bound to be plenty of other kids around, so Bato won't be specially noticed."

Proud that Duško had given me this task, I made for the Tablja as fast as my legs would carry me since it was nearly three o'clock. When I arrived, completely out of breath, I found about fifty grown-ups and as many children already gathered there – news in Cetinje travelled fast. Two Blackshirts were arranging things, putting three chairs in line and measuring the distance between them and the firing squad of some dozen *carabinieri*, already drawn up waiting. At a signal from the Blackshirts, the squad stepped forward a few metres and stood to attention.

A few moments after the clock on Vladin Dom struck three, the condemned men appeared, chained together. They looked around eagerly, obviously hoping for a last sight of family and friends in the crowd. Duško had asked me to look in particular at how his lame friend bore up. At first, as they slowly made their way to the centre of the Tablja, he limped badly, but the closer he got to the chairs the more easily he walked, until in the end his lameness was scarcely noticeable. To get a better view, I pushed my way to the very front of the crowd, which stood as close as the guards would allow. Now I could clearly see their faces and hear them calling to one another.

"Shall we have a song, brothers?" cried Duško's friend, and at the top of his voice led them in the old song about outlaws captured by the Turks languishing in prison while awaiting a violent death:

"Durmitor, Durmitor, lofty mountain! Has my house fallen down or my love married another…?"

For a moment the Italians appeared confused, not knowing whether to interrupt the singing or wait for the song to end. Then they proceeded with the job, taking out black scarves with which they tried to blindfold the three young men. These broke off their singing and said something I couldn't quite catch, but I guessed they were refusing the blindfolds. The Blackshirts then seated them on the chairs with their backs to the firing squad, but all three stood up and tried to face their executioners. Finally they were forced down on to the chairs and there was a momentary silence.

The *carabinieri* officer raised his hand, then lowered it, setting off a fusillade.

I watched in horror as their white shirts where suddenly ripped to pieces and dyed crimson. Then Duško's friend sprang from his chair and howled in a terrifying voice:

"Shoot, you Fascist bastards! Shoot, I'm still alive!"

A Blackshirt slowly unbuttoned his holster, took out his revolver and shot Duško's friend in the head. Everything fell quiet again.

❦

The following day Mara came with some good news. Hearing of our predicament, Nikola Rolović, a twenty-three-year-old recently graduated lawyer whose family also came from Crmnica, had sent a message that we could move into his house at once, since he wouldn't be needing it for a while. Mara confided that in a day or two he would be joining Stana and Bogdan 'in the woods'. Later that same day Nikola came to hand over the keys.

"Don't worry about paying rent. What's important now is to get through this alive," he said with a reassuring smile.

I couldn't imagine this good-looking, urbane young man with a neat moustache, elegantly dressed in an expensive suit and hat, wandering around the woods and mountains with a rifle over his shoulder.

Next day Duško and his friends carried all our goods and chattels to our new home, just a few doors away. The ground floor of the house, which was much more spacious and better decorated than the upper, was occupied by the Lopica family. The father had been a doctor at the Prince Danilo Hospital in Cetinje until he was operated on for cancer of the throat and lost his voice. Now he was able to communicate only in whispers. From her manner it was clear that Mrs Lopica strongly disapproved of her new upstairs neighbours. Our family, blacklisted by the authorities, was regarded as dangerous, and she was afraid of our bad influence on her three sons and two daughters. The eldest boy, a year or two older than Duško, was exceptionally tall, even by Montenegrin standards, and was generally called by his nickname, Duruz (Lofty).

The upper floor, that could be reached only by an outside flight of steps, had an entry hall, two small rooms and a kitchen.

From the large house by Black Rock we had moved into less spacious accommodation with Father Vukmanović. Now our living space was even more cramped, reduced to bare essentials, but we felt happier and more secure here, not dependent on anyone and, more important, not having to pay rent. Even so, life got more difficult with every passing day. As a 'Partisan family' we did not receive rations, like other people, and the barbed wire around the town prevented our Crmnica 'relatives' from getting food to us.

A totally unexpected visitor turned up one day: a Moslem friend of Father's from Mitrovica named Baškiri. He was working for the occupation forces, he told us, and after a two-day journey had arrived in Cetinje with a convoy of trucks bringing grain from Kosovo.

"I've brought you thirty kilos of maize," he said, "so you have something to fall back on, if you need it."

Mother thanked him warmly, for need it we certainly did.

Our visitor was a member of Mitrovica's Turkish minority, which before the war had mostly made a living by trade between Yugoslavia and Turkey. Now they enjoyed a favourable status with both the Albanian and German authorities. They spoke Turkish, Albanian and Serbian, and quickly learnt German as well. Baškiri handed Mother a letter from Gina, Uncle Luka's youngest daughter, whom he happened to meet in the town of Prizren just before coming to Montenegro.

"I'll drop by for an answer tomorrow," he said as he was leaving.

The letter, eagerly seized upon and read aloud by Duško, gave us the first reliable news of the fate of our family in Kosovo. When Yugoslavia capitulated, Albanian nationalists had taken up arms against the Serbs and Montenegrins: some of them had been slaughtered, others driven out of their homes before their houses were torched and their land was seized. A group of them had come upon Uncle Djuro working in his orchard in a village near Mitrovica. He had been tied up, beaten unconscious and left for dead. Then they had burnt his house and everything in it. During the night, Djuro had come round, managed to free himself, and in his injured state make his way to the town.

They had then moved on to the next village where our tall Herzegovinian relative, Rikalović, lived, the one who had offered to escort us to Plav. When he saw the Albanians coming, he quickly sent my cousin Velika and their four young sons through the maize fields in the direction of Mitrovica and himself stayed behind to give them time to escape. For more than an hour he held the Albanians back with his accurate fire. When he finally ran out of ammunition, he was struck down by a hail of bullets.

Uncle Luka, Aunt Maša and their daughters Milica and Gina had narrowly escaped a similar fate. Gina wrote that her family and other relatives who had survived the massacre were now in Mitrovica, where the Germans had placed the Serbs and Montenegrins in a kind of ghetto, so that in a way they were protected from the Albanians. Mother's parents, sister Mileva, and brothers Jovan and Marko with their families had all survived, but Marko, who as a policeman had antagonised a number of Albanians, had fled to Serbia proper to save himself.

"Well," commented Mother, "Petar was right. We've got what we were asking for. If we'd tried to get on better with the Albanians, there wouldn't be all this bloodshed now. Golubović and the army thought they could settle things, and this is the result. The army's gone off and left the people to pay the price, just as Petar foretold."

Gina's letter also told us that she had just married a tailor called Voja living in Prizren, a member of an old Serbian family that had been in Kosovo since the Middle Ages, when Tsar Dušan made Prizren the capital of his extensive empire. The 'old Serbs', she added, were in a better situation than the colonists, who were the main target of the Albanians. Guessing, quite rightly, that food would be in short supply in barren Montenegro, she offered to take Aco or myself to live with her while the war lasted.

Duško and Mother discussed the pros and cons of this proposal at length. In the end, Mother decided it would be better for Aco if he went with Baškiri to stay with Gina and her husband: he would probably be safer and certainly less hungry. "I may be making a mistake," she added, "but who knows in a war where's the best place to be."

Mother packed up a few clothes in a bundle for Aco and when Baškiri returned next day for the reply, asked him to take her youngest child:

"If you hand him over alive and well to Luka's Gina, the whole of our family will be grateful to you till the grave."

Baškiri took eight-year-old Aco by the hand, assuring us he would take good care of him. After kissing him goodbye, Mother and Nada began sobbing, so Duško stayed behind to calm them while I went with Aco. A line of trucks loaded with various goods covered by tarpaulin was waiting by the monastery. At the front and rear were German armoured cars to provide protection on the journey.

"Up you get, Aco!" said Baškiri, helping him to climb into the back of a truck, where he squatted down in a corner, small, skinny, his big dark eyes brimming with tears.

"Don't cry, Aco," I shouted as the engine started up. "It'll be better there, you'll see."

I waved until the trucks were out of sight, and wept.

❧

The Italians seemed to be bringing in further reinforcements almost daily and making serious preparations for a counter-offensive. After the defeats suffered by his forces in Greece, Mussolini couldn't swallow another military failure at the hands of tiny Montenegro.

By a combination of threats and cunning – *divide et impera* as Uncle Mihajlo used to say, by granting various privileges to those families who demonstrated their obedience, the Italian authorities managed to win over a section of the population, mostly those who hoped that with Italian help the old kingdom of Montenegro could be restored. From among these they formed the National Guard, whose members in the beginning were not asked to take part in joint military actions against the Partisans, "only to defend your villages and homes against possible attack, robbery and arson". In Cetinje, a number of young men enrolled in the Guard, accepting Italian weapons, money and food in the belief that they would be able to stay out of danger and get through the war more easily. One of these was Dr Lopica's tall eldest son. Now there were two families on opposite sides living in the same house. Duruz had the duty to defend Cetinje from any Partisan attack, while Duško in his clandestine organisation was busy planning one.

❧

Nada and I continued to get up at dawn and sell Mother's doughnuts. One morning, standing by the unfinished building intended to be the new high school but turned by the Italians into barracks, we watched the soldiers of the Messina Division getting ready for their departure to fight the Partisans. With our empty tray and our pockets full of liras, we stayed to listen for a while to the short-legged Calabrese singing their melodious songs in hoarse voices. When off duty, they would spend hours standing around in circles facing inwards, heads together, arms on one another's shoulders, singing long-drawn-out, melancholy, southern songs about love and happiness, and anxious mothers waiting in Calabria for their sons.

When we got home, Duško questioned us, as usual, not only about how much we'd earned but about how many and what type of troops had left that morning, how they were armed and what direction they had taken.

⁂

It was difficult to enter Cetinje, but one of our 'relatives' from Crmnica somehow managed it. The soldiers at the check-points were not always equally strict, and sometimes they intentionally let someone in or out of town in order to shadow them, establish who their contacts were and whether they were carrying secret messages. Our 'relative' brought us some food but also, and more important, some wonderful news: Stana was alive and well! With her battalion, which was moving around the Crmnica and Lovćen regions, she had survived several clashes and punitive expeditions.

Our visitor then gave us some news that greatly saddened us. Early one morning soldiers had unexpectedly arrived at Bukovik and rounded up all the young men they found there, a dozen or so, all under twenty. Among them was Jovo Radača, son of the man who had saved my father in the battle of Taraboš: he had come from Stana's battalion to visit his mother just for one night. They tied them up and shut them in the school.

"When his comrades heard that Jovo was in Italian hands, they sent a message to the commander of the punitive expedition offering to exchange him for an Italian officer they were holding. The Italians then shot all the youths except Jovo. His mother, Milica, hoped that her youngest would be saved and spent all day in front of the school, waiting for the exchange. But then all of sudden the whole lot got up and started back where they came from, and Jovo was brought out of the school and shot before his mother's eyes. What went wrong at the last moment, why he was not exchanged, nobody knows."

Our visitor also brought us news of other friends and acquaintances – in wartime, even more than in peace, information circulated rapidly by word of mouth and he was clearly in contact with the Partisans. We heard that Father's friend Pero Popović had been among those seized after two Italians were killed near his house in Bar. In reprisal for this, males over sixteen in the neighbourhood had been rounded up, chained together, driven by truck just outside the town, and executed by firing squad. Thanks to the fact that a Turkish sabre had cut off his hand, Pero managed to slip out of the chains and when the truck slowed down, jumped out and ran for cover in a nearby wood. The soldiers, taken by surprise, fired after him but he escaped and found his way to the Partisans.

"Many people have been executed in Crmnica," our visitor went on. "They even picked up that drunkard Lukin and shot him. But people who were there and saw it say that, when they got ready to fire, he was more sober than he'd been for years. When they stood him up against a wall, the officer in charge took pity on him – he knew Lukin was innocent because he was always drunk – and offered him a bottle of brandy. Lukin took it, they say, then flung it at the wall. The bottle broke into a hundred pieces and Lukin didn't swallow one mouthful. Then he turned to the officer and said, 'I should have done that years ago!' "

Duško, frowning, his head bowed, listened without saying a word.

That evening, when we were alone, Mother shed tears for young Jovo, pitying his mother, who had witnessed his untimely death, and his father Ilija, working in some mine in America, who might never know what had happened. Then she reminisced about the happy days spent in Pero's house in Bar after her marriage:

"Now he's wandering in the hills with the wolves, and Petar is lying in gaol, waiting to be shot."

We didn't touch the food from Crmnica we had received that day. Everything at all nutritious that we managed to lay hands on was kept to take to Father.

"Let him share it with his comrades," Mother used to say. "God forbid it should be his last meal."

For as the fighting intensified and more Italians were killed, the number of hostages taken out to be shot mounted. The executions were carried out in the open space on the edge of town known as Donje Polje (Lower Field). The bodies were thrown into a common grave and just covered with earth.

❧

After a string of successes in the six months following the insurrection, the Partisans had managed to gain control over many villages and extensive areas of Montenegro without serious losses. Perhaps becoming over-confident and underestimating the Italian forces, they set their sights on capturing a town. Their goal was Plevlje, a small, predominantly Moslem town near the meeting point of Montenegro, Serbia and Bosnia, which the Italians, unknown to the Partisans, had fortified with the help of the local Moslems. Who actually ordered the night attack on Plevlje without having sufficient information on the town's defences was subsequently never made clear. After a short battle, several battalions, among them one from Cetinje, entered the town. Just as they thought they would celebrate another easy victory, they were mown down in the streets by a storm of machine-gun fire from the curtained windows and walled courtyards of the Moslem houses where the Italians were concealed.

A few days later, when the full toll had been reckoned, it became clear that some five hundred fighters had been killed or wounded and that the flower of Cetinje's youth had died that night.

We first learnt of this tragedy from Mara, who came in wringing her hands, sobbing and lamenting:

"My Bogdan's been killed at Plevlje! My little Milovan has lost his father. What am I to do now? Where am I to go?"

"The Plevlje massacre" as it came to be called, soon left its visible mark on Cetinje, where many now wore the mourning kept in chests and cupboards in case of a death in the family or hastily-made skirts and blouses sewn from any black material they could find.

A day or two later Ljuba and Vicko came to see us. As soon as she entered, Ljuba burst into tears.

"What's happened?" we asked in one voice, all dreading to hear that Father had been shot or Stana killed.

"My brother Savo was killed in Plevlje," Vicko replied simply. "I wanted to go to fight instead of him, but he wouldn't listen. He never carried anything heavier than a violin in his whole life."

As Vicko went on talking about his brother, I kept imagining Savo wandering lost through the dark streets of Plevlje, knocking on someone's door to ask for shelter or the way out of town, and being shot down on the threshold. I thought, too, of his pretty Czech wife who would never see him again, and perhaps would never find out why he didn't return to Prague.

The disaster at Plevlje was a major setback for the Partisans and boosted the Italian occupiers. Apart from the Greens, who hoped for the restoration of King Nikola, the Italians were now joined by Chetniks, supporters of the Serbian crown and Serbian dominance of the Kingdom of Yugoslavia. In the early days of the uprising in 1941, the Chetniks, led by the Royal Army officer Draža Mihajlović, began in Serbia to fight the Germans in partnership with Tito's Partisans. After several months, however, they withdrew from any active combat, abandoning the Partisans, and reached an accommodation with the Germans and Italians which gradually grew into collaboration with the occupiers. The Italians could now rely on Chetnik as well as Green support in Montenegro. In all parts of Montenegro, including Cetinje, units of Chetniks were formed as part of Draža Mihajlović's movement. These were armed by the Italians and sent to fight the Partisans. For the most part they were made up of former Royal Army officers, policemen and other supporters of the prewar regime. In Cetinje, the criminal band of Vlado Kokotan provided the core of this unit.

❧

And so we entered into the long, cold winter of 1941-42. Mošo and Gojko Kruška came to see Duško from time to time, but they never went out all together: it was forbidden to move about in more than twos. One day I happened to listen in on their talk. Knowing they could be arrested at any time, they were discussing how to escape from Cetinje when it was surrounded by barbed wire and when military patrols were cruising around day and night, stopping people and asking for their papers. They agreed that their only chance was to try to get through the wire in a section that was less closely guarded. Just then Duško noticed me but, like the last time, he motioned me to stay.

After they left he called me aside for a serious talk:

"If I stay in Cetinje any longer, Bato, I'm certain to be arrested. Tomorrow I'll try to get out somehow and you'll be left with Nada and Mother. It's vital you and Nada keep on selling doughnuts, and whatever else you can lay your hands on. You're a better salesman than I am, better at dealing with the customers! Help Father if you can. Keep going; we mustn't give up. As Grandpa Filip always used to say, we're of good stock. You'll manage!"

"You just go, Duško, and don't worry. I'll look after Mother and Nada, and take what I can to Father, so he doesn't starve."

"Then I'll try to get out tonight," said Duško, and gave me a big hug.

All next day I waited in a fever of expectation, wondering whether Duško had made it to the Partisans, where he would probably be safer, or would return to us, as I hoped deep down inside. Just before curfew my secret hope was fulfilled: Duško slipped stealthily into the house, so as not to be seen by our neighbours, especially tall Duruz. He made some excuse for his absence to Mother, then told me quietly, so that she and Nada wouldn't hear, that his contact had not arrived and might have been arrested. He would have to try again as soon as possible. I felt proud that my brother was confiding in me, treating me as though I, too, was a member of the resistance movement.

A couple of nights later we were woken by a commotion in front of our house: a group of *carabinieri* were gathered there, shouting to one another. We could also hear the voices of Vlado Kokotan's Chetnik police. Duško made for the back window, hoping to jump out and escape, but an instant later the door crashed open and several men rushed in, overpowered him and flung him to the floor. After handcuffing him they dragged him up and pushed him out of the room.

"Criminals!" Mother shouted. "Take me, not him. He's still a child!"

While this was happening, I was cowering in a corner of the room, weak with fear, repeating to myself over and over: "Please, God, don't let them kill him!"

※

Next morning, as soon as the curfew ended, Ljuba burst in, sobbing:

"Last night they arrested Vicko! They beat him up and took him away. Nobody knows where he is, or if he's alive."

"And Duško, too, my child," said Mother in an anguished voice and began lamenting in the age-old Montenegrin manner, in turn begging God to save her son, and then cursing and renouncing the Almighty for allowing this misfortune, all the time crossing her arms and beating her breast.

We waited on tenterhooks for several hours in the hope that Mara would come with news. When there was no sign of her by mid-day, Mother dispatched me:

"Bato, my son, now it's all up to you. Run and ask around town if anyone knows where Duško and Vicko are being held. Maybe we could take them some warm clothing. In this bitter weather, Duško will die of cold."

Without waiting, I grabbed my short winter coat, which I had already outgrown, and dashed out. Snow had been falling heavily, blanketing the streets and blocking the entrances to houses and yards. On a snowy slope in front of the government apartments, Olga was enjoying herself sledging. I ran over and, just to say something, asked:

"Have you seen my brother Duško? They took him away last night."

Olga in her white fur coat, leather boots, smart woollen cap and gloves, only shrugged indifferently and went on pulling her sledge. I ran off to look for some of Duško's friends: they would surely know where he was and how to contact him. I made for Mošo's house as fast as my legs would carry me. For a moment I paused in front of Lame Talaja's shop: there were no longer any bicycles in the window and the door was boarded up. I pictured him in some Italian prison, waiting for one hundred and one years to pass.

I knocked on Mošo's door for a long time before it was opened by his half-deaf grandmother. From her I learnt that Mošo, like Duško, had been arrested in the middle of the night and now everyone was out looking for him.

My last hope, then, was that Gojko was at home and would have some news: as he was the smallest and youngest of Duško's friends, perhaps he had not been picked up. He was also my favourite, being less grown up than the others and always ready for a joke. He often teased me, asking me whether there was any girl in my neighbourhood I had taken a liking to.

After my first bang on the door-knocker I heard steps approaching. The front door was flung open and there was Gojko Kruška with a grim expression on his face. He didn't say a word of greeting, I supposed because he was so upset about his friends.

"Gojko, Mother's sent me to say Duško was arrested last night. So were Mošo and other friends. Can you help find out where they're being held?"

Before I could go any further, Gojko cut me short:

"Don't expect any help from me. I couldn't care less where they are. If they've been locked up, they must have deserved it. You just tell your mother and everyone else that Gojko Kruška doesn't want to get dragged into their dirty communist dealings and he'll report to the police anyone who comes knocking on his door asking about them.

And you, Bato, keep away from me from now on. Your family are no friends of mine."

The door then slammed in my face and I was left standing there, speechless with astonishment. For some time I waited shivering on the doorstep, expecting the door to open again and Gojko's grinning face to appear. I knew he was fond of jokes, but this seemed to me a strange moment to play one when his friends were under arrest and Mother was waiting anxiously for news. Finally I concluded that something terrible must have happened to Gojko, that he had gone mad like several other young people in Cetinje.

∞

The only person I could turn to now was Mara. Again I set off running and luckily found her at home in the tiny one-storey house, just one room and a kitchen, where she lived with her little son Milovan. At once she pulled me inside, sat me down by the stove and handed me a bowl of watery, but wonderfully warming soup. She had been going around town all morning, she said, to check who exactly had been arrested in the previous night's raids. Next day, she hoped, they would find out where everyone was being held and see what could be done to help them. Then she sent me home, accompanying me to the yard gate:

"Be very careful, Bato. They don't ask your age if you're from a Partisan family."

I made my way home slowly: there was no longer any need to hurry, and I had to think what to say to Mother. Suddenly a brilliant idea struck me. Olga's parents were friendly with Italian officers in the Cetinje administration: we often saw them coming to visit. They were our neighbours, just across the street, and I'd seen Duško talking to the father several times. He could easily get my brother out of prison. All he had to say was: "Let the lad go. I know him. He's only just seventeen."

Excited and buoyed up by this thought, I started running again. As I entered the apartment building it was already growing dark on that short, overcast February day. My heart pounding, I stood in the hallway before the door of their flat. From within I could hear the sound of a piano. Dared I knock and interrupt the playing? It would be wiser to wait until it stopped. Olga was being given a lesson by her mother, whose sharp voice I heard correcting mistakes. As I could tell from the difference in the playing, she was sitting beside her daughter at the piano and demonstrating how it should go. When there was a pause, I rang the smart white bell the Petrovićs had brought from Italy, and heard the mother call out in Italian:

"Olga, don't open the door!"

There was the sound of keys being turned and bolts drawn. However many locks did they need, I wondered, when we managed with only one, and that one broken since the police burst in. Finally the door opened and I saw Olga's tall, good-looking father with her short, dark-complexioned mother standing behind him and peering suspiciously at the unexpected caller. I also glimpsed Olga, come into the hall to see who it was.

"What do you want, lad?" her father asked.

"I'm a neighbour from opposite. My brother Duško's been arrested. You know him, sir, I've seen you talking to him. If you would help to get him out of prison, we would be eternally grateful."

Seeing that Olga's mother was straining to understand, I switched to Italian, in which I was by then quite fluent thanks to all my practice with the soldiers.

"My grandma was Italian," I added, in the hope of winning her sympathy. This certainly didn't work for she stepped from behind her husband, thrust one hip forward, and shouted:

"If he's in prison, he must have stolen something. The court decides on these things, not us!"

"He's not a thief, *signora*," I protested. "He's a political prisoner."

Hearing the word 'political', she became almost hysterical:

"Be off with you! All communists deserve to be in gaol!"

I glanced towards Olga, but she had disappeared, perhaps ashamed of her mother's shouting. Seeing how downcast I was that my hope had been dashed, the father gave me a kindly pat on the shoulder and explained, almost apologetically, that he was not involved in politics and there was nothing he could do to help:

"If I tried to intervene on behalf of those who are arrested, there'd be a long line of relatives in front of my door."

Slowly, dragging my feet, I made my way downstairs and out into the street, where it was already dark at five o'clock. Then I remembered that Mother had been waiting for news all this time and must be out of her mind with worry, thinking that something had happened to me too.

"I didn't find out anything," I called from the doorway, my voice hoarse from the cold, "except that Gojko Kruška has gone out of his mind, or is pretending to be mad so as not to be gaoled. Mošo and lots of others have all been arrested."

Nada had gathered a few branches for the stove so we could warm ourselves. Though I didn't feel hungry, just dreadfully tired, I ate the bowl of cabbage soup and piece of bread Mother had kept for me before I fell fast asleep. In the middle of the night I woke and started thinking about Duško. Fear gripped my heart. If I lost my beloved brother, I could never be happy again. And how could I possibly take his place, look after Nada and Mother? He was strong, good at judo and boxing, and I was younger, weak, without experience. All the same, I had to try. I had promised him.

Next morning the three of us discussed our situation. There was nothing to be done, we decided, but go on selling as many doughnuts as possible. Other Partisan families were exchanging their furniture piece by piece for flour and other food – peasants were still allowed to enter the city under strict control to sell produce at the market. We had very little furniture because of our constant moving around: after Mitrovica we had never had time to set up home properly. In the early months of the occupation we swapped for food all our non-essential clothing except Father's uniform. This Mother kept carefully in a chest, regularly checking for moths, in the hope that one day he would need it again.

As we were talking things over, Mara came with the news that Duško, Vicko and about a hundred others arrested the same night were being held in the cellars of Vladin Dom (the Government Building). This imposing edifice, built to house Montenegro's ministries and Parliament, was completed in 1910, when the Principality of Montenegro was proclaimed a kingdom on the occasion of Nikola's fiftieth year as ruler. Now, it seemed, its large cellars, mostly used for storing coal, were to serve as a prison since the gaol at Bogdanov Kraj was already packed. One of the building's porters had seen them being brought in, followed by several prisoners from Bogdanov Kraj who were given the task of shaving their heads. Then they had been forced to take off their clothes, which were boiled in large cauldrons over fires in the yard, and had spent the whole day naked in the cellars, waiting for their clothing to be returned.

When I heard this, I ran at once to Vladin Dom. Unlike a few days before, there were wooden sentry-boxes on either side of the basement entrance. Two *carabinieri* in fur-lined greatcoats that reached the ground were standing guard, every now and again walking towards each other, exchanging a few words or lighting up cigarettes, then walking back. Watching them, I hatched a plan.

Next morning, with a full tray of doughnuts I walked quickly towards the guards, getting as close as I could to the ground-level windows of the cellars. At the top of my voice I kept shouting "Hot doughnuts!" in the hope that Duško somewhere inside would hear me and know I was carrying on and wouldn't let him down. The two sentries seemed pleased to see me and beckoned me closer. As I approached I went on crying my wares, knowing full well that at ten degrees below zero my doughnuts must be like lumps of rock.

"Let's have a look," one of guards said, taking off a thick woollen glove.

"Hot doughnuts!" I yelled again.

"Hey, stop shouting, boy! We may be a bit hungry but we're not deaf. How much are your doughnuts?"

To keep them interested I gave a lower price than usual and they started digging around among the doughnuts.

"Hey, these aren't hot; they're stone cold!" the guards protested.

"They were hot when I left home half an hour ago. They cool down quickly in this weather."

"Well, never mind, give us five each."

"Help yourselves, take the biggest ones," I offered generously.

While they were busy picking and choosing, I strained to get a good look into the cellars through half-frosted window-panes. I could just make out a crowd of men walking about in overcoats or with blankets over their shoulders, with scarves tied round their heads, but I couldn't recognise anyone. I was staring so intently into the cellars, I didn't notice when the guards handed me the money.

"Here, take it! What are you staring at?"

"My brother's in there. Can I just take a look?"

Without waiting for a reply, I pushed my face up against the cold glass.

"That's enough, boy! Take your doughnuts and get lost! You can't hang around here."

I picked up the tray from the frozen ground, bawling "Hot doughnuts!" several times as I did so, then made off, sure that Duško must have heard me.

That bitterly cold winter there was hunger in Cetinje, particularly among the Partisan families, almost all of whom had someone in prison. While others were given a meagre monthly ration of flour, oil and sugar, even this was denied to 'enemies of Italy'.

Cetinje's open-air market still functioned on Wednesdays. It was here we bought food with the liras we earned, and learnt from the peasant women what was happening in the villages around. They were allowed to enter the town with their donkeys through the two check-points after the Italians had subjected them to a thorough search and often helped themselves to a bit of cheese or dried meat.

Mother, Nada and I used to go early to the market in the hope of buying a little lard, oil and flour for doughnuts, but most of all to find out from the peasant women if Stana and her battalion had passed through their village. We had to look out for women we knew and trusted, for even enquiring about Partisans could end you up in front of a firing squad. One market day we met a woman we knew from the Katun village of Štitari: her sons had been at school in Cetinje with Stana and Duško. She was pleased to see us and, taking care not to be overhead, told us that Stana had spent the night in her house not long before:

"Your Stana is a famous Partisan, and better than any man, brave and proud, and as pretty as a picture. My sons are with her. There's a lot of heavy fighting going on, Milica. Hundreds of troops are going round burning and killing, and with them our traitors, local people who show them all the paths and tracks. We're waiting for our turn to come at Štitari. There are terrible times in store for us."

The uprising spread throughout Yugoslavia. Partisans attacked and captured towns and villages, disrupted communications, and prevented the occupation forces from consolidating their hold over the regions under their control. The capitulation of Yugoslavia had not pacified the country, as Hitler had expected. On the contrary, only three months later it erupted into a new theatre of war. In view of the region's military-strategic significance, Germany and Italy undertook a large-scale combined campaign to crush the Partisans, throwing into action their whole available war machine, which included troops of their many allies and collaborators: Bulgarians, Hungarians, Albanians, Russian White Guards, Yugoslavia's ethnic Germans, Croatian Ustasha forces, Bosnian Moslems, Montenegrin Greens, and Serbian and Montenegrin Chetniks.

The fiercest battles at the beginning of 1942 took place in Montenegro. The occupiers' military operations were backed up by propaganda activity. A newspaper called *Hell or Communism* in banner headlines called upon the highlanders to free themselves from "communist heathens imposed on them by Judas Iscariots". Its message, repeated daily, was that the Jews had sold the Montenegrins to aetheist Bolsheviks and British imperialists. The allusion was to Moše Pijada, a leading figure in the Partisan movement, and the many other Jews who had joined the Partisans, among other reasons, to save themselves from the fascists. *Hell or Communism* was full of reports of the immorality of Partisans who "make love in churches, burn sacred icons and defile altars. Any children born of such sin are immediately murdered and buried."

One morning Mara brought us a copy of this paper. A large photograph on the front page showed Stana riding a white horse over the corpses of old people, women and children. Riding towards her, also on a white horse, was Peko, commander of the Partisan forces in Montenegro. Mara warned Nada and me not to go out for the next few days.

"They faked the photo," she explained, "but ordinary folk don't realise that."

The paper also called on Montenegrins to come to their senses and see where the true interests of their family and clan lay:

"Only in peaceful conditions will the authorities be able to ensure regular supplies, which are now disrupted by Partisan attacks on trucks. The food which the Italian Administration sends you is being stolen by the Partisans, leaving you and your children hungry. Help to get rid of the Bolshevik heathens, and you will be able to travel freely to visit your relations in villages and towns throughout Montenegro. It's up to you decent Montenegrins to make your choice: either to live a peaceful and secure life or to perish in the flames of war, together with your innocent children, and all because of the selfish interests of the Jews, Bolsheviks and British."

Loudspeakers around the town constantly reported the immense sadness of Queen Elena because of events in her native land. Her Majesty's great wish was that hostilities would cease so that she could come to Cetinje and stay among her relatives and people. By playing on the Montenegrins' vanity, emphasising their link with the Italian Court, while at the same time subjecting them to arrests, executions, oppression and hunger, the occupiers gradually managed to turn a section of the population against the Partisans.

Wednesday afternoon. Mother and Ljuba were putting the finishing touches to the huge pan of thick bean soup that had been simmering for hours, steaming up our small flat. Finally they took it off the stove and tipped the contents into two smaller pans. One of these, with a large loaf Mother had baked earlier, would be taken by her and Nada to the Bogdanov Kraj prison for Father; the other pan and a loaf Ljuba and I would carry to Vladin Dom for Duško and Vicko. Each pan of soup weighed several kilos, so we lugged it between us.

In front of Vladin Dom dozens of women and children, all with similar pans of bean soup, were waiting for the prison officers to start taking in the food. Each pan had a label with the name of a prisoner written in large letters. When we were all nearly frozen from the long wait, the heavy oak door creaked open. Pushing forward to get in out of the cold, some stumbled and spilt the food they had brought on the parquet floor. The guards were not bothered by this: they knew prisoners would come along later to scoop it up and eat it.

Finally we all got inside the large reception room, where eminent guests, princes and rulers, had been welcomed in the time of King Nikola. The guards made us stand in line and place our food in turn on a table, where they stirred it with long-handled wooden spoons to check there were no weapons or messages inside. Then, with terror in our hearts, we all went together into an adjoining room to collect the dirty pots and pans from the previous week. The women recognised their own and when they went over to it, some of them let out blood-curdling shrieks and wails: if there was food still inside, it meant that the prisoner had been executed.

By taking and shooting hostages, the Italians put terrible psychological pressure on the Partisans. Their dilemma was whether to continue fighting and put the lives of their family at risk or to give themselves up, abandoning the cause and sacrificing themselves. Some did return home and surrender, but the majority stayed on 'in the woods' to fight, bearing the heavy burden of responsibility for the fate of their loved ones.

The Italian occupation forces introduced draconian measures against all who harboured Partisans, gave them shelter, food or medical treatment, or aided them in any other way. From the immediate family, these measures were soon extended to other relatives and then to the whole village, which was collectively punished for such actions by any individual. This punishment most commonly took the form of sending all the inhabitants to one of the many prison camps that were springing up throughout Montenegro.

Constantly harried by superior enemy forces, exposed to daily bombardment from the air and ground attacks by the Italian troops and local collaborators, the Partisans in Montenegro gradually lost ground and suffered heavy losses. However brave and determined, in the terrible winter conditions these young men and women were no match for the modernly equipped army of a major military power. Partisan attacks were ineffective against the tanks and armoured vehicles that rumbled along all the roads of Montenegro.

Nada, Mother and I were now almost isolated, apart from a narrow circle of Partisan families. Most of our acquaintances and former friends no longer visited or helped us, our neighbours avoided us, for fear of coming under suspicion themselves, and the Partisan families kept their heads down. Vlado Kokotan, still police chief, and his gang took part in all arrests and executions, denouncing their fellow citizens to their Italian masters.

One day I saw an astonishing sight: Gojko Kruška, wearing the same Italian uniform as Kokotan's men, was hurrying along with this group, probably off to arrest someone. Being the shortest among them, he almost had to run to keep up. Was it possible that he could have changed so much, sold himself, lost all pride and self-respect? Now I understood his strange behaviour in slamming the door in my face: he hadn't gone mad, as we all thought, but out of cowardice had gone over to the stronger side and betrayed his friends. If Gojko Kruška was capable of that, who could be trusted?

Early one morning Mara arrived looking very downcast to tell us that the young lawyer who owned our house had been killed in Crmnica:

"Now there's treachery even among Montenegrins – something that was never known in bygone times. Nikola was killed by a traitor in the same unit, stabbed in the back. Then the man ran off to join the Italians, probably thinking they would overlook his time with the Partisans because of this crime. Or perhaps he'd been sent by them. They try to infiltrate our ranks whenever they can. The death of Nikola is a great blow for our movement: he was one of the main organisers and leaders in Montenegro."

I remembered his words when he came in his elegant suit to hand over the flat keys and tell us there was no need to pay rent: "What's important now is to get through this alive."

A few days later Mara brought us more depressing news:

"The Partisans can't hold out in Montenegro much longer. The Chetniks have joined with the Greens, and both are fighting alongside the Italians. And the Germans are helping them too. For the time being we can't expect any help from the Russians. The news broadcasts say the Germans have pushed them back to the gates of Moscow, but I don't believe it. If it's true, there's nothing left but for all of us to commit suicide. Without the Russians we can't survive. If great Mother Russia can't stop the Germans, what hope is there for little Montenegro?

"Well, because of all this, my dears, it may well happen that our people leave Montenegro temporarily, move to Bosnia and link up with the Bosnian Serbs, who are being chased around and slaughtered by the Moslems and Ustashas. They need someone to rally and lead them, and who better than Montenegrins? Over there we could fill up our ranks: in recent fighting we've lost many comrades."

"Surely the Partisans won't leave Montenegro, Mara?" exclaimed Mother, horrified. "Why, then, did they start the uprising at all, free half the country, get schoolchildren to join them, if now they're going to leave us to the mercy of those criminals? Why have so many young lives been cut short? What did your Bogdan die for?"

"You mustn't talk that way, Milica!" Mara broke in. "The Partisans are fighting for the whole country, for Yugoslavia, not just Montenegro. We have to think of the others – the decent Croats, Moslems, Slovenes and other nationalities who share our ideas and want to live together with us after the war. We must draw a clear line between them and traitors of whatever nation or religion."

"Well," said Mother, calming down a bit, "if you're certain of what you're saying, Mara, perhaps we three could somehow get out of Cetinje and join Stana and her comrades. We can't help Petar and Duško any more, and up in the mountains these two children may have a better chance of surviving."

Hearing Mother mention this possibility, Nada and I both jumped at the idea and begged Mara to help us reach Stana before she left Montenegro. We knew we would find many acquaintances among her fellow fighters, for when the uprising was launched, almost all her friends from the senior years of Cetinje teacher-training school had gone into the Partisans together. In Stana's battalion, we had been told, was sixteen-year-old Danica Popović, who for several months had lived with us in the house by Black Rock, together with her younger sister Vjera. Their father, a friend of the family from our time in Kolašin, had sent the children to stay with us for a while and attend school in Cetinje. Soon after, within a month of each other, both parents had died of tuberculosis. We were glad that Stana was again able to look after Danica, as we had done when she was grieving for her parents. We had all become very fond of her for she was a sweet-natured and exceptionally pretty girl, with dark curly hair, black eyes and a pale complexion. She had a beautiful singing voice and played the violin – music was a compulsory subject at the teacher-training school. The doctors pronounced the Popović children to be healthy, but from time to time Danica's pale cheeks would become strangely flushed, and I overheard Father saying to Mother that she would not live long. Tuber-culosis was the most common disease in Montenegro at that time and the one people feared most.

We immediately got all excited at the prospect of seeing Stana, Danica and other friends, and of moving with them to Bosnia, so escaping from the hunger and constant fear of our life in Cetinje. However, Mara, our mentor in all things, quickly dashed our hopes:

"There are many refugees in the woods already, Milica, lots of sick and wounded, elderly people, women with small children… They're a great handicap for the fighters and their numbers will have to be reduced somehow, not increased. What would we do there, except be-come a burden, hanging on to them and hindering them from carrying on the fight they have begun?"

Mara had heard that all who were not fit, for whatever reason, to carry guns and stand long forced marches would have to stay behind in villages with reliable people or in caves, where food would be brought to them, until the Partisan forces returned from Bosnia.

"Don't you worry, Milica," she said before leaving. "You know it's my duty to look after you. And if anything should happen to me, someone else will take over the very same day."

That evening I turned in very early. By the weak light of the bare bulb in the kitchen which we kept burning all night, I lay down fully dressed, as we now did in case of an emergency. Though tired, I couldn't fall asleep. The silence of the winter night was broken by the occasional barking of some starving dog and by the sound of Olga's piano. Even I could tell that her playing had improved, and now and then I recognised a melody. Lulled by the music, I gradually fell asleep, resolving to find some pretext to talk to her next day.

Before dawn we were woken by shouting in the street. Was this a nightmare repeating itself? Still half asleep, we all three ran to the front window. Just like when Duško was arrested, the house was surrounded by *carabinieri* and Vlado Kokotan's men. My first thought was that they had come for Mother. Someone must have reported her activities with a group of women who collected and cooked food for prisoners. Once again the police broke open our front door – more easily this time as it had never been properly repaired. Several of them burst in, brandishing revolvers, but instead of Mother they made for Nada. As they were taking her away, Mother managed to grab the black fake-fur coat she had kept for best before the war and throw it over Nada's shoulders. It all happened so fast there was no time for protests or curses: Mother's main concern at that moment was to protect my sister from the cold.

Since Duško's imprisonment, Nada's friends had come more often to our house to cheer her up. The most frequent visitors were Miška and Anka, both fourteen, like Nada, and from Partisan families. Two of Anka's brothers, aged eighteen and nineteen, and one of Miška's brothers had been killed in battle soon after the start of the uprising. They were both good-looking girls but very different: Miška exceptionally dark, olive complexioned, with lively black eyes; Anka pale and delicate, with wide blue eyes, quite unlike most Montenegrin girls with their strong features and sturdy build.

I often sneaked up to eavesdrop on their whispered conversations. It was a great relief whenever I discovered that they were not talking about sentimental matters but discussing how to help the movement and people in prison. As the only male left in the family since Duško's arrest, I felt it my duty to look after Nada and make sure that in the abnormal conditions in which we lived she did not do something that could harm the family's good name. Only recently, Vjera, Danica's younger sister, who was barely sixteen, had caught the eye of one of Vlado Kokotan's gang. Left without parents and almost destitute, frightened of being arrested because of her sister in the Partisans, she accepted his attentions and soon, it seems, fell in love. She could now be seen walking around Cetinje with him, to the horror of Partisan families.

"There's a fine thing!" Mara exclaimed. "While her sister's in the woods with the Partisans, there she is going round openly with that criminal."

My father's words on the first day of occupation were deeply engraved on my memory: "The most important thing is that those who survive this war can afterwards walk with their heads held high, their honour unsullied."

The morning after Nada's arrest, I again went running around town. At Miška's house, the story was the same: she, too, had been taken away during the night.

I found Anka at home, scared and upset after hearing of Miška's arrest:

"They didn't come for me," she said, almost apologetic that she was still at liberty.

Her father kept one of Cetinje's inns, which stayed open day and night:

"The Italians would rather see Montenegrins drunk than sober," he would joke.

Anka believed that he had given one of his regulars a large bribe to keep her out of gaol. Money, people said, could save your neck. Unfortunately we had none, nor any jewellery or other valuables: Father had spent all he could spare on our education, declaring that this was the best investment for the future. Now, it seemed, without money there would be no future.

Having filled up all available prison space, the Italians had rapidly built a large camp at Donje Polje, the large field where executions were carried out. The prison camp was surrounded by electrified barbed wire and had raised wooden guard posts, each with a machine-gun, at regular intervals around the perimeter. From Niko the interpreter, who once more came to our aid, we learnt that this was where Nada had been taken. He couldn't tell us how long she might stay there because it was considered a transit camp. We knew that there were others of the same kind in all districts, including Crmnica. As these rural camps were more vulnerable to Partisan attack, the Italian authorities were transferring prisoners from them to Albania, where they would meet with little assistance if they escaped.

Mother, quite unlike herself, now spent much of the time weeping. While she had children to defend, she was like a she-wolf. I remembered her at the market in Mitrovica, walking proud and tall, with two revolvers tucked in her belt, while we young ones clustered round her. But times had changed. Then, Father had been powerful and by our side; the whole of Montenegrin Mitrovica was with us. Now she was alone and helpless, living in constant fear for the lives of her family. In Mitrovica the Montenegrins had been united against a common enemy: the Albanians; now they were fighting among themselves.

One morning Ljuba came to tell us news she had heard from one of her husband's relatives that all the prisoners in Vladin Dom were to be shipped to Italy. Mother, horrified, began weeping. Ljuba tried to console her:

"They may be better off in Italy, Mother, than here, at the mercy of traitors who would like to slaughter them all if they could. They say army barracks somewhere down in the south are being turned into prison camps. It's much warmer there, so at least they won't die of cold."

Mother then implored Ljuba to find Niko and beg him to arrange for us to see Duško to say goodbye, perhaps for the last time.

"I've already pleaded with him, for both Duško and Vicko, but it's not in his power."

A few days later Ljuba came again to tell us that during the night all the prisoners, in chains, had been taken by truck to Bar and put on board a vessel bound for Italy.

Through a prison guard, Niko passed a message to Father informing him of Nada's arrest and Duško's internment in Italy. The guard, who had joined the police so he could serve as a link between the prisoners and the movement, reported that Father had sent a letter to the Italian Command requesting that he alone be held hostage – and shot if necessary – because of Stana, and that his two minor children be released. He received no reply, but ten days later he was lined up with a group of hostages who were told that they would be shot next day in reprisal for the killing of four Italian soldiers in an ambush.

We heard about this horrifying news from all-knowing Mara, who had contacts everywhere. She told us that the executions would take place on an empty stretch of ground near the unfinished high school:

"All day yesterday, prisoners were made to dig the frozen ground, and the Blackshirts didn't let anyone go near."

"I know the place," I cried. "I'll go there tomorrow and if I can't get close enough for him to see me, I'll shout to him from a distance. It'll make it easier for him…"

That evening Mother and I sat mostly in silence beside the kitchen stove. As if in a daze, from time to time she spoke the names of my brothers and sisters, even Milan and Branko who had died as infants in Mitrovica, or mentioned the Austrian camp in Stari Bar, the little towns where we used to live.

Before dawn I slept a little, but as soon as day broke I got dressed as warmly as possible: I didn't know how long I would have to wait in the freezing cold, hiding in some bushes. I felt a desperate need to tell someone what would happen to Father at noon and decided to confide in Rajko, a boy who lived nearby. True, his father, a pre-war gendarme, was on the opposite side, carried a gun and got food and pay from the Italians, but he was a quiet kind of man who had never done anything bad to anyone. Though Rajko was two years younger than myself, I preferred him to his elder brother, who was my age, because he was very lively and bright. We often argued about the Partisans, Chetniks and Greens. Like the official propaganda, he blamed all the shortages on the Partisans, and I energetically defended them, certain that I had nothing to fear from Rajko. In general, I felt I could say anything to friends of my age, even children of our enemies, without fear of being reported. With grown-ups it was a different matter. Children were more loyal and sympathised with me because of the family's troubles.

When Rajko heard what I had come to tell him, he at once started putting on his outdoor clothes, saying: "Hang on a minute, I'm coming with you, to keep you company."

Then he went into the kitchen, closing the door behind him. A minute later his mother opened it:

"Come in, Bato, and sit down. You boys can't go out in this cold on empty stomachs."

Before us on the table she put several large slices of bread spread with a thick layer of lard and sprinkled with plenty of salt and red paprika pepper.

"What can I say, my poor Bato? I'll go to see Milica. My Lazar has gone off with the Guard to some place where there's fighting with the Partisans. But he'll never get blood on his hands, never aim his gun at anyone except to defend himself. He didn't join the Guard willingly, but to save our children from starvation. What else could he do, being a gendarme? If he'd refused, he would have ended up like your poor father. They say the Italians have it in for Petar because, when they called on the young people who had been led astray to come back from the woods, and promised to pardon them, Petar sent a message to Stana telling her on no account to return to Cetinje. Word of this got round, for your Father is a well-known person, and many other young people besides Stana followed his advice."

Rajko and I ran to the execution ground by a roundabout route, for fear that someone would stop us from seeing Father. In the distance we could make out an Italian soldier standing guard in the snow by a pit or trench. Judging by the amount of fresh earth piled up on one side, it was deep and wide. Stealthily, we made our way to a hillock about fifty metres from the guard. Concealed behind this we could see the whole of the soldier, so we knew we would be able to see the hostages as well. Rajko kept glancing at his father's pocket-watch, which he had brought with him. Precisely at noon, two trucks covered in tarpaulin drove up. Several Blackshirts jumped out and set up a machine-gun. It was not like at the executions at the Tablja at the start of the uprising when they'd shot the three young men caught while asleep in the village of Bjeloši. Then there had been a whole squad on parade and they had gone through all the ritual – blindfolds, chairs so the condemned could sit with their backs to the firing squad, and other ceremonial – so that the public could see how 'humane' the Italians were. Clearly no longer concerned about their 'civilising role' in Montenegro, they had now dispensed with all this in favour of the machine-gun, which could dispose of a large number of people more simply and efficiently.

Then the first group of hostages, bound together, was pulled out of a truck. I stopped breathing, paralysed with fear as I looked for Father. I could see the faces of the hostages quite clearly. Some of them looked little more than Duško's age; others were much older, unshaven and unkempt. Some wore city overcoats, others, peasant homespun. Father was not among the first group. We both gave a great sigh of relief. The soldiers pushed the hostages forward and lined them up on the edge of the pit. An officer raised his arm and lowered it. The machine-gun started stuttering and before our eyes pieces of clothing and flesh, fragments of skull, began flying in all directions. Under the impact of the bullets, the bodies mostly toppled into the pit. From the trucks we heard first one voice, then others, break into the old fighting song that had become the battle-hymn of the movement: "Woods are green, flowers in bloom; Montenegro's going to war…"

In the next group, I could clearly see a bearded priest in his long black robe, but not Father. The singing from the trucks grew louder and stronger. The hostages, too, sang as they were led to the edge of the pit. Then a third group was brought out, again without Father. Each time the same horrifying scene was repeated, though the firing seemed somehow to go on longer and longer and the pieces of clothing and flesh to fly a greater distance from the bodies.

Finally the last group emerged. They, too, were singing.

"We used to sing when the Turks cut us down. What else is there to do but sing?" whispered Rajko, just to say something to console me.

In the grey light of the gloomy winter day I could see Father wearing his police overcoat, once so smart but now creased and shapeless and without its gold epaulets.

"Shall we call to him now?" asked Rajko.

"Not yet. Wait a moment, something's different."

We watched in surprise as the Blackshirts freed the hostages from their bonds: they hadn't done this before shooting the other groups. The prisoners stopped singing, which puzzled us even more. It all became clear when the Blackshirts gave each man a short army shovel and indicated that they should bury their comrades. They tossed the earth into the pit, pausing every now and then to pick up remains that had fallen around the edge and place them with the bodies. After about half an hour, when all the earth had been shovelled into the pit, the hostages were herded back towards the trucks. They moved slowly, casting backward glances at the common grave. When it was Father's turn to climb into the truck, another prisoner offered him a helping hand. Before he could jump down inside, I ran forward and shouted as loudly as I could in a voice hoarse with the cold: "Dad! It's Bato!"

Rajko joined in, yelling: "Petar, Petar Tomašević!"

Father paused, turned towards us, and then raised both arms. Rajko and I waved back furiously and he managed to give us another wave before soldiers pushed him out of sight inside the truck and raised the back-flap.

We stood for a while, watching the trucks trundle off in the direction of the prison. Rajko looked at his father's watch:

"We've been here two and a half hours," he marvelled.

Trembling with cold and shock at all we had experienced and seen, we walked slowly towards the execution spot. All around on the blood-stained snow parts of bodies were scattered. A great pool of blood marked the area where the hostages had stood.

"If we leave all this," I said, "stray dogs will come and gnaw their remains and drag them round the town, to the everlasting shame of the whole of Cetinje."

So we ran around picking up the pieces that the big machine-gun bullets had torn from the bodies and the fragments of skull.

"When they were shot in the head, half of it was blown off," said Rajko. "We can't scoop up all the brains."

We collected everything we could in one spot and with our frozen fingers dug a hole at one end of the pit. Carefully we buried the remains, stamping down the earth. While we were doing all this, we couldn't help getting blood all over our clothes, so we crept home by back streets, hoping not to meet any police or soldiers.

Eager to tell the joyful news that Father was still alive and had waved to me, I dashed into the flat. At the sight of me covered in blood, for the first time in her life my mother fainted. When she started coming round, I shouted:

"I'm fine, Mother! It's not my blood. It's from the hostages who were shot!"

Several minutes later, when she had quite recovered, I realised I hadn't yet told her the main thing: Father had survived.

Next day Rajko told me that his mother had suffered a similar shock, thinking that he had been wounded during the executions. After this, Rajko and I became even closer friends and spent much of our time together. Mother liked him because he reminded her of Aco with his bright, black eyes and restless high spirits, and now that my brothers or sisters were no longer around, I had someone to whom I could confide almost everything, knowing he would never tell.

Soon after we found out how Father had come to be in the group for execution. The guard had reported to his contact that the older prisoners – men of forty or more – had agreed that they would try to save the young men in their teens and twenties from execution, at least for a while. In the crowded cells they hatched a whispered plan. The prison officers would receive orders from above to shoot a certain number of prisoners in reprisal, but they could not connect names with faces. Anyway, it was all the same to them as long the number was right. So when the list of names of those condemned to execution was read out, Father and the older men stepped forward instead of the youngsters.

Mara didn't come to visit us for several days. This was unusual, so I got worried that something had happened to her. When I suggested going to her house and asking her neighbours if I didn't find her, Mother grew agitated:

"For heaven's sake don't go looking for her, unless you want to get her into bad trouble. She'll come as soon as she can."

Finally, when I insisted, she whispered to me in the strictest confidence that Mara had gone to meet our people 'in the woods', passing through the block with an axe and some rope on the pretence of cutting firewood. There was a chance that she might meet Stana or at least bring back news of her.

We had not had any message from Stana for ages. From time to time we heard about the movements of her battalion, the fighting that was going on almost continuously, the death of Partisans we knew – the sons or daughters of family friends. Still, we had the feeling that Stana was not far away, that she was roaming the hills almost within sight, and this kept us going, gave us the strength to endure the hunger and cold, to face up to the dangers all around us. That was why we so dreaded the thought of her leaving for Bosnia. Times had changed. Armed and at liberty, she was now the pillar of the family, our hope for survival, while Father, helpless in prison, could no longer be counted on.

"Listen, Mother," I said. "If Mara makes contact with Stana, I could pass through the block like she did and be with Stana for just a day or two, not to leave you alone for long."

I was half expecting Mother to flatly forbid this, but she seemed indecisive:

"If I knew it was safe, I'd say go at once. But I daren't, for if anything happened to you I could never forgive myself. These are terrible times when a mother no longer knows how to advise her children for the best.

You're only twelve, but you know as much as a twenty-year-old before the war. You must make up your own mind."

One morning soon after, Mara arrived, tanned by the mountain sun and wind, and bringing good news: she had met Stana.

"She's well, but she worries a lot about you. She blames herself for all your troubles and hardships. But now there's nothing to be done but go forward."

"And is she going to Bosnia?" I asked impatiently. "Will she be passing near Cetinje?"

"Indeed she will," Mara assured me. "In about ten days' time her battalion will be at the village of Štitari, to collect fighters from the Katun area. Then they'll join up with the rest of the Lovćen Detachment and go west into Bosnia. The detachment has about fifteen hundred fighters, they say, divided into several battalions, operating in the Cetinje, Bar and Kotor districts. But they're having a hard time of it: the villages have been plundered and burnt so people haven't enough food for themselves, let alone for others. Many of the fighters in Stana's battalion are from Crmnica. Petar would be glad to hear that."

When Mara finished her account of her journey, I announced in a very determined voice that I was going to Štitari to meet Stana.

"Don't worry, I'll come back as soon as I've seen her," I added, noticing Mother's anxious gaze.

Mara did her best to dissuade me, but seeing my mind was made up, promised to help me reach the village.

"The road is pretty dangerous now. There are plenty of soldiers wandering around the Katun area, and you could easily run into Chetniks. They're drunk most of the time and can hardly wait for an excuse to pull out their knives."

Bato Tomašević, photograph
taken in Podgorica, late
December 1944, when he
was on his way to Albania
with his unit

Reluctant Partisan

The few days before I was to leave I spent mainly with Rajko, his brother and other boys in the neighbourhood. I longed to call them together and announce that I would soon be among the Partisans, or at least to confide in Rajko, but I had sworn not to say a word. For this reason I was unusually quiet and especially avoided talking about the Partisans.

In preparation for my meeting with Stana, Ljuba made me a warm jacket and plus-fours out of Italian army blankets. From an Italian soldier who needed a bit of spending money I bought some heavy, metal-tipped army boots, several sizes too big, which I wore with two pairs of thick, hand-knitted, woollen knee-socks to protect me from frost-bite up in the mountains.

Early one morning Mara arrived with an axe and some rope and for the tenth time gave me instructions on which way to go, which houses to call at on the way, how to avoid Italian and Chetnik patrols:

"When you come to the block, say you want to collect firewood for your mother. And when you come back, wait and take a good look around before you approach the ramp, and don't forget to carry a bundle of wood! You must tell the same story and stick to it, even if they roast you alive, otherwise we're all finished. You'd better leave straight away to get as far as possible by daylight. It would be risky for Milica and me to see you off. Good luck!"

I hugged Mother and Mara and off I went, excited and scared in equal measure. It was a clear sunny day, which is what we'd been waiting for, so I wouldn't get caught in a blizzard in the mountains. I glanced towards Olga's windows: there was no sign of her. Walking to the check-point, I imagined how it would be if I could tell Olga what a dangerous journey I was undertaking. Maybe this would impress her and make her think about me.

Cheered by the March sunshine, the *carabinieri* at the block were in a good mood, joking and singing snatches of song. They didn't bother to ask where I was going, but waved me through. I walked away from the ramp as quickly as I dared, in case they had second thoughts and called me back.

After several hundred metres of brisk walking, I paused, out of breath, and cast a quick backward glance to see if I was being followed. Cetinje lay behind me in the sunshine, enclosed by its hedge of electrified barbed wire that would kill you if you only touched it, they said. I had no idea what lay ahead, but I was glad I'd set out.

Mindful of Mara's warnings, I kept my eyes open for the enemy. How could I explain what I was doing so far from town in an area without any trees, only naked rock and snow? The Cetinje women cut their fuel in copses close to town, and here was I heading for the bare hills that sloped steeply down from the Katun area and its villages, still in Partisan hands. There was only one track leading upwards so I could hardly get lost. This rough path, so narrow two loaded donkeys couldn't pass on it, had been created over the centuries by the people of the Katun villages taking the easiest route down to Montenegro's little capital. I walked steadily higher, but every now and again there was a sudden sharp dip and I had to dig in my boots to stop myself slip-sliding out of control into some crevice. After a while I found myself on a level patch of land with a couple of small houses, just as Mara had described. The larger, built of rough stone and thatched, had no chimney: smoke from an open hearth was escaping through holes along the length of the roof. I approached cautiously and waited for a while behind a rock, as Mara had advised, in case there were Italians or Chetniks inside. Just then a middle-aged woman came out carrying chicken feed and went towards the stone hut nearby. I summoned up my courage and stepped forward. She didn't seem at all surprised to see me:

"You must be Bato. Welcome! Mara sent word you'd be coming. It's a good job you didn't arrive yesterday. We had some uninvited guests: a Chetnik patrol, about a dozen cut-throats. But never mind that. Come inside, poor child, and warm yourself by the hearth. A lad of your own age will come later to see if you've arrived and take you to Štitari. You mustn't stay here long in case those murderers come back. From your face and hands they'd see at once you're a town boy. And you don't talk in our peasant way."

On first entering the cottage, all I could see was smoke.

"There's a south wind today, so the smoke comes back," she explained. "I'll have a go on the bellows: that'll soon do the trick."

When it was bit clearer I could see that the whole house was just one fairly large room. Along one wall was a rough wooden bed with a straw mattress covered by a threadbare blanket. In one corner stood a barrel and a number of empty tin cans containing water that served instead of jugs. In this barren area there was little water, and every day the women used to sling barrels on their backs and walk, perhaps for an hour or two, to the nearest spring. The roof beams were blackened by smoke and soot. Before the war, there had usually been hams and other smoked meat hanging from the beams, but by this time it had all been hidden, eaten or stolen.

Katun was considered the poorest part of Montenegro. Seen from the Lovćen side, the whole region resembled a stormy sea of stone, with almost no trees, apart from a few around houses that the owners had planted and carefully nurtured. In the small patches of earth collected in hollows they grew excellent potatoes, for which Katun was famous.

"I'll put a couple of potatoes to bake in the ashes, son, so you don't leave our house hungry," she said. "I've nothing else to offer you."

I had just finished eating the potatoes when my guide arrived.

"I'm Vido," he said, welcoming me with a firm handshake and kissing me three times on the cheek. He seemed a little older than myself and from his clothes and speech I guessed he was a village boy.

"Let's get going straight away, while it's still daylight," he proposed.

I thanked my hostess and we set off at a fast pace for the village of Štitari.

As we walked, I began thinking about meeting Stana and remembering the day she had left to join the Partisans at the age of nineteen. Dressed for a journey into the countryside and wearing the French beret from her school uniform, she had hugged each of us in turn, teasing us as she often did, smiling broadly and showing her beautiful white teeth – the finest in the family. None of us, except Duško, had any idea she was not planning to return in a few days, that the uprising was soon to begin.

Father had seemed moved by her warm embrace: displays of affection were not common in our family. He adored Stana, but at the same time was a little in awe of her cleverness, her strength of mind and will, her stubborn determination to do what she believed right. She had been the best student in the teacher-training schools in Kragujevac and Cetinje, had a good knowledge of French and played the violin, practising assiduously, since this was a compulsory school subject, to make up for her acknowledged lack of musical talent. She was not strikingly beautiful, like Ljuba, but her radiant smile and charm attracted young and old alike. Father used to say that she would be able to "pick and choose a husband from the whole of our lovely Yugoslavia", and imagined her happily married with children of her own – the ambition and dream of most girls of her age, but not Stana. On a trip to Prague she had met a young man of President Masarik's family with whom she corresponded, as with many other of her contemporaries abroad who shared her ideals.

She used to have long talks with Mother, who liked to listen to her daughter's views on the role and equality of women, since they were close to what she herself had felt and voiced long ago, in quite different circumstances, as a young wife in Crmnica. Of all the children Stana was most like Mother in appearance: tall, strongly built yet slim, with pronounced cheekbones and a determined chin. I used to listen in as she spoke passionately about the changes there would be in our country if progressive people came to power: no one nation or religion would be above others; education would be for rich and poor alike; society would care for the aged, the sick and those without work.

Mother would listen in admiration, but from time to time she would break in with comments like: "Eh, my Stana, you're out of your mind! When will this ever happen?"

I remembered Mother giving advice drawn from her own experience of life:

"Now you've finished your schooling and you're independent, people will take you at your own worth, respect and value you as much as you do yourself, neither more nor less. It's up to you to set the standard."

⁂

Vido interrupted my thoughts, as though guessing their subject:

"I'm not sure Stana will be able to get from Crmnica to Štitari. Large forces are heading towards us, they say. Milovan Čelebić keeps urging the Katun people to hold out. He says this offensive will pass like the last two, but some villagers are wavering: people are starving; bombs are flattening and burning their homes. But Štitari is still solid, thanks mainly to Milovan. He's a friend of Stana's and you'll be staying with his family."

I walked fast, but Vido walked even faster. Knowing every stone, he was sure-footed, while I was cautious, afraid a twisted ankle might stop me from reaching Stana. Sometimes he had to wait for me to catch up.

"You walk very well," he said to console me. "You'd be a good Partisan."

"Then how come you're not a Partisan when you're faster than me?"

"I am," Vido replied. "I'm a Partisan runner. That's why I've come to fetch you. Runners are young, our age. We mostly carry messages between units. Sometimes, when there's fighting, we go with the bombardiers when they creep up at night to throw grenades into bunkers and dug-outs, before the main force attacks."

"And how old are the bombardiers?" I asked my knowledgeable companion.

"Anything from your age to sixteen, seventeen. We runners are often both, depending on what's needed, but there are experienced bombardiers who only do bunkers."

As we talked away the sun went down behind Lovćen, which we could see clearly as we walked, just like from our house by Black Rock. As long as it was in sight I felt somehow more secure. Night fell swiftly.

"Is it safe to go on in the dark?" I asked. "Do you know the way, so we don't get lost?"

"You town boys!" laughed Vido. "You're scared to go out at night, afraid of the dark, the devil, witches... But the Partisans have turned night into day. At night you march and attack; by day you sleep, rest, and hide from planes and artillery."

"I'm not afraid, I just asked," I countered, but in fact I was trembling with fear, thinking of enemy bullets which, when they hit you, blew off half your head or bits of your body.

Suddenly the silence was shattered by a loud voice:

"Halt! Who goes there?"

"Partisans! Don't worry!" Vido replied.

"Give the password!"

"Stavor!" Vido shouted.

"One person step forward."

Vido whispered that I should stay put while he approached the guards.

"Oh, it's you, Vido," said a friendly voice. "Have you brought the lad from Cetinje?"

"Come forward, Bato," Vido called.

By the faint moonlight I could make out three young men with rifles over their shoulders wearing homespun peasant clothes and unfamiliar caps. Mara had told me that if I met any Partisans in the woods, I would be able to recognise them by their caps with a five-pointed star in front, "like the ones worn by the proletariat in the Russian Revolution". The young men pumped my hand and enquired about the number of enemy troops in Cetinje. After ten minutes or so we moved on.

"Now you're in the Partisans, Bato, at liberty," one of them called after me.

His words made me realise that I was now enjoying that precious freedom everyone living in slavery dreams about. I felt a warm glow. At the same time I wondered how it was possible that all those enemy soldiers, the fighting, the prisons, the executions, were because of young men like these, armed just with rifles. How could they stand up to tanks and big guns, like the one outside Father Vukmanović's house?

Suddenly I noticed some pale flickering lights ahead: the flames from open hearths glowing through narrow windows.

"Here we are at Štitari!" my guide announced with satisfaction.

Vido took me to Milovan's house. I was surprised and pleased to find that his mother, Lepa, was the nice woman at the market who had told us about Stana.

"Welcome to our home, Bato," she said with a kindly smile. "Warm yourself by the fire. You mustn't fall ill because we've no medicines left!"

There were already several Partisans sitting around the fire. Some distance away, propped against the wall, were their rifles with ammunition. Beside each was a broad leather belt with hand-grenades attached: small red oval Italian Ballistas and pear-shaped Kragujevkas, collected after the capitulation of the Yugoslav Royal Army. They all got up to greet me and made a place for me by the fire.

"So you're Stana's brother!" said the one who looked to be the oldest, a man of about thirty.

"I'm Andrija, a friend of Stana's. I know your father, and Duško. Danica will be coming to see you any moment now. She was pleased to hear you were on your way here."

It was the same Danica, a close friend of Stana's, who had often spent the night with us: when Stana had left Cetinje it was supposedly to visit Danica and her widowed mother in a nearby village. From there, a few days later she had gone into the Partisans.

The moment I saw Danica I felt more at ease.

"How you've grown, Bato!" she cried, hugging me. "We'll have to see what to do with you until Stana arrives." Then, turning to my guide, she added: "Look after your new comrade, Vido. Show him how things are done and what goes on here when we're not fighting. Take him to the Command Post."

Vido looked pleased Danica had entrusted him with the task of introducing me to Partisan life. Danica, it turned out, was not a member of the local Partisan company, but had come for a few days to organise educational activities.

Close to midnight, our hostess threw one more log on the fire and said we should sleep. From a large wooden chest she pulled out a number of Italian army blankets and some shabby sheepskin rugs to spread on the mud floor. I looked around, wondering whether to get undressed, and Danica seemed to read my thoughts:

"We're billeted around all the houses, from three to six in each, depending on the space. We sleep in our clothes because of the cold, and because you never know when you may be taken by surprise. Here in the village it's quite safe because we have guards all around, but it's not always so, especially when we're on marches. Come and lie down by me, Bato. Nobody has a special place. We're like brothers and sisters in one big family. If you need to get up in the night, call Lepa to go with you. Never go outside alone in case the starving dogs attack you."

As soon as we had all settled down on the floor, I fell fast asleep, exhausted by all the walking and excitement of the long day. When I woke up, I was the only one left on the ground, though several others were sitting by the fire drinking 'coffee' made of roasted grain.

"Good morning, Bato," said Lepa. "Did you sleep well? You must have found the floor hard last night, but you'll get used to it!"

She handed me a bowl of maize porridge and some warm milk.

Shortly after, Vido arrived looking quite different from the day before: he wore a Partisan cap with a five-pointed star and had a revolver and grenades at his waist. Over his shoulder he carried a short Italian rifle of the type that Duško and his friends had made fun of, saying they were toys for children, not weapons for grown men. It seemed, in fact, just the right size for Vido. It had a bayonet which sprang out when you pressed a button.

Vido then took me to the Command Post:

"It's in the primary school, together with all the other people's authorities in Štitari."

He emphasised 'people's authorities', and, guessing that I had no idea what this meant, he hastened to show off his knowledge:

"It's what the Russians invented during their revolution. Before, in the old, rotten Yugoslavia, there was nothing like it. The city bourgeoisie didn't care about the countryside, didn't pay any attention to the villages. Now the people in the village decide about everything. In the school, besides the Command Post, there's the People's Committee, the Youth Committee, the Party Committee, and lots more. Ask Danica;

she'll explain it better than I can. This evening she's going to give a talk to the women. Now they are all active, engaged in politics, not just looking after the house and the hens like before."

Some of Vido's expressions seemed strange to me, but I was soon to become familiar with them.

To reach the school at the far end of the village we passed about thirty thatched, rough-stone cottages, smaller and poorer than the houses in Crmnica. We met lots of Partisans on the way. Being younger, Vido saluted them first, with a clenched fist, not a flat hand, as soldiers did before the war. Sometimes he also called out: "Death to fascism!" to which they replied in equally ringing tones: "Freedom to the people!"

Inside the school all the doors bore signs, hand-printed on paper. The first was 'Command Post'; opposite was 'People's Committee', and so on, each classroom housing another of the new Partisan organisations.

Vido knocked on the first door and opened it wide, without waiting for permission to enter. An older Partisan was sitting at a table.

"Comrade Commandant," Vido addressed him in a loud voice, giving a clenched-fist salute, and added another rousing: "Death to fascism!"

The commandant stood up and saluted back.

"On the orders of Danica, I've brought you Bato from Cetinje, the brother of Stana Tomašević, for you to receive him and assign him a place."

The commandant looked me up and down, shook hands, and said:

"Welcome to the Partisans, Bato. You're a bit on the young side for any heavy duty, but now you're here, stay with the others. Vido's not much older, after all."

I suddenly realised, with an unpleasant shock, that he believed I had come to join the Partisans. How could I explain, without appearing a coward, that I just wanted to see Stana and then return to Cetinje, where my mother was anxiously waiting for me? I decided it was best to keep quiet for the time being and let Stana do the explaining when she arrived.

"Let him report to Company Commander Stevan, so you can be together," he said to Vido. Then turning to me added in a kindly voice:

"We all eat together from the same cauldron during the day, and in the evening they'll give you some supper where you sleep."

Vido next took me to a larger house on a knoll above the village where a dozen or so members of his company stayed, while the rest slept in other village houses:

"We meet here every day about noon, talk a bit, and then go to eat. After our meal we all come back and have a 'reading hour' with discussion."

Seeing I looked blank, he said this was when various texts were read out and everyone had to say how they understood them, and if they didn't, the company delegate would explain.

"That's how we improve ourselves," he added. "The Partisans aren't here just to fight but to learn how to govern the country after our victory."

Commander Stevan, who looked about twenty, also shook hands warmly and welcomed me to the Partisans. 'Well,' I thought, 'there's nothing to be done but accept it and behave as they expect.'

One of the company they called the intendant took me into a room where he showed me a number of caps and told me to choose one.

"Our women make them out of homespun cloth and sew on the five-pointed star made of red cotton material. To tell the truth, they've been so busy we have more caps than we have heads to put them on!" he joked.

The first cap I put on fitted perfectly, so there was no need to try on others. Then he handed me the same type of rifle as Vido's and an ammunition belt with twenty bullets:

"Someone in the company will teach you how to handle it. For the time being you won't be needing more bullets, at least we hope not."

I said I didn't need any teaching as my father had instructed me.

Scarcely believing what was happening to me, I fastened on the ammunition belt and slung the rifle over my shoulder. All of a sudden I was no different from the rest. They, too, wore their ordinary clothes, city or peasant, or a mixture of the two – whatever they had on when they joined the company. The only thing we all had in common was our cap with the red star.

When Vido and I set off to take a walk through the village, for the first time I felt grown-up and responsible. I thought about Olga, Rajko and all the other neighbourhood children. What would they say if they could see me now with my rifle and cap?

※

When it was getting dark I noticed village women, alone or in twos or threes, hurrying in the direction of the school. They were all dressed much the same: plain black kerchiefs tied under the chin, leather peasant sandals and thick hand-knitted stockings. Their long skirts and short jackets with wide sleeves were made of coarse woollen cloth woven at home. None of them wore winter coats, for these would only hamper them as they hurried about doing their many chores. Nor did they wear any gloves, so their hands were rough and red with the cold.

"Come on, Rada, you'll be late!" "Hurry up, Zorka, the 'converence' will start without you!" they called to one another.

I heard the word 'converence' for the first time and was about to ask Vido what it was when Danica appeared with several friends. Noticing my rifle, she at once came over:

"I see they've armed you already! No matter, you can hand everything back before you return to Cetinje."

"Could I come to your 'converence', to see what it's about?" I asked, realising that this must be connected with the talk Danica was due to give to the women.

Instead of replying she burst out laughing, gave me a hug, and led me into the school. One classroom was already packed with peasant women: about fifty sitting on school benches and standing around the walls. I stayed at the back by the door and Danica went to the teacher's desk. They all fell silent and listened attentively when she began to speak, first of all talking about all the sacrifices they had been making:

"All the burden of cooking, washing and sewing for our fighters has fallen on your shoulders, in addition to all your other duties. Many of you have entrusted your sons and daughters to us, and are anxious about what will happen to them. But I must warn you that this is not the end of your sacrifices, just the beginning. Only now are the really hard times coming. Traitors to our people, together with the Italians, are burning villages, putting women, children and old people into prison camps. We mustn't hide anything from you, because without your help there can be no victory, no better times, only darkness and slavery. And so, my dear comrades, if some great force pushes us out of Štitari one day, it will only be for a while. Your sons will return as avengers, stronger than they have ever been."

"We won't give in, Danica, even if our menfolk do!" called out a peasant woman near me. Her interruption set others off, and they started jumping up from the benches, all shouting approval and agreement at the same time. Danica begged them to sit down, so they could talk over important matters calmly, one by one:

"We've got time, until dawn if necessary, for everyone to have their turn to speak."

But again a dozen women jumped up: they all had something to say that couldn't wait.

At that point the door opened slightly and Vido peeped in. He beckoned me to come outside.

"That's enough listening to the women," he said with a grin. "Let's see what the amateur society is doing."

Again another new expression, but I kept quiet, not wanting to appear ignorant and stupid when I had attended Cetinje High School, said to be the best in Montenegro.

Putting a finger to his lips, Vido pushed open another door and whispered:

"We mustn't disturb them."

A score of young people were gathered in the classroom. All the young men or boys wore revolver holsters and grenades attached to their leather belts, so I could see they were active Partisans, while the girls just wore ordinary peasant clothes.

A moment or two later a huge man, almost two metres tall, entered. To my astonishment I recognised Vaso Spahić, an actor of the Cetinje theatre company: he had come to the high school just before the war to give a Njegoš recitation, which had delighted pupils and teachers alike. Though

Vaso played various roles in the theatre, he was best known for his recitations of the poetry of Njegoš, whom he resembled in appearance.

"I know you, sir," I said when he extended his large hand.

Hearing I was from Cetinje, Vaso seemed very pleased:

"I'm sure you know how to sing and have a good ear, not like these here, who were fast asleep when God gave out musical talent. I'll need you to sing and recite something. Come tomorrow to show what you can do, and if you like, be here in an hour's time for a rehearsal, to see what we're preparing. The Command has given me permission to take anyone who may be of any use to the theatre. It's just as important as fighting. Before we came to the Katun villages, nobody had ever seen a performance, or even knew the theatre existed, although they live just a few hours' walk from Cetinje. It's important to show that the Partisans are not like other armies, that they want to educate people in every way."

With Vido's guidance I soon saw this for myself. He showed me the various classrooms where courses of all kinds were held: literacy, hygiene, nursing, child care – there seemed to be hardly any practical subject not covered.

At the appointed time, Vido and I returned for the rehearsal. Several dozen people, Partisans and others, who had been attending various courses or meetings, had stayed to see this. The audience, separated from the 'stage' only by some improvised curtains made of several blankets, waited impatiently for the start. Finally, the curtains parted and a neatly dressed young Partisan came on stage, stood to attention and shouted:

"Death to fascism, comrades!"

"Freedom to the people!" everyone responded in a deafening chorus.

Vaso then made his appearance. He stood perfectly still, like a great statue, except that he lowered his thick black eyebrows in a frown, and with finger and thumb twisted his moustache. The expectant audience waited with bated breath. Vaso cleared his throat and then thundered out: "Duke Draško in Venice!"

At these words, everyone roared with laughter. Though most of them were illiterate, they all knew 'Mountain Wreath' more or less by heart.

This section of Njegoš's work was about a theatrical performance in Venice in which he made fun of Italians: their small stature, plumpness, affected manners and frivolity, as he saw it. In expectation of their attack on Štitari, Vaso wanted to remind those present that the great Njegoš had not thought very highly of Italians.

⁂

Next day I turned up at the appointed time.

"Have you ever sung in public?" Vaso asked.

"I used to sing in church and in the choir of Cetinje Monastery."

Hearing this, everyone, including Vaso, burst out laughing.

"Don't forget to mention that when you apply to join the Party," someone joked, causing more laughter.

"Fine, Bato," said Vaso, seeing I was put out. "We can make good use of what the priests and monks have taught you. I've had a hard job finding these boys and girls for the choir. First you stand at the side and listen. We're preparing a concert for the Lovćen Detachment. When your Stana arrives, we'll surprise them."

At once I started imagining how wonderful it would be if Stana were to see me first of all as I was singing in the choir. She would be sitting in the audience and afterwards she would come up and hug me.

"Now, comrades, let's get going. We'll sing 'I'm proud to be a Partisan' and then 'From Lovćen eagles fly'."

I listened as they sang with more enthusiasm than tunefulness. During a break Vaso asked me whether I knew those songs. I said I did: Partisan families in Cetinje used to sing them quietly in their homes.

"Well, here you can sing your heart out. There's nothing to be afraid of, not even the audience: they won't boo because they've never heard anything better! Go ahead then."

As I nervously cleared my throat, he gave me some advice:

"What's important is to sing loudly, so everyone can hear. They think the loudest singing is the best. And they care more about the message than the melody, so make sure every word is clear."

At a signal from Vaso I began "I'm proud to be a Partisan' at the top of my voice. Judging by his expression he liked my singing, and when I finished everyone clapped, making me turn pink.

"Well done, Bato! It was worth waiting for you to join us. Now we've found the voice that was missing, I know how we're going to start. After 'Death to fascism!' Bato will sing the first few lines alone, then everyone else will join in."

When we finished practising the songs, Vaso again turned to me:

"I suppose they taught you to recite in high school?"

This time I was confident he would be satisfied since my Serbian teacher had always praised my recitation and held me up as an example to others. In fact, it was mostly from my father that I had learnt to recite. I told Vaso I knew a lot of poems by heart, but I could easily learn new ones if necessary. Again he signalled me to begin, and I adopted the proper upright pose Father had taught me:

"'We'll fall, brothers, and drown in blood' by Djuro Jakšić, and 'Freedom will come, from death, from the grave' by Aleksa Šantić," I announced.

When I finished, Vaso and my new comrades couldn't praise me enough. Proud and happy, I felt I had quickly gained an important place in their 'amateur society' and that life in the Partisans was the real thing, full of enjoyable activities and true comradeship. I would be very sorry in a few days' time when I had to return to the grim, enclosed, dangerous life of occupied Cetinje. But, then again, how could I leave them when I was so badly needed? How to tell them I hadn't meant to join the Partisans, only to see Stana and go back home?

That evening, back in Milovan's household where I was still sleeping, Lepa greeted me with a broad smile:

"I hear, Bato, that you're good at singing and reciting, so the show will be even better. Well, if it wasn't for the Partisans, we wouldn't know such things existed. Now, every day when we've milked the sheep and goats, we go off to the Command Post to see what's happening. You can always hear and learn something there."

That night, not long before dawn, we were all woken by a tremendous noise and jumped to our feet.

"Is that thunder or guns?" Lepa asked in alarm.

We listened hard. Some moments later the thunderous noise was repeated, but this time you could clearly make out the distinct sounds of the firing and the impact.

"Not thunder, worse luck," answered Andrija. "Somewhere in Katun there's fighting going on; they've brought up their big guns. We've got a few mortars, but no field guns. That's the Italians and Chetniks using heavy artillery against our positions."

We sat round the fire again and strained our ears as the cannon and mortars sounded at short intervals. When it was daylight, a fighter came to report to Andrija:

"A large enemy force left Cetinje for Katun. Our people have blocked their advance and there's heavy fighting on Mount Šimunja."

Andrija, Danica and the few other Partisans sleeping at Milovan's hurried off to the Command Post to get more information and see what was to be done if the enemy broke through our defences. I left with them, but made for my company's house, where the other members billeted out like myself were already gathered. When I entered, Commander Stevan was speaking to them:

"From the sound of the firing, the way it echoes round the mountains, the fighting seems to be some distance from Štitari. All the same, we must strengthen the guards."

Listening to the commander, I became alarmed at the turn things were taking and whispered to Vido:

"If I have to be on guard, I'd like to keep with you, if possible."

"Don't worry, I've already spoken to Stevan about that. I'll tell you what to do when the time comes."

The commander told us to stop talking as he had something else to say:

"Look out for planes today! Don't stay out in the open or go round in groups. Try to keep near some shelter in case of bombing."

Around midday, as he had foreseen, from the direction of Podgorica a number of Italian bombers, Savoys, flew over the village and were lost to sight behind the nearest ridge. Just after there was a series of loud explosions as they dropped their load on Partisan positions. Less than an hour later another wave of Savoys flew low overhead and the same thing was repeated.

"They want to soften up our fighters before an attack," commented Stevan. "It looks as if villages are less important to them for now than our lines of defence. Still, we must take precautions. They can easily change their minds and drop their bombs on us."

In the course of the afternoon reports of the fighting on Šimunja reached the Command Post. The enemy forces from Cetinje were being held by the well-armed and well-organised Katun Partisans. The battalions fighting there already had experience in battle and knew every square metre of ground, every goat track, so they could easily move around and attack the enemy from the rear when least expected.

"As soon as it gets dark, our people will counter-attack," Vido declared confidently.

Danica, seeing me outside the Command Post and guessing I was scared, came over to encourage me.

"We're expecting the arrival of four of our battalions: the Jovan Tomašević and Coastal battalions from Crmnica, and the Carev Laz and 13th July from Cetinje, so it'll be much better," Danica told me.

This news filled me with excitement: my meeting with Stana was very close.

As the night wore on, more and more shells were fired. Soon after midnight, in the distance we could see bursts of tracer bullets going in the opposite direction, which meant, they said, that our forces were moving against the enemy, just as Vido had forecast.

At one moment everything fell quiet.

"Our people must have got to their guns and mortars," Vido explained.

Soon after a fresh series of explosions followed, different in intensity.

"That's our bombardiers throwing grenades at enemy positions. After that the older and stronger Partisans will move in and you'll hear the crack of revolvers – rifles are no good close up. And if it comes to hand-to-hand fighting, they'll use their knives. Then everything depends on who keeps his nerve. So far our knives have got the better of the Italians and Chetniks, and so they will tonight."

I was amazed that somebody scarcely older than myself had learnt so much about warfare so quickly. Sure enough, everything went as he said: grenade explosions, followed by revolver shots, and then silence.

"Now they're stabbing the Italians and Chetniks," Vido added gleefully.

I shuddered at the thought: ever since being slashed in the leg by an Albanian boy at school in Mitrovica I'd had a horror of knives and couldn't imagine myself using one.

After some time, no sound came from the direction of the fighting: a sign that the Partisans had gained another victory. Long after that Vido and I stayed in front of the Command Post, listening to the Partisans and peasants talking. They all agreed on one thing: the events of that night were only the first of many battles to come.

The following day more details came in from Šimunja. When the bombardiers burst in among them, the enemy, in a state of confusion, had begun to retreat rapidly towards Cetinje. Casualties had been heavy. Four ambulance trucks of wounded had been driven to Kotor instead of Cetinje, so as not to demoralise the troops there.

Over the next few days events moved fast all over Montenegro. Groups of peasants set off secretly at night from their villages to surrender to the Italians. In return for their help in driving the Partisans out of Montenegro, they were promised that their homes and families would be spared in future fighting. They were also given a few liras and some flour for their starving families.

Most of these peasants placed themselves under the command of Krsto Popović, a prominent leader of the Greens who had been in exile with King Nikola in Italy. After the King's death, he had returned and lived in hiding from the Yugoslav police in his native Katun area. When the Italians arrived, Popović, a strong personality of imposing military appearance, placed himself at the head of the Greens in the hope of reviving the Kingdom of Montenegro. And so the Greens, as well as the Chetniks, took sides with the occupiers in fighting the Partisans.

Krsto Popović had a grown-up son, Nikola, who was a communist. He had joined the uprising at the very outset and was now a Partisan leader in the Katun area. The rift in this respected family split the Katun peasants into those who were for the father and those who were for the son. For the first time in Montenegro, opposing forces led by a father and a son fought against one another.

To take some of the pressure off the Katun Partisans, Nikola Popović and his battalion undertook to attack an enemy stronghold towards the coast at Gornje Orahovac, part of the defences of the Gulf of Kotor. After fighting all night, they destroyed the garrison, killing and wounding a large number of Italians, taking forty-seven prisoners and capturing a considerable quantity of arms and ammunition. Three Partisans were killed and ten wounded, among them Nikola Popović.

These two victories at Šimunja and Gornje Orahovac helped to boost morale among the Katun Partisans and their supporters, but they did not essentially improve their position, which was becoming graver day by day.

In one battle about that time Nikola Popović's battalion directly confronted a much larger force under his father. At one point the father and son were close enough to recognise each other, but the fighting continued, with more or less equal losses on either side. The fight against the occupier in Montenegro had now become, at the same time, a fratricidal struggle.

❧

One evening I went along to a meeting in the Command Post. About a hundred peasants from the Katun villages and hamlets were gathered there to discuss the present difficult situation and the choice facing them: to continue their support for the Partisans and accept the consequences for their homes and families, or to throw in their lot with the Greens and Chetniks under the Italians.

The meeting was to be addressed by a Partisan commissar who had arrived in Štitari that afternoon. He was, they said, a prominent pre-war communist from Virpazar, a shoemaker by trade. The trouble started as soon as he began speaking about the struggle shifting from Montenegro to Bosnia.

"All the Serbs there will join our ranks," he said, "and there will be Croats, Muslims and others, regardless of nationality or religion, who are eager to fight for a new Yugoslavia and want to live together with us after the war."

This reminded me of Mara, who had spoken almost the same words to Mother. They were probably what all political activists were supposed to say, to explain to people, so as not to lose their support.

"Does that mean, commissar," someone interrupted, "that you want us to leave our homes, our wives and children, unprotected, so they can all go up in flames, while we fight for other people's homes, wives and children? I see that you're not from our village, so it's easy for you to talk."

The speaker was an older peasant with moustaches, obviously an influential man in the area, for after him most of the others voiced their agreement. They were all ready to fight to the death to defend their own village or even other villages, as far as Montenegro stretched, but not a foot further.

"You young people go, and good luck to you, but we'll stay home and protect our own. We're not yet ready to die for any other religion, and nor were our forefathers, thank God," another older man declared.

The meeting went on for a long time and there were sharp words exchanged between the commissar and several of the peasants, who criticised him for putting the good of others before the good of Montenegrins. When it finally broke up, the commissar had failed to gain support for the move to Bosnia.

Shortly after, Vido called me aside and told me, so as not to be overheard:

"We've got orders tonight to get rid of those two who turned the peasants against the movement."

Around midnight Commander Stevan divided us into two squads of ten.

"The squad leaders know what's to be done; they'll instruct you when you get near the houses. These men are enemies of the people and we must show them no mercy."

Was it possible, I wondered in total disbelief, that Partisans, too, killed ordinary people? It was hard for me to realise that those two older villagers who had argued most strongly against leaving their homes and families were to be killed that very night. I didn't see this as some kind of treachery against the movement and I couldn't bear to witness, let alone take part, in their deaths. Anyway, I wasn't a real Partisan. I was only in the company temporarily, until Stana came.

And so, when my squad reached the house of one of the men, I immediately volunteered to stand guard outside. Before my eyes I pictured the respectable-looking peasant with moustaches speaking out freely at the meeting, little guessing it might cost him his life. I imagined him sitting beside the hearth and telling his family, and perhaps a worried neighbour or two, what had gone on at the meeting, who had said what. If only Danica and Andrija were around, I thought, they would certainly stop this injustice, but both of them had left Štitari that morning to return to their own units.

The silence of the pitch-black night was broken by a burst of revolver shots which echoed around the hills long after the firing stopped.

Next day I heard from Vido that he had already been on several similar assignments, and that in a pit by the school on Mount Stavor there were at least a dozen "enemies of the people" whose bodies were thrown there after execution.

ॐ

The Command Post in Štitari was in constant touch through runners with a group of Partisans on Mount Stavor. When it was my turn to carry the post there one moonlit evening, I had to pass by the school. Long before I reached that grisly place I was filled with dread: would those executed men, drenched in their innocent blood, rise up and lead me from the path into some Chetnik trap, so I met a worse death than theirs? As I grappled with my fears, a voice boomed:

"Halt, who goes there?"

"Partisans!" I replied, and at once heard rifle shots mingled with curses. In a tenth of a second it flashed upon me that this place, which the Partisans had held the day before, was now in Chetnik hands. Instantly I turned and as fast as my legs would carry me, leaping from stone to stone, made off towards Štitari. When I eventually had to stop, breathless and exhausted, I reflected on my near escape from death. I had probably been saved by the fact that there was a large rock between them and me, and also because somehow, without thinking, I had followed Commander Stevan's advice:

"When anyone stops you to ask for the password, better say 'Partisans', not 'Partisan'. If they think you're alone, they'll call you forward, then shoot you or take you prisoner. If they think there's more of you, they'll open fire straight away, and if you're not hit straight off, you'll very likely get away."

I felt very grateful to Stevan for this useful tip on how to survive!

The rest of the night I spent wandering around in a daze, losing my way and finding it again. Several times I took cover when I heard voices, but in the darkness I couldn't make out whether they were Partisans, Chetniks or families fleeing before the approaching storm to stay with relatives in even more out-of-the-way and therefore safer places.

As it was growing light I reached some level open ground just above Štitari and saw a crowd of men, women and children huddled together, sleeping in the snow. Beside them were a few sheep, goats and donkeys. Refugees! Where had they come from and where were they going?

When I finally reached the company, Commander Stevan, Vido and a few others there greeted me with delight:

"So you're alive!" Stevan exclaimed. "We thought the Chetniks had got you."

"Where are the rest?" I asked.

"You may well ask! Last night most of them ran off home. The enemy have taken Stavor and blocked the route of the Lovćen Detachment, so they're going to Bosnia another way instead of through here. We've been left to look out for ourselves."

Realising that I wouldn't see my sister, a terrible feeling of panic swept over me and I started trembling uncontrollably. Stana had always protected me when I got into trouble with Father or Mother, putting a comforting arm around my shoulder and reassuring me: "Nobody's going to lay a finger on you, Bato, while I'm around!" Now, when I most needed protection, she was not there.

"How can I get back to Cetinje?" I wondered aloud, my quavering voice betraying my fear.

"You haven't got a hope, even if you grow wings," Vido answered. "There's a big army coming towards Katun. You can't get through to Cetinje, and I can't get to my village. We just have to try to save our skins, so that the hungry wolves don't gnaw our bones up here among these rocks. The best thing is to try to catch up with the Lovćen Detachment before they get to Bosnia."

"I'll go with you, Vido. But do you know the way, so we don't run straight into the enemy?"

"I think we'd all three better go along with the refugees," joined in Stevan, who came from the same area as Vido. "They have the same idea and they know all the paths. And there will always be something to eat with them, when some animal drops dead. Then, at the right moment, we can leave them and go our own ways."

So the three of us banded together in the hope of reaching our families alive. I knew, though, that it would be much easier for the other two to stand the journey. They could walk all day in the rain, and then joke and sing while they lay down by the fire to dry off. Nothing bothered them. But I was used to changing into dry clothes as soon as I came home wet, even just sweating from play.

All day fresh groups of refugees kept arriving. Most of them were elderly men – very few young ones – women and children.

"They set fire to our houses, slaughtered our livestock. They wanted to slaughter us as well, but we managed to get away," they reported quite calmly, accepting all the hardships of abandoning their homes as a necessary part of every war in Montenegro from time immemorial.

That evening the three of us, who seemed to be all that was left of the company, sat warming ourselves by the hearth until late at night. We talked mostly about our families, as though suddenly remembering the existence of a different world which had become remote and unreal. At last Stevan, older and more experienced – he had joined the Partisans at the start of the uprising and had already survived two enemy offensives – told us we must get some sleep, but first he wanted to say a word or two:

"Tomorrow we'll let the refugees go on ahead. If the crowd gets through, so shall we. If they come under attack, you keep with me, because I don't know yet what orders I'll give. Hand-grenades and re-volvers will be more useful than rifles. We'll defend ourselves, not the refugees, because they'll have an escort company to look after them. More than that I can't tell you now. The enemy control all the roads in Katun, so we'll have to follow paths and tracks through the snow. We have no contact with any other of our units. But the main thing is to follow the Lovćen Detachment going north."

The moment we lay down by the embers, Stevan and Vido fell fast asleep and started snoring, as though they hadn't a care in the world. But the warmth at once brought out the lice in my shirt, which began crawling around and biting my skinny body. As I tossed and turned, I wondered whether I should ever get used to these tormentors. I couldn't wait for daylight to set off for Bosnia. Exhausted in mind and body, I did eventually get some sleep before Stevan woke us and offered us some of the 'coffee' he had made by boiling roasted rye grains in water, "so you won't walk on an empty stomach".

In our cloth shoulder bags we packed what underwear we had, a pair of thick woollen socks knitted for the fighters by peasant women, a bit of bacon and some dried mutton that had been put aside for long marches. Then we went out into the cold April morning to find that fresh snow had fallen during the night. In the highest parts of Katun you can sometimes find snow until July.

As soon as I got out in the cold, the lice stopped biting. I cheered up at the thought that they wouldn't bother me for a quite a while: there wouldn't be any warm hearths on our march.

When we reached the place where the refugees had been sleeping the previous morning, there was hardly anyone there: only two or three elderly people too weak to go further and a couple of younger women, one of them in labour.

"A company of soldiers came and they all started off together at dawn," an old man with a white beard told us. "I've got this far but I can't go another step. Let them shoot me on this spot – better to die here than roam around foreign parts at my age, so nobody knows where my grave is."

"No matter if they started early," Stevan said. "We'll soon catch them up. They can't move fast with the wounded, the children and the animals they've brought along for milk."

Sure enough, after a couple of hours we caught up with the column of refugees. The company that had been sent to protect them was commanded by a lean young man they called Bajo, perhaps a year or two older than Stevan, with thick black curly hair and large, dark, sunken eyes. His company numbered some thirty young men and girls aged from about sixteen to twenty-five. Half of them led the way, while the rest, with him, guarded the rear. The long straggling column was made up of twenty to thirty families, perhaps a hundred people, whose homes had been burnt, and several dozen wounded Partisans, some walking, some carried. There were also some who had been in people's committees or active in the movement in other ways. All together there must have been about two hundred of them.

Less than an hour after we joined the refugees, a number of Savoys appeared out of the blue from the direction of Podgorica. Before most people had time to take cover, they swooped down, dropped a dozen small bombs on us, and vanished beyond the mountains as swiftly as they'd come. Most of the bombs fell all around on the rocks, making a terrifying amount of noise. Though only two hit the column, this score was more than enough. One killed two children and injured their mother: covered in blood she was screaming and trying to revive them. The other bomb killed a peasant and injured a loaded donkey, which kept struggling to stand up and braying pitifully. Commander Bajo and two nurses in the company went to comfort the mother and bandage her wounds, but she refused all help:

"If you can't bring back my children, leave me to die here with them."

Bajo had two runners, scarcely older than myself, near him all the time. Now, expecting another air attack, he ordered them to run along the column and shout to everyone to scatter in small groups away from the path in case the planes came back. Not long after they did, dropping a further load of bombs and firing a few rounds from machine-guns. Luckily, this time no-one was hurt.

"That's why it's better to march at night," Stevan commented, "but because of the wounded and small children they have to travel by day, even though it's much more dangerous."

"It's important the three of us keep together," Vido put in, and turning to me added: "I know this kind of country better than you do. If we have to, we'll hide out in some cave until the worst passes."

He no longer had any need to poke fun at me and show off: his superiority was evident. Anyway, his thoughts, like mine, were fixed on one thing: to catch up with the Lovćen battalions, in which he had two older brothers. With the famous Lovćen Detachment, we agreed, we'd be safe from the Italians and Chetniks, we'd be real Partisans, not like until now, in a company made up of local peasants who ran off home as soon as things got rough.

Stevan, for his part, kept giving us advice:

"If the worst comes to the worst, keep one bullet for yourself: it could save you from torture. If you find yourself surrounded with no way out, take the pin out of a hand-grenade, but hold it tight so you don't drop it. When you see there's no hope and you're done for, let the devils get really close to you, then open your hand and blow up yourself and them. The more you take with you, the better for your comrades."

As I listened, I remembered Father saying exactly the same – the Montenegrin's eternal fear of not taking 'a life for a life' and not dying like a hero.

As dusk was falling, Commander Bajo called all the heads of families together:

"Find the best places you can to spend the night, but on no account light any fires, to attract the enemy. I know it's hard without a fire when you have sick people and children, but you'll have to manage somehow. Keep close together in groups; put the children and old people in the middle for warmth."

Soon after the runners came up to report:

"Comrade Commander, everyone's settled down. Guards have been posted."

The exhausted people, young and old alike, could hardly wait to fall asleep in the snow. Despite Bajo's order, some of the heads of families collected a few dead branches and lit fires. All around, children, cold and hungry, were crying. Their mothers and grandmothers held them close, to warm them with their own bodies and comfort them as best they could. In less than an hour the flames of a dozen 'forbidden' fires were flickering like the forked-tongues of serpents in the folk tales.

Stevan told us to gather as many branches as we could, shake off the snow and lay them on the ground beside a big rock that would serve as a wind-break:

"The branches will keep us off the snow and frozen ground. We must huddle together to keep warm, like dogs do."

Then he covered us with a sheet of tarpaulin from an Italian army tent that we had brought with us and crawled underneath himself. It was good to be with someone who knew about such things, I reflected. Without those two, I would have probably got lost and almost certainly perished from cold and hunger. As I was dropping off to sleep, Stevan muttered:

"We must keep our distance from these refugees. When it gets light, the Savoys will be after them again."

Luckily the enemy were not close by and didn't see our fires, so the children, sick and wounded were able to get a bit of warmth.

I spent the first night of my life sleeping in the open, in the snow and cold at a height of a thousand metres above sea-level. Still shocked by the bombing and the sight of the dead children, for hours I drowsed in a strange half-dreaming, half-waking state, waiting to hear the roar of guns and mortars. Whatever happened to the donkey? I wondered. Did anyone help it to get up?

These recent scenes became confused in my mind with the bombing of Cetinje the previous April: the twisted body of our young neighbour Stanka floated before my eyes. That had been the start of the war, exactly a year ago, when the family were all still together in the house by Black Rock.

Early next morning, the runners dashed up and down shouting at the tops of their voices:

"On the move, comrades! Let the stronger and healthier help the weaker!"

I noted that there was one advantage to sleeping outdoors in the cold: I hadn't been bitten by lice.

As we three walked along a little apart from the column, we kept glancing at the sky.

"We're safe as long as the clouds stay low, but it looks like they're lifting, so keep your eyes open," Stevan warned.

"I don't think we ought to stay with these people more than a day or two or we'll die together with them. They're bound to attract planes, guns and troops," said Vido. "Why don't we see when we can get away? If we travel on our own at night, perhaps it'll be easier to push through to Bosnia."

Stevan at once agreed with this idea, and it made sense to me, too.

Around mid-day the sun broke through the clouds, which had lifted enough for aircraft to fly beneath them. We hadn't long to wait before fighter planes appeared over the mountainous horizon, swooped down on us and started machine-gunning. These were followed by bombers, and this time bomb blasts mingled with explosions of cannon and mortar shells. Again there were several dead and wounded, children screaming for their mothers and mothers for their children.

By now I had worked out how to save myself during air attacks. Without waiting to be told by Stevan or Vido, I leapt into the nearest hollow in the rocks and lay low until the danger passed. Luckily, in that stormy sea of stone there was plenty of shelter. I repeated Father's words to myself: "During bombing, those who panic and run are more likely to get killed." But it was extremely hard to control myself when bombs were falling out of the sky and coming straight at me, so it seemed. At that moment I felt such panic I didn't care what happened as long as I could run headlong from that spot.

"What you can't hide from, in a pit or anywhere else, are mortar shells," experienced Stevan told us after the attack had passed and the column was on the move again. "Mortars are the deadliest weapon for mountain warfare. It's our bad luck the enemy has hundreds of them and we don't. You can aim them so precisely that the shell lands right in the middle of a fire where frozen people are warming themselves, or in a cauldron where beans and nettles are cooking. Mortars have killed more Partisans than all other weapons put together."

When the column had been ordered to stop for an hour's rest, one of the tireless runners dashed over to us:

"Who's the leader of you three who don't belong to our refugee column?"

"Let's say it's me," answered Stevan. "Why do you ask?"

"Well, then, bring your comrades over to our commander. He wants to have a word with you."

"I don't like the sound of that," Vido whispered to me.

Stevan stood to attention and saluted Bajo, even though they were of the same rank.

"We were waiting for the Lovćen battalions, to withdraw to Bosnia with them, but they bypassed us, so now we're trying to catch up," he explained.

"It's good you're with us; we'll soon need every fighter," Bajo answered. "Ahead there are Italians and Chetniks and we'll have to fight our way through. I've had orders to take into the company all fighters we come across who've lost contact with their units. From now on you're one of us."

"Understood, Comrade Commander," Stevan replied, giving the clenched-fist salute.

"And we thought we were going to escape!" Vido muttered to me afterwards. "Now there's nothing for it but to get killed with all these people and their donkeys. But take my advice and keep your eyes open, try to remember every path and fork, every landmark, in case we get separated and you want to go back."

After the first shock of realising we would share the fate of the refugees, Vido and I both felt somehow safer. We consoled ourselves that with this crowd at least we wouldn't get lost. Along the paths and tracks we travelled there were no signs to tell us which direction we were following. Various heads of families took it in turn to lead the way according to who was most familiar with the area we were passing through. They chose the route carefully, keeping as far as possible from villages, from where the enemy might attack us.

According to the plan which Stevan had discussed with Bajo at length, we were making for the northern part of Katun that was still partly in Partisan hands. This was the poorest area of Montenegro: an uninhabited rocky wilderness, with scarcely any vegetation and a harsh windy climate. Though this route offered the greatest safety from enemy attack, it was a catastrophe for the hungry refugees. The small reserves of food brought by families and Partisans were nearly exhausted, so there was no choice but to begin killing the animals. The company intendant decided that the first to be sacrificed should be the donkey wounded in the bombing, which was still recovering. At a given signal, several fighters threw themselves on the animal and pinned it to the ground while its throat was cut, with strong protests all the while from the family who owned it, since they would now have to carry its load.

The donkey was quickly cut up and the meat, distributed among the groups, was eaten almost raw. The other donkeys, it was at once decided, were to be slaughtered and eaten in turn so that the refugees and fighters could survive until they reached Bosnia. Somehow everyone was convinced that then all our troubles would vanish, there would be no more danger, hunger and cold. It was this faith that gave us all the strength to go on.

For some days we were lucky in one respect: the weather was cloudy and rainy, so we were spared aircraft attack. This was a great relief as we could move forward steadily, without breaking to take cover when planes appeared. We had time to stop and rest, to gather firewood and anything edible – herbs or berries left by the birds. All that time as we crossed the barren highlands, whipped by bitter winds, we never saw a living soul, or even a wild animal of any kind.

When we stopped for the night, all along the column lights began to glimmer. After the first day Bajo did not try to ban fires, realising that strict Partisan rules could not be applied to the refugees. Several families gathered around each fire, on which they put a large pot filled with snow. When this melted, they threw in a bit of lard, any green stuff that had been found, a few potatoes and anything else they had that was fit to eat. The steam from the boiling liquid carried the scent of herbs, especially fennel, which grows all over Montenegro. Children and the sick and wounded were given this watery soup first, then the others. All the while the fire was burning, more branches were thrown on to make a cheerful blaze. Then the heads of families would roll themselves a cigarette, light up and recall various events in their hard lives.

One evening, as Vido and I were sitting with a group around a fire, an elderly man began to talk about prophecies he had heard from older villagers when he was a boy and which were now coming true.

"A hundred years ago, they said, there was a black monk that could tell all that was going to happen in the future, down to the last dot. He knew when the Turks would attack Montenegro and how the fighting would end. He could tell to the day when some famous man would be killed and in which battle. He could see a hundred years in advance, and foretold that 1942 would be the worst year in our history. For the first time brother will fight against brother, father against son, he said. Once again people will have to flee, this time not from the Turks but from traitors. There will be hunger and misery everywhere. But after that, salvation will come like sunrise from the East, a great army will come to help the wretched, suffering Montenegrin people. There will be happiness and good fortune for all who live to see that joyful day. Well, that's what the black monk foretold."

※

Gradually we made our way north, leaving Katun and heading for Grahovo, scene of the famous battle in 1858, when five thousand Montenegrins defeated thirty thousand Turks. Remembering Grandfather's harrowing story, I consoled myself that Italians did not cut off ears and noses, but just shot you, which I felt was a less painful fate.

One morning the weather suddenly cleared up and we saw blue sky for the first time for days.

"Now wait for the Savoys!" said Vido, but strangely enough, none appeared. Instead of bombers we heard the rumble of guns.

"It'll be hard from now on," Stevan warned us, "so you two be careful. In front the Italians are waiting for us, together with the Chetniks of that treacherous Vasojevići clan."

Vido began singing loudly a popular rhyming couplet which describes the clan as famous for plundering, and a dozen of the younger refugees joined in.

This brought us to the attention of the head of a family, a tall, craggy man of about fifty, with huge strong hands roughened by field work. He came over and asked us our names, then introduced himself:

"Call me Rade. If I can be of any help, let me know."

Shells were falling some way off and exploding with great force, but nobody took much notice. We were well on our way to Bosnia, and that was all that mattered.

"You know what," Rade said to us confidentially. "About an hour's walk from here, up above the path, there are some houses where relatives of mine live. I want to drop in on them, and you could come along and help me carry back some potatoes to keep my family from starving. I dare say they'll give us something to eat as well."

At the thought of getting some proper food, we attached ourselves to Rade, doing our utmost to keep up with his long strides, so as not to lose sight of him. My fear of getting lost was as strong as my longing for food.

In the late afternoon his relatives' houses came into sight. Before approaching, we all three paused to look around for any danger. When we took a better look, with the light falling from behind us directly on the houses, we were shocked to see that they were nothing but burnt-out

Partisans crossing
a river in Bosnia
in 1943

shells, without roofs or doors. Rade took a deep breath, crossed himself and exclaimed:

"Oh, holy Basil of Ostrog, help my relatives wherever they be now!"

Then, turning to us:

"We've no reason to waste time here."

It was almost dark before we got back to the refugees. As soon as Bajo's runners saw us, they called out in chorus:

"Where've you two been? Commander Bajo's looking for you."

I thought this was strange because he'd never sent for us in the dark before. Something important must have happened.

The whole company and the heads of families were gathered together. By the light of the moon I could make out their worried faces. Bajo was talking:

"We know there's a large force of Italians and Chetniks in front of us. Tonight we must take extra care with the watch, stay together and keep awake. We'll move at three in the morning, in the hope of taking them by surprise and getting past without casualties. Young children will have to be carried in arms and the wounded on stretchers. And mind you don't leave behind anyone sleeping. Now, forward the bombardiers."

Seven youths and a girl stepped forward and stood to attention.

"You'll go ahead of the company to their bunkers and dug-outs. We're told that they are mostly beside the path, to stop Partisans and refugees passing. We've no choice; we have to go that way. After you the whole company will advance in force. Only Stevan, his runners and the younger heads of families will stay behind to protect the rear. If we get through, I'm sure they will too."

While Bajo was speaking and calmly giving orders for the coming show-down, I started to shake with fright. So this was the first battle my father had talked about. Fear when a person first went into battle was usually forgiven and forgotten; later it was called cowardice.

"Bombardiers, go and get some sleep now," Bajo told them in an almost fatherly voice. It was quite normal for them to get special care and treatment even when there was no battle, because of their importance. I looked at them standing there so calmly, giving no sign they were aware of the extreme danger of their mission. Among them was a lad of Vido's age everyone called 'little Ivan'. Though shorter and skinnier than myself, he was said to be even more fearless than the rest, running ahead of them to throw his grenades into the bunker openings. I wondered in admiration what had made him become a bombardier, for bombardiers were not chosen – you had to volunteer.

"Check your rifles and other weapons," Bajo went on. "And when we attack after the bombardiers, run in pairs and shout your heads off, so they think there are more of us."

Stevan, Vido and I sat by a fire at the very back of the column with a few others, including Rade. One of them had a railwayman's pocket-watch which he kept taking out to look at. Each time someone asked him: "How long till three?" he would answer: "Another two hours", "Another hour and a half", and so on until it was nearly three. Then Stevan jumped up and groaned:

"If only I could take a swig of that *loza* my old dad makes."

"You're in luck, my lad," said Rade. "I've got a bottle in my saddle-bag. I've been keeping it for wounds, but this is as good a time as any to drink it."

He ran off to his loaded donkey, which was waiting impatiently to start, undid the saddle-bag and pulled out the bottle.

"Here you are, Comrade Stevan. It may not be as good as your father's, but it'll cut through you like a Montenegrin sabre!"

The bottle passed from hand to hand until it came to me.

"I don't drink yet," I admitted sheepishly.

"Well, there's no better time to start, nor ever will be," said Rade with a laugh. "Gulp it down. You'll feel better."

I did as he said, and at once started spluttering and coughing.

"What is it, young fellow? Doesn't it like you?" Rade joked, and everyone laughed. "Better to laugh than cry at a time like this," he added.

"It burnt my throat," I protested, afraid they would think me a complete weakling, but at the same time I felt a warmth in my stomach calming my agitation at the thought of what lay ahead.

After that it seemed an age before anything happened. Then, not far away, there were several flashes and hand-grenade explosions.

"Well done the bombardiers!" shouted Rade.

Trembling with nervous excitement, I told myself: 'If you get through this, you'll live to be a hundred.' I remembered from my father's story, often retold, that these were the words he spoke before his first battle.

The explosion of grenades continued with even greater intensity. This was because both sides were now throwing them, not just our people, Stevan explained. The horizon was blazing, just like during the battle on Šimunja, only that had been somebody else's battle; this was ours.

I pictured 'little Ivan' striking fear among bearded Chetniks and Italians, and wondered how he got to be so brave. I wished I could be like him.

The grenade explosions were now joined by the stutter of machine-gun fire, the crack of rifles and revolvers.

"We didn't surprise them and get through at the first try," Stevan commented. "They were ready waiting for us, well dug in. They knew we were coming. If our people don't get past before dawn, they'll mow them down. If the company were on their own, they could easily avoid the enemy by going a roundabout way, but dragging this crowd of people with them, they've no choice but to pass by the machine-guns."

"Why else do they call themselves the People's Army?" asked Rade, taking offence at Stevan's remark. "Sure they could do better on their own, but what would happen to the refugees, the women and children? If they didn't take care of the people, what difference would there be between Partisans and Chetniks?"

We waited for the runners to come to keep us informed, as promised, but there was still no sign of them. During fighting, they usually ran forward and back keeping contact between the front line and those at the rear guarding non-combatants, supplies and donkeys. Behind the distant hills it was already starting to get lighter.

"If the runners don't come soon, you go, Vido, and see what's up," said Stevan.

Just then one of them dashed up and saluted him:

"There's a large force of Italians and Chetniks, and not many of us. The bombardiers attacked their bunkers twice, going right up and inside, but they couldn't knock them all out. Both times Bajo and the company went in after them, but the enemy managed to throw back all our attacks. Bajo sends word that before dawn the company will move round behind the bunkers and attack the enemy from the rear. You should get the children, the old and the wounded under cover among the rocks, to protect them from guns and mortars, and wait until we call you to move."

"Did we suffer any casualties?"

"Two killed and three wounded. And one bombardier missing: he didn't come back after the first attack so the Chetniks must have wounded and captured him. If he'd been killed outside the bunkers, someone would have seen him."

"Who is it?" Vido asked.

"Little Ivan. Yesterday was his fourteenth birthday."

"It would be a bad thing if, heaven forbid, something happened to our brave Bajo, but we'll manage without the others," said Rade.

Several other peasants were standing nearby, leaning on the carbines they had brought from home, rolling cigarettes and frowning, not saying a word. They waited to hear what else the runner had to say before hurrying off to move their families to shelter among the rocks, as Bajo had instructed. Veterans of earlier wars, they trusted their commanders and carried out their orders without question.

"You just tell Bajo we're ready for the enemy. There's nothing else I can say," said Stevan.

Suddenly the sky grew brighter and the tops of the mountains, still covered by thick snow, glowed with a silvery light. Stevan dashed around, calling all the heads to get their families hidden behind bushes and rocks. He posted Vido and me on either side of a large stone, like a boulder.

"We don't know which direction those sons of bitches will strike from. I'm placing people so they won't get taken by surprise. You stay on different sides of this stone, but if necessary you can join up. Look out for each other; now you're on your own. I have to be with the family heads – they're the only army and protection we have."

"Can you hear me, Bato?" called Vido from the other side of the boulder when Stevan left.

"Yes, I can hear you. What d'you want?"

"I wanted to tell you to keep one bullet and one grenade. You may need them."

"I will, Vido. I know that."

I was about to say something else when shells started falling around us.

"It'll be worse when the mortars start," he shouted.

At that moment I felt a terrible need to tell him I was afraid, that I wished I was on his side. It would be easier if we were together, but Stevan's order had to be obeyed. I looked around me. If we came under attack from the rear, as Stevan said might happen, I was well hidden. He had put Vido and me in the second line of defence to protect us as much as possible.

"From the firing, it sounds like our people are attacking from the rear," shouted Vido.

Then for a while it was impossible to hear anything for the noise of shells falling all around.

"They must see us from some hill because their aim's getting better," Vido yelled.

Stevan was running from one head of family to the next and encouraging them:

"That's fine! You're well positioned, so keep where you are. And you two," he called from the path, "shelter from the mortars."

From the way he was hurrying I guessed he was expecting an attack very soon. Some shells fell close by, scaring the donkeys and goats, which scattered in all directions. The women ran to catch them, regardless of the danger, for without goat's milk their children would starve in a week.

"Bato, can you hear me?

"Yes, Vido. Go on!"

"When the shelling stops, they'll attack us. But I want to tell you something else…"

At that moment there was a tremendous blast as a mortar shell struck the other side of the boulder.

"Vido! Vido!" I yelled. "Are you alright?"

There was no reply.

"Vido, answer me!"

Again, only a deathly silence. The guns, too, had gone quiet for a moment. I steeled myself to walk round the boulder. All I could see was a large dent on its surface.

"Vido, where are you?" I called in panic.

As I looked around to see where he was hiding, I saw, hanging from a branch, part of a leg, torn off below the knee.

Overcome with horror, I shouted at the top of my voice:

"Stevan, Stevan! Help! Vido's dead!"

Suddenly, as though in answer to my frantic calls for help, I heard the sound of singing. 'It's our people coming, just in time, but too late for Vido,' I thought.

I looked and there, marching along the path, about fifty metres away, was a group not of Partisans, but of Chetniks. With their long hair streaming under their black fur caps with the death's head badge in front, they looked like dark birds of prey – the ravens of Kosovo Polje flashed across my mind. The heads of families at once opened fire, surprising and scattering the Chetniks.

"Let the traitors have it!" yelled Stevan.

Rade joined him, the two of them urging the peasants to stand fast and save their families. I began firing myself, the first time I'd ever shot at human beings.

Stevan rose from his cover and shouted:

"Chetnik whores! Italian-arse-lickers! You'll pay one day!"

From the other side came answering insults:

"Wait till we get you, Stalin's bastards. Where's Moša to help you now?"

Curses and bullets rained from both sides. Then there was a kind of stand-off as the Chetniks realised they couldn't dislodge us without suffering heavy casualties. After a while, some Italian reinforcements turned up, and were obviously discussing with the Chetniks how to surround us. I kept repeating: "I'm not going to die like Vido. I must get home to Mother."

After what seemed an eternity, one of Bajo's runners rushed up to tell Stevan that the company had cleared the way and now held all the bunkers. The refugees were to move off at once and Bajo would lead them and the company ahead, while Stevan and the heads of families stayed in the rear holding back the Chetniks.

Stevan at once shouted the order to Rade:

"Get all your people moving straight away, and you and the other heads stay to defend the rear."

Gladdened by this news, the men passed the word to their women and children to set off at once after Bajo's runner.

In a lull in the firing, Stevan came over to me:

"Now you're all alone, poor Bato. If you see we're all going to get killed, you hide among the rocks and afterwards try and get back home. Forget about Bosnia. The enemy will be waiting round every bend. I can't see anyone getting there alive."

I lost all track of time as we went on defending the refugees' withdrawal. At one moment I heard Rade say to Stevan:

"Now my family's safe, I'm not sorry to leave my bones here!"

Stevan repositioned the peasants behind the rocks that protected them so that every attempt to advance by the Chetniks and Italians was checked by a round of fire from the well-placed carbines. But how long could we go on defending ourselves like this? Stevan said we must hold out till dark, when we would be able to steal away and follow the company. The enemy must have realised this too, and stepped up their attack. I remembered Vido saying:

"At night they drink, eat and sleep. They haven't the guts to attack in the dark, so then we're safe."

Suddenly Chetniks and Italians were advancing on us from all sides: we were surrounded. They had had plenty of time to carry out the encirclement, and they had plenty of men to do it with – dozens of them seemed to be springing out of the ground. As they closed in, Stevan, and then the peasants, began shouting and throwing grenades. The enemy faltered for a moment, then realised that we were using our last weapons, and came on again. Stevan stood up. The heads of families did the same, throwing their last grenades and firing revolvers. I could see Chetniks and Italians falling, but our people too. Stevan was hit. He tried to get up, but several Chetniks, knives drawn, leapt on him. I knew he would open his hand. The grenade blew up Stevan and the Chetniks.

Now there was hand-to-hand fighting, but the peasants, weakened by hunger, were no match for the well-fed Chetniks. Some of them tried to flee in the direction of the column and their families. The sight of Stevan's death left me numb, unable to move. Somehow I found the strength to squeeze into a gap beneath an overhanging rock.

Breathless with terror, peering out from my hiding place I could see Chetniks trying to catch Rade. An agile highlander, with his long legs he leapt from stone to stone, like a mountain goat chased by wolves. He kept glancing left and right to find a way of escape, but Chetniks were all around him. Now that our rear-guard was broken, they had joined together to capture the last defiant peasant who was still resisting them. I could hear the excited cries of hunters who smelt blood, their shouts and curses:

"Get the bastard! Don't let him get away! Take him alive so we can skin and roast him, like a wild boar at Christmas."

Seeing there was no way out, Rade jumped on to a bigger rock so that he was a little higher than his pursuers. From his belt he pulled out his knife, his last weapon, and stood there, tall, glaring, bareheaded – his cap lost in the chase – waiting for them to draw near. In his strong, bony hand the blade of the knife flashed as he made passes with it. A dozen of them rushed him, dragged him down and stabbed him to death.

As I lay, frozen with fear, under the rock, the last words I heard him speak kept ringing in my ears: "Now my family's safe, I'm not sorry to leave my bones here!"

Far in the distance, among the hills, the long column of refugees was on its way to Bosnia. His wife must surely keep stopping to look back in the hope of seeing Rade hurrying to catch up with her and their four children.

As daylight faded, the Chetniks and Italians moved off, not in the direction of the refugees but where they'd come from, carrying their dead and wounded.

Throughout that cold highland night I kept repeating: "I want to live. I must live." That was what Father had said after he was wounded at Taraboš, and he had survived. In a kind of delirium, I could no longer tell reality from nightmare. Was it really true that Vido had been blown to bits by a mortar, that Stevan was dead, that I was left here alone in the mountains with no hope of reaching Bosnia and Stana?

At long last day dawned, chilly and damp. I had to get home, but how would I manage without Stevan and Vido? And if I made it, would they know in Cetinje I'd been all this time in the Partisans, and shoot me? I started to feel terrible pangs of hunger – all the events of the past few days had completely suppressed this feeling. Wondering how long it was since I'd last eaten, I suddenly remembered Levi, the Jewish grocer in Mitrovica, and the little green book. Father had told him I could take whatever I wanted to eat on credit. Why hadn't I done so? Maybe one day I would go back to Mitrovica, and Levi would remember me and let me take as much as I liked. At that moment I thought I'd be able to eat everything he had in his small, overcrowded shop. But would Father be alive then to pay the bill?

This painful thought brought me out of my reverie and I forced myself to start walking, though my legs would hardly carry me. I passed the mutilated bodies of Stevan, Rade and several other peasants. The Chetniks had stripped them and taken everything they had. I remembered Vido singing about their clan being the leaders in plundering. Now I could see for myself that plunder was the real reason they went to war. When they fought the Turks, this was called patriotism and heroism. What did they call it now when they joined with the Italians in killing their fellow countrymen?

Slowly and cautiously at first, I set off in the direction of Štitari. I knew that at about half way I had to find a turning towards Cetinje. I felt extremely grateful to Vido for advising me to memorise the way – as though he'd foreseen what would happen. I began to hurry back along this same route as fast as I could, stopping now and then to survey the countryside in case there were any soldiers or other dangers. As I went, I wondered what would happen to Stevan and Rade's bodies. Would someone bury them or would they be eaten by wolves? All I wanted now was to get home to Cetinje, which had taken the place of Bosnia as the goal that gave me the will to go on. Strangely, I no longer felt tired or hungry, or even afraid. As fast as I could I had to get to that cottage above Cetinje where I'd first met Vido. That meeting and my life with the Partisans in Štitari now seemed distant and unreal, like a story I'd been told, not something that had actually happened to me. When I got back, I must wipe it all out of my mind, never tell a single soul, even Rajko, for yesterday I had seen what Chetniks could do to those on the opposite side.

Returning was much quicker and easier because I was going mainly downhill and there was no column of refugees or bombing to slow me down. I began to think about practical matters. Where was I to find an axe and rope to show at the check-point or if I met someone before then? Under the rock where I'd spent the night I'd left the Partisan cap with the five-pointed star that I'd been so proud of. With my roughened hands and face reddened by the cold and wind, I could easily pass for a peasant boy. Even my more refined speech had taken on the rougher tones and expressions of my comrades in arms.

When it was starting to get dark, I came upon a large bush between two rocks and crawled under it to sleep. Well protected from the wind and feeling quite secure, I dropped off almost at once. In the morning, I carefully surveyed my surroundings before setting out to walk. Another day passed without food, apart from a few berries left by the birds. When I was thirsty, I put a handful of snow in my mouth. At nightfall, I again found somewhere to sleep, but it was not as sheltered from the wind and I spent the night shaking from the cold.

Next morning I could hardly get up: I was aching all over and it was difficult to breath. 'If I fall ill now, I'll never get home,' I told myself, and started walking again, but with no idea how far it was to Cetinje. Perhaps a couple of hours later I looked ahead and caught my breath: a great vista stretched as far as the eye could see. On the distant horizon Njegoš's chapel pierced the blue sky. My joy at being within sight of Lovćen, which from now on would guide me to Cetinje, gave me fresh strength and I began running. I paused at a small clearing with three rough crosses, just pieces of wood nailed together. Somebody had raised them recently, someone who knew the dead people. Otherwise he wouldn't have taken the trouble to bury them: I had seen the remains of many dead people left lying where they fell. Above and below the path there were a few houses, all burnt-out shells, and not a living soul anywhere.

Stealthily, in case anyone was hiding nearby, I picked through the charred remains in the hope of finding a scorched crust of bread or anything else I could eat. I was disappointed, but I had one stroke of luck. In one of the houses my glance fell on an old axe hanging on a hook. Nearby, on the same wall, hung a coil of rusty wire which could serve instead of rope.

After several more hours of walking, in the late afternoon I drew near the cottage where I had waited for Vido on the day I left Cetinje. I looked forward to seeing the nice woman who had welcomed me before and to spending the night there beside the hearth. She would surely offer me some of those potatoes baked in the embers, and tell me all the news of Katun and Cetinje. Then next morning, with my bundle of firewood, I would easily get to the Italian block.

When the cottage came into view, I saw at once that it had no roof, but I still hoped for the best. I knew that every few years, a thatched roof would be set on fire by sparks from the hearth and the owners just came out and waited for it to burn. Next day, relatives and neighbours would help them to remake it. That's how it had always been in Montenegro. But I was in for another bitter disappointment. From close up it was clear that it had burnt maybe two months ago, perhaps at the time of the fighting on Šimunja, when the sky glowed red from burning houses, bombs and mortars. Where were the peasant woman and her husband now? Had they joined some group of refugees heading for Bosnia, or been sent to one of the camps in Montenegro or Albania? I lay down by the cold hearth in that burnt-out home. Even if I had had matches, I wouldn't have dared to light a fire. Exhausted, starving and utterly miserable, I tried to get some sleep before the fateful day ahead.

Next morning, now the moment of my return was drawing near, I became more and more worried about being recognised at the Italian block. I decided it would be safer to cross in the afternoon, and say the morning guards had let me out to collect fuel, though I was unsure if they still changed at mid-day. As I went, I began collecting firewood.

Try as I might, with my blunt axe I failed to chop off a single branch, so I had to pick up what I found on the ground and break off what I could. Somehow I managed to make a bundle with the length of rusty wire. All this time I saw no-one. The villages around Cetinje had been torched and their inhabitants sent to camps, so that the occupiers could more easily control the approaches to the town.

⁊⁊

It was a clear sunny day, just like the one when I left Cetinje, though by now the snow had vanished. I could tell the time roughly by the sun, and when it crossed its zenith I swung the bundle of firewood on to my shoulder, pushing the axe handle underneath to support it and make it easier to carry. As I drew near the block, my heart started pounding; I could hardly breathe. Trying to look as small as possible, I lowered my head, half-hiding my face behind twigs with dried leaves. It was important not to show any sign of fear. The tanks that had guarded the check-point were no longer there. Now the Partisans had withdrawn to Bosnia, there was no danger of attack. Several *carabinieri* were hanging around the block-house. The ramp was down so I had to wait.

"*Buon giorno!*" I said, doing my utmost to sound natural. At that moment I was just as terrified as when the Chetniks and Italians were attacking us.

"Where do you live?" one of the guards asked.

I explained in Italian where I lived and that I had been to collect some firewood, as he could see for himself.

"How come you speak Italian so well?" he enquired, surprised.

"My grandma was Italian. She taught me when she was alive."

He stared at me strangely, looked me up and down, then said:

"Put down that wood and wait here till I get back."

'Now it's all up,' I thought. I knew he would come back with the list of people who'd crossed that morning, find out I was lying, and then it would be questioning, beatings, prison… I thought of making a run for it, but if I tried, they'd quickly catch me or shoot me.

After a couple of minutes that seemed endless, he came out of the block-house carrying not a list of names but half a loaf of bread and an open can of meat.

"Eat this up. Looks like they don't feed you at home, or perhaps you're ill? You need fattening up a bit."

"I'm ill," I muttered, taking the food, pushing it in my cloth bag and hurrying off, afraid that this kindly Italian might want to drive me home in a police car. With my last ounce of strength I heaved the wood on to my shoulder again and made for home, still not believing my luck. All of a sudden I was overcome by hunger and could go no further. I dropped the wood, broke off a sharp stick and in a flash had dug out and swallowed every last morsel of tinned meat. Then the bread disappeared.

I felt a warmth in my face and stomach, followed by shivering. As I got nearer home I began shaking all over and ran faster and faster to get warm. In my feverish state, I imagined that the war was over, the killing was past, and that round the dinner table I would find the whole family waiting. What could I say? Why was I late for dinner? Because of the war, of course. They would understand.

Two Years of Terror

When I opened my eyes, the first thing I saw was my mother's big, strong hands. I recognised them at once, without looking at her face. I remembered them well from earlier illnesses, smoothing my hair and cheeks, making me feel completely safe. The realisation that I was back in my own bed, with my mother beside me, was like a wonderful dream come true.

"Something stinks!" were my first words.

"That's good, son. It means you're better!" Mother replied. "Thanks be to Almighty God, you're alive! You haven't got a gram of flesh on you, but never mind: eagles haven't got much flesh either. You've been fighting for your life for a whole month. I nearly lit candles for you, like we did when you were small. But you wouldn't give in. You're the kind who always survives. That smell is from the paraffin oil I rubbed in your hair to kill the lice. You had thousands of them: every inch of your body was covered in bites. Mara and I took turns rubbing you down with alcohol, to clean the bites and bring your fever down."

During the next few days Mother filled in the details of my homecoming and illness:

"I heard a noise on the steps, so I opened the door. I swear to God, at first sight I couldn't believe it was my Bato. There you were, dragging a bundle of firewood up the steps, wheezing and gasping for breath. You didn't recognise me, and when I touched you, your body felt on fire. But I said to myself: I'm not giving up the last child left to me. Mara ran around to find some *loza*, to rub on you to bring the fever down, since there's no other medicine, then I rushed to Doctor Gerasimović's.

"When he examined you, the Doctor said he'd never seen anyone so badly bitten by lice. 'How did you let him get in such a terrible state?' he asked. Of course, I couldn't tell him the truth, so I had to take the blame for neglecting you."

Mara came every day to find out how I was. One day she brought news of Stana:

"I'm telling you, in the strictest confidence, that some of our comrades have been sent back from Bosnia to Montenegro. They've split up into threes and are hiding out in the Katun area. Stana's good friend Veljko Mićunović is in overall command. Well, Veljko told some people that Stana was wounded in both legs, but it's alright – the bones weren't broken and she'll get over the wounds."

After recovering consciousness, I spent another month in bed, getting up now and then to look out the window whenever I heard the roar of a motorcycle: Crazy Dima was speeding up and down Njegoš Street again! Sometimes I would sit by the window facing the government apartments, but there was no sign of Olga or her parents. Perhaps they'd gone to Italy on holiday. Rajko, my faithful friend, visited me almost daily. He never asked where I'd been for so long, for which I was grateful. From him I got the latest neighbourhood news: the children from Partisan and Chetnik families no longer hung around together. It seemed that the parents, by their talk at home, had finally managed to destroy our childhood friendships. Now the two groups fought each other with fists and stones. Rajko hadn't joined either side, probably because of me.

※

One day, Mother brought two lodgers, a brother and sister named Lubarda, to live in one of our two rooms. The Lubarda family was from the nearby village of Ljubotinj, but like ourselves had been colonists in Kosovo, from where they had managed to escape when Yugoslavia capitulated. The sister, Mila, a small, pretty girl of fifteen with large dark eyes, paid more attention to her appearance than other girls of her age at that time and sometimes even wore lipstick. She had come to attend Cetinje high school, and her eighteen-year-old brother, Miro, was enrolled in the teacher-training school. Mother explained that payment was to take the form of much needed food, which their father would bring us once a month.

Their father, exceptionally short in height and temper, had got into serious trouble in Ljubotinj. When a fellow villager made some slighting remark in public about his lack of inches, he had thrown a hand-grenade at him, killing several people. By enrolling in the Greens and joining the Guard, he managed to avoid being arrested and tried for this, but from then on, under the code of the blood feud, he and other males in his family were marked men and went in constant fear of their lives. Whenever he brought food for the rent, he would first empty his pockets of several small red Italian hand-grenades, Ballistas, then place his revolver beside them on the table, before unpacking the cloth bag in which he carried flour, bacon, dried meat and beans.

I liked Mila because she was always smiling and animated. We used to have long conversations when she came back from school. Though a couple of years younger, I was much better informed, especially on historical events: I had moved around a lot with the family and learnt much from my father, a mine of information. Impressed by my superior knowledge, she was always questioning me and asking for advice on various matters.

With her brother, however, I never managed to establish any contact. He seemed to me to be always tense, listening for something, as though afraid that the relatives of the men his father had killed might suddenly burst into the house with their guns. No-one would harm his sister, he knew, for in Montenegro, as in Sicily and Albania, revenge for spilt blood was taken only against males. But he believed it was only a matter of time before someone came for him. It was for this reason, I supposed, that Miro, a good-looking, freckle-faced young man, was so withdrawn and quiet.

When they had been living with us for several months, one day he came back from school earlier than usual and didn't say a word to anyone. Mila asked him why he was so silent, but he didn't reply. Then, out of the blue, he announced that he was going away.

"Where to?" his sister asked, alarmed. "Has something happened to Father?"

"Not to him, but it will to me if I stay here, so I've heard. I have to protect myself. I daren't tell you or anyone else where I'll be, so don't question me."

Then he packed up his things and left without saying goodbye. After that we didn't see or hear anything of him for a whole month, until one morning I caught sight of him wearing the uniform of the Greens and carrying an Italian rifle standing guard in front of the army barracks.

I ran home to tell Mila this news, adding that the Partisans would kill him for this when they came.

Mila listened and quietly began to weep:

"It's all the same to him, poor thing, who's going to kill him: Greens, Chetniks or Partisans. Though if he has to die, it would be best for all of us if it was done by those to whom my crazy father owes blood."

⁂

After Nada's arrest, her friend Anka often came to see Mother.

"You haven't been selling doughnuts for a long time, Bato," she commented one day, when I was well again. I explained that now the soldiers mostly came and went at night, and, besides, there was a lot of competition. At the beginning Nada and I had been alone, and business had been quite good, but now there were more than a dozen sellers, all from other Partisan families who were as needy as we were.

A day or two later Anka presented Mother with two hens, which she said were good layers, so we would have a few eggs to eat. At the same time she took some liras out of her purse:

"This is from Red Aid, Milica. We couldn't spare any more: now very few of our people have anything left to give."

Mother locked the hens in a shed in the yard, so no-one could steal them, and sure enough, just as Anka said, they at once started to lay. With the liras I went the next Wednesday to the market. As usual the peasant women had laid out their meagre produce: a few small bags of flour, bottles of olive oil, chunks of fat bacon nibbled by mice, flour-coated dried figs… I had just started haggling over the price of a bag of flour, when four strange women appeared and immediately attracted everyone's attention. With their dyed hair, heavy make-up and brightly

coloured dresses, they seemed quite out of place in wartime Cetinje. They came up to the peasant-woman I was bargaining with and asked in Italian for fresh eggs. I translated this, and when they saw that I understood Italian they were very pleased: they had been in Cetinje several days, they explained, but hadn't yet managed to buy a single fresh egg.

"What kind of country is it where you can't buy eggs?" they asked.

I translated this, and the peasant-woman answered sharply:

"Tell them the Italians have stolen all our hens and now you can't find one anywhere for love nor money. Before they came, we had hens and eggs as many as you like!"

Hearing this, the Italian women turned away in a huff and one of them addressed me:

"Can you get us a regular supply of fresh eggs, boy, so we won't have to deal with these rude peasants? We'll pay you well. We're tired of wasting our valuable time looking for eggs."

Cetinje: on the left, the Government Building (Vladin dom). Its cellars were used by the Italian occupiers as a prison during the Second World War. Photograph from c. 1950

I agreed at once, seizing this unexpected chance to earn some money. One of them explained where they lived:

"There's always a guard in front of the house, so you must say we've told you to come, otherwise he won't let you in. Get some eggs and bring them as soon as you can."

What luck, I thought, that Anka had brought those two hens at just the right moment, as if she'd known.

Next day, with a large wicker basket containing just a few eggs, I made for the house where they said they lived. I was amazed to see a line of soldiers, a hundred metres long, waiting to go in. Had I got the address wrong? Were the men waiting for their pay or special rations, or were they going to be deloused? I remembered seeing soldiers lined up in front of the new high school, and several women in white over-alls with something like a bicycle pump spraying them with the white powder that was said to kill lice like nothing. I went up to a guard and explained I was bringing eggs for the ladies. He burst out laughing:

"What do they want eggs for? They've got more than they need!"

"How come?" I asked. "Only yesterday they were looking all over Cetinje for them."

"Do you see all those standing in line? Everyone is bringing them two as a present."

Still completely in the dark, I climbed the steps to the door at which the soldiers were waiting. When I knocked on it, they started shouting:

"Hey, boy, you can't jump the queue. Wait your turn with the rest of us!"

The door was opened by a women dressed in white, just like those with the pump. When I explained my mission, she led me inside. In the entrance hall the first thing I saw was four soldiers hurriedly unbutton-ing their flies and putting on condoms. Utterly confused and embar-rassed, I stopped, not knowing where to look, and whether to run away or wait. Just then the door of the main room opened and there were the four Italian women from the market, sitting on or getting up from four divans arranged around the large room, while four soldiers came out taking off condoms, which they dropped into a bin. Like the day before, the women were heavily made up and carefully coiffed. But while their upper garments were neatly pressed and buttoned up, below these they wore nothing at all. At that moment they started putting on something like pantaloons.

"Stop them coming in for a while," said the one I'd talked to the previous day.

"But what about the four ready with their condoms on?" asked the woman in white.

"Let them wait. They're young and can get it up any time."

I glanced at the four young soldiers and they glared back at me for causing this delay. The woman in white said they would have to be patient a minute as the boy had brought eggs for the ladies, so they could make face masks from the yolks.

"Come in, boy!" the ladies called out, pleased to see me. "Are the eggs really fresh? No rotten ones there?"

I assured them our hens had laid the eggs that very day and apologised for the fact that there were only four. I offered, however, to bring them four every second day, and this suggestion met with their approval.

"What shall we give you for them? How many liras?" they wanted to know.

I knew I mustn't waste this opportunity, for I would be stuck with whatever price I set. I answered that I didn't want money, but if they had any left-over stale bread to give me for the hens, the eggs would be bigger and better.

"And for Mother and myself," I quickly added, "if you have any kind of food, cans of meat and beans, some cheese or something like that…"

One of the women looked into my big basket and seeing the four small eggs nestling in the bottom, said with a smile:

"You don't expect us to fill up your basket for only four eggs, do you?"

"I didn't have a smaller one to bring. And if you have any old army shirt or some clothing you don't need…"

"Just listen to him!" she broke in. "Every time he opens his mouth he asks for more. Soon he'll be asking us to pay him in kind!" They all roared with laughter.

With a basket full of stale bread for the hens, a loaf fresh enough for us to eat, and two cans of meat, I ran home as fast as I could. When I showed Mother, she could hardly believe I'd got all that in exchange for four eggs:

"They must be good and decent women, Heaven preserve them!"

Before Mother had finished blessing those "good and decent women", I dashed off to Rajko's house, impatient to recount my experience, and asked him to come outside as I had something important to tell him. Hearing this, his anxious mother barred our way and started warning us not to do anything forbidden —everybody had enough trouble already. When we finally got outside, I had to recount my story in great detail several times.

"You didn't really see them naked, did you?" he kept asking incredulously.

"Yes, I did," I assured him, "but only half: I saw their bottoms but not their tits. They don't let the soldiers touch them with their dirty hands."

"Can't you take me with you next time, so I can see with my own eyes?" he begged.

"Not possible, Rajko. They won't let two of us inside. But if you like, you can come with me to the house and see the soldiers, and you might even see the women if they look out the window."

It seemed a long time to wait until the next visit to my new acquaintances. All next day I kept going out to the shed to see if the hens had laid. Supposing they suddenly stopped, just to spite us, I thought fearfully. It was not the benefits of trade that most interested me, but the chance to pay another visit to the *kupleraj* [whorehouse] as the people of Cetinje called it. The news that the Italian Army had opened such an establishment spread like wildfire round the town, and titillating stories about it began circulating even among the children. Besides politics, we suddenly discovered another interest of which we had scarcely been aware. I was twelve and Rajko ten. It was time, we decided, for us to become better informed on this subject.

When Mother finally found out where our food supplies came from, she started to cross herself and marvel that such a thing was possible in respectable Cetinje:

"It's an evil time when foreign whores and thieves are in power. Don't bring any more bread – they're bound to touch it with their dirty hands. If you must go there, take canned food."

When news got round that I was privileged to pay regular visits to the *kupleraj*, my status shot up. I became the envy of all my contemporaries, from Chetnik as well as Partisan families. Ideological differences were brushed aside when it came to this all-absorbing new topic, to which I alone held the key, having seen with my own eyes what other boys could only imagine.

Cetinje's *kupleraj* was denounced by respectable citizens as an insult to their honour. Even so, women walked past the house, to see for themselves that such a thing was possible, making the sign of the cross and spitting contemptuously as they passed, especially if there was a long line of soldiers impatiently waiting. Men of all ages went out of their way to stroll by, in the hope of catching a glimpse of something interesting that would break the monotony of their daily lives. However, it was the children who mostly hung around in front of the *kupleraj*. When the ladies took a break from work to go for a stroll or buy something, they were regularly followed by a couple of dozen boys calling out insults. When the women tired of this, they turned round and shouted threats and curses, and if this had no effect, they would raise their skirts and show their backsides. This provoked roars of laughter, cheers and applause, so that their progress was like that of circus entertainers walking through a town to attract visitors to their show.

One day Mara, who was involved in the distribution in Cetinje of a clandestine news-sheet – much of its contents gleaned from Radio Moscow – told us that Stana's brigade had launched an attack on the Croatian town of Kupres, which the Ustashas and Germans had strongly fortified since it was the 'gateway to Split' and the Adriatic Sea. In the fighting, which lasted several days and ended in our defeat, about a hundred

Partisans died and one hundred and fifty were wounded. Among the dead was seventeen-year-old Danica.

"Perhaps it's better for her to end bravely like that than die from tuberculosis, like her poor parents," was all Mother could say in consolation when we heard this sad news.

At that time, the summer and autumn of 1942, the Montenegrin Partisans were fighting in Bosnia and Herzegovina, alongside local forces and units from Serbia and Croatia. According to Radio Moscow, the total Partisan forces in Yugoslavia numbered 150,000, Mara reported with pride. But a few days later, from the same source she heard some sobering news which she relayed to us:

"In Yugoslavia there are now 50,000 German elite troops specially trained for mountain warfare, 340,000 Italian troops, 90,000 Bulgarians, 28,000 Hungarians, and about 250,000 Ustashas, Chetniks and Greens. This adds up to 850,000 well-armed troops, nearly six times as many as the Partisans. They said at the end of the news that all these figures came from German military reports."

In the absence of any sizeable Partisan force in Montenegro at that time, the Italian administrators tried to normalise life for themselves and 'loyal Montenegrins'. Once again, like before the insurrection, brass bands played and unarmed soldiers marched up and down Njegoš Street, singing and eyeing the Cetinje girls. Security in the town was maintained by those we called 'turncoats' or 'traitors'. It was they who served as guards and made arrests for the Italians – Vlado Kokotan and his gang still leading the way in this.

My father, together with other hostages, remained in gaol in Cetinje, waiting to be summoned for execution. We found out that Nada was in a prison camp in Kavaja, Albania, while Duško was in a camp at Colfiorito, near Perugia in central Italy, but we had had no news of Aco since his departure by truck for Mitrovica.

The loudspeakers relaying Radio Cetinje blared out Italian songs and various announcements to the population, who were gradually being Latinized, like the Albanians before them. A number of young men were selected to go to Italy for further education, among them Duruz, the eldest son of Dr Lopica. Partisan families regarded acceptance of this schooling by the occupiers as treason, and Mara said darkly that sooner or later they would have to pay for it, even if the Partisans had to go to Rome to catch them after the war.

One day Mrs Lopica approached Mother and said almost apologetically:

"My son is not against you or against your fight. Much less is he for the Italians. He only wants to survive in these terrible times, not die for no good reason."

❧

The new year of 1943 brought more than usually heavy snow that almost buried Cetinje. People had to dig deep tunnels from their houses to the streets so they could get around. The dry, powdery, sparkling white snow delighted the children, who ran through the tunnels calling to one another and playing hide-and-seek. Smaller children and girls slid down the great mounds of snow on trays and sledges, screaming, colliding and tumbling off.

In the yard of the government apartments, several girls were making a snowman. Seeing Olga among them, I seized this opportunity to speak to her. At first I stood apart watching, trying to get up some courage. What pretext could I find? Then one of the girls accidentally knocked down most of the snowman they had been fashioning so carefully. When the others started scolding her, I stepped forward and offered to rebuild it. As their fingers were frozen by then, they readily agreed. As if by chance I stood next to Olga and set to work. For a while I kept quiet, but then I ventured to look at her and remark:

"I haven't seen you around for a long time. I thought you'd gone back to Italy."

"No, we haven't," she replied, "though Mama would like Father to be transferred."

"I guess your mother doesn't like Cetinje. What about you?"

"It's all the same to me. Mama wants to live in Italy, but Father likes it better here. Have they let out your brother?" she asked unexpectedly.

"No, but now he's in some camp in Italy."

Then I was at a loss what to say next – something that never happened when I chatted for hours on end with Mila – but I wanted desperately to keep the conversation going.

"Are you going to live in Cetinje after the war or go back to Italy?"

Suddenly it seemed to me important to know this.

Instead of answering she began smiling – the first time I'd ever seen her smile.

"As soon as the war ends I'm going to Italy to look for my brother."

"I must go home now," Olga said, but then added: "Sometimes I see you standing by the window."

"That's so I can see you," I finally dared to admit.

"Why's that important?" she asked, pretending not to understand my reason, though I had a feeling she was pleased. "Now I really must go," she said and ran into the house.

From then on I spent more and more time by the window. Whenever I saw her, I waved, and she waved back. How she had grown, and got prettier, in the time I'd spent in the hills and ill in bed!

For some time I had been helping Mara by carrying a clandestine news-sheet from her house to a cigarette kiosk near the high school run by a friend of Duško's, an exceptionally short young man everyone called Mijo Mali (Little Mijo). But so I could come and go without arousing suspicion, she insisted I had to go back to school. My new class teacher turned out to be Professor Grabovski, the one who had prepared me for the high-school entrance exam in mathematics, and given me the questions in advance. With his white beard, divided in the middle, and neat suit, he cut a distinguished figure. He was still failing pupils so that he could afterwards coach them, but now his payment was a little flour and lard, and he no longer took any pains to hide the fact.

As I had lost a year of schooling, all the others in my class were a year younger, except for a boy called Raco, a tall, strong lad with gleaming white teeth and light blue eyes. He had escaped to Cetinje with his father from some place in Kosovo where they had lived until the war.

Raco and I hit it off at once, partly perhaps because we were both from Kosovo, the children of Montenegrin colonists, and older than the rest of the class.

Every day after lessons, Raco and I would hang around talking in the school yard. We were regularly joined by a class-mate, Pušo Zorić, who was the headmaster's son. Partisan families held it against his father that he co-operated with the Italian educational authorities and forbade pupils to engage in politics. He was a strict teacher, insisting that pre-war standards of behaviour should be maintained, so he was not popular with the pupils either. Pušo was a frail, rather sickly boy, left slightly lame by some childhood illness, but very clever, polite and well-informed. As he lived with his parents and brother in the *gimnazija* building, it suited him to stay chatting with us in the yard.

Less than a hundred metres from our school, on the same street, stood the 'English Legation', now the residence of General Pirzio Birolli. Every day the three of us, leaning against the iron railings of the school yard, would observe with interest all the comings and goings in front of this attractive building. Sometimes, when the weather was fine and warm, Pirzio Birolli would drive off or arrive in his large open limousine. Each time, Raco and Pušo would sigh and exclaim in chorus: "What a fantastic car!" and I would always add: "Yes, my father went to prison in it. Pirzio personally sent it for him as a mark of respect."

Then we would all three fall about laughing.

When we went to school in the afternoon shift, after classes we watched 'prominent citizens' of Cetinje coming to visit the General. I guessed that he held important talks in his residence, for these were all well-known collaborators. But Pirzio Birolli had other interests besides war and politics. Quite often we saw a certain Mrs Kusovac drive up in his limousine with her beautiful fifteen-year-old daughter Gina. Pušo, who somehow knew everything that was going on, told us there was a lot of talk in town about some relationship between the General and young Gina, encouraged by her mother, a well-educated and cultivated woman who spoke several languages. There may have been no truth in this, but the story fired our imaginations.

"How on earth could anyone as beautiful as Gina have anything to do with that fat-arsed old general?" we marvelled.

⚜

One Saturday Mila's father was expected to come from Ljubotinj bringing food for her rent. When he didn't come that day or the next, Mila, in tears and fearing the worst, begged me to look for her brother at the barracks. To my surprise, there were no soldiers there, nor anyone who could tell me why the barracks were empty. As usual, Mara knew the answer. When I got home, she was there, looking very worried and telling Mother that in the last two nights, in the greatest possible secrecy, the Italian troops, together with Green and Chetnik units, all in full fighting gear, had left by truck for Herzegovina, to join up with large German forces preparing an offensive against the Partisans.

"The news we're getting isn't good," Mara said. "The main body of our forces is being driven out of Bosnia, and is marching through deep snow in the direction of the Neretva river. All the way, day and night, they're being bombarded from the ground and the air. There are some four thousand wounded with them – they can't leave them to be captured and slaughtered – so they can only move slowly."

We told Mila that her father and brother had probably gone with their units to Herzegovina, since the Italians were mustering all available troops for the forthcoming major battle with the Partisans. This was confirmed by Rajko, who said they had come for his father in the middle of the night, barely giving him time to say goodbye to his family.

All through January we heard only dire news of constant fighting, hunger and Partisan losses. Then, in the middle of February, our newssheet reported a change in the fortunes of war:

"Our forces have managed not only to avoid encirclement by crossing the Neretva, but to destroy the bulk of the Chetniks [in Herzegovina] in hand-to-hand fighting."

⚜

For the rest of February our spirits remained high because of this great Partizan success on the Neretva. But in March we heard that the Germans and Italians, with the help of Bulgarian and quisling units, were already launching a further offensive, the fifth, with forces totalling some one hundred and twenty thousand men. Its aim was to surround and destroy the biggest concentration of Partisan forces, numbering twelve thousand fighters and wounded, half-starved and poorly equipped, who were withdrawing eastward towards the Sutjeska river. Marching through snow in the high mountains along the border between Herzegovina and Montenegro, they spent days and nights in the open, under constant air attack. Close at their heels were German battalions of the Prince Eugene Division specially trained and equipped for highland warfare. All the news coming through at that time filled us with gloom.

"The Germans and their allies are throwing huge forces against us," Mara reported. "The radio says Hitler has ordered the commander of all troops in the Balkans, General von Löhr, to come from Greece and personally direct operations to wipe out Tito and the communist 'bandits' once and for all. The Partisan fighters are not just Montenegrins. There are Muslims, Serbs and Croats, people from all over."

Cetinje Radio kept announcing the complete destruction of "Partisan bands". We knew that Stana's Fourth Montenegrin Brigade was in that enemy encirclement and that she must be somewhere in the long column of exhausted fighters who were being attacked not only by the Germans but by an equally dangerous foe: typhoid fever.

Italian military reports claimed that the Partisans had been completely surrounded in the Mount Zelengora area and only a few small groups had succeeded in fighting their way out and escaping annihilation. These, they said, had no hope of survival, for all the villages in the Partisan rear had been evacuated in advance of the fighting, so that they had no food supplies and were reduced to eating grass and roots.

Ten days after this, some of the people 'evacuated' before the start of the offensive – mostly older peasants and only men – began arriving in army trucks, accompanied by Blackshirts, and were driven into the camp at Donje Polje where Nada had spent some time before being sent to Albania. The trucks kept on coming for several days, packed with men who were only skin and bones. As the trucks went by, they called out: "Help us, brothers! We're dying of hunger. We've eaten nothing for days."

With Mara and members of other Partisan families, I ran around town collecting crusts of bread and other scraps, perhaps put aside to feed poultry, which we tossed into the incoming trucks. When the camp was crammed full, the trucks stopped coming and we started taking what food we could find to the barbed-wire fence. The Italian guards were less strict with these peasants than with political prisoners, and they let us come close to the wire and talk with the inmates.

One day someone told us that a prisoner by the name of Musić, from Nova Varoš, had been enquiring after the Tomašević family. I at once remembered the blacksmith and his three sons, but what could one of them be doing among peasants from a distant region? We thought of Musa, Duško's friend, whom we'd seen being led away in chains by the police just as we were leaving town. Mother and I hurried off to the camp and asked a man by the wire to shout out the name Musić. The cry was taken up by others and before long we heard a voice replying. Eventually, a man of about twenty, emaciated and with sunken eyes, like the rest, pushed his way through the crowd and introduced himself as Ramo, the second of the Musić brothers:

"I knew your Stana and Duško well in Nova Varoš, and I remember this lad. Is it Bato or Aco?"

We threw a couple of boiled potatoes and some bread over the wire, but others grabbed the potatoes and Ramo managed to catch only the bread:

"Never mind, this'll do me. Everyone here is just as hungry."

Then, lowering his voice, he told us he had been with the Partisans until recently, when the Germans had scattered his unit. After hiding in a village for a while, he had been rounded up with the rest. There were other Partisans in the camp, he said, but they were all keeping their heads down, mixing with the peasants, so they wouldn't be shot as communists.

On our next visit he told us the sad fate of his elder brother Musa.

"As you know, Milica, Musa was a bigger communist than anyone in the whole of the Sandžak province. He was the first to go into the Partisans. I followed, then Hajro, who's the same age as Bato here. Then, last year, in Eastern Bosnia, Musa was shot by his comrades. You may well ask why! He was wet and hungry, and he went into a peasant's house and helped himself to a change of clothes and something to eat. Partisans are strictly forbidden to take even a plum from a peasant, because we have to show people we aren't thieves like the Chetniks and Ustashas. Punishment for Party members is much harsher than for others. When he saw that the men in the firing squad were in tears, he

Funeral in Cetinje of Italian soldiers killed fighting the Partisans said: 'Stop blubbering! I deserve the death penalty. Long live our just struggle and our Party!' Those were Musa's last words."

I asked about my school friend Hajro and learnt that he too had joined the Partisans and been hit in the knee during a battle. The Germans searched for the wounded with dogs and shot everyone they found, regardless of age and sex. Hajro had managed to hide in some bushes and so avoided the fate of the others. Several days later, when the Germans had left and his leg had somehow healed by itself, he was found by his comrades.

Mother and I visited Ramo almost daily, bringing him food and trying to cheer him up. We felt somehow close to him, for he reminded us of happier times when we had been all together in Nova Varoš. We guessed he must be suffering because of his brother's death and in constant fear that his Partisan past would be discovered. One day when we came, the Italians had taken him away. We never saw him again.

ã€

After days of fearful uncertainty about the fate of the Partisan forces fighting around the Sutjeska, we learnt that they had managed to break out of the encirclement, that Tito was wounded but had survived, and that the fifth enemy offensive had also failed in its objective. The news-sheet reported that our forces had regrouped and were marching in two directions: some heading back to Montenegro, the others returning to Bosnia. It was now known that over eight thousand fighters, more than half the Partisan force, had lost their lives in this battle, but Hitler's favourite, Von Löhr, had failed.

We wondered, with dread in our hearts, whether Stana was with those who had managed to fight their way out or among the thousands left lying in the snow.

A small number of sick and wounded Partisans began returning to villages around Cetinje and were hidden by relatives in outhouses or nearby caves. One of them brought word that Stana had been wounded a second time, but had managed to rejoin her brigade, which had turned back into Bosnia.

After the failure of the fourth and fifth offensives to wipe out the Partisan movement, relations between Chetniks and Italians underwent a sudden change. The Italians, afraid the Chetnik leaders might betray them and start negotiating with the allied forces, now fighting in Southern Italy, began arresting and deporting prominent Chetniks. One day we were shocked to hear that Uncle Mihajlo was among those arrested and interned somewhere in Italy. This was, in fact, the first news we'd had of him since he fled with his family to Podgorica at the start of the war. Knowing he was a great Anglophile, it was hard to imagine him collaborating with the Italians.

⁂

September 1943. The long, hot summer was drawing to a close. The peak of Lovćen with the little chapel on its summit gleamed in the rays of the late-afternoon sun. Bare-footed, I was idly kicking around a ball made of rags in front of the house, glancing from time to time at the government apartments across the way in the hope of seeing Olga. There was no-one else out in the heat. At one moment, I happened to look along the side street leading from our corner house to the street parallel with ours and was surprised to see a large number of soldiers moving along it, coming from the direction of Donje Polje. I went closer. They looked somehow different from usual, serious and downcast, as they hurried along in no proper order. Some of the soldiers were almost running. Where and why? I wondered in alarm, suspecting some kind of trick. Perhaps they were going to carry out raids on houses. Right after the first group came another, driving before them about twenty big, strong mules loaded with rifles, mortars and boxes of ammunition. Plucking up courage, I ran towards them to ask what was happening. When they noticed me – the street seemed otherwise deserted – they started waving their arms and shouting:

"*Ragazzo, dove sonno i Partigiani*? We're from the Venezia Division. The whole Division is joining the Partisans."

"What Partisans?" I answered in Italian. "I don't know anything about the Partisans. Why ask me?"

"Don't worry, boy, the war's over! Do you understand? *Italia finita!* Done for! Tell us how to find the Partisans. We're all communists. *Vive il Communismo!*"

Amazed by what I was seeing and hearing, for a moment I was speechless. I still couldn't believe my ears, but from their desperate expressions I knew it was no trick. I pointed the way and told them to take the same little path I'd followed to get to the Partisans over a year before.

"The Germans are coming, boy," one of them shouted. "Coming from Albania and Greece. If they catch us, they'll put us in camps or shoot us. With the help of the Partisans we'll get back home to Italy. *Povera Italia!*" And with that some of them began to weep.

I left the Italians hurrying off in the direction I'd pointed, and rushed home to tell Mother the wonderful news. I passed a couple of people and without stopping shouted out: "Italy's fallen! Italy's fallen!" When I reached Olga's house, I felt I had to tell her, too, but then it struck me that for her and her parents the news would hardly be welcome. Perhaps they had already heard it and were now speeding along the road towards Kotor and Italy with their fine furniture and piano, hurrying to escape the Germans, together with soldiers of the shattered Italian army. I'll never see her again, I thought, never hear that piano in the evenings.

From the threshold I shouted the glad tidings to Mother, who flung out her arms wide, hugged me and started sobbing for joy:

"Bato, son, I never believed I'd live to see the end of this terrible war, that we'd all come through and be together again…"

I quickly interrupted her, for I realised she thought the war was over:

"Listen, Mother! The Germans are coming, do you understand? They haven't capitulated, only the Italians. They're coming from Albania and Greece, the soldiers said. They'll be in Cetinje any time now."

"What nonsense, son! Why would they come to Cetinje when we were under Italy?" Mother protested, refusing to accept this disappointment.

"They'll take over Cetinje and all Montenegro in place of the Italians. But forget that now and let's hurry to see whether Father will be let out of prison."

At the yard gate we met Mara, out of breath with running, who had come to tell us the news and accompany us to the prison:

"There's no time to lose. We must get the hostages released and send them into the hills before the Germans arrive."

We found a crowd of women and children already gathered in front of the big iron gate, impatiently waiting for it to open. As yet, no-one had come out, but a lot of Blackshirts had gone in.

"The royal army units have scattered," said Mara, "but not Mussolini's Blackshirts. They're still Hitler's allies, damned fascists! They'll want to take control of the camps and prisons and hand them over to their new masters."

It seemed that Mara was right, for the Blackshirts kept delaying opening the gates, wanting to negotiate. This went on all night. When they saw that the crowd was getting steadily bigger and becoming threatening, at dawn they let out the first small group of prisoners. To our great joy we spotted Father among them. Painfully thin, his hair quite grey, he walked with his head bent, appearing in no hurry. At forty-eight he moved and looked like a sick old man. When he caught sight of us, he came over, still without hurrying, and hugged us for a long time. After more than two years of awaiting death every day, his feelings seemed to be numbed and he could not even express joy at being free at last.

"Where are our other children, Milica?" he asked in a calm, quiet voice.

As we walked home, we told him all we knew about everyone.

"It was the uncertainty that almost killed me," he said. "I'd left you to fend for yourselves, unprepared for the war, when you needed me most. Night after night I lay awake, wondering how you were, what you were doing. I was only two hundred metres from home, but divided from you by those damned thick walls, unable to discover what was happening, suffering like a bird whose nest has been destroyed and fledglings scattered."

Father had not lost the poetic turn of speech that seemed to come naturally to him in times of high emotion.

"Leave that now, Petar," said Mara. "Unless you want to be shot by the Germans as soon as they arrive, you must get out of Cetinje straight away. I've been asked to tell you that the comrades value highly your behaviour in prison and you will be welcome in the Partisans in spite of your anti-communism before the war."

Father had never shown much tenderness towards Mother, and now, after two years' separation and all he had been through, he seemed even more distant. He talked with her about the house and children in a cool, somehow detached way, as though not particularly glad to be with her again. Sensing this, Mother said:

"Well, my Petar, this war has killed everything fine that we had – more than that Austrian war, when you and I first met."

Before we had been in the house more than half an hour, we heard distant gun-fire.

"That'll be the Italians, or the Partisans, or both together, stopping the Germans from entering Cetinje. Now the Germans are their common enemy," said Mara.

As soon as Father had eaten something, he opened the old wardrobe to get out a change of clothes and saw his police dress uniform that Mother had managed to preserve and not sell for food. For her and the rest of us, it had symbolised our pride in our father. He took it out, turned it around and examined it for a minute or two, and then said:

"Don't keep this any longer, Milica. There will be no going back to our past life. That police has served its turn. Sell the uniform for what you can get."

Then he set off slowly, without any show of spirit, to join the Partisans. As I watched him until he was out of sight, I realised that our family life would never be the same again: the war had changed us all.

That day and the next, the Germans drew closer and closer to Cetinje. Along the way they came under attack from the Partisans, who had rushed as many of their forces as possible into Montenegro, as soon as they heard of Italy's capitulation, so as to seize the Italians' arms and supplies. Of the eight Italian divisions fighting in Montenegro, they managed to completely disarm six. The other two went over to the Partisans to fight against the Germans. In the days before the Germans arrived, everybody seemed to be moving about the town at all hours. We children from Partisan families went around collecting weapons from the fleeing Italians, who readily handed them over, wanting only to get rid of them and set off home. Members of the underground then carried the arms and ammunition to nearby villages for the Partisans, who were once more surrounding the town. We even went into the barracks and asked openly for grenades, guns and ammunition.

"How come you're all Partisans now, and yesterday you all swore you didn't know them!" joked a sergeant when Rajko and I asked him for a grenade or two. "Are you going to ask the Germans for some when they come?"

"Not likely!" I replied. "Before they reach Cetinje they'll get the grenades you give us as a present from the Partisans!"

"Well, in that case, wait a minute," said the sergeant. He disappeared inside the storehouse and came out holding a large rucksack full of red Ballistas.

During those two days, the more resolute officers and sergeants led off their entire units, fully armed, to join the Partisans.

Overnight, the whole of politically divided Cetinje became pro-Partisan, with the exception of Vlado Kokotan and his band, who went to ground somewhere to await their new masters. Young people streamed out of the town, some to take refuge for a while in villages, to escape the new danger that loomed; others to join the Partisans. Among the latter were some Greens, whose movement had collapsed with the capitulation of Italy. Our neighbour Duruz, returned from Italy, was one of these, Mrs Lopica came to inform Mother. After that, she became much friendlier.

❦

For several days I hadn't seen Raco. I went to look for him and found him in front of the high school talking with Pušo, discussing what would happen when the Germans came. Raco seemed depressed, for his father, commander of a unit of Greens, had been away for some time up in the Katun region and now would be unable to return to Cetinje.

"My father thinks it would be best if we all went back to school, and protected ourselves with books, not guns, while the Germans are here," said Pušo. "If we cause trouble, they'll come and take us all out of school and shoot us, like they did whole classes at Kragujevac, in 1941."

Pušo was referring to the German massacre of 8000 people one day in 1941 in the Serbian town of Kragujevac – nearly half its population. When they had rounded up everybody they could find in houses and streets, the German troops entered the *gimnazija*, where lessons were in progress. They marched whole classes with their teachers out of town where soldiers were already machine-gunning the population. The headmaster, Professor Pavlović, who happened to be a teacher of German, horrified at the sight, began to protest loudly in perfect German. An officer, taken aback, ordered him out of the column, saying that his life would be spared. A pupil who miraculously survived the slaughter recounted that Professor Pavlović indignantly refused this offer, preferring to share the fate of his fellow-teachers and pupils.

Then the talk turned to people we knew who had left town in the last few days.

"You'll never believe who's gone into the Partisans," Raco said. "Crazy Dima!

"I was out in the street when he rode past on his motorbike, all dressed up in his leather suit, gloves and goggles, and with a big rucksack on his back. 'I'm off to the Partisans! Back soon!' he yelled to some fellow near me. 'How's he going to get up those rocks on a bike, unless it grows wings?' this man says to me. 'Now you know why the great Russian Empire fell.' "

"Do either of you know where little Gina's gone?" Pušo broke in.

"Must've bolted to Italy with that fat-arsed general," I guessed.

"Not a hope! Pirzio Birolli turned his back on her and all his Cetinje friends. Her mother has sent her off to stay with relatives in some village until things quieten down here."

"And what about your Olga?" asked Raco. "Has she sent you a postcard from Italy, asking you to come to visit?"

"No, she's still here. I met her today. Her father doesn't want to go anywhere until the war's over, and then he'll see. Her mother would have gone back with the first group, Olga says, but she couldn't bear to leave all their furniture and the piano, for fear the neighbours would carry them off."

As we chatted about who had gone and who had stayed, we heard bursts of machine-gun fire from near the park beside the Palace. We ran to find out what was happening, and saw Italian soldiers firing in the direction of the Budva road. At the same moment we heard and saw the first of the heavy German tanks roaring down it. The Italians backed away and began shooting again, but the tanks did not return the fire, if they even noticed it.

"Run home quick!" I shouted. "The Italians haven't a hope against tanks." We turned and fled our separate ways.

The gunfire went on for a short time and then stopped. As I sprinted along empty Njegoš Street, keeping close to the houses for shelter, people were lowering wooden roller blinds and closing shutters, taking things from their yards indoors and bolting gates. Before I reached home, tanks and Zündapp motorcycles with sidecars appeared at the end of the street. It was like the first day of the occupation, in April 1941, when the Germans and Italians had entered Cetinje together, but this time the Germans were alone and the Italians were firing at them.

The Germans' prime targets in the first few days were the remnants of the Italian forces. Those who resisted or tried to hide were hunted down and shot on the spot. The rest were treated ruthlessly, humiliated in every possible way, imprisoned and taken off to camps, as though the Germans wanted to punish their former allies for leaving them in the lurch just when they were suffering setbacks on all fronts.

The local people were left to the mercy of the Chetniks, whom the Germans had 'resurrected' as their allies, and the police under Vlado Kokotan. The new Chetniks were not from Cetinje or Old Montenegro – these had been almost wiped out on the Neretva – but were brought in from the Vasojević region bordering on Serbia. When not fighting the Partisans, Mara said, they carried out raids into Bosnia, killing Moslems and Croats, supposedly in reprisal for Serbs who had been killed, though the main reason, in fact, was plunder. And so the Italian and Green authorities in Cetinje were replaced by German and Chetnik. The Chetnik newcomers, long-haired, thick-bearded and unwashed, their curved daggers at their belts, swaggered around the streets making threats against their former friends, the Greens. One morning, we three boys came upon a prominent Green lying in the street with his throat slit.

But the real danger for the Germans and Chetniks remained the Partisans, now well equipped with Italian arms and finally aided and recognised by the British.

To our great satisfaction, Radio London reported more and more about the successes of the Partisans, who were now tying down thirty-three complete German divisions. Prime Minister Churchill dispatched Brigadier Fitzroy Maclean to Tito's Headquarters as head of the Allied Military Mission to coordinate joint military actions in the Balkans. The group of British officers parachuted into free territory controlled by the Partisans included Churchill's son, Randolph, and a number of military experts. The Chetniks began to be qualified as collaborators with the German and Italian forces, and their commander, Draža Mihajlović, was dismissed by King Peter II and the royal government-in-exile in London.

Over half a year had passed since Mila's father and brother left to fight the Partisans in Bosnia and there was still no news from them. After some time, we heard from a peasant that he had been together with them in the battle on the Neretva. Their Green unit and some Chetniks had been trapped in a valley by the Partisans and mown down by machine-gun fire. He himself had escaped, but as for them, he couldn't say.

Mila was tormented by the uncertainty, and also anxious because she owed rent for half a year, though Mother kept telling her not to worry:

"No matter, Mila. You eat with us whenever we have something. One more or less doesn't make much difference."

One day, a relative of Mila's finally turned up from Ljubotinj bringing some food. He also brought some news that upset and saddened us: young Gina had been sentenced to death by the Partisans for being Pirzio Birolli's mistress, and publicly executed a few days before.

"Have the Partisans gone mad?" Mother asked in dismay. "She was only a child. Surely they didn't shoot her?"

"Yes, Milica. When they put her in front of a firing squad, she stood there calm and defiant, not crying or asking for mercy, looking straight into the gun barrels. I've never laid eyes on a more beautiful girl in all my life.

"They shot a number of others," our visitor went on. "Mostly those who came recently from Cetinje. One of them was that lanky son of Dr Lopica, your neighbour."

"It can't be true!" Mother broke in, horrified. "He went there to join them of his own accord!"

When Mara arrived later that day, we bombarded her with questions.

"In wartime there are bound to be mistakes," she replied defensively, as if we were blaming her for the death of Gina and Duruz. "Those who have just got out of Cetinje are responsible. They're settling scores among themselves. Many of them don't belong to our movement in their hearts."

When Mrs Lopica heard of her son's death, for days she roamed about the house weeping and lamenting. From that time on she again stopped talking to Mother.

The Partisans steadily tightened their hold on the territory around Cetinje. The Germans no longer had the strength to undertake major offensives: their primary objective now was to keep control of the main roads connecting their garrisons and outposts that safeguarded their troop withdrawals from Albania and Greece. They were forced to abandon more and more areas to the Partisans, the only real threat they faced in the Balkans.

Every day German detachments demonstrated their presence to the citizens by marching up and down Njegoš Street in perfect step and singing the same song: "Heilo, heila, ha, ha!" But I noticed a difference between them and the athletic, blond young men who had so impressed me in 1941. These soldiers, towards the end of 1943, were a mixed bunch: tall and short, old and young, fair and dark. I wondered aloud what had happened to all the handsome blond soldiers.

"Left on the hills of Bosnia and Montenegro," Mara replied proudly, "but most of all in the deep snows of Mother Russia."

⚘

Cetinje, too, was buried in deep snow that winter, like the previous one. Menacing long icicles hung from all the eves. I was in a melancholic state of mind brought on by the approaching end of the year, 1943. Not long before I had turned fourteen.

One evening, just before curfew began, Mara with little Milovan came running up our steps. I had rarely seen her looking so distraught.

"Is there anyone here but you? Is Mila in?" she asked urgently.

Hearing that Mila was spending the night with a girlfriend, as she had been doing quite often lately, Mara looked relieved.

"Good! I'll sleep here with Milovan. Something dreadful's happened and they may come round to our houses looking for us this very night. Gojko Kruška's been caught! They've got him in gaol at this moment."

"Serves him right, the scum!" was Mother's first reaction. "But wait a minute! How can be he caught when he's one of Vlado Kokotan's gang, going around with them arresting people?"

Then Mara explained that Gojko had never been a turncoat: it was on Party orders that he had posed as an anti-communist and managed to get himself into the police. Now he had been unmasked and she was terrified that under torture he might name names. In that case, she and other underground workers could expect immediate arrest.

"Well, Mara," Mother replied, "I always found it hard to believe that Gojko, Duško and Mošo's friend, a lad from an honourable Montenegrin family, could turn traitor."

While I was glad that I could again regard Gojko as a friend, the news of his arrest shocked and also frightened me. For the first time I was fully aware of the danger of being a member of the movement, which I, as a messenger, considered myself. I'd heard that the Germans had shot members who were only fourteen. We stayed awake, fully dressed, for most of that night, listening for footsteps approaching the house.

Next day the whole of Cetinje was talking about Gojko's arrest and speculating whether he would withstand the torture he was being put to by Vlado Kokotan and his former colleagues. Ghastly details of this leaked out and made my blood run cold. They kept torturing him in various ways until he lost consciousness, it was said, but so far they had got nothing out of him.

Days passed and there were no fresh arrests – a sign that Gojko was still holding out. Then Mara told us that the Germans had taken over, determined to break him: it was evident that for three years he had been at the centre of underground activities in the town and could supply them with many names.

Still dreading what every new day might bring, we entered 1944. When the Germans finally realised that Gojko would never speak, he was sentenced to death by public hanging.

The thirteenth of January dawned grey, cold and misty. The snow was slushy under foot; the damp chill crept into the bones. On such days, as a rule, people went out only on essential business. But that day was different. All citizens, including Gojko's mother and sister, had been ordered to attend the hanging, so the streets were thronged with people heading towards the market-place. When I arrived, there was already a large crowd gathered in a wide semi-circle, muffled up in whatever warm clothing they could find, shifting their weight to keep their feet from freezing. Bearded Chetniks in their black fur hats with the familiar death's head badge, armed to the teeth, were lined up in front of the crowd, separating it from a group of booted and helmeted Germans in long green greatcoats. The metal plaques round their necks were engraved with the word '*Feldgendarmerie*'.

Some soldiers were making the final preparations, securing and testing the rope fastened to the massive overhanging branch of a great linden tree. Finally, a tall, thin captain, an Austrian by origin, came to make a personal check. He was a familiar figure in the town for he spent much of his time walking round the streets and peering into yards accompanied by two gigantic men armed with automatic rifles. If any passers-by made the mistake of coming near him, he would lash them on the head and face with his whip. Those who didn't seem sufficiently respectful, or who appeared to him suspicious in some way, got beaten up by his escort and taken off to prison.

Exactly at the appointed hour, an open army truck turned slowly from Njegoš Street into the market-place. I ran alongside to get a closer view of Gojko. He was not alone: beside him stood a young man of about the same age. Gojko was singing. His thin face with large, sunken eyes bore the marks of terrible suffering. His hands were bound behind his back and he was lightly dressed for the bitter weather, though he appeared not to notice the cold. As soon as he caught sight of the crowd, his eyes brightened and he began looking around with an expression that seemed to me like pride. Seeing the Chetniks lined up he started singing again, a mocking refrain that promised the Chetnik 'black ravens' that they would soon see 'black days'.

The truck stopped right underneath the improvised gallows, with its back facing the crowd. The tailgate was let down and the captain climbed up, checked a second rope that had now been secured, and took charge of the two condemned men. I squeezed my way to the front. The second prisoner was taller and heavier than Gojko, with dark curly hair and a deathly pale face. He stood motionless on the truck, looking round at the crowd, but showing no emotion and never uttering a sound. Somebody behind me whispered he was an Albanian from Skadar who had been captured carrying messages from the Albanian Partisans to our people in Montenegro. Perhaps he was in a state of shock, I thought, finding himself suddenly facing death amidst strangers in a foreign country.

Unlike him, Gojko, in front of his own people, was never quiet for a moment, shouting threats and curses at the Chetniks, police and Germans, and breaking into Partisan songs. Two chairs were positioned on the truck underneath the ropes. The captain put the noose around Gojko's neck first, and to keep him quiet punched him in the face. Blood trickled from his nose down over his mouth and chin, but Gojko kept singing and cursing traitors who would pay the price one day. The silent crowd watched in awed admiration. The Germans had intended this hanging to serve as a warning to others, but Gojko's unbreakable spirit had spoilt their plan. Infuriated, the captain struck him again, but with no effect.

Then from the crowd a child screamed: "Gojko! Gojko!" He started, recognising the voice of his seven-year-old sister Beba, and looked desperately around until he saw his weeping mother and sister waving to him among the mass of frozen people.

As loudly as he could he shouted back: "Mother! Beba! Don't cry! Be proud of me!"

The angry captain pulled the chair away from under his feet and as the body fell struck a heavy blow that broke Gojko's neck. A moment later the Albanian messenger suffered the same fate. Two lifeless bodies swung slowly in the bitter January wind that sweeps down from snowy Lovćen. As I made my way home, I felt immeasurably sad, yet proud that I had known Gojko, that he had proved himself a loyal friend of Duško, Mošo, and Lame Talaja. In Cetinje that day everyone was saying that Gojko had won his war, defeated the German might and the mad Austrian captain.

After the hanging, no-one was allowed to approach the bodies for four days. Gojko's mother and sister, frozen from the cold and numb with misery, stood all day long at a distance from the gallows, gazing at his stiff corpse that was gradually turning to ice. Towards evening on the fourth day the body was released for burial. An old horse-drawn cart was found to carry Gojko to the cemetery, where friends had dug a grave. Mara, who had joined the small group of family members at the burial, later recounted how his little sister had taken off her coat and put it over him, to keep him warm in the grave.

The body of his Albanian comrade in death remained hanging there for a couple of days more, then disappeared during the night.

Good news began arriving from the battlefronts. The Chetniks and Ustashas, together with the Germans, were suffering defeats in all parts of the country.

The war was definitely going our way, but for us in Cetinje there was little else to be cheerful about. Vlado Kokotan and his police, trying desperately to halt the inevitable, or venting their fury at the prospect of defeat, intensified their terror against the remaining members of Partisan families. The Germans no longer trusted them, but still let them get on with the dirty work in which they were so proficient: spying on, arresting and torturing their fellow citizens. The Germans then took over the interrogated prisoners, tried and condemned them, and carried out their execution, either by hanging or by firing squad, depending on the number to be liquidated.

The sound of firing from the execution ground was now heard daily.

"Whose soul has departed from his body?" Mother would wonder aloud. "Whose mother is left to mourn till her dying day?"

Besides this fear and insecurity, in the first three months of 1944 we, like other Partisan families, faced starvation. German troops were forbidden to buy anything from the local people, so I had no hope of selling doughnuts. I spent more and more time digging through the snow in untended gardens and vegetable plots in the hope of finding a frozen head of cabbage or anything else edible.

One day I recalled seeing Italian soldiers roasting sparrows on skewers. We had never eaten sparrows in Montenegro, but I decided to give it a try and set out with my catapult and a pocketful of stones for Queen Maria's Park, which seemed a suitable and secluded place for my hunting expedition. I was feeling very pleased with myself, having killed several and stuffed them in my pocket, when suddenly I saw the Austrian captain, Gojko's hangman, and the two giant members of the *Feldgendarmerie* walking along the path towards me.

"Halt!" they all bellowed. My first impulse was to run, but my legs turned to jelly.

"What's that in your pockets? Empty them!" the captain ordered, speaking quite good Serbian. "What! You've been killing innocent little birds! What harm did they do you? I'll teach you a lesson!"

And with that he raised his whip and began beating me mercilessly on the head and shoulders. I gritted my teeth, determined not to cry out or beg for mercy. I was just praying he wouldn't kill me now the war was nearly over.

Montenegrin peasant woman with her sole means of transport in the harsh Katun region above Cetinje

Finally, having exhausted himself and his anger, he lowered his whip and said:

"Be off with you, little savage, before you end like the birds."

Fully expecting to be shot from behind, I dashed off in a zig-zag line into the nearest cover.

When I arrived home, bruised and bleeding, Mother greeted me with the news that Ljuba, who had been lying low in her mother-in-law's house all this time, had managed to get out of Cetinje dressed in peasant clothes with a group of women driving donkeys from the market, and was now on her way to the Partisans.

Next morning, I went off to Mara's as usual to collect the news-sheet, typed on thin paper so it could be folded up very small, and take it to the tobacco kiosk. I was never told where she got it from – someone or group of people in the town with a wireless and typewriter, both strictly banned, risked their lives daily to produce it. Nor did I know what happened to it after I passed it on to Mijo Mali, so that if I was caught and tortured, I could incriminate only two people. By the time I arrived, she would have read and memorised it.

As always she was pleased to see me:

"Our brigades are getting closer to Cetinje, Bato. Wherever they appear, more and more people – young and old, men and women – are joining them. If the English hadn't started sending us food and weapons, we wouldn't be able to feed and arm such a huge number."

After handing over the news-sheet, I decided not to go to school, which I was now attending very irregularly, but run off to the market-place to see if I could pick up a few vegetables lying around. I was bending down, peering under a counter in the hope of finding a discarded cabbage leaf or fallen potato, when a voice just behind me made my heart sink:

"What are you looking for, boy? Lost something?"

I straightened up to find myself face to face with Vlado Kokotan and a couple of his men. All through the occupation, it seemed, I had been running away from an encounter like this, but now I was cornered, all avenues of escape were closed. With a kind of numb resignation, I abandoned myself to my fate.

"I know you, we've been keeping an eye on you," said Vlado in a menacing tone. "You're one of the Tomaševićs, aren't you? Would your father be Petar Tomašević, by any chance?"

I mumbled that he was, unsure whether this was a good or bad thing in my case.

"So you're the son of that traitor who turned communist! Well, now I'm chief of police, not your father, and I think we'll try to get a bit of information out of you, with the help of a few beatings! Tie him up, we'll take him to the station!"

At the entrance to police headquarters, several German soldiers were chatting among themselves and, separately, several Chetniks. Together they guarded the police building and kept an eye on one another. A middle-aged man with a scar down one cheek opened the door for us. From his bundle of keys I guessed he was the gaoler. He took one look at me and turned to Vlado:

"You must be short of big fish if you have to catch tiddlers!"

As I stood waiting in the hall, I remembered bringing Father his lunch there. Then it had been clean and tidy; now everything was filthy, and the glass panels of the internal doors were mostly broken. Though I'd hoped I would never fall into Vlado Kokotan's hands, I had nevertheless prepared myself for that eventuality. Facing the test on which my life would depend, I kept reminding myself of Mara's words: "Whatever happens, never change your story."

After a while, I was taken into Father's former office, where his successor was sitting at the big polished walnut desk. He observed me for a while, as though considering how to deal with me, then stood up, strolled over, and unexpectedly gave me two stinging slaps on the face.

"If you don't want more, tell me at once where your father is."

"When he came out of prison, he went with an Italian column to Mitrovica, to our relatives, to look for my younger brother, Aco…"

Vlado curtly interrupted my carefully rehearsed story, picked up the whip of plaited leather, like the Austrian captain's, which he always carried round town, and started hitting me mercilessly, all the time cursing and threatening to kill me on the spot. Instinctively I covered my face, but my head and ears remained unprotected.

When he stopped, I touched the spot on my head that hurt the most and saw that my fingers were covered with blood.

"Many people have tried to deceive me. Now they're sleeping underground – and that's where you'll be unless I get the truth! I'm a patient man, but only up to a point. Now tell me again where your father is."

I began repeating my story word for word: "When he came out of prison…"

He motioned me to stop and spoke in a calm, almost fatherly voice:

"I don't enjoy beating you. Look how skinny you are! There's nothing for a man to hit. We know very well your father isn't in Mitrovica, we've made enquiries. Now, tell me exactly where he is, in what village and whose house, and you can go home."

Parrot-like, I began repeating: Mitrovica… our relatives… my brother…

This time I added that we hadn't heard from Father, so perhaps he'd never got there, perhaps he'd been killed on the journey…

Another vicious beating followed. I was near collapse when he paused again:

"Well, boy, it looks like you've made up your mind to leave this world. Perhaps you think I'm joking? Others thought so too, but they're not alive to tell the tale. But let's forget your father for a moment and turn to something you know more about. Those messages you carry for the communists – now you just tell us who gives them to you and where you take them."

At that very moment someone came in and had a word in his ear.

"I'll give you one night to think it over," he said as he got up to leave. "But don't make us wait too long. Just remember, you'll never get out of here alive until I get a list of those names."

In solitary, I looked around the cell dimly lit by a bare bulb hanging from the high, dirty ceiling. Generations of prisoners had passed the time by spitting on their cigarette ends and flicking them to make them stick on to the ceiling, which was still covered with them. Among the many signatures and messages on the grimy walls, I made out some familiar names, such as Vlado Dapčević, the communist agitator my father had arrested at the market.

My head seemed to be splitting with pain, my swollen ears on fire. I carefully patted my scalp: the blood had congealed. Utterly worn out, I lay down on the bare floor and at once fell fast asleep.

When I woke up, I had no idea how long I had slept and whether it was night or day. I started worrying about the next interrogation. I knew Vlado was only guessing about my being a messenger. Otherwise Mara and Mijo would already be under arrest. Would I be able to stand the pain without betraying them? Unless I did, Mijo would be hanged and Mara, dear, good, wonderful Mara, would kill herself. Then, if I myself got out alive, people would point at me and say: "That's the cowardly little Tomašević who betrayed his friends and disgraced his family…"

I could only hope they didn't actually torture boys of fourteen by breaking their fingers and putting red-hot bayonets between their teeth, like they did with Gojko Kruška.

Days and nights passed, and still I was not taken out for questioning. Every now and again the gaoler would push some food into my cell. Each time I asked him something: what time of day it was, why I was being kept there when I'd done nothing wrong, whether I was going to be questioned again…

"Don't be in a hurry, boy," he'd say. "Just eat up and keep quiet. Better to spend a few days in solitary and wait for Vlado to cool off."

"But I'm innocent. I was brought here by mistake. All I was doing was looking for cabbage leaves under the market tables. Mother's waiting for me at home and worrying. She has a bad heart and she'll die without me."

Gradually my conversations with the gaoler got longer and I sensed that he felt sorry for me. I decided to play that card for all it was worth, every time mentioning my sick mother all alone at home. One day, he finally told me that Vlado Kokotan had gone off with the Germans some fifteen days before, soon after my arrest, and had not yet returned.

"They've been interrogating people in villages around Cetinje. I hear they've collected a big bunch of new prisoners, but heaven knows where we're going to put them. We're overcrowded as it is."

I saw my chance and seized it.

"Why don't you ask someone to let me go home for a day or two, until Vlado comes back, so I can see Mother. I'm afraid she'll die all alone there. You can be sure I'll only be at home. Where else would I go?"

"To tell you the truth, boy, if they'd asked me, I'd never have locked you up in the first place. What harm can a kid like you do, all skin and bones? But about letting you go home for a couple of days, I'd better talk with someone, though perhaps I don't need to. I'll see."

This ray of hope filled me with such excitement I almost choked. Could I possibly be that lucky? I paced up and down the cell until, completely exhausted, I lay on the floor and slept. I was woken by the sound of a key turning in the lock and the familiar voice of the gaoler:

"Come on then, boy, run off home to your mother and don't budge outside the house!"

❧

A pale, late February sun was setting behind Lovćen when I got outside. I took a deep breath of fresh air and began to run, but after a few steps had to stop. For the first time I, who always ran everywhere, hadn't the strength. I made my way home walking and trotting in turn, all the time glancing over my shoulder in case they had changed their minds or it was all a cruel joke… I decided it would be safest to spend the night at Mara's and try to pass through the block next day.

Mother nearly fainted with joy when I appeared at the door. I told her briefly what had happened and that I had to leave at once. Without more ado, she tied up some clothing for me in a bundle and then began collecting some things of her own.

"What are you doing, Mother?" I asked in surprise.

"I'm going with you. All I have is there, the whole family. Anyway, I can't stay here, waiting for them to arrest me."

We were about to leave the house, carrying a blunt old axe and some rope, when Mila unexpectedly appeared. Her face lit up when she saw me:

"Bato, dear, you're back! How wonderful! We've been so worried about you. But where are you off to at this hour? You can't collect firewood in the dark."

"No, we're going first thing in the morning. We'll be back in the afternoon," I added unconvincingly.

Suddenly guessing our real plan, Mila looked shocked and scared:

"You're escaping from Cetinje and leaving me alone! Well, go if you have to. You've got somewhere to run to, but there's nowhere for me to hide. If Father and Miro were alive, it might be different. But they got themselves killed, and for no good reason. It's all so stupid and senseless. I curse the day we ever came to this damned Cetinje, to escape the Albanians and get slaughtered by our Montenegrin brothers."

"Don't, Mila!" I protested, trying to stop her outpouring of misery and bitterness. "We'll meet again soon. Perhaps your people aren't dead and it will all turn out right in the end."

"Don't talk rubbish, Bato! We'll never see each other again, except maybe in the next world. After the war, you'll say to people: 'There was once a family called Lubarda, but they all got killed because of their stupidity!'"

"Hush, Mila, it's tempting fate to talk that way!" Mother broke in.

"You go, Bato! I was hoping you'd be in Cetinje to protect me when the Partisans come."

"Don't worry, Mila! Nothing bad will happen. The Partisans won't harm you."

⁊

Helpless to comfort Mila, we left hurriedly, knowing we had to get to Mara's before curfew. She was overjoyed to see me, and after hearing my story agreed that we ought to leave early next morning by the same check-point I'd used two years before. Now our people would be easier to find as they were all around the town, she said, but we should beware of Chetniks pretending to be Partisans by wearing caps with five-pointed stars.

Next morning we hugged Mara and Milovan goodbye.

Stana Tomašević in Drvar,
Bosnia, in May 1944, by the
British war photographer John
Talbot. This picture was dropped
as a leaflet over occupied Europe
to encourage local resistance

Winners and Losers

Slowly, fearfully, we approached the road block. The Italians had always swallowed the story about gathering firewood, but would the Germans? I glanced at Mother, tall and gaunt in her long, shabby, frayed skirt, her face grey and drawn. I was wearing the same clothes, now outgrown, that Ljuba made for me out of Italian army blankets when I first went to the Partisans, and a school cap with the number two on it, indicating that I was a second-year pupil and twelve years old, not fourteen – Mara had thought of this at the last moment. My great fear was that one of Vlado Kokotan's police would be at the check-point and recognise us. Two big German Tiger tanks were positioned where the smaller Italian tanks had once stood. To our huge relief, the German guards just waved us through.

It was almost nightfall when we neared Čevo, a little place on a plateau that had been the scene of much fighting with the Turks in past centuries. We knew it was now in Partisan hands.

"Halt! Who goes there?"

"An old woman and a child," Mother answered, as agreed in advance.

Half a dozen young men appeared out of the semi-darkness. By their tidy dress and clean-shaven faces we recognised at once that they were 'ours', not Chetniks. When we told them why we'd left Cetinje and that we hoped to find Stana and Father, one of them was assigned to escort us to the local commander in Čevo. In the village, dozens of camp-fires were burning and crowds of young people were sitting around them or milling about. Our escort told us that the Tenth Montenegrin Brigade, in which there were many Cetinje people, was stopping there just for the night. They would be setting off next morning in the direction of Podgorica to intercept Germans units trying to recapture the town of Nikšić, which the Partisans had liberated just a few days earlier. From the general high spirits, laughter and singing, no-one would have guessed they were expecting a battle next day.

The local commander, a short, thick-set man in peasant clothing with a red star embroidered on his cap, greeted us cordially. He proposed that Mother should stay at Čevo, to help with cooking for the Partisans passing through every day, and I should go to Nikšić, where I would be more likely to learn the whereabouts of our scattered family. Mother protested strongly, realising that for the first time since the birth of Ljuba she would be quite alone, without a single child, but finally she had to agree, with a heavy heart, as it was a Partisan rule that no family members could be in the same unit.

Next morning, before daybreak, the Tenth Brigade assembled, still stretching and yawning, and went off to battle.

"Don't worry," said the local commander, who was among the first to rise, "they'll soon wake up when the firing starts."

Then it was my turn. With two messengers – 'couriers' the Partisans called them – and a loaded pony, I set out for Nikšić, leaving Mother wiping away her tears with the back of her broad hands.

All day I struggled to keep up with the two boys, who were my age or a bit older, and the mountain pony, all of them accustomed to the rocky terrain of the Katun region. Weakened as I was by hunger and prison, I held on to the pony's tail when going uphill, but let go whenever we got to a flatter part in case he decided to kick out to get rid of me.

It was dark by the time we reached Nikšić, but there were no lights in the town, in case of an enemy air raid. My companions took me to the Partisan headquarters and explained to the man on duty that I was Stana Tomašević's brother who had escaped from Cetinje and wanted to find his sister before being assigned to a unit. At the mention of Stana, the man at once took me into the office of the local commander, who pumped my hand and wished me welcome. Stana would soon be in Nikšić, he said, as she was to speak at a big public meeting that was scheduled. In the meantime, he would ask Veljko Mićunović, a good friend of hers, where I should stay.

Turning the handle on his field telephone, he tried for a long time to get in touch with him. Veljko, he mentioned by the way as we waited, was an important comrade, head of OZNA for the whole of Montenegro, the Gulf of Kotor region and the Sandžak.

"OZNA, in case you don't know, is the Partisan police force, just formed. They interrogate German and Chetnik prisoners, as well as suspected enemies of the people."

Finally, he got Veljko and handed the apparatus to me. For the first time in my life I was speaking on the telephone!

"Welcome, Bato!" said Veljko. "Your father's here in Nikšić, and Stana will come in a day or two. Let someone bring you over to me in the morning and I'll make sure Petar is here!"

❦

Nikšić was full of Partisans, all in new British uniforms, which I saw here for the first time, with shining boots, leather belts and British machine-guns. The only thing Partisan about them was the cap. The two messengers handed over some papers at OZNA headquarters and said goodbye. A guard led me across the spacious courtyard of the large house, which was crowded with men, all with their hands bound together in front of them. By their uniforms I at once recognised Germans and Chetniks, and there were a few civilians as well. It was the first time I'd ever seen Germans and Chetniks tied up and I found the sight very strange!

"Veljko and other comrades will question all these, then decide what to do with them," the guard explained. "I reckon most of them will be shot. That's the job of the Escort Company. What else to do with them? Every day there's more and more, and we have no place to put them nor food to feed them."

He took me through another door and then into Veljko Mićunović's office. The head of OZNA was a dark-haired man in his twenties, of medium height – rather short for a Montenegrin – with penetrating black eyes, a very pale face and a thin moustache. He rose to greet me with a kindly smile and soon put me at my ease, telling me Father would be along soon and asking me about life in Cetinje.

"I need a messenger," he said after a while, "who will be around most of the time to do various things for me. He would sleep and eat with our Escort Company, like all the rest. If you want to stay with us, we'll take you. There'll be a bit of fighting, but more chasing after bandits!"

I accepted his offer with alacrity, for I immediately liked his firm, quiet voice and courteous manner.

Soon after, someone came to say Father had arrived and led me downstairs.

"I can't believe it's you, Bato! How you've grown! And how thin you are! When they said you were in Nikšić, I almost died of happiness!"

I asked him if he had news of the family.

"We're slowly getting together, Bato. Stana will be here soon. Ljuba's with her unit. Nada, I know, has come back with the internees from Albania, and I'm trying to find out where exactly she is. I spend all my time looking for my children instead of fighting!"

"What about Duško? Tell me all you know about Duško," I interrupted impatiently.

"I heard from Stana that she met him at Drvar in Bosnia last May, at the time of the German airborne attack, when they tried to capture Tito. He survived that – his unit defended Tito, the High Command and the British mission against the paratroopers the Germans dropped. He managed to escape from the camp in Italy and joined the Italian and then our Partisans. But tell me, how's Milica?"

I said she'd stayed at Čevo to cook for the Partisans.

"Poor thing, she's suffered a lot," he said, then changed the subject.

"Don't worry, my Bato, everything will sort itself out in time. We have to be patient. The war's still on, many fighters are dying every day. It's not certain all of us will survive."

Then he told me about a big performance to be held that evening in the Nikšić theatre.

"We must go to celebrate your arrival. You're sure to meet half Cetinje there."

I looked at him in his British uniform with the Partisan cap and thought how odd it was that he, who had spent years hunting down communists, should now be wearing their badge. Throughout the occupation I had often dreamt of being with Father, but in my dreams he was always wearing his glittering police dress uniform. Now he seemed quite ordinary, without the aura of authority I remembered from childhood.

When we arrived at the theatre that evening, a score of Partisans, armed to the teeth, were standing in front of it,

"From tomorrow they'll be your comrades," Father remarked. "Those are members of Veljko's OZNA. While we're in the theatre, they'll be standing guard."

The large auditorium was lit by dozens of bright lights – I'd never seen so many all in one place, nor so many Partisans gathered together: there must have been two hundred of them. Every face seemed to glow

Participants in the Yugoslav Youth Congress held in the Bosnian town of Drvar in May 1944, when an attempt was made to capture Tito by a German airborne attack. In the centre: Stana Tomašević, leader of the Montenegrin Youth delegation

with happiness: the scent of victory was in the air. As Father said, I recognised many people from Cetinje; some former students now wore the insignia of higher-ranking officers. When the audience finally settled into their seats, the commander of recently liberated Nikšić took the stage, saluted the Partisans and welcomed the members of the Soviet and British military missions. Mention of the Allies was greeted with tumultuous and prolonged applause. Behind him, at the back of the stage, were three large photographs – Stalin, Churchill and Roosevelt – and a huge banner inscribed: 'Long Live Our Allies!'

The performance that followed, with choral singing and recitations, was just like a better-prepared version of the one I'd been rehearsing at Štitari. This was not surprising since it was under the direction of my old acquaintance, the Cetinje actor Vaso, whose huge figure with arms outstretched blocked our view of half the choir when he was conducting. They sang "I'm proud to be a Partisan" and other familiar songs with such power and passion that tears came to my eyes. Vaso, in Montenegrin national costume, again recited appropriate passages from Njegoš in his deep, resonant voice, creating the thrilling illusion that it was the great poet himself speaking.

"More, Vaso, more!" the audience shouted after each piece glorifying the people's struggle for liberty. I felt immensely proud that I was now truly part of that great movement spoken of so often by Mara, Duško, Gojko Kruška… This was the happiest moment of my life!

During the interval, when people moved around greeting one another, I noticed that Father, not yet fifty, was one of the oldest there. Younger men and women, many of them friends of Stana and Duško, came over to shake hands, and Father introduced me to each of them proudly as his younger son who had escaped from gaol in Cetinje three days before.

One older Partisan, nearly Father's age, said quietly while shaking hands:

"I know how you feel, Petar. I've been through the same. And in the pride of his youth, too!"

These words struck a kind of chill. When the lights went down and the concert resumed, I kept thinking about them. What did the man mean? Was he talking in general about the victims of the war? Then suddenly I knew: he was speaking about Duško. Duško had been killed! All the feelings I had been bottling up during the war, so as not to show weakness to the enemy, all my grief and fears, suddenly erupted within me like a volcano when I realised that Duško was no more. As the choir on stage sang rousing Partisan songs, I began to weep, at first silently, to myself, so no-one would notice. Then, as the tears flowed, I covered my face with my hands. Finally, I could hold back no longer and started sobbing aloud… Father quickly led me outside.

"Duško's dead! I know he's dead. Tell me the truth!"

I waited for him to say, as he'd done so often in my childhood, that I was not to worry, he would put everything right. Then I'd believed there was nothing he couldn't do, even bring someone back to life. But the miracle didn't happen. Father just looked at me in silence with tears in his eyes, then hugged me:

"Yes, Bato, it's true. Our Duško is dead, slaughtered by Chetniks, and on the very border of Montenegro. He never lived to reach home, to be with us all again, as he wanted. No-one's looking at us, son. Just let it all out. I know it's hard for you to bear…"

Next morning I reported at OZNA headquarters and was taken into Veljko's office.

"Sit down for a bit, while I call your superior officer," he said.

I sensed he was showing me special attention and kindness not just because of his friendship with Stana, but because he knew about Duško.

In came a shortish, very powerfully built officer, with a swarthy complexion, neatly trimmed moustache and black eyes that all the time darted here and there.

"I'm Mugoša," he introduced himself, giving me a bone-crushing handshake. "Now we'll get you dressed like a real Englishman," he added with a smile. "You're as skinny as they are, anyway! Have you ever seen a live Englishman?"

I said no, only in films, quite forgetting about the mining colony in Mitrovica.

"Well, tomorrow you'll come with me to the frontline towards Podgorica and you'll see them there."

He took me off to the '*intendatura*' – a word I didn't dare attempt to pronounce for a long time – and an older women Partisan named Višnja gave me several pairs of trousers and jackets to try on. Even the smallest were at least two sizes too big.

"Never mind," she said, "Marko here will soon fix that. You just pick out some boots, a shirt and a cap that fit."

Half an hour later I stood before the mirror in the small work-room of the Partisan tailor and could hardly believe my eyes. Was that really me looking so grown-up and serious in that perfectly fitting English uniform?

"Now all you need is your weapons – grenades, revolver and rifle – and you'll be a proper Partisan," said Marko. "Only mind how you handle them. Plenty of our lads have accidentally killed each other!"

Not wanting to be thought ignorant, I told Marko I'd been in the Partisans back in 1942, but all my comrades had been killed and I had returned to Cetinje. He shook his head as he listened, as though not quite believing my story:

"All the same, be careful! It's for your own good."

When my transformation from civilian to soldier was complete, Mugoša was sent for:

"Well, Bato, now you're a real Englishman, except the English haven't got a red star on their caps. They will have, though, after the victory of the proletarian revolution. That's why we sing the song: 'Montenegro and England will be proletarian countries!'" Then, turning to Višnja: "Burn his old clothes at once. They must be full of lice."

"Certainly, Comrade Mugoša, straight away! And when we manage to kill off all the lice here, England will have a proletarian revolution!"

"You just mind what you're saying, Višnja, if you've any sense!" Mugoša, suddenly stern, reprimanded her for this joke. "People have been shot for less than that!"

He then took me into a long building occupying all one side of the courtyard of OZNA's headquarters. Formerly used for storing timber – the owner of the house had operated a saw-mill – this was now the barracks of the Escort Company. Along its entire length, straw mattresses were ranged against the walls, each covered with British army blankets. Instead of pillows, there were Italian army rucksacks, some of the huge quantity left over after the capitulation.

When Mugoša entered, the Escort Company, numbering around fifty, all stood up. He introduced me to them, and a thin young man of about twenty came over to shake hands first:

"I'm Martinović, company commissar. And this is Rade Nikić, corporal, Ilija Vuković, messenger… But I can't introduce them all now, Bato. You'll soon get to know them."

The messenger, Ilija, spoke up:

"If comrade commander agrees, we could make a space for Bato to sleep next to me."

"That was my idea, too," said Mugoša. "You're the same age, so you'll get on well."

Ilija and I were the same height and equally thin. He had arrived only a few days earlier from the little town of Šavnik, way up on Durmitor, the highest mountain in Montenegro, and was the messenger of Veljko's deputy.

That evening, as we lined up waiting for our food to be dished out from a big cauldron, Ilija stood in front of me and the corporal, Rade Nikić, behind me.

"Do you smoke, pal?" the corporal asked at once.

When I said I didn't, he seemed pleased:

"That's very good! Don't go starting if you haven't smoked up till now. I'll always stand behind you, Bato. They give you ten English cigarettes with your food in the evenings. You tell them you smoke and give your cigarettes to me."

Two women Partisans were standing by the cauldron, one, not much older than myself, ladling stew into our mess tins, and an older one doling out bread and cigarettes. When it came to my turn, she asked:

"Do you smoke, comrade?"

Hesitantly, unconvincingly, I said that I did.

"That's not good for you. You're skinny enough without that. Better give it up!"

I began to mutter something in justification, when Nikić spoke up behind me:

"And why should you care, comrade, if someone smokes? Your job is to hand out fags to those who do. Let others worry about our health!"

Sheepishly I took the ten loose cigarettes, which had an unusual scent, and when we'd moved away, passed them to Nikić:

"You're a real pal, Bato. You can always count on me. From now on I'll keep an eye on you."

❧

Next morning, before daybreak, I was woken by Nikić shaking me:

"Come on, Bato, time to move!"

'He's already looking after me because of the cigarettes,' I thought.

Outside, the rest of my squad of ten, which Nikić as a corporal was in charge of, were already lined up. Nearby a large, battered, pre-war truck was rattling and belching out clouds of smoke. We got in, having plenty of space to sit on the benches fixed to each side. Commander Mugoša and Commissar Martinović joined us.

"We'll be going as far as we can towards the frontline by truck," Mugoša explained. "Then we'll hide it among the rocks, so the Germans don't shoot it up, and proceed to OZNA battalion headquarters on foot. With a bit of luck, they'll give us some food and a glass of Chetnik *loza* or German Schnapps, depending on what they've captured! Then we'll bring the German and Chetnik prisoners back with us."

The day dawned fine and cloudless. About half an hour after the sun rose, we heard the drone of aircraft.

"Don't worry, comrades," said Martinović, "from the engines I can tell they're not Stukas but American Douglases, making for Podgorica. Tens of thousands of Germans, withdrawing from Greece and Albania, are concentrating there. If it weren't for those planes giving them no peace, the Germans under General von Löhr would have retaken Nikšić by now. He's the one who nearly wiped us out in the Fifth Offensive."

As the sound of exploding shells grew louder, I knew we were getting close to the front.

"That's the English batteries pounding the German positions," said Mugoša. "As agreed with us, the English guns and American planes are helping us stop them from moving north towards Nikšić."

Soon after, we found a place to conceal the truck and set off on foot along a steep goat track towards OZNA headquarters. When we reached the top of the hill, down below a vast panorama stretched as far as the eye could see: a broad green valley through which the Zeta river wound its way to the little town of Danilovgrad and on to Podgorica. At that very moment, as we stood there, it was again being bombed by the Americans. We could see the planes flying in formation over the town and dropping their deadly load.

The wide Zeta Valley was enclosed on both sides by a long chain of rocky hills which gradually got lower towards Podgorica. On the hills nearest to us, the enemy lines with dozens of small concrete bunkers were clearly visible. When we reached OZNA headquarters – a wooden barrack protected from shelling by two huge rocks – we met the commander and commissar, who at once invited us to sit down for a rest and something to eat and drink.

"That's just what we need!" said Mugoša and Martinović in chorus. From their relaxed and familiar attitude, I could tell they all knew one another well.

When we were seated at a table knocked together from rough boards, they began discussing the fighting with Germans and Chetniks in several sectors towards Nikšić two days earlier.

"They were testing us, to see if we're strong enough to defend Nikšić," commented the commissar. "Von Löhr is withdrawing all their forces from Greece and Albania, and we're blocking the way. They pressed us so hard our OZNA battalion had to join in the fighting, although we're here for quite another purpose. By agreement with the English, we do the reconnoitring, gather information on the enemy's strength and disposition, their plans of attack, movements, so that the allied planes know where to strike. We get our information by questioning peasants in the surroundings and from captured Chetniks and Germans. Earlier, prisoners were interrogated by the units, but since the formation of OZNA, they hand them over to us. We've got eight Chetniks and four Germans from the latest fighting."

"Who captured the Germans? How did they get separated from the rest?"

"Two of them were brought in single-handed by a fellow called Dima from Cetinje. Until recently he was with another unit, but they sent him over to us on suspicion of being a double agent. Now he's with us as a kind of fighter and suspect at the same time!"

At the mention of Dima, I couldn't help saying that I knew him well, and his Russian parents. We children in Cetinje used to call him Crazy Dima, and people were very surprised when he left to join the Partisans.

The commander, interested, called the guard to bring Dima, to check if he was the person I knew. Ten minutes later, Dima appeared, broad and powerful, his face tanned by the sun. He was still wearing his leather flying suit and the same leather cap, now with a red star on the front. He glanced around at the squad. I saw he hadn't recognised me, so I decided to keep quiet.

"Are you going hunting again tonight, Dima?" asked the commander.

"I think so," he replied seriously. "But the first line of bunkers is now well guarded, so I'll go deeper behind the lines. I'll need to leave earlier, as soon as it gets dark. But I won't be able to bring any prisoners back from there. They'd notice me."

"Do you want anyone to go with you?"

"I don't need anyone, comrade commander. I'm better off by myself."

He offered Dima to sit with us a while, but he refused and remained standing.

"Well, if you won't sit down, you'd better be on your way. Good luck and take care! See you tomorrow morning!"

Dima left, his head held high, as when he entered. Mugoša wanted to know how he had captured the two Germans and what he planned to do that night.

"He's not like the rest. He sits alone all day, not speaking unless spoken to, lost in his own thoughts. But when night falls, Dima comes to life, cleans and checks all his weapons ten times. Somehow he's a different person. Then he goes off without a word to anyone, with an automatic rifle over his shoulder and two knives in his belt. At dawn, here he is again, with a load of German guns and grenades. Sometimes he brings in a German prisoner or two as well."

"How does he manage it?" everyone asked in astonishment.

"God knows! He creeps up close to a bunker like a cat, slits the guard's throat, then bursts in while they're asleep and stabs them to death before they have time to come to their senses. In the narrow bunker, they can't shoot because of the others. It wouldn't help anyway – he's as quick as lightning. That's how he spends his nights. Nobody orders him: he does it off his own bat."

"Maybe he's not a spy, but one of those crazy adventurers," commented Commisar Martinović.

I asked him later what 'avanturist' meant and he explained:

"They're some types from the West who don't know what to do with themselves. They're not communists like us, so they have no cause to fight for. They just get killed for nothing, like that Dima will."

After Mugoša and Martinović had had several minutes' talk apart with the battalion officers, the prisoners were brought to us, two by two, their hands tied. The German soldiers, in uniform but bare-headed, led the way: a pair of tall fair young men no more than twenty, followed by a middle-aged man with a gash not yet healed down one cheek and a younger, very short man. Of the eight Chetniks, only two had beards.

"When you're going to be caught, you cut your hair and shave off your beards!" Mugoša jeered. "Is that so you'll look like gentle lambs? As we all know, a wolf changes its coat, but not its nature."

"Here, take along this civilian as well," said the battalion officer. "Someone brought him in last night from Kotor. They say he's a war profiteer, that he's worked for the occupiers all through the war and got rich."

We escorted the bound prisoners to our truck and helped them climb on board. Only the smallest German refused, pushing roughly against the soldier who offered him a helping hand. He struggled to get on by himself, but the back of the truck was too high for his short legs. Then Janko Durmitorac, the tallest in the squad, stepped forward, grabbed him by the collar with one hand and the seat of his trousers with the other, and tossed him into the truck. The man picked himself up and started shouting threats and curses.

"Listen to that little squirt yelling at us! He reminds me of their Goebbels! We'll see what kind of hero he is when he's standing in front of a firing squad!" said Nikić angrily.

The last prisoner in the column was the 'war profiteer', a plump, balding, older gentleman in a well-cut dark suit.

"I'd be grateful if you would help me up," he said. "It's good we're going to Nikšić. This business will quickly be cleared up when we get there. I'm not an enemy – quite the contrary – I've always been a communist sympathiser, even before the war."

"Fine, fine, you just sit down and later we'll see who and what you are!" replied Nikić, who was in charge.

The thirteen prisoners squatted close together on the floor of the truck while the squad sat around on the benches, machine-guns at the ready.

As soon as the truck moved off, the civilian asked:

"Has anyone perhaps heard of the Riviera Factory in Kotor? It manufactured Merima soap before the war, and produced olive oil with the same brand name."

Nobody answered, so I spoke up:

"I have. Why do you ask?"

"Well, I'm Engineer Vučković, the owner of that factory," he said, addressing me but speaking loud enough for everyone to hear.

"A rotten capitalist!" exclaimed Durmitorac. "Making soap for gentlefolk! Up in the mountains we never saw any of your city soap. Mother used to make ours from pigs that died."

All the way to Nikšić, Engineer Vučković kept assuring us that his arrest had been just a mistake by the three-man Partisan patrol that had picked him up near Kotor on his way to a wedding a couple of days before.

Back at headquarters, the courtyard was full of fresh prisoners brought in during the day. We left ours among them, and Mugoša sent me off to ask Veljko what to do with the civilian. The guard outside his door told me to wait: "Veljko is just now interrogating a well-known criminal."

Soon after a bearded Chetnik, hands bound, was brought out by two members of the Escort Company, and I was shown in.

I quickly told him about Engineer Vučković and asked if he would question him, to see whether there was some mistake, since he seemed to me to be speaking the truth.

Veljko listened, smiled, and said:

"You'll make a good interrogator when you've had a bit of experience. We need the kind who use their heads, think things over, and don't just decide on the spot – though in war you often haven't the time to do otherwise."

Bato Tomašević (front left) with other members of the OZNA Escort Company in liberated Cetinje, December 1944. Front right: Ilija Vuković

After considering a moment, he added:

"In the case of your civilian, since we know nothing about him, we'll wait for a day or two until we get a report from our people in Kotor."

"Where's he going to sleep, Comrade Veljko? He's a civilian and an older man?"

"There's nowhere else but in the courtyard with the others, where it could be wet and windy, or maybe with the Escort Company."

"Shall I tell Commander Mugoša that he can sleep with us?"

"No, I'd better do that. This will be the first time we've had a possible enemy sleeping with the fighters!"

I called Engineer Vučković aside and told him that Comrade Veljko had been very understanding and would personally question him as soon as he found time. In the meanwhile, he could sleep with us in the barracks instead of outside with the rest. Taking this as a sign that he might soon be released, he was greatly cheered and thanked me again and again.

A whole month passed, events succeeded one another with unbelievable speed, but Vučković was still sleeping in the company barracks, where he now seemed quite at home. He was pleasant to everyone, and we had all got used to having him around and standing in line with us for food and a ration of cigarettes, which he too, being a non-smoker, gave to Nikić.

After our evening meal, Ilija and I would sit listening to interesting stories from his eventful life.

"I never got married because I put all my passion into my business, building our factory, making the best soap in Montenegro, and olive oil equal to the finest in Italy. I never had any time for women or marriage."

He told us of his fine house in Kotor, of the many customers from all over the country and abroad who used to visit him before the war, none of them leaving without a gift.

"When the war's over, I promise that the first time you come to stay with me in Kotor, each of you will get the finest Italian bicycle as a gift, though nothing can repay all your kindness to me. If it hadn't been for you, Bato, I would have died from sleeping outside in the yard. Not to mention being taken away by mistake with all those who go off somewhere every evening."

After lights out, while I was dropping off to sleep, my thoughts would dwell lovingly on the Italian bicycle with the silvery mudguard that Italian officers used to ride through the streets of Cetinje. The promise of such a bicycle was one more reason to hope the war would soon be over.

❧

A few days after we brought the thirteen prisoners, Veljko called me to his office:

"Well, Bato, the day of your meeting with Stana has finally come! She's just arrived in Nikšić and she's on her way over here to see you."

So excited I could hardly breathe, I waited for her outside the building. I had not seen Stana for more than three years, since the start of the uprising, and now the minutes seemed like hours. Then she suddenly appeared and ran towards me, arms outstretched, calling: "Bato, little brother!" We kissed and hugged, Stana murmuring words of endearment as she had always done when I was little. Then she held me at arm's length to take a good look:

"You were just a boy when we parted, and now you're a man!" she said with a grin.

With her were several other young women Partisans, among them a couple of her school-friends from Cetinje. Instead of the uniforms and berets of the teacher-training school, they were now, like Stana, smartly turned out in British army jackets with Partisan caps.

Stana first questioned me about Mother. When I said she was at Čevo, she was overjoyed:

"We must bring her here as soon as possible. And there's some more wonderful news: Nada's been found! She's with a medical unit that should be arriving in Nikšić very soon. You see, Bato, we're getting together again. As soon as Mitrovica is liberated, we'll look for Aco."

"And Duško's grave," I added.

At the mention of Duško, Stana's eyes filled with tears:

"I'll never forgive myself for Duško's death, Bato. As long as I live I'll blame myself for not saving him, not helping him get back to Montenegro, to transfer to some Montenegrin unit, as he asked me to. He wanted to be closer to us, to the family. I met him by chance at Drvar. Can you imagine? In the middle of the battle, when we were fighting to save Tito and the Supreme Command from the German paratroopers, I bumped into my own brother. After the enemy were wiped out, Duško and I met up again. He'd survived the battle and there he was, tall and slim, with a machine-gun over his shoulder. I was so proud of him. Then we parted. I didn't ask for him to be transferred, as he wanted. I was ashamed to, afraid people would think I was trying to save my own brother, while other young men were dying all around."

⁊

A month passed with ever increasing danger of Von Löhr's huge forces breaking through in the direction of Nikšić. The townspeople were in a real panic. Veljko informed us that the town might fall any day, so it was essential to pack up all important documents to take with us, and burn the rest. All the prisoners we were holding would have to be interrogated. Those who were young and had committed no serious crimes should be released, and the others shot, since we would be unable to take any of them with us.

The next few days Ilija and I with other members of the company spent all our time escorting Germans, Chetniks and civilians to be questioned and then back to the prison, the same building in which Partisan-family hostages had been held before the liberation of Nikšić. From there they were either released or taken for execution to a small level stretch of ground behind the prison wall. One afternoon we took a group of German prisoners there.

"Well, krauts, you're getting a taste of your own medicine now," said one of the squad as he made ready to fire. "This is how our sick and wounded felt when you shot them in cold blood."

The German soldiers gazed steadily into the gun barrels, without a word of protest, resigned to their fate. One of them, an extremely short man, I recognised as the soldier captured by Dima who had protested when getting into our truck. At the command: "Take aim!" the small one, drawn up to his full height, raised his arm in the Nazi salute and shouted: "Heil Hitler!" just before the command: "Fire!"

"A midget he may have been, but he had balls enough for two big men!" someone commented.

⁊

Then, unexpectedly, my squad was assigned a completely different task: to wait for British aircraft that had begun making night flights from

Marshal Tito with Brigadier Fitzroy Maclean, Chief of the British Military Mission (centre), and RAF Air Vice Marshal Elliot at Bari airport when returning from a meeting with Prime Minister Winston Churchill in August 1944

Bari, bringing weapons, food and wounded Partisans who had been treated in British military hospitals in southern Italy. The planes landed at an improvised airfield – just a stretch of flat ground between Nikšić and Danilovgrad. It was our duty by day to gather and cut enough wood to build a dozen bonfires around the edge of the landing strip. About midnight, as soon as we heard the sound of engines, we lit the fires and waited for the heavy British transport planes to touch down with a deafening roar between the lines of beacons. When they came to a stop, drawn up to attention in front of the cabin, we waited impatiently for the door to open so we could welcome the crew with a clenched-fist salute and the greeting: "*Smrt fašizmu!*" ["Death to fascism!"].

The British crews grinned and waved energetically, thankful they had once more crossed the Adriatic and landed safely. When they set foot on the ground, we would dash over and offer them some strong *loza* in Italian metal flasks. They took a swig from these, coughed, and, wreathed in smiles, shook hands warmly all round.

Then the Partisans recovered from their wounds would begin to descend from the plane, dressed in new British khaki uniforms, with long greatcoats. They were a mixed bunch, from teenage boys and girls to older men with greying moustaches. Before dawn, Partisan messengers would arrive with sturdy mountain ponies to take them back to their units.

One night, by the flickering firelight, I recognised Duško's great friend Mošo among the wounded leaving the plane. His head was bandaged and he was leaning on a stick. The thought flashed through my mind that my brother might be with him, that Father had been misinformed, so when I ran over to him my first words were to ask for Duško.

"He stayed behind in Italy, Bato. In Colfiorito, where we were in the prison camp. When we got out of the camp, he wanted to come with us, but he was too weak and ill, coughing up blood. The local doctor and his wife took him in, to look after him. I got away and walked all the way to Yugoslavia, I can't tell you how, and then all the way south to a village near Cetinje. It was just my luck the Germans bombarded the village that very night, and I was wounded in the head and the leg."

We spent the rest of the night talking. I told him Duško's story, as much as I knew of it at that time, and for a while he couldn't speak for grief. Then he recounted some of his narrow escapes on the walk of fifteen hundred kilometres from Colfiorito to the Cetinje area, his capture by the Germans after he was wounded, his escape from Cetinje hospital with the help of a friendly nurse before they had time to interrogate and shoot him. That was how he managed to rejoin the Partisans. Afterwards he was flown back to Italy for medical treatment.

Mošo then asked for all the news I had of Cetinje. Most of all he wanted to hear about the hanging of Gojko Kruška, his bravery in the face of death.

"Look after yourself, Bato," he said when it was time for him to go. "Let's hope we'll meet again soon in Cetinje, when we'll have all the time in the world to talk. Only Cetinje will never be the same again without Duško, Gojko and all the other wonderful friends. Never again, Bato, at least for me!"

After we'd been at the landing strip about two weeks, sleeping in tents when not on duty, we were sent back to Nikšić. We heard that our forces had launched a counter-offensive and the town was no longer under threat.

❧

On arrival, we found the courtyard of OZNA headquarters empty: no German prisoners or Chetniks. When we went into the barracks, the rest of the company jumped up to greet and question us. Ilija and I made our way to the end of the long room where we had left our beds and Vučković. There was no sign of him or his mattress.

"Where's Vučković? Has he gone back to Kotor?" I asked.

"No, he wasn't released. We shot him!" said one of the company who always volunteered when a firing squad was needed.

"Why?" we both cried, shocked.

"Veljko agreed he should stay with us until a report came from Kotor," I protested.

"Well, you see, Bato, the report never came," intervened Commissar Martinović in a quiet, serious voice. "And when it looked like we'd have to get out of town in a hurry before the Germans arrived, Vučković was taken out with some others who probably hadn't done much wrong either. Another one was that Russian of yours from Cetinje, Crazy Dima, who used to attack German bunkers all alone at night. He was handed over to us for questioning. He stood there without blinking, as though it had nothing to do with him. Only, just before the squad fired, he shouted: 'Long live the great Emperor of Mother Russia!' As you know, they suspected him of being a double agent. From what he shouted you can see that, after all, he really was an enemy and counter-revolutionary."

That night I couldn't sleep for thinking about kind, harmless Vučković and Dima, who had remained crazy to the last. When I finally dropped off, I dreamt that the war was over and Dima and I were having a race in Cetinje: Dima on his motorcycle and I on a new silvery Italian bicycle given me by that fine gentleman, Mr Vučković of Kotor. Dima's motor kept choking and letting out clouds of smoke so it could hardly go, while my bicycle glided forward soundlessly at great speed, carrying me to the winning post. Then I woke up and realised there was no longer any motorcycle or bicycle…

❧

The old road from Kotor to Cetinje with its hair-raising serpentine bends

On 20 October 1944, guns suddenly started blazing all over Nikšić. We grabbed our weapons and dashed outside, thinking the Germans had unexpectedly broken through and there was fighting in the streets. To our astonishment, we saw Veljko and other officers standing at the open windows, laughing and firing their revolvers into the air. They shouted down to us in the courtyard: "Belgrade's fallen! Liberated! The Red Army and Partisans joined up near Belgrade. Victory is at hand!"

Overjoyed, we danced around the yard, hugging each other and letting off our own guns.

Events now followed one another rapidly. Under pressure from Partisan forces, the German army withdrew from Montenegro. Town after town passed into Partisan hands.

One morning Mugoša ordered the company to assemble in the yard. We lined up expectantly: almost daily we were kept informed of the latest important and exciting news from battlefronts in the country and in Europe. Then Veljko appeared and announced that next day the company would be leaving Nikšić for Dubrovnik, then on to Kotor and Cetinje:

"All these places have been in our hands since a few days ago. Now we're a regular army, not outlaws. But be very careful, comrades, when we enter Dubrovnik tomorrow, not to let off your rifles or cause any damage, for Dubrovnik is a museum of a city, famous around the world."

He also said we should take extra care to be smartly turned out and well-behaved, so the people of this ancient city wouldn't think we were wild men from the hills.

In Dubrovnik we found the Partisan liberators of the city singing and dancing in the main street, the famous Stradun, with the local people in an atmosphere of joyful festivity. These scenes were repeated in the old walled city of Kotor, where we stopped only briefly before boarding two British army trucks. Slowly we began climbing the dangerous serpentine road leading from the Gulf of Kotor up the steep mountainside towards Cetinje. The trucks were driven by two fighters who had been through an army 'crash course' to learn to drive. The sons of Montenegrin goatherds, they were completely ignorant about machines and technical matters: all they knew was how to turn on the engine, press the accelerator and hold the steering wheel. Everything else was left to providence.

We had laboriously negotiated only half a dozen of the sharp bends when the front truck stalled and stopped. The driver lifted the bonnet and a crowd of us gazed with curiosity at the engine, never having seen its like before. Nobody had the least idea what to do.

"We should have kept those Englishmen who brought the trucks, got them to drive us to Cetinje," said Nikić, looking worried.

"Better if we'd got Russian trucks; they wouldn't have stopped!" Commissar Martinović commented. "Capitalist trucks can't compare with Soviet ones."

When we were losing hope of continuing our journey, Mugoša, who knew a bit more about motor vehicles than the rest, shouted to the driver:

"Hey, pal, have you any fuel in the tank?"

The driver checked and then declared, almost proudly:

"I'll be darned, there isn't a drop!"

"Well, comrade, let me tell you something," said Mugoša. "Even Soviet trucks won't go without fuel, let alone capitalist ones!"

Petrol was poured into the empty tank and the trucks crawled on up the steep, narrow road on the Kotor side on the mountain. As our inexperienced drivers braked abruptly on each bend, most of the fighters, unused to this kind of travel, looked both sick and scared. When they started throwing up, a number of them jumped out and declared their intention of getting to the summit on foot, taking short-cuts: "We'll wait for you at the top!"

After picking them up, we drove on to Njeguši, a village of a score of thatched stone houses, from which originated the Petrović family, rulers of Montenegro from 1696 to 1918. It is from this place, where he was born, that the country's greatest poet, Vladika Petar Petrović, is known as Njegoš.

⁊⟪

When I caught sight of Lovćen with its little chapel, I was as excited as when we first arrived in Cetinje after Father's 'wanderings in the wilderness'. It felt like coming home. Soon I would see Olga and Mila, Rajko and Raco… Wouldn't they be mightily surprised to see me! The Escort Company, recovered from the serpentines, began singing songs about Lovćen, one after the other, until we reached the outskirts of town. As we drove in, I saw that the unfinished high school, used as barracks by the Italians and then the Germans, was now empty. In the distance I could make out the government apartments. How I wished Olga would look out of her window and see me in uniform! As the truck passed our house, I wondered if Mila was up there at that little dormer window. But there was no sign of either of them.

When we stopped, Mugoša's powerful voice boomed out:

"Here we are, comrades. That fine house over there will be OZNA's headquarters and we'll be sleeping in the courtyard building." He was pointing to the 'French Legation', which the French had supposedly built by mistake in Cetinje instead of Cairo.

As soon as I'd left my kit, dusted myself down and tidied my hair, which I had started combing upwards so as to look more grown-up, I ran to our house, only a couple of hundred metres away. I rushed upstairs and tried the door, but it was locked: Mila must have gone out, perhaps to her girlfriend's house. I next tried Rajko's. He opened the door and his mouth dropped open:

"Mother, come and see who's here. You won't believe your eyes!"

They both hugged me, looked me up and down and bombarded me with questions.

"This is a great day for us," said Rajko's mother. "Now we need Petar, Milica and the others to come home, and we'll all be good neighbours again, as we used to be…

"When the Partisans were entering Cetinje, my husband got frightened and fled, even though he never did anybody any harm. Now we don't know where he is, or whether he'll ever come back alive. I'm afraid he won't, because we heard that the Partisans shot some people they caught running away. A lot of people got out of town at that time, all those who weren't on your side, though many of them weren't against you either."

When Rajko and I were alone, I asked him at once about Mila and Olga. He hesitated a moment, and then blurted out:

"Your Mila ran away and got killed, without any need."

Horrified by this news, I asked how it had happened.

"When the Partisans were coming close, the Germans drove off in their trucks, a great long column of them, towards Rijeka Crnojevića and Podgorica – that was the only road still in their hands. At the back of the column, there were two trucks packed with people who wanted to leave, some of them with good reason, some with no reason at all. My father and Mila were among them. We heard afterwards, from someone from Rijeka Crnojevića, that the truck stopped there, by the market, for fuel and when it started off again with a jerk, somehow poor Mila fell out and hit her head on the curb. They left her there to die by the roadside. There was no-one even to bury her. They say some Gypsy took her body away on his cart."

"And Olga? Is she alright?" I asked, shaken by this story.

"A lot's been going on here in the last few days, Bato. The same day they entered Cetinje, the Partisans went around houses with a list and picked up twenty-five people, took them to Donje Polje and shot them. Olga's father and mother were in that group. Some people came and carried away their things, even that piano, though what good it'll do them, except for firewood, heaven only knows. Olga went off with one of her father's relatives. Nobody knows where. They say her mother never stopped screaming all the way to the execution ground."

The shocking news of Mila and of Olga's parents left me speechless. After a while I asked him to let me know if he heard anything of Olga, and to come and see me at the French Legation where I was staying.

"What are you going to do with your house? Why don't you stay there, so you're nearby?" Rajko asked.

"We shan't do anything with it. The house isn't ours: it belonged to the lawyer Nikola Rolović who was stabbed in the back at the start of the war. Anyway, there's nothing of value in it. All we had that was worth anything we exchanged for flour and oil. They took Duško off to prison from that flat, and Nada too. We'll never go back to live there!"

Rajko listened gravely, with sadness in his eyes, as though he realised that this was the end of our childhood companionship, the parting of our ways.

⁊⁊

From Rajko's I ran off to see Mara. She hugged me, with tears in her eyes, and excitedly called Milovan, who was playing in the street. Recognising me at once, even in my uniform, he threw himself upon me and wouldn't leave my side. I looked around the tidy room, noticing the freshly whitewashed walls. Mara, too, looked neat in a new black dress.

"I want everything to be just-so when Bogdan's comrades come, so they see I haven't neglected myself and Milovan or the house," she smiled, guessing my thoughts.

Then she recounted with pride how the Partisans had attacked Cetinje one night and that next morning red flags were flying from all the main buildings: "Everyone came out into the streets to cheer them. I thought I'd die of happiness. The young people danced the Montenegrin *kolo* in the market-place. They leapt up so high they touched the branches of that linden tree on which Gojko Kruška and the Albanian messenger were hanged, side by side. The traitors who did that tried to run away with the Germans, but luckily our fighters intercepted the trucks near Podgorica and killed a lot of them, together with the Germans. But Vlado Kokotan, the worst of them all, and some of his murderous lot just vanished."

"I was told twenty-five people have been executed here in Cetinje. Did all of them deserve it?" I asked.

"I reckon they did, all of them! Among them was that Father Vukmanović whose house you lived in for a while. Who knows what came over him to turn Chetnik. They say his brother Svetozar is with Tito, a member of the Supreme Command. I don't know who, in fact, drew up the list: probably not Cetinje people but those from the villages around. Fifty-seven of our fighters, mostly from Cetinje, died liberating the town."

⚹

From Mara's I went in search of Raco. I had never been to where he lived and didn't even know exactly where it was. His father may have wanted it that way, to protect his son from some vendetta. We had always hung around in the high-school yard together with Pušo, whose family lived on the top floor of the school building, so now I ran up the stairs to find Pušo. When I knocked, the door opened to reveal several men and women wearing mourning sitting around a table. Seeing me in uniform with my machine-gun over my shoulder, they stood up quickly, as though afraid. Pušo's mother, who had always been very nice to me, came forward:

"Come in, Bato, come in. You're not to blame!"

"What's happened?" I asked, bewildered.

At that moment Pušo appeared with a black ribbon in the button-hole of his jacket.

"The Partisans shot Father," he said in a trembling voice. "Let's go out in the yard."

"I'm so sorry! I just wanted to surprise you with my uniform and machine-gun!"

I tried to explain and apologise in one.

"Never mind! You always belonged to their movement. But as long as I live, I'll never understand why they killed Father. All he did was try to make kids to go to school, keep out of trouble, and not get mixed up in politics while the war was on. And for that they called him a collaborator and shot him."

After a while Pušo cheered up a bit:

"I'm glad you've come to see me, Bato. Though we belonged to different camps, we never quarrelled because of that; it never spoilt our friendship. You've won, but people say the British won't allow communists in the middle of Europe for very long. They'll turn against you and drive you out of power. The Greens will be called back to take over Montenegro, and the Chetniks the rest of Yugoslavia, under King Peter."

"Don't you believe it! There's no power on earth that can budge the Partisans now. Hitler couldn't do it with his SS, all his tanks and planes and guns. Who's going to stop us when we have an army of nearly one million? And anyway, the Russians wouldn't leave us in the lurch. They're stronger than all the rest of the world put together. Better not let anyone hear you talking like that, Pušo, or you might land in trouble."

"There we go, Bato, talking politics again! We Montenegrins are an accursed race. We can't carry on a conversation about anything except politics, even though it may cost us our lives."

Before I left, I asked him about Raco, but he hadn't seen or heard anything of him for several weeks.

❧

On my way back to the company, I bumped into Dr Gerasimović.

"Good afternoon, Doctor. You've probably forgotten me. I'm Petar Tomašević's son. You treated me when I was very ill a couple of years ago."

"Of course I remember you," said the doctor, looking pleased to see me. "But what's a boy of your age doing in the army?"

Instead of answering, I told him:

"I met your son Dima on the frontline towards Podgorica not long ago. His comrades told me he was a real hero, going into enemy bunkers at night and capturing Germans single-handed."

The doctor's face lit up. I didn't, couldn't, tell him the rest of the story, of his son's sad fate.

"That's wonderful news, wonderful that you've seen my Dima, that he's alive!" He could hardly speak from excitement. "His poor mother spends days and nights on her knees, praying for his safe return from the battlefield. When I tell her that you've seen Dima, that he'll soon be home with us again, she'll stop grieving and be happy once more, just like when Dima was with us. Thank you a thousand times, dear boy, for this marvellous news."

The next month or two were spent in Cetinje, standing guard in front of the French Legation and maintaining security at large public meetings, sessions of the newly-formed Montenegrin Government, and theatre performances. Wherever I appeared, my school friends and the kids from the street gazed at me with admiration and envy. Everyone wanted to be in my company, to be seen with me. During the early evening *korzo*, which was crowded with strollers once more, I noticed the girls of my age looking at me with interest. All this made me extraordinarily happy, proud and pleased with myself. It was a wonderful, indescribable feeling, after all the suffering and fear, the sacrifices and risks, to return as a victor, to be on the winning side that the whole world acclaimed as heroes and the only real force of resistance in occupied Europe. I seemed to be walking on air, floating in the clouds, borne up by the thought that I had not let down Grandpa Filip, Father and Duško, that I, too, had contributed to the family's honour and reputation.

One night I was on guard duty at the entrance of OZNA headquarters. Veljko and the other officer-interrogators were working late as usual, trying to keep up with the files piling up on their desks. Since the whole of Montenegro was now liberated, they had a huge number of cases to deal with. In the prison where they had held Father and so many others, there were a lot of Chetniks and a few Germans. Our company no longer had to escort prisoners as we had at Nikšić: that was now the duty of a separate prison service. Our new state was gradually taking shape.

Some time after midnight, I was called to Veljko's office.

"I'm going to tell you something, Bato, that nobody else must know for the time being. In a few days I'll be leaving with Mugoša for Belgrade, where there's a lot of work waiting for us. We have to travel through Albania and Macedonia, since this is the only road to Belgrade open at the moment. Do you want to come with us, or would you rather stay in Cetinje? The fighting here is over, so you could catch up on your schooling."

Without hesitation I said I would rather go with him.

"Fine, if that's what you want," he said. "Mugoša has to select a squad of ten to come with us part of the way, stay for a while in Albania, and afterwards join us in Belgrade. The Albanian Partisans are forming their own OZNA, modelled on ours, and the squad may be able to help with this. There are several of our instructors already there. The Albanian comrades are now our great friends: we have the same programme, the same ideals. For now, don't mention Belgrade even to your great pal Ilija. When he hears you're leaving, just say you're going to fight in Albania.

❦

The news that popular Veljko was to leave for Belgrade shortly cast a gloom over the Escort Company. They guessed this meant that the unit would change and its members would gradually disperse, returning to their homes, since the fighting in Montenegro was over. They wondered whether they would find their houses burnt and families scattered, whether they could ever be happy there again, living as they had done before the war.

One snowy morning in December 1944, I hurried out to say goodbye to Rajko, Mara and Pušo: I was due to leave Cetinje with the chosen squad at noon. The first person I met in the street was Rajko, on his way to see me:

"Bato, hurry! I've found Olga. I was passing the cake shop this morning, and there she was, washing the window."

Without waiting to hear more, I rushed off. I knew the cake shop well because Father used to take us children there as a treat once a month when he got his salary. When I came near I stopped: there was Olga in her mother's winter coat polishing the large plate-glass display window.

"Olga!" I called. "What are you doing here?"

Instead of replying, when she saw me she began to cry. She was taller and thinner than before, and dejected looking, nothing like that pampered, protected little girl in the white fur coat who had been sledging when I went searching for Duško. My heart thumping, I was too confused to say anything. After a while she wiped away her tears and smiled. Now she was much prettier, more like her old self.

"You ask what I'm doing? I'm the cleaner here. And what about you? Why did you go off without saying goodbye? Anyway, it's good you're back again."

"I'm afraid I have to leave for Albania this afternoon, but I'll be back soon."

This was the first time I caught myself lying. Until then I'd always told the truth – except to the enemy. But now I looked straight into her tearful eyes and told a lie. Perhaps it was because I didn't want to hurt her; perhaps because I hoped she would keep thinking about me, counting on my return, and we could postpone our love until after the war.

"But you've only just come! Why can't you stay in Cetinje?" she said, her face clouding over.

I explained that though Montenegro was liberated, other parts of the country were still occupied.

"Isn't Montenegro big enough for you? You'll never come back, never, I know that," and again tears trickled down her pale cheeks.

When I left her, I told myself that the Revolution was more important than love, that I must stick by my comrades till the end.

❧

At noon we said farewell to the rest of the Escort Company who were staying behind. The saddest moment for me was parting from Ilija, who like myself had heard a few months before that his elder brother had been killed.

"You've been like a brother to me, Bato, like the one I've lost. I know you're going to Belgrade, and leaving me here." He had tears in his eyes.

Then the squad piled into one of the trucks that had brought us to Cetinje and set off for Albania. This time we had a more experienced driver: Avdo, a Moslem from Podgorica mobilised when the Partisans liberated the town, who had owned a truck before the war. Leaving Cetinje, the truck passed the house at Black Rock from which the Italians had ejected us, and I remembered Uncle Mihajlo and his family. I was glad we would be stopping in Podgorica for an hour or two: I hoped I could see Aunt Vasilija, Dragica and Dragan. I didn't know where they lived, but I could ask our relative, the lady photographer Slavka, with whom we had spent the night on the way from Nova Varoš to Cetinje.

We stopped for a break at Rijeka Crnojevića, which was decked with flags, fluttering in the wind even from houses burnt in the fighting to liberate it. There was no-one about: in winter the few inhabitants retired to their homes early. I wandered along the pavement by the market, hoping somehow to find the place where Mila had struck her head on the curb, as though there might be a plaque marking the spot. I remembered her words of reproach as Mother and I were leaving: "You've got somewhere to run to, but there's nowhere for me to hide."

As we drove on to Podgorica, I began thinking about Olga again, wondering why I hadn't stayed behind in Cetinje – I could easily have told Veljko I'd changed my mind. I could have helped Olga get over the loss of her parents and find a better job. If she was with me, people would have overlooked the fact that she was the daughter of a collaborator. So why had I left? There could be only one answer: I was part of a mighty movement, a great rushing river that was carrying everything before it, sweeping me along with a power far greater than any sentimental personal feelings, bearing me towards the new and unknown.

In Podgorica we found devastation. Almost nothing but ruins and bomb craters was left of the small town I'd visited five years before. Looking for the sign 'Photographer's Studio', with a heavy heart I made my way among heaps of stones and scattered household possessions in the area near the river where Slavka lived, I remembered. Here and there, an isolated house – its walls cracked, window-panes broken – was still standing. By a miraculous chance, one of these houses was Slavka's. When she opened the door, she didn't recognise me in uniform and fully armed.

"Slavka! It's me, Bato! I came to see if you're alive!"

She gave a shriek of delight, pulled me inside and started questioning me about all the family. Then it was my turn to ask about Aunt Vasilija and my cousins. Slavka paused for a moment, as though trying to find the right words, then simply said:

"Vasilija and Dragica were killed, and Dragan left town with the Chetniks. It was in the bombing by our allies, the Americans, damn them! I don't think they got more than a handful of Germans, but hundreds and hundreds of our people were killed, women and children. And those who survived aren't fit for anything, either crippled or half out of their minds. Anyone would be, after what we went through for a whole month, with bombs raining down on us all day. Vasilija and Dragica were killed the very first day of the bombing. In a way it was a mercy; better than if they'd lived through all that and then died in the end. Dragan was saved because he was playing chess in the park at the time. When he ran home, as soon as the bombers passed over, all he found was the house in ruins and the scattered remains of his mother and sister. Poor Dragan somehow found two sacks and collected them up for burial, bit by bit, as best he could. Then he carried them in turn to the cemetery, dug a grave and buried them together. Afterwards he came hurrying over to see whether I'd survived the bombing. I gave him some water to wash as he was covered in blood and a glass of *loza*. He said he was leaving Podgorica that very moment and never coming back. He wanted, above all else, to find his father, if he was still alive, so he was going to join the Chetniks.

"That was the last I saw of Dragan. When I think of him, not yet seventeen, wandering all alone in the wilds, my heart bleeds. That's what this damned war had brought us to, Bato: families and friends divided – you in the Partisans, Dragan with the Chetniks. But both of you will always be equally dear to me, wherever you are. Let me take a photo of you, Bato, in your fine uniform. I'm only sorry I didn't photograph Dragan before he left."

꧁

From Podgorica to the Albanian frontier, a distance of some twenty kilometres, the road runs through the fertile Zeta valley as far as Lake

Skadar [Shkodra]. Several Albanian fighters waiting for us at the border greeted us with the clenched-fist salute. Then they shook hands warmly and looked admiringly at out British uniforms and new weapons. They were still dressed as we had been earlier, in a mixture of peasant and town clothes, and armed with the old types of Italian weapons we had discarded after the Allies began supplying us. It turned out that their interpreter had failed to appear, and so we had no means of communicating. In desperation, Nikić asked if any of us could speak a bit of Albanian.

"We're all from the other side of Durmitor," said one of the squad. "Anyway, you don't expect a Montenegrin to learn Albanian, do you?"

"I know a word or two," I admitted. "We lived in Kosovo when I was small."

As our truck bounced along the dusty road towards the town of Skhodra, I searched my brain for Albanian words and expressions. I wished our Albanian comrades good morning, asked them how they were, what they were called, how old they were, how many children they had – in short, all the usual courtesy questions I'd heard or used as a child. Delighted with this, they shook my hand again, laughed and slapped me on the back. Then they started talking all together, plying me with questions I couldn't understand. Instead of answering, all I could do, using my limited vocabulary, was to tell them the name and age of each of the squad, that we were from Montenegro, that we were not hungry – anything I could think of to fill up the time.

"Just listen to that Bato!" Nikić exclaimed, much impressed by this nonsensical conversation. "Whatever they ask he knows the answer. You see what it is to be a learned city boy, not ignorant peasants like us!" To my great relief, at Shkodra a proper interpreter was waiting who knew Serbian better than I did. This was Murat, a teacher of Serbian, whose Montenegrin ancestors had converted to Islam during Turkish rule.

"Welcome, Montenegrin comrades, to democratic Albania!" he greeted us. "First we'll have something to eat in the headquarters canteen, then we'll take you to the houses where you'll be sleeping. We'll stay two days in Shkodra and then go on to Tirana and other places."

After a meal of boiled mutton and bread, Murat, carrying a flash-lamp, led us through dark, unpaved streets to the homes of people who had been ordered to put us up. At the first house, Murat banged loudly on the heavy wooden double doors with massive iron locks. When the head of the household appeared, holding a paraffin lamp, the two of them had a lengthy conversation before one of our number was ushered inside. As we walked to the next house, I asked Murat why they'd talked so long.

"It's wartime and you never know what ideas people may get. Some-one may take a fancy to your nice uniform and your new weapons. That's why I have to tell each householder that he is personally respon-sible for his guest. If anything bad happens to you, God forbid, his family will be broken up and his house burnt down. That way, he'll take better care of you than we could!"

I was the last to be billeted. The large house, obviously belonging to someone well-to-do, perhaps a merchant, was divided into two parts: left for the men and right for the women. My host led me into a spa-cious room with rugs on the walls, a heavy wooden bed, also covered with kilims, and a small table in the corner with a wash-basin and jug. Beside it hung a white linen towel with an embroidered border. To be on the safe side, since I couldn't lock the door, I put my machine-gun under my pillow.

For the first time in my life in a foreign country, and in an Albanian house, I slept very lightly, woken by every creaking sound and by every dog that barked in the neighbourhood. As I lay in the dark, I wondered what it was like, that city for which King Nikola had sacrificed ten thou-sand Montenegrins, one third of his army, in the First Balkan War.

Murat spent most of the next morning gathering together our scat-tered squad, since some had overslept. Finally Nikić got us all into line and marched us to headquarters. This part, Murat told us, was just a suburb of Shkodra, where the houses were crooked and the streets muddy. The centre was quite different, for after annexing the country the Italians had built up the city so as to show people that life was better under their occupation.

The appearance of Montenegrin Partisans in the streets caused something of a stir. Children followed us in droves until Murat managed to shoo them off. At the city headquarters we were given a festive welcome: an archway decorated with embroidered towels and flowers and a huge banner with the words: 'Long Live the Partisans of Montenegro and Albania!' In a large room a long table was laid out with an abundance and variety of food seen in Montenegro only at pre-war weddings. Was it possible, I wondered, that in Albania they were eating all this wonderful food during the war while we were on the edge of starvation? But, of course, we had been under the harshest occupation regime, while here the Italians had been paving the streets, filling the shops with goods. They had considered the country part of Italy ever since that day in 1939 when we had watched our soldiers in Nova Varoš travelling on ox-carts to the frontier, ready to go to war over the loss of political influence in Albania.

After the speeches of welcome, the squad couldn't wait to get stuck in to this feast, but Murat warned us that it was the height of bad manners to start before the host. All our eyes now turned to the local commander sitting at the head of the table, looking pleased with himself and not at all hungry. Nikić resorted to cunning:

"Our Albanian comrades were lucky to have such an abundance of food: they didn't have to fight on empty stomachs, as we did in Montenegro."

When Murat translated this, our host got the message, smiled, and took a mouthful of bread dipped in salt. Without more ado, the squad fell on the food like a swarm of locusts, stuffing sweet and savoury together into their mouths, until only empty plates were left on the table. Our hosts watched this with a kind of fascination.

We left headquarters with full stomachs and high spirits to walk to the centre of town, passing neat, whitewashed Turkish-style houses with overhanging upper storeys. The shops were full of goods of all kinds, some displayed in the street on wooden counters; the shopkeepers were standing in doorways crying their wares; women in the streets were wearing make-up, silk stockings and high-heeled shoes. I was amazed at how different everything was from just across the border in Montenegro.

As it was a market day, Murat took us to the main market place. We could hardly push our way through the dense crowd of shoppers and the vendors offering soft drinks and oriental sweetmeats, which they carried on trays balanced on their heads or hung round their necks. Suddenly, in the midst of the crowd I caught sight of a familiar figure: an older man with a white beard parted in the middle. He was carrying a tray of doughnuts and shouting to attract customers like the other vendors. Unable to believe my eyes, I went closer. Yes, it really was Professor Grabovski, the Russian mathematics teacher who had prepared me for the high-school entrance exam.

"Professor! Professor Grabovski!" I shouted and starting pushing my way through the crowd. Hearing his name, the old teacher looked around. Seeing an armed Partisan heading in his direction, he dropped his tray of doughnuts and fled. In a moment he was lost to sight in the crush.

Nikić, who happened to be beside me, asked with interest:

"Who was that old fellow you just frightened to death?"

When I told him he burst out laughing:

"Even I would have been scared, seeing you coming at me with a machine-gun, let alone some old teacher. The poor fellow must think OZNA sent us here specially to hunt him down. He'll spend the rest of his life on the run! After escaping from the Russian Revolution, I don't suppose he wants to lose his grey beard in another one."

The rest of the day I thought about Professor Grabovski, who must have fled from Cetinje out of fear of the Partisans. I bitterly regretted frightening my teacher and kept hoping I might see him again, to assure him that he was in no danger, that he could freely return to Cetinje, for the time of executions had in any case passed.

While we were taken back to the same houses to sleep, I asked Murat if he knew a young man from Shkodra called Musa Buta. I explained that he had been captured as a Partisan messenger and publicly hanged in Cetinje. His family might not know of his fate, and I could tell them how he had died.

"I've never heard of him," said Murat, "but, in any case, better not to look for the family. Let them believe he is still alive; leave them something to hope for."

I said nothing more, but I was sure that one day they would long to know where, when and how their Musa had lost his life.

⚜

Early next morning we piled into our truck and Avdo, the driver, turned the crankshaft, which was needed to start the engine in cold weather. With a great deal of spluttering and banging, amidst clouds of exhaust fumes we set off for Tirana. I felt I was beginning a real journey into the unknown – I didn't count Shkodra since I had heard talk of it from earliest childhood and it was somehow familiar.

It was night when we reached the Albanian capital. Murat led us into a school, where we were to sleep all together in a large classroom. Tired out by the long journey, on which we had been stopped many times at military check-points, we quickly fell asleep, fully dressed, on straw mattresses on the classroom floor.

Next morning we got up early, eager to see the city, but Murat kept delaying our departure, telling us not to hurry, to get ourselves spruced up, to wait a little longer… Around midday, two Albanian Partisans, armed to the teeth, suddenly burst into the classroom and stood to attention on either side of the door. They kept glancing down the corridor in the direction of the entrance. A few minutes later, surrounded by bodyguards, the Albanian Supreme Commander, Enver Hoxha, and his wife appeared. We recognised him at once from the large photographs we'd seen in various places in Shkodra. Amazed and confused by his unexpected appearance in our midst, we quickly got ourselves into line and stood to attention. With a smile he motioned us to stand at ease.

Before we left for Albania, Veljko had briefed us about him: he was thirty-two, a 'French scholar' who had been dismissed from a diplomatic post in Belgium because of his pro-Soviet sympathies and had then taught French in some Albanian town. Veljko said he was important for us because he was the founder of the Albanian Communist Party, which now worked closely with our party on the same ideological platform.

Slim and youthful in his well-cut uniform, his thick, dark hair brushed back and brilliantined, he looked more like one of the smart Italian officers who had eyed the girls in Cetinje in the early days of the occupation than one of our own weather-beaten commanders. His young and pretty wife also seemed to us too elegantly dressed for a Partisan.

He spoke for a while to Murat, who then translated:

"Comrade Enver Hoxha welcomes you, his Montenegrin comrades who have come to fight in Albania. United, we'll defeat the enemy more easily, and after the war we shall live together in a community of brotherly states…"

At the words "fight in Albania", I noticed Nikić's expression change.

"…Now these comrades from our OZNA will show you around the city," Murat continued, "and Comrade Enver and his wife would like to take Bato home to offer their hospitality to Comrade Stana's brother."

"Tell Enver that Veljko needs us urgently in Belgrade, so we can't stay to fight in Albania," Nikić whispered to me as he was leaving.

"I will, Nikić. You can be sure of that," I whispered back, feeling slightly ashamed that I was being treated differently from the rest because of my sister, and also quite nervous about spending the day with the Albanian leader.

❧

When the others had gone, Enver Hoxha and his wife, Namxia, came over and embraced me, then conducted me outside. As we appeared, the crowd gathered in the street cheered and clapped their leader, who waved back. The gleaming black limousine waiting for us reminded me of the one General Pirzio Birolli used to drive around in. Murat and one of the guards got in the front beside the chauffeur, while I sat between the Hoxhas in the middle of the spacious back seat. Several more guards, armed with machine-guns, followed us in an open car. I could hardly believe that I was riding around in such state and in such exalted company. As we glided almost noiselessly along broad boulevards flanked by tall, handsome buildings, the Hoxhas pointed out the more important ones. I exclaimed at the width of the avenues – several times that of Cetinje's main street.

"The Italians built these for us," Hoxha responded with a smile. "They thought Albania would always be theirs."

Several guards were waiting for us in front of the building where they lived. Through a big iron gate we entered a large courtyard enclosed by a high wall and climbed a flight of wooden steps to the first floor. The large sitting room had divans around the walls and colourful rugs covering the floor. Enver Hoxha took off his holster belt, placing the revolver on the floor by his side, unbuttoned his tunic, and leant back comfortably amongst the divan cushions, telling me, through Murat, to make myself at home. His wife went off to the kitchen and soon reappeared carrying a large tray with Turkish coffee – real, aromatic coffee, a jug of brownish sherbet and a plate of still warm baklava.

When we were all served, my hosts started questioning me about Stana, who was evidently well known in Albania.

"My great wish is to make her acquaintance as soon as possible," Namxia declared. "I hope we shall meet shortly at some youth conference in Montenegro or Albania. Like Stana, I'm particularly concerned with the youth movement."

"Our Montenegrin comrades have always served as examples to us," Enver Hoxha added.

Then the Hoxhas talked for a long time about meetings with these comrades in the course of their clandestine party work, Murat translating. I soon felt quite at ease, for both were very natural, pleasant and attentive, listening to what I had to say and asking my opinion. There seemed to be the same spirit of comradeship in Albania as at home, where all were treated as equals, regardless of age.

Enver then asked about the situation in Montenegro, Comrade Veljko and the activities of OZNA. I replied as best I could, and he commented:

"We in Albania also have enemies from the old regime that we must quickly eliminate, so they can't hamper the building of our new society."

At this point he turned to Murat and talked for quite a while. Murat translated:

"Comrade Hoxha would like you to stay with him until the end of the war, and the rest of the squad could stay too. They would serve as a good link with Montenegro. Comrade Hoxha admires their height and strength, as though they're carved out of oak."

This offer took me completely by surprise, but I realised I had to do my best to reject it without giving offence. I remembered what Nikić had whispered and, choosing my words carefully, I said that the squad would like to do this, but we were Veljko's personal guards and he was waiting for us in Belgrade with some urgent special duties. For this reason alone we would like to return to Yugoslavia as soon as we could.

"Well, if that's how it is, you leave when you like, though I'm sorry you can't stay longer," he replied.

Then there was another longish conversation with Murat:

"Comrade Hoxha says you should spend the night as his guest in the Hotel Daiti, so you can get some proper rest. I'll come at eight tomorrow morning to take you to your comrades."

This proposal also alarmed me: I had never stayed in a hotel and had no idea how I was supposed to behave. I would have given anything to sleep with the squad on the schoolroom floor, but felt I couldn't refuse the Albanian leader a second time. I thanked him and his wife profusely for their kindness and accepted their generous hospitality. They stood up, embraced me again, and accompanied me to the courtyard gate:

"Perhaps you'll come back to Tirana. Whenever you come, you'll be welcome. Just let us know."

As we were driving to the hotel in the black limousine, Murat remarked:

"Enver and his wife must have really taken a liking to you. You're a polite young man. And you know what to say and how to please people. It's a great honour to be sent to the Hotel Daiti. Only Enver's highest guests stay there!"

The entrance to the large, modern hotel, blazing with dozens of lights, was guarded by several armed members of the security police. When Murat had a word with them, they politely stood back to let us pass. In the huge lobby, a man in a dark suit was playing a grand piano. For the first time I rode in a lift. From my white-walled bedroom with shiny black furniture a door opened into a bathroom with a washbasin, bath and lavatory. I had never seen anything like it before except in films.

"Now I'll fill up the bath with hot water and you can have a good soak," said Murat.

"I'm not dirty," I protested, though I hadn't been up to my neck in water since the time, just before the war, when we children splashed in the cold mill pond at Rijeka Crnojevića. At our various houses we had never had a bathroom, only a privy in the yard and a tin bath in which the male and female members of the family had washed separately in the kitchen once a week, standing up and pouring water over one another's heads.

Now, stretched out in warm scented water in the large white tub, I realised how delightful it must be to live in a rich society where people could take hot baths whenever they felt like it. I recalled Mara telling Mother once that after the war all the houses in Cetinje, and not just the government apartments, would have bathrooms. This made me think of Olga, who must have splashed around in her bathroom just like I was doing now in the Hotel Daiti in Tirana. The strains of the piano drifting up to my room from the hotel lobby made me even more sentimental and lonely.

As soon as I rejoined the squad next morning, I gave a detailed report on my visit to the Hoxhas. When they heard that Enver had said we could leave when we liked, it was generally agreed that we should set off without delay, before some Albanian commander got involved and decided otherwise. However, when Murat heard our decision to leave at once for Macedonia, he insisted we stay at least ten days: our Albanian OZNA comrades in various places were waiting impatiently to show us how they operated and how they were combatting enemies of the Albanian people. There were a lot of these, he said, mostly men who had worked for the Italian police, imprisoning, torturing and executing members of the Communist Party. Now they were hiding out with relatives in mountain villages and had to be hunted down.

For the next ten days we toured various places and OZNA command posts. Our Albanian colleagues were eager to demonstrate and discuss with us their methods of uncovering, capturing and interrogating enemies. They were most surprised to hear we did not resort to beatings and torture to extract confessions – Veljko had strictly forbidden these methods used by the pre-war police. But, in other respects, their work was much the same as ours in Montenegro: searching for outlaws, bringing them in for questioning, then releasing or executing them. In Albania, as in Montenegro at that time, human life was cheap and anyone with a gun could take it with little risk of punishment.

⯎

When we returned to Tirana and the day came for us to leave, Murat said he would have to accompany us to Macedonia as we'd never make it without an interpreter. We realised the wisdom of this when our truck was stopped by one check-point or patrol after another. Experienced Murat had got hold of all the right papers, including Enver Hoxha's signature on a travel permit.

"If any of you gets separated or lost, he's done for, so keep together at all times," Murat advised.

The road from Tirana led via the small Albanian town of Elbasani through a mountainous region to Struga on the shore of Lake Ohrid in Macedonia. We soon found out why Murat had been keen to come with us: he had a sister living with her husband and children in Struga and had not seen them since the start of the war.

Though the journey was only one hundred and thirty kilometres, it took us most of the day. The narrow, winding, unpaved road was dangerously slippery in winter and every few kilometres there was another ramp. When the soldiers saw our truck coming, they would line up with their machine-guns at the ready. After a word or two from Murat, however, there was a lot of hand-shaking and back-slapping, and they would immediately bring us something to eat and drink. This always ended with our men from Durmitor putting away a great quantity of their brandy, to the general admiration of our hosts. In the best of spirits, not to say half-tipsy, the squad progressed from one check-point to the next.

"Communism," proclaimed Murat, who had also downed more than a few glasses, "unites all nations and creeds better than anything else in history. Better than kings and emperors, sultans and generals; better than all the victories and conquests and treasures of this earth. Glory be to the great Lenin! Our nations should be eternally grateful to him and raise a million monuments in his honour."

The winter sun was setting on Lake Ohrid when our merry band reached Struga and regretfully said goodbye to Murat. Well, I thought, we've passed through Montenegro and Albania, and here we are in Macedonia. I remembered the stories Father used to tell about places here: "When Tsar Dušan in the middle of the 14th century conquered Macedonia, Thessaly, Epirus and Albania, he was crowned emperor of all Serbs, Greeks, Bulgarians and Albanians in the city of Skopje. But that was not enough for him, so he set out to conquer Constantinople. If he hadn't fallen ill and died on the way, he would have ruled the whole Byzantine Empire."

As children we loved to hear stories about the medieval Serbian hero from the Macedonian town of Prilep, the giant Kraljević Marko, who slaughtered dozens of Turks with his heavy mace, and shared his wine with his favourite steed, Šarac.

In the famous battle of Kumanovo in 1912, the Serbs got their revenge for the defeat at the battle of Kosovo five hundred years earlier. At Kumanovo, Father liked to remind us, the Serbs lost 30,000 men, the same number as at the battle of Kosovo. The only difference was that after Kosovo the Turks stayed in Serbia for a full five centuries, whereas after Kumanovo they left Serbia forever.

The train journey from the southern border to Belgrade had taken about fifteen hours before the war. Now the train wasn't running because the retreating German forces had destroyed all the wooden sleepers with a heavy iron hook dragged behind the last wagon of the last train.

The next four days we journeyed north on foot – most of the time, by hitching lifts on army trucks and peasant carts, and, finally, by train on a small section of narrow-gauge track the Germans hadn't destroyed since it was only a local line.

All along the road to Belgrade people were moving in the same direction, returning to their homes from remote villages where they had taken refuge with relatives during the occupation. Mothers with children, elderly couples, all carried with them large bundles of bedclothes and other portable possessions.

Towards evening on the fourth day, the sun broke through and in the clear cold winter air we could see the distant outlines of the capital spread out on low hills.

The truck we were travelling in dropped us on a hill on the outskirts. From there we could make out the confluence of the Danube and Sava, the great rivers glittering red in the fiery sunset, beyond that the endless Pannonian Plain, and down below, the city itself.

"Belgrade! Belgrade!" we shouted, hugging one another, rejoicing that we had finally made it.

"Well, comrades, I've brought you safe and sound to the capital of our new, mighty Yugoslavia," Nikić declared proudly. "Now we're all together like brothers, no-one can ever separate us!"

As though we had suddenly grown wings, the squad set off at top speed for the city, eager to tell Veljko and Mugoša that we had arrived, that we had carried out our assignment in Albania to the best of our ability, and that we were now ready for new challenges.

The Price of Victory

We wandered through the centre of Belgrade, marvelling at the size of the buildings. Some of the biggest – the multi-storey Albania Building at one end of Terazije Square, the Royal Palace, the National Museum – and many others were badly damaged by bombing or in the fighting to liberate the capital two months earlier. Heavy bombing by the Germans in 1941 and by the Allies in 1944 had cost tens of thousands of lives. We stopped for a while to watch the water spouting from the large Terazije fountain, enclosed by elaborate wrought-iron railings, raised by Prince Miloš Obrenović, the crafty despot who had won Serbia's complete independence from the Turks. There were crowds of people but no traffic at all, apart from the occasional noisy old tram, which we gazed at fascinated, this being the first time we'd ever seen one.

It was only a short walk from Terazije to OZNA's Belgrade headquarters, an imposing seven-storey building on the corner of the street named Obilićev Venac [Obilić Crescent], after Miloš Obilić, hero of the battle of Kosovo. At the entrance we were told that Veljko and his judicial investigators, as they were now called, even though they were all still in uniform, were to be found on the third floor.

After waiting ten minutes in the company of a lad of about my age called Golub, a Serb from Croatia, we were shown into Veljko's office. He had always been quite reserved in his relations with his men and now he seemed even more so, only shaking hands instead of embracing us. At Nikić's suggestion that he should make our squad solely responsible for his personal safety, he answered that the Montenegrins couldn't take over the whole of Belgrade:

"This is the capital of Yugoslavia, so there have to be Croats and Slovenes, Macedonians and members of other nations at all levels in all organisations, including OZNA. Now Mugoša's coming and he can assign you where he thinks best."

Unlike Veljko, Mugoša made no effort to conceal his pleasure at
seeing us again and hugged us all warmly:

"Welcome, boys! I was beginning to think you'd come to a sticky
end in Albania. Now you've arrived, you'll stay with me. In the work
we're doing, I'll feel safe with you beside me on our raids." Then, turning to Golub: "Take them to Brankova Street. You can make room for
them there with the rest of the Escort Company."

The company was housed conveniently near headquarters in a
large, marble-clad building towards the bottom of Brankova Street,
which runs steeply down from Terazije to the Sava river. Before the
war it had been occupied by well-to-do people. On the fourth floor
we found about twenty company members relaxing on their beds in
various rooms.

"You could sleep in my room," Golub suggested, probably because
we were of the same age. "There are six of us already, but we'll make
space for another bed."

When his five room-mates, all older than us, came back from some duty, he introduced me as Bato Crnogorac [the Montenegrin] – it was common to call people by the area they came from, like we called 'Durmitorac'. I had just arrived from Albania, he added.

After shaking hands, the five of them, dressed as they were in their uniforms and boots, threw themselves on their beds "to take a rest from racing around town".

"How well do you shoot, Crnogorac?" one of them asked, and without waiting for an answer, drew out his revolver, took aim at a dark spot on the ceiling, and fired. The bullet struck its mark.

"Now, my hero, let's see what you can do!"

I aimed, fired, and missed.

"That's because mine's a small Beretta, and yours is a long-barrelled German Parabellum," I said in excuse.

"Here's the Parabellum for you," he said, and tossed it on to my bed.

I took it and fired. This time the shot was very close, but still not as good as his.

"You practise here every day, Ivan, and for Bato it's the first time," Golub said in my defence.

Then all the others started shooting practice and I saw that the high ceiling and walls of the spacious room were peppered with holes.

"Who were you after today?" Golub asked.

"Who else but bandits?" answered Ivan.

After supper in the canteen next door, Golub and I went to Terazije to join the crowds of Partisans and Belgrade people, mostly young, who were singing and dancing the *kolo* well into the night. Golub told me that this had been a regular thing every evening since the liberation of the city.

A few days later it was my turn to be on duty outside Veljko's office. I was sitting on a bench there with Golub and Ivan, my two new Croatian friends, when a tall, bony, elderly man in a well-cut suit appeared.

"I am Prince George Karadjordejvić," he announced. "Would you be kind enough to inform Colonel Mićunović of my arrival?"

"Comrade Veljko isn't a colonel any longer. He's been promoted to general," said Ivan.

"My sincere apologies and congratulations," the courteous gentleman replied.

I gazed at him incredulously, wondering if this was some kind of joke. I knew there were no longer any princes – we were supposed to have got rid of them forever. Comrade Veljko was out, but expected to return shortly, I told him, so he could either wait or come back another time, whichever suited him.

"With your permission, I'll sit here with you and wait."

He sat down and observed me for a while, then asked:

"How did you join the Partisans so young?"

I began explaining that in Montenegro it had been like that in all wars, when he interrupted me:

"I knew at once from your speech that you're from Montenegro. I'm Montenegrin, too, on my mother's side. She was the daughter of King Nikola."

"Then, are you the brother of King Alexander who was killed?" I couldn't stop myself asking.

"Better that I were not," Prince George replied. "We had nothing in common. He was a bad brother and a bad king. Only now has Yugoslavia got a real ruler. I have had several long talks with the Marshal. As soon as he arrived in Belgrade, he invited me to call on him and asked my advice on various matters."

Then the conversation returned to Montenegro:

"I have often wondered whether it wasn't a great mistake that Montenegro joined Serbia and lost its independence. But the Marshal told me that this will soon be put right through a kind of federation."

Our talk was interrupted by the arrival of Veljko. Prince George stood up and saluted:

"General, sir, I have come to see you on the recommendation of the Marshal."

Smiling, Veljko shook hands and politely ushered the visitor into his office, where they stayed for a long time.

While I waited, I recalled what Father had once told Duško and me about Prince George. He was said to have a violent nature and during the First World War to have killed an adjutant in one of his frequent fits of uncontrollable rage. Some people thought this story was invented by the Prince's enemies, who for reasons of their own wanted to put his younger brother, Alexander, on the throne. In any case, George was declared mentally incapable and kept in confinement. It was believed that the officers behind this were the same ones who had murdered King Alexander Obrenović and Queen Draga in the royal palace in 1903 in order to put the Karadjordjević family on the throne. This ended the rule of the Obrenović family, which had reigned for most of the 19th century.

After this, Prince George came to visit Veljko several more times and they became very friendly. There was always a chauffeur-driven car waiting for him in front of the main entrance – a gift from Marshal Tito, so that the Prince would not be obliged to walk or use public transport.

"Tomorrow we're off to the Srem front, to First Army headquarters, to see if they've caught any big fish – some Chetnik leader or one of those German generals who shot innocent civilians," Mugoša announced one morning. "We'll stay three or four days. I've got several good friends at headquarters, and a close relative of mine is with the Russians, so while we're there, I'll try and get to see them."

He then described for us the situation at the front:

"On our side, besides our own forces, there's a Russian unit with planes, tanks and Katyushas, and a Macedonian corps. The Montenegrin Division includes the Italian brigade formed from soldiers who joined us after the capitulation. On the German side, under our old friend Von Löhr, there are Chetniks, Ustashas and Domobrans [Home Guards]. We reckon there are about three hundred thousand troops on each side. Fighting has been going on ever since the liberation of Belgrade, but the main battle is still to come. That's when we shall have to break through the enemy's seven lines of trenches in the flat marshy Pannonian plain, laid with mines, to get through to Zagreb and Ljubljana, so the whole country is free."

Next day, our ten-man squad climbed into an open personnel carrier captured from the Germans; Mugoša sat in the cabin beside the driver. It was cold and our progress was slow. All round were blackened fields of maize, scorched by Russian and German flame-throwers, and the burnt-out remains of tanks. We kept having to stop to allow other vehicles to pass: Russian trucks transporting Katyushas under tarpaulin; groups of heavy tanks; trucks carrying our troops.

We had not gone more than thirty kilometres across the plain when we heard the sound of shelling. This grew gradually louder as we approached the front. From time to time, Russian planes flew low over our heads towards enemy lines, and returned after dropping their load of bombs, making for the military airfield at Batajnica on the outskirts of Belgrade.

When our vehicle stopped, Mugoša jumped out and signalled us to follow him on foot. We were going first to visit the Russian Katyusha battery where his relative was serving as some kind of liaison officer.

Marshal Tito with his generals on the Srem front inspecting the Yugoslav Partisan forces before the final push against German armies under General von Löhr, early Spring 1945

Life and Death in the Balkans

"How does he know Russian? Was he sent to one of those Party schools in Russia?" someone asked.

Mugoša chuckled: "He knows about as much Russian as a cow knows English! He never budged from his village till the Partisans turned up one day. But why should a Montenegrin bother to learn Russian when we understand one another without words?"

It was getting dark when we reached the Russian base, a large wooden barrack half buried in the ground, where we came upon about fifty soldiers. Among them was Mugoša's cousin, Mišo, who was delighted to see us and introduced us to the Russians. "Have you brought any vodka?" they clamoured. Mugoša, who had been there before and knew what to expect, had carried with him a ten-litre demijohn of Serbian plum brandy. First their commanding officer, a burly major, raised the heavy demijohn with one arm, took a long swig and passed it back to Mugoša. With equal ease, he did the same. Then the cheerful Russians, lined up according to rank, drank in turn, all of them attempting the same feat of strength. Those who had to use both hands came in for a lot of good-natured ragging. After a while Mišo took us to a separate room used for staff meetings. We couldn't wait to ask if we could see the famous Katyushas.

"No, they're night birds that only come out after midnight!" Mišo replied. "By day the Russians keep them heavily guarded and under wraps. This is their secret weapon: even I'm not allowed to examine them, though we're the closest of allies. Just after midnight you'll see them like shooting stars with fiery tails lighting up the sky. They have some way of directing them so they destroy everything before them – not a foot of ground is left untouched."

We talked all evening: Mišo was eager to hear news from Belgrade, and we were interested in the Russians.

"It's not easy with them: they're giving our Command a lot of headaches," he confided. "Russians are good comrades, and when it comes to fighting no worse than Montenegrins, but they'll drink anything that's not water. Groups of them wander around at night and go into houses, especially out-of-the-way farms, looking for wine and brandy, and raping any woman in sight. Nothing's sacred to them. They don't seem to care that we're allies. The peasants have started keeping guard and shooting any Russians that try to enter their houses. You can imagine what problems this causes!"

As most of us were dozing off around midnight, we were brought wide awake by a terrifying, ear-piercing, hissing noise, like all the snakes of the world.

"Don't worry, comrades," Mišo called out, "that's your Katyushas! They'll go on like that, taking off from their tracks, for more than an hour."

We all dashed outside and a few moments later the second round of rockets was launched not a hundred metres away from where we stood. Rooted to the spot, we gazed in awe at those fiery comets hurtling at unbelievable speed towards the enemy lines. Suddenly all was pitch-black and eerily silent for a few moments, before the next onslaught began. Mara had been right, I thought, when she promised we would get Russian help. Only it had come more slowly than expected – too late for her Bogdan and our Duško.

The next two days we toured other units and headquarters in our truck. The scenes were much like the first day, only the closer we were to the frontline, the more troops, tanks and heavy artillery we saw, all moving like a great river in the direction of the iron wall of tank-traps in front of the enemy trenches. The only vehicles going the other way, towards Belgrade, were trucks marked with big red crosses carrying the wounded. The commotion grew ever greater, the gunfire ever more deafening. Planes roared low overhead. Then we heard machine-gun fire and grenade explosions, a sign that we were very near the frontline. We saw bewildered soldiers, none more than twenty I thought, drawn up, awaiting the final order to advance and attack.

"Eh, poor lads," Mugoša muttered, "just another mouthful for the hungry German dragon. None of them will see tomorrow. Thousands are dying in useless attacks on the enemy lines, although it's obvious we're not yet strong enough to drive the Germans from their entrenched positions. Many are high-school kids, completely inexperienced, who joined us as volunteers during the fight to liberate Belgrade." Then he turned to the rest: "There's no place here for us. This isn't the Partisan war we fought in the Montenegrin highlands."

We jolted along in our truck heading for the next command post. His mention of Montenegro made me think of my scattered family, the loved ones and friends who had died or disappeared, how the war had divided us into Chetniks, Greens and Partisans. These thoughts are the last thing I recall before I was swallowed up in total darkness.

⁂

When I opened my eyes, through a kind of haze I saw clouds moving across the sky above my head. I was lying on my back and being driven somewhere. Trying my utmost to remember where I was, I struggled to raise myself, but an excruciating pain shot through my head and everything went black again. Then I heard someone speaking, but the words made no sense. The pain in my head was agonising, unbearable. Suddenly I understood that this was not a nightmare, like the ones I often had, but really happening. But why all this pain? I opened my eyes and tried to speak, but no words came out. Through a mist that gradually cleared I saw people with bandaged heads and blood on their faces. It flashed into my mind that these were the wounded, the ones who went past in trucks. But what was I doing among them? I slipped back into darkness.

Next thing I felt and heard someone hammering on my head, trying to break my skull. 'Ustashas or Chetniks?' I wondered in my half-conscious state. 'I'm going to die like Duško!' More terrible, unbearable pain.

"We've done the best we can," someone said. With a supreme effort I opened my eyes. Men in blood-stained white gowns were already moving to another patient. Some nurses lifted me on to a trolley and pushed me off somewhere.

"This lot have been operated on; those over there are still waiting," I heard one of the nurses explaining.

I realised with relief that I was among the first group and at once felt better: I had survived an operation, the worst was over, I would get well! But where were Mugoša, Nikić and the rest?

Time passed. Somehow I knew it was night, but couldn't tell whether I was awake or in some nightmarish world. At dawn the pain in my head began to get worse, minute by minute, until I couldn't stop myself crying out. I knew there was something seriously wrong, some change the doctors hadn't foreseen. The nurse who came gave me a couple of tablets and assured me that in a few minutes the pain would pass. I waited, but it soon became so unbearable I called her again, begging her to find a doctor. I longed to die rather than go on suffering such agony. Things around me grew misty, out of focus. As if in a deep cavern I heard faraway voices. Then again the hammering on my skull, which was splitting with pain.

⊱❦

As the darkness lifted, the first thing I made out was the anxious, tear-stained face of my sister Stana.

"You're awake, little brother. It was high time! Now everything will be alright. You're in the military hospital in Belgrade. The wound got infected so you had to have a second operation. Mugoša and Nikić have been to see you several times."

I tried to move my head, to see where I was lying, but the effort was too painful.

Bit by bit, I learnt more from Stana, and realised that without her I would probably have died. She had spent a whole week by my bedside as I lay unconscious. Though the medical staff worked round the clock, they were completely overwhelmed by the number of wounded being brought in daily from the Srem front and could devote very little time to individual patients. Thanks to Stana, I had been moved from the floor in a corridor to a tiny room with just one other bed. She had given her blood for a transfusion and had persuaded the doctors to give me another transfusion next day, she said – this time the donor would be her friend Zina.

After a while, Stana left to get a few hours' rest and catch up with what was happening at the headquarters of the Yugoslav Youth Organisation, where she was Secretary of its Central Committee. That evening she came again with Mugoša, Nikić and Zina. The doctor who accompanied them declared that I was now out of danger and would make a gradual recovery, with no more permanent damage than a scar on my scalp.

"His father has a similar souvenir of the last war, which he got at the same age," Stana told him, then turning to me: "This is Zina, who's giving you some of her blood tomorrow. I'm sure you won't mind getting the blood of such a pretty girl."

Zina asked with a grin what would happen when her mild Jewish blood mingled in my veins with Stana's wild Montenegrin blood. Mugoša said he and Nikić were ready to be donors as they had more than they needed of real proletarian blood – every drop of it red. While everyone was laughing and joking, clearly glad to see me alive, the door opened: two nurses carried a patient into the room and laid him on the other bed.

"We've nowhere else to put him," one of them said, as though apologising for disturbing us. "Both his legs have been amputated above the knee. When he comes round, Bato will have some company. They're much the same age."

When Stana and Zina left, Mugoša finally told me what had happened:

"Our daft Avdo drove straight towards the enemy lines! When the Germans opened fire, he turned round fast and drove back like crazy. He was trying to avoid a bomb crater when he lost control and the truck overturned. We were all thrown clear and landed in mud, with no harm done, but you happened to hit your head on a sharp stone by the side of the track. It was real bad luck – there wasn't another stone in sight! But you were lucky in one way, because an open truck carrying wounded was just leaving for Belgrade, and we managed to get you into it, and Nikić with you, to make sure you got to a hospital. But the main thing is that you're alive and in one piece. It could have been worse!"

That night I couldn't sleep for a long time for thinking about what had happened, and the strange chance that both Mila and I had fallen out of trucks and hit our heads on stone. I wondered whether she, too, could have been saved if she'd had some Nikić to take her to hospital. Around dawn I was woken by a commotion in the little room. I gathered that my neighbour was in a critical condition. I watched as two nurses, one young and clearly inexperienced, the other older and motherly, fixed up the bottle with blood above his head as he moaned and rambled in delirium.

"The crisis will last several days, but he's young; he'll probably pull through," the older one said. "It'll be much harder for him when he wakes up and finds out what he's lost."

Over the next few days, Stana, Nikić and Mugoša came to visit me regularly. On one visit Stana mentioned finding a flat where Mother and Nada could live when they came to Belgrade, and Aco, too, when he was found.

She asked whether I would like to live with them, so we would be together with Mother again. After she left, I began to wonder why she hadn't mentioned Father at all when talking about our reunion. Why wasn't he with Mother? But then I thought it was probably because the war was still on and he had duties somewhere else.

Next evening my neighbour regained consciousness. He opened his eyes and looked around, clearly trying to work out where he was and, then, why he was in hospital. He kept quiet at first, and then spoke to me in a weak voice:

"It hurts. It hurts badly. Was I wounded?"

"Yes," I replied, "but you'll be alright. They operated on you."

"Where am I wounded? Is it the legs?"

I said it was.

"I thought so. I have terrible pain below my knees and in my feet."

I wondered how that could be when they had amputated his legs above the knees, but said nothing.

"Will I be alright? Did you hear the doctors talking about me?" Without waiting for an answer he went on: "I suppose it'll hurt for a while and then stop. What are you called?"

"Bato," I said, "Tomašević."

"And I'm Pero, Pero Popović."

Another strange coincidence, I thought, for Father after he was wounded in the head had been lying beside another Pero Popović, but that Pero had lost only one hand, not two legs.

The older nurse came in:

"You've woken up, dear boy! Are you feeling better, my love? Now auntie will look after you and stop it hurting."

Encouraged by her tender words and kind voice, Pero asked where in the legs he was wounded and if he would be able to walk again. Instead of answering, she supported his head and quickly got him to swallow some tablets with water.

"We'll talk about your wounds tomorrow. And then you can ask Bato."

Pero wanted to ask something else, but the nurse hurried out of the room. I saw that she had tears in her eyes.

"Why did she say to ask you, Bato?" he began, but he was already yawning from the strong dose and in no time had sunk into a restless sleep.

I thought for a long time about what to say when he asked me about his wounds. It was not yet dawn when he called to me:

"Bato, I feel awful pain in my legs and feet again. Tell me the truth: are my legs all there? I can't sit up enough to feel them."

"No, Pero, they're not all there. They were badly injured when you stepped on a mine; the doctors had to cut them off above the knees."

Pero let out a terrible howl, fell silent for moment, then began to sob and lament his fate.

In the following days, all the staff and my visitors did their best to comfort and console him. The doctors promised he would get artificial legs and walk again, after a bit of practice, so nobody would be able to tell the difference. Stana said that his comrades would help him to complete his schooling and find a job. Mugoša assured him that he would get a medal for bravery. As the days went by, he became gradually more resigned to the life of an invalid.

"You know, Bato," he said, "they sent us towards the German trenches over minefields. They knew the Germans had laid landmines every step of the way in front of their positions, to stop us attacking, but they didn't care. They wanted us to clear the way with our bodies before the great battle everyone's talking about. Well, I did my bit in clearing the mines. I lost my legs, but at least I stayed alive; thousands of others died – some from mines, others from the German gunfire that waits for every attack."

⁂

One afternoon there was a knock on the door and Stana entered with a beaming smile that showed her beautiful white teeth.

"You've got some visitors, Bato. Shall I let them in?"

Behind her I caught sight of Mother and Nada, both in new English uniforms. Stana stood back to let them rush in and hug me. I hadn't seen my youngest sister for almost three years, since they had dragged her off to prison in Cetinje. She was much taller, but painfully thin.

We discussed future plans. For the time being, Mother would be cooking in the youth canteen, Stana said, and Nada was to go on a nursing course. Soon, when the war was over and I was out of hospital, we would all be together again, in Belgrade.

"Where's Father now? When is he going to join us?" I asked, impatient to see him.

"We don't know yet. We'll find out soon. You just get well and don't worry about anything," Stana replied.

When Stana and Nada moved away a little to talk to Pero, I said quietly to Mother:

"As soon as I'm better, we'll go off to Kamena Gora to look for Duško."

⁂

In the three months I spent in hospital, Pero and I became firm friends. He was from a remote village in northern Montenegro. After the fall of Italy, like many other youths in this area he joined the Partisans. Until he was wounded, he had fought with a company attached to the Italia Brigade. Eventually, fighting all the way from Montenegro, they reached the Srem front in Vojvodina.

Pero and I spent a lot of time in the corridor of the surgical clinic, where patients waited their turn to have their wounds dressed. The waiting didn't bother us: on the contrary, it was like an excursion into the wide world. After about two months we noticed that the number of wounded being admitted was now much smaller, and from this we gathered that there was a lull in the fighting on the Srem front. Then, one night, we were woken by a lot of shouting. I helped Pero tie on one wooden leg, and with the aid of crutches he made his way with me to the main hospital corridor to find out what was happening. This broad corridor was again crowded with wounded waiting for emergency treatment, their temporary bandages soaked with blood. The groans and screams of scores of wounded combined with the shouts of doctors and nurses calling one another and racing frantically around.

"It's begun!" cried Pero excitedly. "You don't know, Bato, what I would give to be in the front line!"

I knew he was referring to the long-awaited push on the Srem front after six months of trench warfare. Next day, the breakthrough of the German lines near the small town of Šid, a hundred kilometres west of Belgrade, was the sole topic of conversation among our visitors. According to Mugoša, the enemy forces were now in full retreat and the town of Vukovar had already been liberated, opening up the way to Zagreb:

"Now, nobody can stop us. The end of the war is in sight!"

The next month brought thrilling news of our victories in the final battles of the war. But for me the greatest joy was to hear that Aco had been found: he had somehow ended up in the new Partisan Navy in Dalmatia.

Pero and I spent long hours talking about what we would do after the war.

"I can't go back to my village and spend my whole life sitting in front of the house, like my relative who lost a leg in the Balkan war," said Pero. "I remember him sitting there on the threshold, staring into space, thinking his own thoughts. That's where some Italian patrol found him and shot him one day in 1942."

Though on other European fronts the war ended with the capitulation of the Third Reich on 8/9 May 1945, in Yugoslavia it lasted another six days. It was not until 15 May that the German Balkan group commanded by General von Löhr, together with Chetnik and Ustasha forces, which were encircled between Celje and Maribor in Slovenia, finally surrendered to the Partisans. To the last, Von Löhr with some 300,000 German and quisling troops, the largest force ever amassed in the Balkans, had been trying to reach Austria and surrender to the British and Americans. And so Hitler's celebrated general lost his game of cat and mouse with Tito and the Partisans: he failed to capture and kill Tito, as he promised Hitler, but was himself taken prisoner, tried and executed.

The end of the war was celebrated in Belgrade by the firing of guns and dancing in the streets that went on for two whole days. From our hospital room window, Pero and I made our contribution until we had used up all our bullets. When it finally went quiet, the two of us were left lying in our hospital beds listening all night to the groans and screams of the wounded dying in agony.

Another month passed until I was finally discharged. I put on the new uniform Mugoša had brought me a few days before, trying not to show my great joy at leaving hospital in front of tearful Pero.

"Cheer up, Pero. You'll soon be moving to a hostel for invalids. We'll see one another and stay friends."

I crossed the large hospital courtyard and showed my discharge paper to the elderly guard, who opened the iron gates to let me pass.

"All the best, young comrade," he said in a fatherly voice, and saluted me.

In steep Nemanjina Street I stopped to watch a long column of German prisoners-of-war of all ages walking slowly up it. Some Partisans no older than myself were in charge of them. From the same direction an ancient truck loaded with coal was noisily approaching. The prisoners looked round and, seeing the truck, all moved to one side to let it pass. One of the prisoners, a thin, middle-aged man, stopped right beside me. As the truck drew level with us, he swiftly stepped forward, bent down and put his head under its back wheels. I heard a loud crack as the skull split open and saw his head turned in an instant into a mess of bone, blood and brains. Some of this splashed on to my new uniform. Other prisoners picked up his body with its mangled head and carried it with them. The column slowly moved on up the hill.

In a state of shock I shakily made my way to the centre of town. I felt somehow strange and empty. The end of the war had brought sadness as well as joy. Things would never be the same again. Our company and squad would be dispersed and the wonderful Partisan comradeship would be lost for ever. The column of German prisoners-of-war I had just seen conjured up in my mind's eye another column of prisoners, as I pictured them, marching through the little Italian town of Colfiorito. I had to go in search of Duško…

We knew that Duško had been killed near a tiny village in the mountainous region of Kamena Gora [Rocky Mountain] on the border of Serbia and Montenegro. Before the war, the journey to Kamena Gora would have taken only a day by car, but Mother and I travelled for over a week by various trucks and on foot, sometimes having to take roundabout routes to avoid pockets of Chetniks and Germans. In this area a notorious band of Chetniks was still very active. Its leader, a former Partisan named Belica, had for some reason gone over to the Chetniks during the Fifth Offensive in 1943. Since then he and his band had slaughtered numerous Partisan supporters in the remote villages of this wild highland region, entering their homes at night and slitting their throats. The local inhabitants still lived in fear of them, so that, mainly because of Stana, we were given an armed escort and two horses for the last part of our journey.

For a whole day we struggled upwards through the snow that still lay on Kamena Gora in early June. With the help of our escort, not long before dusk we managed to find the hamlet and the house of the peasant named Obrad to which Germans and Chetniks had brought my wounded brother after the battle. Obrad, his wife and two sons, one of them my age, made us very welcome and offered us food. Then Obrad told us all he knew about Duško's last hours.

"The Germans brought him just in front of our house, handed him over to the Chetniks and left straight away. He was wounded in the head and could hardly stand. His face was pale and he was so weak he had to lean against the wall to keep from falling. One of the Chetniks took his diary out of his bag and started turning over the pages and reading bits of it aloud to the others who were standing round. They all laughed whenever he read something insulting Duško had written about Chetniks. One of them was a fellow with wavy hair they called Vlasta. I heard him telling the others he'd known Stana before the war, when her father was serving in Plav."

After the Chetniks withdrew next day, Obrad found Duško with his throat slit in a nearby copse and covered him temporarily with a few branches, but it soon started snowing and a pack of hungry wolves devoured the body.

"I'm afraid you won't be able to bury Duško," he went on. "A dozen other Partisans were killed in that little wood on the same day. The wolves tore them all to pieces, dragged them around, so you won't be able to tell which are the remains of your son and brother."

Early next morning Mother and I made our way to the copse, where tracks of wild animals were visible in the snow. We searched the area and found human bones but, as Obrad said, there was no way of knowing whose they were. Then I remembered that about a year before the war started, Father had taken both of us to the only dentist in Cetinje to have our teeth checked – something out of the ordinary at that time, for most people went to the dentist only for extractions when they had bad tooth-ache. Afterwards Duško and I had peered into each other's mouths and I knew exactly which of his teeth had been filled. After searching around for some time, in a small hollow I found a skull with some hair still attached and other bones. The skull had all the teeth and one molar with a filling.

"Mother, I've found Duško!" I cried. She came running over, took the skull from me and cradled it in her arms. For the rest of the day she refused to be parted from it. We gathered up the rest of the bones nearby and buried them next day in a corner of the primary school yard in the little place named Kamena Gora, like the mountain. We stood for a long time beside the fresh mound while Mother wept and spoke to her eldest son:

"Duško, my son, my sorrow, what a terrible end you suffered! Now you can rest in peace in this beautiful place. You couldn't stay quietly at home, as I begged you, to wait for the end of the war, like many others. Now you would be alive and in a year or so become a teacher. Well, let the schoolchildren now learn from your example…"

We returned to Belgrade consoled that we had found Duško, touched him, and given him a proper burial. But even after this, I still couldn't accept that he would never return one day, alive and well. I continued to go to the railway station to meet trains bringing home survivors of the German camps, hoping against hope, as I scanned their haggard faces, that I would catch sight of my beloved brother among them.

Several months after the end of the war, things were slowly returning to normal, but I was still in uniform. At the beginning of September 1945, Veljko called me to his office and said it was time for me to resume my education. I protested that I had outgrown school, I couldn't sit in a class-room with kids much younger than myself, and in any case I had learnt all I needed to know in the Partisans.

"You'll stay with us, don't worry," he reassured me, "but you must go to school. I've already given orders for you to be relieved of all duties during school hours. And you won't be sitting with younger boys but with comrades from the Partisans who had their education interrupted, like yourself."

The very next day, dressed in a well-brushed uniform and polished boots, with a Parabellum in my holster, I was standing in the crowded old tram that swayed its way with much rattling and grinding in the direction of the Lijon district and the Sixth High School. It was in this building that courses of accelerated study were being held for pupils who were behind in their schooling because of the war. Some three hundred boys and girls between the ages of fourteen and twenty wearing Partisan uniform were gathered in the large schoolyard, making a tremendous din. Among them were young people on crutches who had lost a leg, others with an empty sleeve, some with a black patch over one eye. All of us were excited and a little nervous about this unexpected turn in our lives.

There was sudden silence when the grey-haired director of studies and a dozen teachers appeared on the steps in front of the main door. The director stepped forward and addressed us in ringing tones:

"Dear comrades, you have all been prevented by the war from attending school regularly. We shall do our best to help you catch up with those pupils who continued their schooling in wartime. Through intensive study you will be able to complete two years of schooling in one year. From today, you will be pupils again, and we shall be your teachers. I therefore ask you not to come to school with weapons. Instead of revolvers and hand-grenades, bring a pen and the notebooks and text-books you need. These will be your most powerful weapons in your future life… Now the class teachers will call the roll of their pupils. When you hear your name, call out 'Present' and go to the room with your class number on the door."

As I looked for my classroom, I felt as scared as when I started school in Cetinje. When we had all gathered and sat down self-consciously in the desks, our class teacher, a tiny, frail-looking woman, introduced herself as Julia:

"In our class there are thirty pupils: twenty-two boys and eight girls. I shall be teaching you history. From your birthplaces I can see that many of you are from Montenegro, so history won't be a problem for you. I'm sure you know more about the Second World War, especially in Yugoslavia, than I do. So we'll learn from one another: you from me and I from you. I can only add that I am proud to be your comrade, your teacher, or whatever you decide to call me – I know you can't be simply pupils any longer. You've had a terrible childhood, suffered a lot. Some of you have been badly wounded; some have lost parents, brothers, sisters… I'll do my very best to understand and help you. You are children and grown-up people at the same time, and I have the greatest respect and admiration for you."

From that moment on we all loved our class teacher. She became a real friend to whom we could admit our mistakes and misdemeanours at school, and confide all the problems that were beginning to appear in our peacetime life.

During our very first lesson, when she was reading out the pupils' names so we would get to know one another, I was astonished to hear a name that sounded very familiar. A boy of my age stood up, strongly built, fair-haired, with piercing blue eyes, smiling broadly:

"I'm Hajro Musić from Nova Varoš."

Hajro sat in the front row so he could stretch out his right leg, which he couldn't bend. I recalled his brother, Ramo, in the camp in Cetinje telling me that Hajro had been shot in the knee. I could hardly wait for the lesson to end and remind him what good friends we'd been in Nova Varoš, right up to the day of my family's departure, when the police had arrested his eldest brother, Musa, and Hajro, believing my father was responsible, hadn't come to say goodbye.

"Hajro Musić!" I called to him as soon as the bell rang. "I'd never have recognised you – nor you me!"

"Who would have thought the two of us would be in the same class again, and in Belgrade of all places!" he exclaimed with a broad grin.

We hugged each other and talked about Nova Varoš, mentioning only briefly our family tragedies in the war. We immediately felt close, though almost seven years had passed since our last meeting. After that, Hajro again became my best school friend.

One afternoon, all the classes were summoned to the large assembly hall, which was soon packed with pupils. We were all wondering why we were there when the curtains across the stage at one end of the hall parted to reveal about forty boys and girls, all in British uniforms. Our director of studies stepped forward:

"Let us welcome the return of our Jewish comrades. They have been freed from German prison camps by our Allies and are now back in their native city. Many members of their families did not survive the camps. They died just because they were Jews. In our new society, people are judged good or bad according to their actions, not their nationality, race or religion…"

Spontaneously, we broke into enthusiastic applause to greet our new comrades.

Next day six of them, three boys and three girls, were brought to join our class. In the first lesson, Julia asked them to introduce themselves individually in turn. Up stood a slender, pale, sad-faced boy with black hair parted in the middle – a pre-war fashion now abandoned in favour of the more manly style, as we boys thought, of combing our hair straight back with no parting:

"My name is Gavrilo Deleon. Like other Jewish families, mine lost many members in the war. Luckily, my elder brother survived. Before the war he belonged to a progressive Jewish youth group in Belgrade, and so he joined the Partisans. The Jews in Yugoslavia had somewhere they could go to fight. Those in some other occupied countries of Europe did not have that chance…"

After Gavrilo, Rafael stood up. He was quite different: square and sturdy in build, energetic and cheerful looking. He was followed by Hari, Rahela…

Their stories were all similar, and tragic. Before the war their families had mostly been well-to-do and respected, with a large circle of relatives and friends. Now the individual survivors were meeting up again in Belgrade, where a fellow Jew, Moše Pijade, occupied one of the highest positions in the state.

October 1945 was exceptionally warm and sunny and there were still plenty of bathers on the Danube beaches. A group of us – Hajro, Rafael and three or four others – decided to go for a swim before lessons, which were one week in the morning and the next in the afternoon. Unlike the other Jewish pupils in our class, who showed little interest in sport, Rafael was among the best in ball games and a keen swimmer. We took the tram down to the bridge over the Danube which the German forces had blown up when retreating. It was now being speedily reconstructed by Russian engineers and soldiers as a form of fraternal aid to our country.

For a while we stood in the sunshine, watching the work in progress and chatting to the Russian soldiers, then moved a hundred metres downstream, took off our uniforms and dashed shouting with delight into the refreshing water, still quite warm for October. We stayed in about half an hour, swimming, diving and splashing one another. Being a poor swimmer, I kept close to the bank, in the shallows. Then Hajro, who was always looked upon as a leader in the class, said it was time to get out and go to school. We quickly dried off in the sun and dressed, feeling relaxed and pleased with ourselves. It was then that Hajro noticed a neat pile of clothing on the bank and asked, jokingly, if anyone was going to school naked. Suddenly we all realised that this was Rafael's uniform and he was nowhere to be seen. We started calling him, then running up and down the bank, as far as the ruined bridge, where we asked the soldiers if they'd seen him. "*Nyet! Nyet!*" they replied. The better swimmers pulled off their clothes and started diving, looking for him underwater, for the Danube was very clear in those days.

Our shouts and commotion attracted some men working on a sand-dredger some distance away, extracting sand for the building work on the bridge.

"Whyever did you pick this place to swim?" one of them asked. "There are deep whirlpools here because of the dredging. For sure he's already floating down the Danube to the sea, so you might as well stop looking."

We were all shocked and saddened by his death. It seemed so unfair that Rafael had survived the horrors of a death camp only to vanish without a trace a few weeks after returning safely to Belgrade. There was no funeral, for the body was never recovered. In any case, there would have been no relatives to bury him: they had all perished in Auschwitz. Rafael had been the last surviving member of a prominent Belgrade family.

In November 1945, the day of the first post-war general elections arrived. Belgrade was ablaze with flags and banners bearing patriotic slogans, military bands played, and the whole atmosphere was festive in the extreme. Loudspeakers on lamp-posts urged citizens to exercise their right to vote. Women, in particular, were urged to vote for the first time. Bursting with pride and excitement, early in the morning I hurried to the polling station where I was assigned with several others to guard the ballot boxes. The leader of our group, wearing a red arm-band, had explained the procedure to us the previous day:

"Here you have two boxes. One is for our Popular Front, the other is for reactionaries – we call it the 'blind box'. You must explain clearly to every voter what each box stands for. Those who are against us – vestiges of the bourgeoisie, rotten reactionaries – drop their ball into the 'blind box'. But their votes are only a protest, because there are no other parties, so our Front has no opposition in the elections. All the old political parties were disqualified by collaborating with the enemy during the war."

In front of our polling station in Brankova Street I found a long line of men and women waiting eagerly to be among the first to cast their votes. We guardians of the voting boxes took up our places and at the appointed hour the flower-decorated door was opened. Soldiers and civilians poured in, all smartly dressed for the occasion. The chairman of the commission, an older comrade, searched for the name of each voter on the hand-written list, slowly circled it, and handed over a small rubber ball.

"Each box," he announced, "has an opening large enough for your hand. You are required to put your closed hand holding the ball into each box in turn. Which box you drop it in is a private matter."

From the start of the voting it was clearly audible when the ball landed on the bottom of a box. Occasionally the plop came from the 'blind box'. A member of the commission leant towards me and whispered:

"To be on the safe side, comrade, I'm putting a pencil mark beside the names of those who drop their ball in the 'blind box', so we know who our enemies are."

Our electoral victory was celebrated up and down the country. On 29 November 1945, the Kingdom of Yugoslavia was formally replaced by the

Federal People's Republic of Yugoslavia, comprising six equal republics, which was recognised by the Allies and the United Nations.

※

The momentous year of 1945 was nearly over when a telegram arrived with the news that Aunt Mileva, Mother's sister, was dying in Mitrovica hospital. Mother and I set off the same day. Sitting on the hard, rickety, wooden seat of the train, I wondered what it would be like returning to my birthplace. Grandpa Aleksa, the old warrior, wouldn't be there: he had died at the age of ninety-five just a few months before the end of the war – the fifth he had known in his long lifetime. According to Grandma Jovana, the hardest thing for him during the occupation was to see Serbs and Montenegrins fleeing Kosovo, and their houses and land being taken over again by the Albanians.

"Damned Kosovo," he often used to say, "how many more times will we conquer it and lose it again?"

Then one day he slipped quietly out of this life, without even saying goodbye to Jovana.

In my early childhood, Mitrovica had seemed to me a large town, but now, after Belgrade, it looked a wretched place, like a dirty, overgrown village. Its narrow, crooked streets were scarcely passable and there were no pavements. While we picked our way through the mud to Grandma Jovana's house, I stopped for a moment in front of some places that I recognised.

"There's the Hotel Božur, Mother," I said, pointing to a large, crumbling building. "Isn't that where the English had their ball and Ljuba won the gramophone? Over there's the headquarters where Father worked, and that building was my school…"

While I went along cheerfully recalling places and events of my childhood, Mother, looking thoughtful and anxious, kept quiet. Eventually we reached the small stone house where my grandparents, Aleksa and Jovana, and Aunt Mileva had lived since their arrival in Kosovo some fifteen years before. When Jovana saw Mother, her face lit up and she started crossing herself.

"Is that really you, Milica? I was afraid I'd never lay eyes on you again in this world. And here you are, sent to me by God to ease my sorrow for your poor sister. She died in agony, and all the time she was asking for you."

The little oil-lamp in front of the soot-darkened family icon in the corner of the room was sending out acrid smoke that brought tears to my eyes. This seemed to go with the atmosphere of death and decay in the Rajković home. Just then Mother's brother, Jovan, appeared at the door, a burly, auburn-haired man with a freckled face – a physical type not uncommon in the Montenegrin highlands. He almost wept for joy when he caught sight of Mother. From him we learnt the circumstances of my aunt's death:

"We'd never have got through the war without Mileva. She never married – she sacrificed herself to look after our parents. She didn't mind washing and cleaning for Albanians, doing any kind of work, to help us out so we didn't starve. And she was well-liked by everyone, Albanians and Serbs alike. That's why she was made supervisor of all the shops in upper Mitrovica when the war ended. But she was inexperienced, too trusting; people took advantage of her good nature. Then it turned out there was some money missing – not a large sum, only about a hundred dinars – and she was held responsible. The shame of this was too much for her – she was a proud woman – so she swallowed caustic soda. We took her to hospital, but it was no use, her mouth and throat were all burnt. Before she died, in terrible pain, she managed to tell us that she couldn't face life in Mitrovica with people thinking her a thief."

During that long winter evening, we sat around the stove catching up on all the family news, at the same time keeping watch over Aunt Mileva's coffin.

"Mitrovica was under the Germans, because of the Trepča mine," Jovan told us, "while the rest of Kosovo was under the Italians, Bulgars and Albanians."

We also learnt that Father's brother Djuro, who had been driven by the Albanians from his land and the house he'd built, was keeping himself alive by chopping wood and doing other jobs for Montenegrin and

Serbian households in exchange for a bed and a meal. Barely literate, knowing nothing but farming, he was now little more than a beggar.

"Your new government," said Uncle Jovan, referring to Mother and myself in our uniforms, "won't let the Serbs and Montenegrins come back to the houses and lands they were driven out of during the occupation, because this would mean more trouble with the Albanians. 'Go to Vojvodina,' they say. 'There are plenty of empty houses left by the Germans, and the land is more fertile.' Before the war, we had the army to protect us and Kosovo was ours, but now they tell us the Albanians must have an equal say in government with our people."

Father's eldest brother, Luka, an energetic and capable man who had suffered a paralysing stroke after being driven from his home and land, had spent much of the occupation sitting in the yard of our stone house, cared for by his daughter-in-law Danica. His only son, also named Jovan, always the centre of attention among four sisters, had joined up at the outbreak of war, having been a royal army reservist, only to be captured a few days later and taken off to a German prisoner-of-war camp. When the Allies started bombing Mitrovica in 1944 because of the lead-zinc mine, Luka, unable to move, stayed in the yard while Danica and the others ran for shelter. Believing himself a burden on his family, Luka persuaded a male nurse to give him a fatal injection of poison in exchange for the treasured gold pocket-watch he had brought from America. And so, one day, Uncle Luka met his end sitting in his chair under the old pear tree that Duško and I loved to climb as children. At the end of the war, Luka's son, Jovan, returned from the camp a severe epileptic who suffered daily attacks. At the time we were in Mitrovica, he was undergoing treatment in a hospital elsewhere, so we didn't meet him.

Immediately after the liberation of Kosovo, in November 1944, Uncle Jovan said, there was a general uprising of the ethnic Albanians which the Partisans, aided by the Bulgarians, who had by then changed sides, had a hard time putting down. People said that Tito got the Bulgarians to do most of this, so as not to antagonise the Albanians.

Before we went to bed, I asked about the grocer, Izidor Levi, and his numerous children, who had always been hanging around the shop when I went in to buy something to eat on the way to school.

"You won't find Levi or his shop, Bato," Uncle Jovan replied. "All the Jewish families in Mitrovica and places around – some three hundred souls all told – were rounded up on German orders by the Albanian Skenderbeg Division in May 1944. They were put on trains and taken away. Not one of them has ever come back."

Next day, there were scarcely a dozen mourners at the Orthodox cemetery where my aunt was laid to rest: most of Father's friends had perished in the war. This was the last time I saw Grandma Jovana, who died a couple of years later.

෪

When Yugoslavia capitulated in April 1941 and was split up among the Axis invaders, the Germans took Serbia under their direct control. In need of a figure like Petain in France to make it easier to govern, they picked on General Milan Nedić, who had never hidden his pro-Hitler sympathies. On the instructions of his masters, in August 1941 the self-proclaimed 'Father of Serbia' formed a quisling government, which took over the civil administration and police. In the course of the occupation, over one hundred thousand people, mostly liberation movement sympathisers, were brought from all over Serbia to the concentration camp in Belgrade for interrogation. From there truckloads of prisoners, eighty thousand all told, were taken daily to the execution ground at Jajinci, just outside the city, and shot by the Germans and Nedić's guards.

February 4th 1946. As I looked down from the upper storeys of the OZNA headquarters, in the cold winter sunshine of late afternoon the bitter *košava*, blowing from the east, was tossing flurries of dry snow from the roof-tops. When I was not at school, I still carried out occasional duties. On this particular day, when I went into one of the waiting-rooms outside an investigator's office I came upon a fat, grey-haired, elderly man. As the room was very hot, he had taken off his jacket and was sitting there in a crumpled white shirt, waiting to be questioned. I had seen this prisoner several times before: he was always brought to the building in a closed vehicle, with the highest level of security. A guard I knew told me that this was the infamous General Nedić, who was being interrogated at length to uncover the full extent of his treason. Then he would be put on public trial, so that people could judge for themselves whether the 'Father of Serbia' had served the occupiers or his own nation.

Now the General was sitting on a bench in the waiting room, his chin resting on his clenched fists. From the corridor outside I could hear the voices of the armed guards who were waiting to take him back to prison. We messengers spent a lot of time in these ante-rooms, ready to receive instructions from the investigators to fetch and carry papers and run other errands. While we sat there, we used to keep an eye on any prisoners waiting to be interrogated, but as we were constantly going in and out, they were often left alone for short periods. When the questioning was over, we would escort the prisoner out of the office and again leave him alone in the ante-room while we went to call the guards who had brought him.

It was no different that day. Nobody bothered about the fact that there was a window in the room, looking on to a large square light shaft in the centre of the building. Though the window was big enough for a grown man to climb through, it was on the fourth floor and there was no way out of the light shaft, so escape by that means was impossible. When I was called into the investigator's office for a moment and General Nedić was left alone, he quickly moved the bench beneath the window, climbed on it, opened the window and jumped into the light shaft. Whether he intended to commit suicide or thought he could escape that way, no-one will ever know. In the investigator's office we didn't hear the window opening, only the thud of the body landing on concrete.

The moment we realised what had happened, we were seized by panic over the consequences of our momentary lapse of attention. Leaning out the window, in the dusk we could make out the General's white shirt at the bottom of the shaft.

He was lying face down and still showed signs of life. But how to reach him as quickly as possible? Investigators, guards and messengers ran around wondering what to do, until someone remembered seeing a large coil of strong rope in the building. Someone would have to be let down by the rope and tie it round the General, so he could be hauled up. As I was the youngest and lightest, this task fell to me.

They lowered me slowly down one wall of the light shaft. The closer I got to the General, the more scared I felt. He was still alive, breathing noisily. When I reached the ground and untied the rope, I approached cautiously, stretched out a hand and patted him, in case he had somehow managed to conceal a knife – maybe he was only pretending to be badly injured and would stab me when I was least expecting it. But the General was now quite harmless. The death rattle in his throat echoed round the walls of the enclosed space.

The chill February evening, the agony of the dying man, the significance of this moment – all this made me tremble so much I could hardly raise the General's heavy body, get the rope under him and tie it firmly around his waist. If it comes undone, I thought, he'll fall back and probably land on my head. The people up above kept calling me to hurry, which made me fumble all the more. Finally I gave the signal to pull him up. It took them a long time because of his weight. When it was my turn, they had a much easier task. That was how I became, by chance, witness of the last moments of the 'Father of Serbia'.

Not long after the dramatic end of General Nedić, I was demobilised together with the other messengers of my age group. We were all handed the deeds of houses and land in Vojvodina left by the ethnic Germans. Over six hundred thousand of them had lived in Vojvodina before the war. Some had withdrawn with the retreating German troops, some had fled, some had been expelled. Tito, we were told, had given instructions that former Partisans should have priority in the distribution of this property. The break-up of our squad was a sad moment for us all. Golub, who had lost his family and home in the war, declared his intention of starting a new life in Vojvodina. Mugoša, looking unusually grim on this occasion, called me aside and said that Veljko's orders were for me to report to the new Ministry of Foreign Affairs:

"You know Italian and a bit of German so you'll be useful there." He added that he and Nikić were to stay with Veljko in OZNA. I could tell that he, too, was sad we were all going our separate ways.

An Unquiet Peace

The new Ministry for Foreign Affairs was still in the formative stage when I moved there. It was located in the main street, which immediately after the war had changed its name from King Milan to Marshal Tito. As a 'trusted comrade' I was put to work in the archive of strictly classified material. A good third of all those employed in the Ministry were under twenty years of age. Our working day started at six, when we gathered in Kalemegdan Park, above the confluence of the Sava and Danube, where a famous pre-war gymnast, now a Foreign Ministry official, was waiting to put us younger people through our morning exercises. Then, in vests and shorts, we would run about a kilometre through the main streets to our Ministry in Marshal Tito Street, carrying our uniforms and boots with us – almost everyone was still wearing uniform at that time, even after demobilisation, for lack of any civilian clothes. The whole country was enthusiastically involved in competitions of various kinds at work and in sporting activities. When my working day ended at three in the afternoon, I dashed off to school and had lessons until eight in the evening. Totally exhausted, I then dragged myself back to Brankova Street, where I was still sleeping.

About that time, Mother was allocated a flat into which she and Nada moved. We heard, to our delight, that Aco was due to be discharged from the Navy in a few days' time and would join them there, and I decided to do the same. Ljuba and Vicko were also in Belgrade, where they were reunited for the first time since his arrest and transportation with Duško to the Colfiorito camp. Father had made only one brief visit to Belgrade since the end of the war, and after a talk with Mother, had gone to Kosovo, where he was in charge of the Commission of Enquiry into War Crimes. I realised that something was not quite right between them. At about that time Stana came down with hepatitis from a contaminated blood transfusion given to her for anaemia, and was confined for several weeks to the isolation wing of the military hospital.

One evening in late February, I picked up my few belongings, my revolver, machine-gun and ammunition, and without saying goodbye to my comrades left Brankova Street to move in with Mother. The flat was quite spacious, but in a very dilapidated state. For the first time since Nada's arrest in Cetinje, the three of us sat down for a meal together. As there was nothing to buy in the shops, Mother had brought back some left-over food from the canteen where she cooked. We talked about Aco's imminent return, and I asked why Father wasn't with us, why he had come to Belgrade and left without seeing Nada or myself.

"The war has driven us apart, son, made us strangers. He's found someone else, someone younger, who suffered less in the war, maybe hardly noticed it. He ran away from you and Nada, avoided seeing you, because he didn't know how to tell you, how to excuse his betrayal."

❦

A week or two later, early one Sunday morning when we were still in bed, there was a loud knocking on the front door. Mother opened it and I, half-asleep, strained to hear who had come at that unearthly hour.

"You don't recognise me, aunt," said a male voice. "We haven't seen each other since the day Father took us to Podgorica."

"Is that you, Dragan Rajković?" cried Mother. "We'd given you up for dead!"

I rushed out and we hugged and inspected each other: five years had passed since our last meeting.

That morning Dragan moved into my room. The only piece of furniture was a very large, unsteady, iron bed we had got from the Property Board, which was in charge of distributing household goods that had belonged to the Vojvodina Germans. Dragan and I shared this, covering ourselves with army blankets, our only bedclothes. We used to talk until late into the night about all that had happened in the meantime.

After the death of his mother and sister in the allied bombing of May 1944, Dragan left Podgorica and with some Rajković cousins moved with the Germans and Chetniks as they pushed out of Montenegro towards the West. During the withdrawal, he said, they had to fight all the way, under constant attack from the Partisans, hardly having time to stop and bury their dead. The roads were crowded with refugees and bands of armed men, members of all the different military formations that had fought the Partisans in the course of the war. Everyone was trying to get to the West in the belief that the Allies would accept them as anti-communists.

Eventually, Dragan's decimated group of Montenegrin Chetniks reached Slovenia, and after another six days managed to get to Bleiburg across the Austrian border. There, in a broad valley, they found tens of thousands of Germans, Ustashas, Chetniks and all kinds of other refugees who had arrived before them, packed so close together there seemed to be no space for any more. This mass of people was surrounded by British tanks, their guns pointing inward. Dragan and his group stopped on the fringe, on a little wooded hill from where they could observe the scene. One of their number went closer to ask some Ustashas what was happening and was told their leaders were having talks with the British. All the time British fighter planes were flying low overhead.

After some time, a Partisan officer, standing on a truck with several British officers, addressed the crowd through a megaphone: the war was over, all weapons had to be surrendered at once, everyone would be sent home and nothing would happen to them – only the guilty would be punished.

"Many didn't believe the officer's encouraging words," Dragan recounted, "especially when Partisans with machine-guns started surrounding us, so they began running off into the nearby woods. People started arguing about whether to give up their weapons or keep them and try to escape back home. But most people threw their weapons on to the heaps and resigned themselves to their fate at the hands of the Partisans.

"With several relatives I made off into the woods again, and after walking the whole of the next day through pouring rain we reached Celovec [Klagenfurt], drenched to the skin. Now, after all the hardships and dangers we'd been through in the past couple of months since leaving Podgorica, we finally felt we were safely out of reach of the Partisans. But at the entrance to the town we were stopped by British soldiers, who disarmed us, loaded us on to a truck and drove us straight back to Bleiburg. Now it was clear to us that the British we'd put so much faith in were on the other side.

"Back in that broad valley there were still crowds of people waiting. The Partisans were getting them into columns and taking them back to Yugoslavia. We joined the Montenegrins we found there. Then they brought up some captured horses and gave them to us to lead along the Drava river to Maribor. The British with their tanks and heavy artillery stayed on the other side of the border, and as soon as we crossed it we saw what kind of welcome we could expect in Yugoslavia. If any of the Partisans we passed recognised a person from his village that he had something against, he would pull him out of the column and shoot him on the spot. All the way to Maribor there were scores lying dead by the road: Ustashas, Chetniks, Nedić's men, Bosnian Moslems, Slovenian Home Guards…

"In Maribor we were crammed into an already overcrowded camp. Again we Montenegrins all stayed together. Lots of Partisan officers kept coming round asking our names and looking at us one by one, trying to find people that were on their wanted list. Then they separated all the older men, the women, and boys under seventeen to send them home to Montenegro. Among them was Vjera, the younger sister of Danica Popović who lived with us in Cetinje for a while. Vjera was with a fellow from Vlado Kokotan's gang. When they were taking him away to be shot, she clung to him and wouldn't let go, so they shot her too.

"Then a few days later they lined up all males from seventeen to twenty, me included. 'You're young and you've been led astray, so you won't be punished, only sent into the army,' they told us. Next day we were put on a train and taken to some military barracks near Zagreb. Those who refused to join the army for whatever reason, like our two cousins Mirko and Milutin Rajković, were all shot. In Zagreb I heard from some men who'd been spared that after I left the camp, the Parti-

sans shot tens of thousands of men older than twenty, mostly Ustashas and Chetniks.

"In the army I was given a uniform and cap with a five-pointed star – overnight I was transformed from a Chetnik into a Partisan! Luckily, the war was over so they couldn't send me to the front, only to blow up bunkers and ruins left by the war. When I was demobbed at the end of last year, I felt I had to go to Podgorica again, to visit the graves of Mother and Dragica and tidy them up. I stayed for a while with Slavka, helping her in the photographer's. She said you'd asked about me when you were in Podgorica, on the way to Albania. She was the one who told me about Duško and that you were now in Belgrade."

Dragan lived with us for several months, then one day simply disappeared. Some time afterwards we got a card from Italy, where he had gone in search of his father. Having crossed the border illegally, like many young men at that time who left the country for political, economic or family reasons, or simply to see the world, he spent a year in an Italian refugee camp before he traced his father, Mihajlo, in Australia and joined him there.

⚜

One evening when I got home from school, who should open the door to me but Aco, wearing naval uniform, looking healthy and sun-tanned, and almost as tall as I was, though he was only twelve and I was sixteen. Nearly four years had passed since I'd said goodbye to him in Cetinje, and now our joy knew no bounds.

"Here I am back from the Navy!" he said with a big grin. "I got fed up with being so far from Mother and home, so I asked them to discharge me."

It was a wonderful feeling to be reunited with my younger brother, whose fate had been unknown to us for so long.

In the Navy Aco had acquired some technical knowledge, which he used mainly to play tricks on us, such as wiring up the handles so that we got electric shocks when we opened doors. Sometimes Nada and I got really annoyed about his practical jokes, but Mother always came to his defence:

"Let the poor boy enjoy himself! He never had a chance to play at the normal time."

Day by day our new home became more lively and cheerful as family and friends, scattered by the war, gathered together again. Food and money were scarce, the shops were virtually empty, we had the bare minimum of clothes and furniture, yet after all the horrors of the war, life seemed wonderful. Whenever relatives or friends came to stay for a few nights or a few months, we somehow made room for them. There was never less than six or seven of us living there, so Mother gave up her job as a cook and became a housewife once more, happy to have a crowd around her again.

We were often visited by young people from Cetinje who had come to Belgrade to study or to escape the boredom of provincial life. The former Montenegrin capital was no longer even the main administrative centre: Podgorica, renamed Titograd and being rapidly reconstructed as a modern city, was chosen as the capital of the new Republic of Montenegro. The main reason for this was its closeness to Albania, since there was a plan at the time for Albania to become a seventh constituent republic of Yugoslavia.

Of all the Cetinje students, the one we felt closest to was Duško's friend Mošo, who spent most of his free time in our flat.

"When I see him, it's like seeing my poor Duško again. The two of them were always together," Mother used to say.

Mošo still suffered from his war wounds: he was slightly lame and complained of frequent headaches from the shrapnel still embedded in his skull. Now the war was over, it was as if he didn't see any place for himself in the new society which he had helped to create. He found a lot to criticise in some of his former comrades who now occupied important posts. All he wanted to do was to study literature, write poetry, live a quiet life on his invalid pension. Tall and stooping, with curly black hair, large dark eyes and a pale face, he always looked somehow melancholy even when smiling. In the opinion of Nada's girlfriends, who all rather fancied him, this gave him the air of a Romantic poet.

But poets at that time, like all writers and artists, were expected to serve the goals of the new society, as in Soviet Russia. Sometimes I would go with Mošo, Nada and their crowd to poetry evenings, at which poets who had themselves been through the horrors of war gave readings of their works. Afterwards, at home, someone would read the poems again from the booklets which were handed out free of charge, and there would be long discussions. When they'd had enough of war subjects, Mošo, Nada or one of the others would recite Essenin, the Russian lyrical poet who had welcomed the Revolution and the ideals of the new society, but had become disillusioned with the reality and hanged himself. At that time many idealistic people, Mošo among them, felt a sense of disappointment that the new Yugoslavia was not free from compulsion, injustices and inequalities. Others couldn't settle down to a humdrum life after the war. For whatever reason, there was a sudden increase in the number of suicides in Belgrade in that period.

Other people from Cetinje, most of them friends of Duško, used to come to our house, usually to pay their respects to Mother. One of these was Duda Muhadinović, a young man of athletic build with wavy blond hair and blue eyes – in appearance quite the opposite of Mošo. He stayed for several hours, recalling the time he spent with Mošo and Duško at the Colfiorito camp. From Mošo we had already heard how Duda, together with two Cetinje friends, had made his way back to Yugoslavia. A few days after escaping from the prison camp, the three of them had managed somehow to get hold of automatic rifles and a quantity of ammunition. Travelling through the Apennines, mostly at night, they eventually reached a small place close to Trieste. Starving and exhausted, they decided in desperation to enter a café and ask for something to eat. Unluckily, a dozen Blackshirts who had joined the Germans after Italy's capitulation happened to be dining there. When they saw three armed civilians, they leapt up from the table to grab their weapons, but Duda and his two comrades were quicker and mowed down all twelve of them. They then succeeded in evading the patrols sent out to hunt them down and in reaching the Slovenian Partisans across the border. Because of this feat and similar stories about Duda that I heard from other former Colfiorito prisoners, I was extremely proud of knowing him. I heard from Mošo that Duda now spent much of his time in a small pub in the town centre which was frequented by the Colfiorito crowd. But as time went by and his friends, one by one, found jobs and got married, Duda remained alone, a misfit in the new society.

Early one morning in the winter of 1947, which was exceptionally cold, with heavy snow and hurricane-force winds, Mošo arrived at our flat looking pale and gloomy.

"Duda Muhadinović is dead, Milica," he said. "Stabbed in the heart by some miserable drunk he had a quarrel with in the pub."

We were so shocked that for a time none of us could utter a word, even to ask a question.

"I dropped by to meet him at the pub last evening," Mošo recounted, "but when I arrived he'd already been taken to the mortuary. As I walked in, the publican called to two policemen waiting there: 'This is a friend of his.'

'Some Duda, a Montenegrin, has been killed,' one of them said. 'Come with us to identify him.'

"And so they took me off to the mortuary. All the way there I kept hoping there was some mistake: Duda was capable of defending himself not just against one but against a dozen. But there he was, lying stark naked on the wet concrete floor, with those bulging muscles of his. The man who killed him was half his size, but he took him by surprise."

One morning in March 1947 the newspaper Borba [Struggle] carried a report that several outlaws, among them Dušan Vuković, had been killed in a skirmish with police officers in the Katun district of Montenegro. In the performance of his duties, Commander Mugoša had died a heroic death. This news shocked and saddened me, but less than it affected my great friend from Cetinje, Raco Vuković, who had turned up in Belgrade one day and had been living with us for several months. The atmosphere at home was very strained as he mourned his father, Dušan, and I, Commander Mugoša, who had been so good to me.

Raco, downcast and anxious, wondered whether he was likely to be gaoled, as he had already been for some months in Cetinje at the end of the war, in the hope he would lead them to his father.

"Don't you worry," Mother tried to reassure him, "nobody will ever lay a finger on you while you're in this house."

Not long after that, Raco disappeared. Years later I heard that he had settled in Canada.

⅌

In May 1948 my class took the final exams for the matriculation certificate. When we gathered together in school for the last time, mainly eighteen-year-olds preparing to make our way in life, many had tears in their eyes.

"What are we going to do now we've finished *gimnazija*?" asked Mika, who wore a black patch over one eye and had the scars of gunpowder burns on his face. He had also lost his front teeth when wounded, and these had been replaced in the hospital by a set made of some kind of metal – we called them his tin teeth. "Are we going to meet up again, see one another? In the past three years the class has been like my family – I haven't got any other. What's going to become of us? What's Predrag going to do with one arm, and Handsome Daša without a leg?" (We used to call him 'handsome' because he was always combing his hair in a pocket mirror and trying to look smart to impress the girls.)

A month or so later, I bumped into Hajro in the street.

"Why weren't you at Daša's funeral?" he asked.

"What Daša? You don't mean our Handsome Daša? What happened to him?"

"He hanged himself!"

⅌

Soon after, Stalin's fateful letters arrived. They accused Tito and the Yugoslav Party leadership of setting themselves apart from the international communist movement, betraying the ideals of the revolution, and called for their replacement. One of the Party's responses was to strengthen its ranks by admitting many new members, mostly young people. So, early in July 1948, at a meeting of all Party members in the Foreign Office held in the festively decorated main hall, I was admitted to the Party, exactly four years after joining the Communist Youth in the Partisans, and was presented with the long-coveted little red membership book, its cover emblazoned in gold with the words: 'Workers of the world, unite!'

I felt I belonged heart and soul to the international workers' movement, firmly convinced that one day, when the proletariat gained power in all countries, there would be universal well-being and brotherly love among all nations, races and creeds. Seeing Russia as the leader along that path towards a better world, I was deeply unhappy about the rift that had appeared. In Cetinje with Mara and in the Partisans, hadn't we dreamt that when the war was over we would become one of the Soviet republics? This unexpected turn of events shocked and perturbed all former Partisans, all members of the Youth and the Party, especially those in Montenegro and Serbia, which had strong historical ties with Russia.

The dispute on who was closer to the teachings of Marx and Lenin soon developed into an open conflict that threatened to escalate into war with the Soviet bloc. In an effort to ensure unity in its ranks in the struggle against Stalin and maintain the country's independence, the Party launched the process of 'differentiation', which meant that every member was called upon to make a public declaration of support for Tito and the leadership and condemn the Soviet pressure. The great majority did so, but there were many who openly or privately supported Stalin and thought the Party and country should bow to the Russian demands. Some army officers were prepared to lead forces, whether from abroad or within the country, in overthrowing the leadership. Tito's wartime chief of staff, General Arso Jovanović, was killed on the border while attempting to flee to Romania. Among those captured at the same time was Colonel Vlado Dapčević – the same person Father had arrested in Cetinje market before the war for calling on the Montenegrin peasants to rise against the royal government.

Stana explained to me the causes of the quarrel with Stalin:

"You know, Bato, we all wish this conflict had never happened. But they forced the issue. We can't accept being treated by the Russians in the same way as the Bulgars, Romanians, Hungarians and Albanians, who until yesterday were fighting side by side with the Germans, or like the other socialist states liberated by the Russians, who brought their leaders in their baggage train and put them in power. We paid for our freedom with one Yugoslav in seven – there's no need for me to tell you that. After all, we timed the start of our uprising to help Russia: only fifteen days after Hitler launched Operation Barbarosa. We made him divert some of his best troops to Yugoslavia and slowed down the blitzkrieg, so that the Germans were caught unprepared for the Russian winter. But listen, brother. Be extremely careful what you say, because the struggle with the Russians is going to be long and merciless. The security forces, UDBA, now have special powers. They can arrest, interrogate, search premises, as they see fit. For your OZNA the enemies were Germans, Chetniks, Ustashas and other collaborators; for UDBA the enemies are our former comrades, Party members, people who fought bravely in the war. Soon many of them will be separated from their families and isolated on an island in the Adriatic, until they realise their mistake and the danger from Russia passes."

Soon after the head of the personnel department called me to his office to congratulate me on matriculating and tell me that they considered I would make a good diplomat in the future. First, however, it was advisable to continue my studies. In the autumn a new department of the university law faculty would be opening, the School of Journalism and Diplomacy, which would enrol only selected and trusted young comrades, participants in the war and politically active young people. The central committees of the six republics would each nominate about thirty students, and the Army, Tanjug News Agency and the Foreign Ministry, all together another thirty or so.

"From our Ministry," he told me, "only two are being proposed: yourself and Kosta Hermann. As you know, he's from a German family, but with his mother he joined the Partisans as a boy at the start of the uprising – not all our Germans were for Hitler. In four years' time, when you graduate, you'll be able to return to the Ministry."

Autumn is the most beautiful season in Belgrade. The burning heat of summer gives way to pleasantly warm, sunny days. In the west the evening sky turns crimson as the huge orange sun dips rapidly below the horizon, its rays reflected blood-red in the waters of the Sava and Danube. The trees lining the streets are turning colour. Water melons, grapes, tomatoes and peppers are piled high at the open-air markets and at their cheapest.

One sunny late September day, on my way to enrol at the university, I spotted Pero, my hospital room-mate. He was walking on crutches with one artificial leg – the other trouser-leg was tucked up to above the knee. I called out his name and ran over to hug him.

"We haven't seen each other since the day you left hospital," said Pero in a reproachful voice. "I stayed there another two months, and then they put me in the war invalids' home where I am now. I've often thought about you and waited for you to get in touch. You promised we'd see each other after the war…"

"I'm truly sorry. I've been so busy working and studying," I said rather lamely in my defence. "Where are you off to now?" I asked, just to say something. Lying next to each other in the narrow hospital room, we had exhausted all the subjects connected with our war, and now it was too late to start over again in peacetime.

"I'm going to enrol at the Law Faculty," he said proudly. "I want to be a solicitor."

"Then we'll meet up again, because I'll be at the same faculty," I replied.

In the large amphitheatre two hundred and twenty-seven young people were gathered, the first students of the new School of Journalism and Diplomacy. It took three hours for us all to stand up in turn and say our name and where we came from. Slovenia and Croatia had sent their students in new suits, while the rest of us mostly wore a combination of civilian and military garments. There were also about thirty young men and women, some of them with Jewish names, smartly turned out in military uniforms. In rank they ranged from lieutenant to colonel. We differed considerably in age – between eighteen and thirty. Apart from a small number of young activists drawn from the youth organisation, all had fought in the war or been in prison camps in Italy, Germany or the north of Norway. This first meeting of young people from all parts of the country was an exciting experience that filled us with pride and happiness.

"You are the spirit of the New Yugoslavia," declared our dean, in his welcoming address.

❧

A month after the start of lectures, a meeting of all students was called at the request of the Jewish group.

"We Jewish students, civilians and officers," their spokesman said, "were born, grew up and fought in this country. It is with heavy hearts that we have decided to interrupt our studies and go to fight in another war, for the survival of the new Jewish state of Israel. We believe that with our experience from the Partisans we can make a contribution and help our brethren in their time of greatest need. We are grateful to Tito and the Party for their understanding and for allowing Jews to freely leave the country. Yugoslavia will always remain in our hearts as our first homeland. We will never betray or forget it."

All but three or four left our year and set off for Israel with thousands of other Jews from all over the country. The western press reported that Yugoslavia was the first East European country that permitted its Jewish citizens to leave to help the creation of the new state of Israel.

❧

One cold windy day I was wandering aimlessly around the city centre. There was nowhere to go to get out of the cold and pass the time except the Kasina canteen on Terazije Square, where it was always stuffy and crowded, but warm. People were standing in long lines, first to pay, then to queue up for food. There was a choice of cabbage or beans with a piece of bacon swimming in grease mixed with red pepper. Along with this you got a hunk of bread and a bent aluminium spoon.

I picked up a bowl of beans and looked for an empty space at the high counter where I could eat standing up. It was then I thought that

I caught sight of Olga. Was it really her? I couldn't be sure in the weak light from the bare bulbs, so I moved closer. The girl looked up and started when she saw me, so I knew there was no mistake. Her hair covered by a beret, she was dressed in that same coat of her mother's she had worn the time I last saw her. I noticed at once that her hands, holding a bowl and spoon, were roughened and chapped, with broken nails.

"Olga, I hardly recognised you!" I exclaimed tremulously. "What brings you here?"

"And I hardly recognised you. You've changed, got taller," she replied calmly, as though not at all surprised to see me. "I knew I should bump into you one day. Sooner or later everyone meets up on Terazije, like on the corso in Cetinje."

"When shall we meet again?" I hastened to ask the most important question, before enquiring how she came to be in Belgrade, where she was living and how long she was staying.

"She can't go anywhere without me, or meet any boys," broke in a woman standing beside her whom I hadn't previously noticed. She was wearing a black woollen hood that covered one eye and half her face, but when she turned her head it failed to conceal a large burn scar.

"This is a cousin of mine on father's side," Olga explained. "I've been living here with relatives for the past six months. We both work in a printing house. Look how it's ruined my hands." She must have been aware that I couldn't help noticing this. When her relative turned aside for a moment, Olga leant towards me and asked quietly: "Morning or afternoon?"

"Tomorrow morning, as early as you like. Ten o'clock in this place?" She just nodded in answer.

As they pushed their way through the crowd towards the exit, I already felt panicky. This would be my first real date with Olga, but where could we go in this wintry weather? It would be awkward to take her home: Mother, Nada and Aco were there, and who knows who else. The only quiet place was Stana's flat. What's more, she had a Tesla radio – pride of our new industry – which at that time was accessible only to our leaders. It would be wonderful to sit there together, listening to the radio and talking over all that had happened in the past four years.

I rushed to Stana's office to ask her whether I could spend an hour or two in her flat next day while she was at work – it was warm and close to my faculty, so I could study there in peace.

"Of course you can," she said, handing me a spare key. "I'm not sure when Zuska is coming to clean the place. Probably not tomorrow as she hasn't let me know."

Next day I pushed my way into the ever-crowded Kasina at the agreed time, looking around anxiously for Olga. Would she manage to get out of the house alone or would that cousin be chaperoning her? Worse still, she might not come at all: she may have forgotten, or perhaps she didn't want to see me again. When the hands on the large round clock showed exactly ten and there was no sign of her, my heart sank. I elbowed my way to the door, then back again to the high counter where we had met the day before. And when I had given up hope, she appeared.

"I thought you would have gone, got fed up with waiting for me," she said, out of breath. "I froze to the bone waiting for the tram in the cold wind for over an hour. And when it finally came, I only just managed to get on. People were packed together like seeds in a pomegranate."

My sister lived in Krunska Street, fashionable before the war, with elegant houses that had belonged to the well-to-do. Stana had a two-room flat on the ground floor of one of these. Besides the Dedinje district with its luxurious villas on a hill above the city, Krunska was considered one of the most desirable residential streets in Belgrade.

"Let's go to my sister's place," I proposed. "It's warm and there's no-one home. We can stay until three, when she usually comes back from work."

"Anywhere's better than this crowded place, as long as it's warm," she answered.

As we hurried along the street, she talked away:

"My relatives don't have a clock, so I kept having to run next door to ask the time, so as not to be late. I didn't sleep soundly last night – kept waking up with a start to see if it was dawn. I've been on sick leave for a week, so I've been able to rest a bit during the day. Bit by bit the lead fumes are poisoning me. I don't know how much longer I'll be able to stand it."

The flat was bright and comfortable. Everything was in its place. Stana had always lived like that. I remembered that when we were all together in Cetinje, she was the one who put some order into the household – not easy with such a large family. During the war, she told us, even in the middle of an enemy offensive, she would wash her clothes in any nearby stream and dry them before the fire in a peasant household, just so she would appear clean and tidy before the fighters or before the Germans if she were killed.

"It's something I learnt at boarding school in Kragujevac," she explained.

"How beautiful it is here," exclaimed Olga with a sigh." It's like being back in the government apartment in Cetinje, with Mama and Papa. Our place was like this. Every night I dream how your Partisans came and drove us out of the house, took my mother and father off to be shot, and left me all alone. Mama shrieked and shrieked because they were taking her away from me. And I screamed too. Only Papa kept quiet, said nothing."

"I know, Olga. It was a terrible thing that happened to your parents, and to you. But I remember that your father could have saved my brother Duško if he'd wanted to. We're not to blame for these things and we shouldn't reproach each other over them… Shall I turn on the radio? There may be some music we can listen to."

"Lucky Stana to have a radio! We used to have one."

The radio started playing and I sat beside Olga on the sofa. Just then I heard a key turning in the front-door lock. I hurried to see who it was.

"I'm Zuska, come to do the cleaning."

I had seen this Slovak peasant woman a couple of times before at Stana's. Along with dozens of others, she travelled daily some thirty kilometres from the Slovak village of Kovačica to do domestic work in homes in the capital. Groups of Slovaks, Germans, Romanians and other nationalities from various parts of her realm were settled in Vojvodina over two centuries ago by Empress Maria Theresa, and most had retained their traditional costumes and language. Zuska was now standing there in the doorway in her wide starched skirts in several layers, embroidered woollen shawl, and warm sheepskin bodice.

"I couldn't let the lady know I was coming. The trains aren't regular and on time, so I can never tell for sure if and when I'll arrive," she explained. "I see you've got a young lady here. I won't bother you: first I'll do the kitchen and bedroom, then this room where you're sitting."

"I was so much hoping we would be alone," said Olga sadly.

I was sad, too, and also worried. After my story about studying, how would I explain Olga's presence to my sister when she heard the truth from Zuska? A difference in age of almost ten years made our relationship tender yet restrained.

In our family we never discussed relationships between men and women or made jokes on that subject. I would feel embarrassed in front of Stana and, even worse, I wouldn't be able to ask for her flat key again on the pretext of studying.

Why did Zuska have to turn up just then? Because of her presence nearby, our conversation was stiff and unnatural. Instead of talking about ourselves, we spoke of Cetinje and our mutual acquaintances.

"Did you ever see Rajko Vujović?" I asked.

"Of course. He works in the Obod printing house as a compositor, swallowing lead. He's been named 'outstanding worker' several times – got his picture in the paper. His brother is away studying in Sarajevo, but Rajko still lives with his mother in that same house, near yours."

"Did he tell you about Mila?"

"We never talked except to say 'hello' when we met – nothing more. I heard that she left Cetinje before the Partisans entered, lucky girl. If only we had! Everything would be different now."

"So you don't know that Mila got no further than Rijeka Crnojevića? She fell out of a truck and got killed. No-one knows where she was buried."

"I didn't know," Olga answered, appearing indifferent. "Every day I hear more bad news; it gets worse all the time. God knows how I'll go on living like this, without any joy."

"You're going to stay in Belgrade now?" I asked. "We'll see each other and go out together."

"Shall we come here again?"

"I'm not sure about here, but there's other places."

"I'll go back to work in a few days. It'll be hard to get away from my cousin. I'll try, though I get back from work dead tired and only want to lie down and rest. Are you sure you want us to meet?"

"Why do you ask when you know very well that I do?"

"I'm an ordinary worker, without education, and you've gone further. Look at your hands and look at mine. When you left for Albania, you said you'd come back soon, but I knew even then that we were two different worlds. Still, I waited for a while and hoped."

At that moment Zuska came in to clean the sitting room so we felt obliged to leave. Before we parted, we arranged to meet again the following day at the Kasina. At the appointed time there was no sign of Olga. The tram's probably late again, I thought, and waited for one hour, then two, going out into the street to look around, then going back inside again. Finally, I came to the conclusion that one of us must have made a mistake. Perhaps it was tomorrow, not today. The following day, and the day after, I waited in vain.

I didn't hear anything about Olga for a long time. Then one day I saw her cousin in the street.

"Stop a minute, please! Can you tell me what's happened to Olga? Where is she?"

"My mother didn't want to keep her any longer, so she packed her off back to Cetinje."

❧

When I arrived home one evening I found Mother in tears for the first time since we'd stood beside Duško's grave. From Stana, just back from a trip to Montenegro, she had heard that Father's friend, Pero Popović, had hanged himself:

"He survived a Turkish sabre, got away from an Italian firing squad, got through all the battles in the Partisans, only to take his own life, so that his comrades wouldn't condemn him. Who would have thought Partisans would ever turn against one another, as against the worst enemy?"

I heard the details of the story from Stana a few days later:

"After the war he came home with a medal for bravery and became the mayor of the coastal town of Petrovac in Bar district. When the conflict with the Russians began, he made some ill-advised statements. Then someone told him he was going to be arrested for this, and rather than go to gaol he ended his life."

According to Stana, the situation in Montenegro was alarming. The Montenegrins, always intolerant when it came to political differences and extreme in their reactions, had become polarised over the break with the Soviet Union. Even she had been reluctant to go out in the streets in case she met and was greeted warmly by old friends and comrades who may have declared for Stalin and could end up in prison next day. It was only there, it seemed, that people had taken seriously Stalin's call for the overthrow of Tito – in one area the entire district Party committee had taken to the woods and was waiting for the Russians to arrive!

"I'm doing my best to save some wonderful people who are mad about Stalin," Stana went on. "A couple of days ago I even wept in front of Milovan Djilas [the leading Party ideologue] and begged him to help someone. I remember that he once talked to a group of us about how we Yugoslavs, in our great enthusiasm for Stalin just after the war, had gone too far in copying the Soviet system he created. We adopted everything – the constitution, laws, regulations, even text-books – and started applying them indiscriminately. We accepted the Party monopoly of government, democratic centralism, unity of the legal, judicial and executive powers. We copied Stalin in our lack of tolerance towards people with different views, and in his methods of dealing with them – not ever having known anything much different in these wild Balkans of ours."

"It must have been an important person," I said, "to make you weep in front of Djilas."

"It was the only person I would do that for, and not only in front of Djilas, but before Tito himself: Mara Laković. She came to see me, and she went to your place, but no-one was home. She told me that soon after the war she moved to Vojvodina, together with a lot of other families from the poor northern part of Katun district. She got a house and some land in a village left empty by the Germans near the Hungarian border – the village is now Montenegrin and renamed Lovćenac. She was very active in the local collective farm, and everything was fine until Stalin's letters. Then the same trouble as in Montenegro started among our 'colonists' there. Mara couldn't bring herself overnight to denounce Stalin and the Russians: it was her faith in them that kept her going throughout the war. She came to me for help when she realised she was in danger of being arrested. It was the thought that good, kind Mara could become an innocent victim, that she could lose her belief in everything that Bogdan died for – that was what made me weep."

In the course of our four years at the School, we had to pass thirty exams, more than any other Belgrade faculty. From the outset there was a wonderful spirit of friendship among us: we all knew one another by name and had many shared wartime experiences that brought us closer together than students in other faculties. These friends were from all parts of the country – the Slovenes and Macedonians all spoke Serbo-Croatian well so there were no obstacles to communication. Spending long evenings together, we learnt a great deal about the other republics. After neat, baroque Ljubljana, bomb-damaged Belgrade with its haphazard mixture of styles and general untidiness did not much impress the Slovenes. One of them joked that older Slovenes had still not recovered from the shock they suffered in 1918 when they found out that, instead of Vienna, Belgrade was to be their capital.

"Our people studied in Vienna; many of them worked there. It was always closer to us, both in distance and in culture, than Belgrade. But the Austrians wanted to Germanize us – we had to struggle against that for centuries. Then, in pre-war Yugoslavia, the Serbs wanted to dominate us. Thanks to the Partisan war, we've now got our own republic and equality with the other Yugoslav nations."

Arriving at the faculty one day in autumn 1951, I noticed something strange going on. Instead of the usual relaxed atmosphere, jokes and smiles, people were standing around outside talking seriously in small groups, running from one group to another, making gestures of surprise or incomprehension, whispering confidentially… As soon as he saw me, Bulat, an older friend who had been in the Colfiorito camp with my brother, left a group of fellow Montenegrins and hurried over:

"Last night a lot of students from our year were arrested. They say UDBA's uncovered a den of Soviet spies in the School!"

Among the 230 students of our year summoned to a meeting in the Law Faculty, which had a hall large enough to hold us, an atmosphere of urgency and alarm prevailed. Before it started, people were moving around the courtyard, trying to find out exactly who had been arrested. Then we all crowded into the amphitheatre and waited anxiously for the start of the extraordinary meeting.

A member of the University Party committee stood up to speak:

"Comrades, I must tell you that the enemy has wormed his way even into our ranks. We must show him no mercy. Each of us must ask ourselves who we keep company with, what we talk about, what stands we have adopted on the key questions for the survival of our society and country. We must rid ourselves of all those who have no place in our Party, who support Stalin and do not share our desire for independence…"

After this the arrests continued. I never went to bed without a feeling of dread. In the morning we would find out at the faculty who had been arrested during the night. At Party meetings, which were held almost every evening and sometimes lasted until dawn, we were called upon to publicly condemn our arrested colleagues. At one of these marathon meetings, the younger brother of the highly influential Milovan Djilas accused a dozen of his fellow students, myself among them, of being pro-Stalin, and called for us to be expelled from the Party. Proof of this in my case, he said, was my close friendship with a student who had been arrested. I was fully aware that expulsion might be followed by my own arrest and dispatch to join the other 'Cominformists' on the dreaded Goli otok ('Barren Island') prison-island in the Adriatic. With all the powers of persuasion I could command, I argued my innocence, standing up to speak several times, fighting for survival. When it came to the vote, I was not expelled, but I was summoned for questioning by a special commission of the Yugoslav Central Committee. The first nerve-wracking session – to be followed by many more in the following weeks – lasted a full two hours. The experienced interrogators used all their wiles to trick me into confessing my alleged Stalinist views and treasonable plotting with my arrested friend, who had had plenty of time on Goli otok, they said, to make a lengthy written statement implicating me. In the end, I was told to come back next day.

At once I set off to find Nikić, certain he would be prepared to intervene on my behalf with his UDBA colleagues, who held my fate in their hands. When I knocked on the door of his bachelor flat, as always he was delighted to see me. After hearing of my predicament, he promised to do his best and gave me some advice. Next day, he said, they would ask me the same questions in the same order, and as they would have a verbatim transcript of today's interrogation, they would compare the two sets of answers. If they could find any discrepancies, I would be finished.

"Now go home and try to remember exactly what you said today, and repeat it word for word tomorrow. This is some new American system of interrogation our people have started using. The Americans and the West in general are helping us to stand up to Stalin."

It turned out just as Nikić said and I followed his instructions. The commission's questioning of students, among them some close friends like Bulat, went on for several months. Finally, a year after that first meeting of the whole School, we were summoned together again – our ranks somewhat depleted by UDBA's activities. The chairman of the special commission first read out the names of students who were to be given a final reprimand before expulsion. My name was on this lengthy list, my 'lack of vigilance' being cited as the reason. The commission considered there was hope for these members, and they would be given a last chance to mend their ways and remain in the Party.

"You're not on the list. You've got off!" I muttered with a grin to Bulat, sitting beside me. "And I haven't done too badly."

Feeling tremendous relief, we thought for a moment that this was all the commission was going to announce. But the worst was to follow. The chairman proceeded to read out a list of about thirty students who were to be expelled from the Party and School: Bulat's name was among them. After this, he and the others could expect imminent arrest. In case UDBA called on him where he was living with some Montenegrin relatives, I brought him home to sleep in our flat. Mother, always ready to take in any friend in need, regardless of the political consequences, welcomed him warmly. She had, in any case, a soft spot for Bulat because he would patiently retell every little detail of life in the Colfiorito camp and everything he could remember about my brother.

⁂

One last meeting of our whole student body followed, presided over by the same committee members as the first time, all looking very grave. One of them stood up to make an announcement:

"We have to inform you of important decisions taken by the Yugoslav Central Committee. First, from today the School of Journalism and Diplomacy is closed down. Those who have taken their final exams will be awarded degrees; the rest will be able to transfer to other faculties. Second, from today your Party organisation is disbanded and you cease to be Party members. All of you must return at once to the places you have come from, where you can show by your actions whether you are worthy to be received back into the Party. Written decisions on where you will live and work can be collected from the Committee. That is the end of this announcement. You are asked to disperse quietly."

Speechless with shock, we looked at one another in bewilderment. Until recently we had been held up as an example to others, as the most successful faculty of Belgrade University, which had over fifty thousand students. Was it possible that we were all to be cruelly punished for the mistakes of some of our colleagues? What important person had it in for us? There was talk that lately Milovan Djilas had looked upon the School with disapproval.

Luckily for me, I was among the students who had passed all their exams on time, so I could pick up my degree diploma. At the same time I was handed the written decision regarding my posting. Nebojša Tomašević, it stated, must return immediately to Cetinje, where he will be assigned appropriate duties, as needed. His character assessment will be sent separately.

"Can you give me the diploma and decision for Bulat – he's had to go to Vojvodina?" I asked, not letting on that he had been lying low in our flat since his expulsion. He, too, was ordered to return to Cetinje.

"Our diplomacy will be a lot of use to us there, at the court of King Nikola!" he joked, relieved because it looked as if he would soon be out of reach of the Belgrade UDBA. "And luck's on your side. You'll be with your Olga again in Cetinje."

"Yes, she's there, but it's too late. Nobody waits forever. Rajko wrote me that she's taken up with some Cetinje footballer."

He left for Montenegro as quickly as he could, but I decided I would try to stay in Belgrade.

In the English Department of the Philosophy Faculty, where I had enrolled as a part-time student a year before and taken several exams, the atmosphere was completely different. Though it had almost the same number of students as our School, the Party organisation numbered only a dozen or so. The great majority of students took little interest in politics or had decided it was better to keep out of them. The good-looking, well-groomed girls from pre-war well-to-do families who studied English exchanged western gramophone records and copied down the words of songs sung by Frank Sinatra and other popular crooners. There was no danger of their being accused of pro-Stalinism.

My idea was to enrol as a regular, full-time student of English and with this status avoid having to return to Cetinje, which seemed to me a step backward in life at a time when I was eager to go forward. However, this proved much more difficult than I'd expected, for the break with the eastern bloc was moving us closer to the West, and English was now an extremely popular subject. In order to cope with the demand, the Department had had to restrict the number of full-time students. I asked Stana if she could help, so she contacted the dean of the faculty, the Ministry for Education, the chairman of the faculty council… All of them said they were powerless to intervene, and I had almost given

1930s postcard
showing the
building of Belgrade
University (left)
Philosophy Faculty,
which included the
English Department,
and (centre) the then
Stock Exchange

up hope, reconciled to going back to Montenegro, when one day, in front of the faculty building, I bumped into a young man I knew quite well from Cetinje.

"Where've you been, Vujica?" I asked. "I haven't seen you for ages. Where are you working?"

"Oh, I'm pen-pushing in the records office here at the Philosophy Faculty. Look at my fingers, covered in ink! And what about you?"

I told him I was trying to enrol at that very faculty, and even Stana had been unable to help.

"Why didn't you come straight here and find one of your own folk? We Montenegrins have to stick together. I'll look for your application and before you can blink twice I'll have it finished. Just wait here."

Vujica went inside and reappeared twenty minutes later with my form duly verified and stamped with the faculty seal.

"There you are," he said with a grin. "When you go chasing those pretty girls, don't forget me!"

"Wait a moment, Vujica," I said, unable to believe my luck. "How on earth did you manage it?"

"Nothing simpler, Bato. I just took your application from the bottom of the heap and put it at the top, among those that have been accepted, and entered your name in the register."

From lectures and exams I already knew a lot of people in the English Department. My transfer was especially welcomed by the girls as there were very few male students. But before I had time to get better acquainted with any of them, something unexpected turned up. It was announced that after lengthy talks with our education authorities, the British Government had 'unfrozen' the Serbian Fund, established in the First World War by voluntary British donations to assist the education of young people whose studies had been interrupted by the war. I immediately applied for a stipend as I fulfilled all the conditions: candidates had to be under twenty-four, unmarried, a participant in the war on the British side, and a graduate with a very good degree and sufficient knowledge of English to follow lectures. There were masses of applicants, but very few met all these conditions. When the final choice of five students was announced, I was one of three from the School of Journalism and Diplomacy.

Sir Fitzroy Maclean
and Bato Tomašević,
Argyll, Scotland, 1990

To England and Back

September 1953. After two days and nights of sitting in a third-class train compartment and six hours crossing a very rough Channel, it was a relief to sight the famous White Cliffs of Dover. Two hours later, the boat train drew into Victoria Station. Waiting for me was the driver of Ambassador Velebit, who had been asked by Stana to help me during my first few days in England. When, in 1948, Stalin accused General Velebit of being a British spy, he had expected him to be shot, as was the practice in the eastern bloc, to which Yugoslavia belonged at the time. Instead, he remained at the Foreign Office and in 1952 Tito sent him as ambassador to Rome, and a year later, before his planned first state visit to the West, to the Court of St James.

"The Ambassador said he'd like you to come to see him in the morning." said the chauffeur. "For the rest of today, I can drive you around London. What would you like to see first?"

"If possible, I'd like to visit the grave of Karl Marx. And if we could stop somewhere on the way to buy some flowers…"

After a lengthy drive northward across the city we reached the gates of the famous Highgate Cemetery. Clutching my flowers, I humbly approached Marx's grave. Here lay the remains of a man whose ideas had revolutionised the world and transformed the down-trodden masses into a mighty class who had made their rulers tremble. It was not by chance that the cover of my red Party book carried the slogan "Workers of the World, Unite!"

"I've been wanting to meet you," General Velebit greeted me, shaking hands. "I'm sorry about your School. It was a mistake to close it. Our diplomatic service is in need of well-educated and well-mannered young people. Brigadier Fitzroy Maclean is coming to dinner tomorrow evening at eight o'clock. You come along too, but an hour earlier so you can meet and have a chat with Vera."

When I turned up at the residence at the appointed time, the Velebits – Vladimir, known to his friends as Vlatko, and his beautiful, elegant wife Vera – welcomed me like a member of the family. I realised that this was because of their friendship with Stana. Most of the hour before dinner was spent discussing my forthcoming studies in the city of Exeter at the University College of the South West, to which I had been assigned.

Fitzroy Maclean arrived, tall, thin, ruggedly handsome, dressed in a dark suit.

"I've just come from Parliament. A *loza* please, Montenegrin if you have it. It's cold outside!" He said all this in excellent Serbo-Croatian, then switched to English.

"Vlatko tells me you're the brother of Stana Tomašević. She did a great deal to give the British a better opinion of the Partisans, together with Vlatko, of course. I must tell you a little story about that," said Fitzroy with a smile, leaning back comfortably in the armchair. "When nobody had much idea what the Partisans were like, we parachuted in a military photographer, John Talbot, to take pictures of the delegates attending the youth congress at the just liberated town of Drvar in Bosnia. Talbot brought back a lot of photos, among them some of Stana, who was presiding at the congress. When our officers saw these, they all shouted: 'If this is what Yugoslav Partisans are like, we volunteer to join them straight away!' Stana looked more like a fashion model than a guerrilla fighter! Afterwards, one of her pictures appeared in papers all around the world and showed that the Partisans were not a lot of savages."

I felt it a great privilege to meet the legendary Maclean, promoted by Churchill to become the youngest British brigadier at the age of thirty-two and dropped by parachute into Yugoslavia to head the British military mission with Tito.

As he said goodbye to me at the end of the evening, Ambassador Velebit added:

"When you come back from Exeter, if I'm still here I'll arrange to keep you at the Embassy. After all, you were among the first people at the Ministry!"

🦋

After a four-hour train journey to Exeter through the green countryside of England, I found a room in a small hotel near the station for the next couple of days, until I was due to move into a student hall of residence and start my course. Wandering around this peaceful, historic city, with its Roman walls and magnificent Gothic cathedral, I was surprised to see so many ruined buildings. I wondered what significance the city could have had for German bombers.

"Probably not much," replied the hotel receptionist when I asked about this. "Their main target was Plymouth, forty miles further west, because of the naval base and dockyard. I suppose they just dropped their surplus bombs on any place along the way that took their fancy. Exeter used to be a really lovely old town, but the main thing is that the cathedral wasn't badly damaged. We'll manage to rebuild the rest."

🦋

My hall of residence, Kilmorie, exclusively for male students, was a terrace of large, late Victorian, red-brick houses converted for this purpose. At a table in the entrance hall, waiting to welcome the incoming students, sat the Matron, a rather severe lady in her forties. Her first words were to instruct me where to go to collect a ration book and to hand it over to her, since meat, eggs and some other items were still rationed and students took all their meals in hall.

All the students I came across seemed pleasant and helpful. I was by no means the only foreigner. In the room next to mine there was an oriental gentleman who introduced himself with bows as "Mister Akiho, member of the Japanese diplomatic service. It's good we are settled here," he went on. "Did you also have difficulty in finding a hotel room before coming here?"

"No difficulty," I answered.

"When I reached Exeter, I tried several hotels, but there were no rooms. Then at the Imperial Hotel they told me 'We do not accept Japanese'."

"What did you do?"

"I went to the police, and they gave me a bed for the night. Now I instruct them in judo and other martial arts."

Later, when we became friends, he confided that he had been among the last generation of kamikaze whose take-off had been averted by the surrender of Japan.

When all one hundred and eight members of the hall gathered for dinner that evening, I noticed a number of black students from British colonies. I particularly liked the look of a tall, handsome Nigerian of athletic build named Eddie Enahoro, who became a close friend. He told me he and others from African colonies had been selected by the British to be trained as future administrators after independence. There were also several American exchange students, a couple of them gigantic young men who soon became stars of the college rugby team. All this cosmopolitan crowd were wearing black undergraduate gowns over their jackets, except for myself.

At the entrance to the large dining hall we were greeted by the head waiter in a black dinner jacket, stiff white shirt-front and black bow tie. The other waiters standing around were similarly dressed. The Warden, Professor Spiers, an authority on medieval English literature, and the Matron sat with a number of students at 'high table', on a raised dais at one end, while the rest of us sat where we liked at the rows of tables for ten.

I found myself with nine English students – British, to be more precise, for my neighbour, the first to introduce himself, turned out to be a Welshman named Gary Bach.

"I'm in my second year," he said. "If you have any questions or problems, I'll do what I can to help."

Unlike most of the others, who wore shabby tweed jackets with leather elbow patches and baggy flannels, Gary was smartly dressed and groomed, with a broad, flashing smile that revealed his even white teeth. I took to him at once and ventured to ask whether this was a particularly important dinner: apart from the gowns and the waiters, I noticed that we each had rows of silver cutlery, like at the Ambassador's.

"No, all our evening meals are served like this," Gary replied. "But, as you'll soon find out, it would be better if they bothered less about the service and gave us decent food, and more of it. Their excuse is rationing. Anyway, they say good table manners are more important than good food! By the way, this is what they call 'formal dinner' and you're supposed to wear a gown. You can get one at the college clothing suppliers in town."

I began wondering how I, as a Marxist, dedicated to the abolition of all outdated traditions, could possibly appear in public in this medieval garment, so I refused to conform.

Though Gary and I did not see eye-to-eye politically, there was one subject we fully agreed upon and could spend hours discussing – girls. Tirelessly we watched them pass by Kilmorie from the nearby women's halls as they hurried to lectures in town, or, dressed in their Sunday best, on their way to a service in the Cathedral in colourful frocks al-most down to their ankles and a variety of little hats that I thought ridiculous, but which nevertheless gave them a serious air.

"Listen to me carefully,' Gary once said. 'There are approximately 800 students at Exeter: half boys, half girls. At Kilmorie there are 108 of us, but luckily for you and me, only a dozen or so have girlfriends – the others simply don't bother. So, Bato, you can take your pick! But keep one thing in mind. When you meet a girl you'd like to take out, don't forget to ask first of all what hall she's in, or you may soon come to regret it. You may find yourself walking miles to her hall in the pouring rain or spending your last penny on a taxi. Pretty soon you'll cool off and start looking for someone living closer to Kilmorie."

From Gary I learnt that, except when there were formal balls, women students had to be back in their halls by ten most evenings; male visi-tors were not allowed except for occasional 'exchange lunches' between halls on Sundays, which had to be arranged through our respective Matrons.

There were about thirty in my year studying for the two-year English Diploma, which included lectures on English literature and British history, law and government, as well as practical language classes. Some were graduates like myself, others were taking a year or two off from their studies at home. The majority had wealthy and influential parents who wanted them to perfect their English and pick up something of British ways and manners. Among my friends were the daughters of a Thai prince, a Norwegian ship-owner and a French colonial minister, and the sons of a prime minister of Luxembourg and a Singaporean multi-millionaire – a very different collection of students from the School of Journalism and Diplomacy.

There were other differences as well. I was determined to demonstrate my loyalty to my communist, anti-monarchist convictions. Probably already aware of my views, at the first discussion on what essays were to be written in the forthcoming term, my tutor, Dr Parkinson, proposed:

"You, Mr Tomašević, as a true republican, will write an essay for next week attacking the institution of the British monarchy and giving reasons in favour of its abolition. Stay behind after class to take some reading on this subject."

Then he turned to my fellow student from Luxembourg:

"You, as a royalist, will do your utmost to defend the institution of monarchy from this dangerous republican."

The following week, when I read my essay calling for the immediate abolition of the British Crown, I was pleased to be congratulated by the other students and Dr Parkinson himself. However, to my surprise, they were then equally approving of my rival's essay supporting the monarchy. There must be something wrong with this country, I concluded. How could they allow foreigners to attack the Crown? Where was their patriotism?

At the beginning of each year, the Student Guild organised a dance, known as the Freshers' Hop, to introduce the new students, most of them shy eighteen-year-olds just out of school and away from home for the first time, to the college's social life. With Gary and other new friends from Kilmorie Hall I went along to this event, held in one of the few buildings of the hill-top campus, which in the early 1950s was only just beginning its expansion. Gary told me this was a good opportunity to look for a girlfriend, but not to forget his advice: it was advisable to find one from a nearby hall as this saved a lot of time, as well as money on taxis, when escorting her back after dates. As I was standing alone at the edge of the dance floor, a tall, slim, dark-haired girl came over and asked me to dance. This surprised me, though I felt less flattered when she explained that she was a member of the Student Guild Council, whose duty it was to make freshers feel at ease. She told me she was called Madge, she was nineteen and a final-year student of English Literature. Mindful of Gary's advice, I asked:

"What hall are you in?"

"Hope," she answered

That settled it! I didn't need to look any further as I knew Hope was only a hundred yards from Kilmorie.

Then she went off to do her duty, but later when I saw she was not dancing, I went over and invited her. After the traditional Last Waltz, I escorted her back to Hope, a fifteen-minute walk away. I discovered that she played badminton and tennis for the college teams, and had recently resigned as editor of the college newspaper so that she could concentrate on her studies. Before we shook hands and parted, I asked if we could meet again.

"I won't be going out much this year, but we'll see each other around," she said. "Most days I pass by Kilmorie on my way to lectures down town in the Gandy Street building."

At breakfast next morning, I was congratulated, as a lowly fresher, on having caught the eye of the popular Miss Phillips, member of the Guild Council.

My first year in England passed very quickly. Madge and I met often, but mostly for short periods when she took a break from studying. During the Easter vacation, she took me home to meet her family in the small town of Newton Abbot, only fifteen miles from Exeter. After graduating with honours, in the autumn of 1954 she went to London

University to study for a diploma of education. We were both sad at being separated, but made plans to be together in London when I finished the second year of my course and got a job, as I hoped, at the Yugoslav Embassy. In the meantime, whenever I could I hitch-hiked the two hundred miles to London to see her.

Our patience was rewarded next summer when Madge gained her diploma and a post teaching English at a north London high school, and I was taken on as an attaché at the Embassy. Luckily, Ambassador Velebit was still there and remembered his job offer.

"I'm glad you've come," he said. "Since Tito's state visit our work load has doubled, but the number of staff is the same. You can start tomorrow, and I'll fix it with Belgrade!"

Among the dozen or so diplomats at the Embassy was a university friend, Dobri, who was dealing with legal and property matters. I was assigned to help him in this consular section.

"It's great we'll be together again," he greeted me warmly. "You take any file you like to work on, and leave me the ones that interest you less."

Shuffling through the heap of documents, I came upon a thick file marked 'Trepča Silver Mine Limited, Mitrovica, Kosovo'.

"This one interests me," I showed Dobri. "The Trepča mine was taken away from the English right after the war. My family used to visit the British colony there on Sundays." And I told him about the bulls with rings in their noses that so impressed me as a child, the 'English Ball' in Mitrovica, and the first gramophone in our family which my eldest sister had won as the 'Belle of the Ball'.

My other colleagues were from all the republics and provinces of Yugoslavia: the policy was to have at least one person from each in every foreign mission. There was a wonderful feeling of comradeship amongst us, regardless of rank, which pleased me as I was the most junior member of staff. One day Ambassador Velebit informed us that he was returning to Belgrade and would be replaced by Ambassador Ivo Vejvoda. Everyone was sad to hear this: he enjoyed a very high reputation among the British and the diplomatic corps. As a Partisan general he had taken part in the Tito-Churchill negotiations in southern Italy towards the end of the war. The round of farewell cocktails and dinners began, and at one of these I met Brigadier Fitzroy Maclean again.

"We must have dinner together some time," he said. I was flattered that such an important person had not forgotten me.

After work, Dobri and I often went out for a stroll along Kensington High Street and dropped into one of the Italian-style coffee bars that were opening on every corner at that time. Passing by were 'Teddy boys', curiously dressed in narrow trousers and long jackets with velvet collars, and girls tottering along in high heels with beehive hair-does and heavy pancake make-up that stopped short at the neck – so very different from the youth back home. Then Dobri and I would walk through Hyde Park, observing with keen interest the many groups of prostitutes openly soliciting customers. We would generally end our long walk in Soho, in one of the small Jewish places that sold steaming salt-beef sandwiches on rye bread with gherkins – my favourite food in London.

Madge and I mostly met up at weekends, since she lived far away near her high school in north London and I lived close to the Embassy in Kensington. I had some difficulty at first in finding a bed-sitting room as many of the adverts in the papers said: 'No foreigners'. To visit Madge, I often used an old car that no-one else at the Embassy wanted to drive as it stalled whenever you took your foot off the accelerator. Driving along Oxford Street one day it stopped dead and refused to budge, blocking the traffic. A couple of bobbies cheerfully came to my aid, pushing me several hundred yards into the nearest side street. They tried to restart the car, and when they failed, offered to call a garage. Being permanently short of money, I declined, and instead phoned a friendly Embassy driver, who came to my rescue. I was most impressed by how polite and helpful the police were – a far cry from our militia-men back home.

We at the Embassy, like the British, were much preoccupied with relations with the Soviet Union following the surprising visit of Nikita Khrushchev to Belgrade in 1955. He publicly apologised for Stalin's treatment of Yugoslavia and recognised that there was more than one road to socialism. This represented the triumph of Yugoslavia's independent way, but knowing the Russians well, many Yugoslavs were afraid that this was some new manoeuvre aimed at bringing Tito back into the Soviet fold. Khrushchev's visit was soon followed by the denunciation of Stalin at the 20th Party Congress in Moscow, and the thaw in relations with the West: he and Bulganin visited Britain and were guests of the Queen at Windsor Castle in April 1956. These improved relations were given a set-back by Soviet suppression of the uprising in Hungary later that year. Yugoslavia gave refuge to many fleeing Hungarians, while Premier Imre Nagy escaped the Russians by sheltering in the Yugoslav Embassy in Budapest.

As 1958 approached, Madge and I decided it was high time to end our lengthy, old-fashioned courtship and get married. Yugoslavs were perfectly free to marry foreigners without asking permission, as people had to in the eastern bloc, but there was a rule that diplomats could not have foreign wives, regardless of their nationality. Though the country had accepted western aid to overcome the economic blockade imposed by the Soviet Union and its satellites, there was still deep-seated distrust of the capitalist states and westerners among leaders who had been trained by the Comintern. The mood was slowly changing, however, as more and more people travelled abroad.

Hoping that in my case an exception might be made, I submitted a request to the Ministry in Belgrade, which would decide whether I could stay on if I married an Englishwoman, and asked the advice of Ambassador Ivo Vejvoda, a very cultured man and polished diplomat who had taken over from General Velebit a year before. He had invited Madge and myself to an embassy dinner some time before, when she had made a very favourable impression. Ambassador Vejvoda sympathised with my predicament and advised me to "pop over to Belgrade" and try to get influential friends to put in a word for me.

As it happened, about that time Bela Miklos, a travel agent of Hungarian origin, came to the Consulate to ask for visas for the Manchester

United football team, its manager Matt Busby and other club officials, who were due to go to Belgrade for a European Cup match with the Yugoslav champions, Red Star. He also asked for visas for the crew of the Elizabethan turbo-prop aircraft that had been chartered to fly the Manchester party and a large group of sports writers to Belgrade. Miklos, a pleasant, middle-aged man who was in charge of all the travel and accommodation arrangements for the trip, said it was customary, when a team went to a socialist country, for a junior member of the embassy staff to accompany them, to help with interpreting, customs and other contacts.

"I should be most grateful and feel much easier if you would come along, as our guest, to be the 'tour leader'," he said.

Realising at once this would be an ideal opportunity to try and solve my problem, I accepted with an alacrity that must have surprised him.

Some days later I took a train to Manchester and was met at the station by a smiling Bela Miklos, pleased that I hadn't let him down. The heavy rain, for which the city is well known, combined with dense smog, meant that I could see nothing of Manchester on my first visit. Never mind, I thought, I could go sightseeing on the way back. After I'd checked into a hotel, Miklos took me to the Old Trafford ground to meet Matt Busby, the players and journalists who would be setting out together early next day. Matt Busby immediately impressed me by his warm, straight-forward manner. In the relaxed atmosphere of the club lounge I did my best to answer all the players' questions: what was there interesting to see in Belgrade, what presents could they buy for their wives and children, what were the hotel and food like, was it safe to go out in the evening? As my diplomatic duty and patriotism demanded, I tried to present the city in the best possible light, though well aware that it was probably the least attractive of European capitals after Tirana.

On the outward journey I sat next to Tommy Taylor, United's brilliant young international centre-forward, who moved over a seat to make room for me when he saw I was standing – feeling like the host,

I let all the other passengers take their places first. From my colleagues at the Embassy who followed soccer more closely and were quite envious about my trip, I knew that he was already a celebrity at the age of twenty.

The turbo-prop planes of the Fifties flew at lower altitudes than jet aircraft, so passengers were subject to a lot of unpleasant turbulence. Still, our trip to Belgrade, with a short stop for refuelling in snow-bound Munich, was more comfortable than expected. The journalists, mostly sitting in the tail of the plane, which for some reason they considered safer, were cracking jokes and in the best of spirits, thanks partly to the flow of whisky provided by the steward, Tommy Cable.

At Belgrade airport, at least a hundred people were gathered to welcome the famous Manchester United. Representatives of Red Star were there in force and had brought enough interpreters, so there was no need for me to hang around. The players were bussed off to the new Hotel Metropol, which was already besieged by dozens of football fans – everybody felt this match was a great event for Yugoslav football and the capital. I was relieved to realise I would be free to spend next day talking to people at the Ministry.

But my talks there were completely unproductive. It was admitted that a few exceptions had been made in the past, but only for 'bigger fish' than myself, for a couple of ambassadors, on Tito's personal intervention. I would have to choose between marriage and career.

When I explained the situation, the members of my family were more in favour of the latter, on the grounds that as a young diplomat I could take my pick of pretty girls from any part of the country.

"What's wrong with our healthy, good-looking Montenegrin girls?" Mother wanted to know.

Quite unexpectedly, in view of his position, one of the few to advise the opposite was Slobodan Penezić, Zina's husband and Stana's friend, who was Serbian Minister for Internal Affairs.

"If you love the girl, Bato, don't waste time running round asking for advice. Marry her! You'll find another job. Remember my words: the greatest success in life – much greater than any career – is to find personal happiness. A person who fails in that is a failure in life."

Next day I went to see the match as the guest of Red Star's manager. The stadium was packed and the pitch soggy from heavy rain. Two minutes after the start, Dennis Viollet struck a pass from Tommy Taylor past Red Star's celebrated international goalkeeper Beara. The home fans were struck dumb. Worse was to come. After fifteen minutes, Bobby Charlton fired in one of his cannon-balls, and just before half-time the same player curled a corner kick into the net. In the second half, the lack-lustre Red Star suddenly seemed to wake up and completely dominated play. Three times goalkeeper Harry Gregg had to fish the ball out of the net. The final result, a three-three draw, meant that United, who had previously won their home match against Red Star, went through to the next round of the European Cup. Even so, the Belgrade players were satisfied to have held the English champions to a draw at a time when English football was at its peak.

That evening Red Star gave a dinner for both teams and officials at the Skadarlija Café, famous for its Gypsy music and grilled meat. Outside it was a cold, dank February night, but inside there was a tremendously warm, lively atmosphere, a feeling of real camaraderie.

When we boarded the Elizabethan next morning, the journalists again made for the tail, while the players mostly occupied the middle section. All the seats faced the pilot's cabin except the four nearest to it, intended for cabin staff, which faced the passengers. I sat down in the front row, directly opposite the steward, Tommy, with whom I'd chatted on the outward flight. While flying to Munich, I reflected that this trip had done nothing to resolve my dilemma.

As we approached the airport, one of the two attractive stewardesses announced that we would be stopping to refuel and would be served refreshments in the terminal building. When the party re-boarded in cheerful mood, looking forward to getting home to Manchester, we returned to the same seats. The laughter, shouts to friends and buzz of conversation were soon drowned out by the engines starting up. It was around 3 p.m. on Thursday, 6 February 1958.

From where I sat by a circular window I could see the powerful propeller beginning to turn, its sharp edges only a few inches away. It gave me an uncomfortable feeling. There were a number of mechanics standing round the plane, bending over and examining something. Then they moved away. It was still snowing heavily, as it had been when we landed. All I could see through the window was large swirling flakes and an expanse of white against a darkening sky.

The roar of the engines reached a crescendo as the plane accelerated for take-off, then abruptly decreased, as though it had lost power. The pilot started braking and with some unpleasant jerking and sliding we slowed down and came to a halt. Our captain apologised and told us we would have to return to the terminal, where we would be offered further refreshment, until the maintenance staff identified the problem. Out we got, but ten minutes' later we were summoned back on board, the captain assuring us that all was now well.

With a deafening roar the Elizabethan gathered speed, but when the moment for take-off came, the engines again lost power and we slithered and skidded along in an alarming fashion, stopping at the very end of the runway. After the plane taxied back to the terminal, it was a relief to feel the ground under our feet as we made our way to the building again.

"I suppose this time they'll take a proper look," Tommy Taylor remarked to me as we waited for yet more refreshments offered by the company. But after only five minutes we were called back to the plane and these were left on the tables untouched. I wondered uneasily what kind of technical problem it was that could be fixed so quickly. The others must have been thinking the same, but the British, noted for their self-control, went on with their banter and jokes. I had a feeling, though, that the jollity was now a bit forced.

As we prepared for take-off for the third time, I noticed that several people got up and quickly swapped seats. There was an air of tense expectancy. The engines started up again; the propeller began turning, scattering the big snow flakes. The steward Tommy and I glanced at each other, and for some reason he said: "Shall we change places?" We both stood up at once and swapped seats, so that I had my back to the pilot's cabin.

The aircraft started moving, gradually gaining speed. The roar of the engines grew louder and louder until at last we seemed to be airborne. Then the sound changed and we began crashing. Afterwards I was told it lasted only fifty-four seconds, but it seemed to me like a lifetime. I remember trying to stand up, but failing. The lights went out. In the dark, bags and cases in the racks started falling on our heads and I lost consciousness.

I came to when I struck the ground. At first I couldn't grasp what had happened; I wasn't even sure I was alive. As I tried instinctively to get to my feet I realised I was still belted into my seat: together with it I had been catapulted about a hundred metres by the force of the explosion. Somehow I managed to release myself and remove a piece of metal wrapped around one knee. When I stood up I found I had no clothes on – even my lace-up shoes had been ripped off by the blast – and I was covered in blood. I looked around to see where the others were. Behind me there was nothing but white fields; in front, scattered sections of the plane and a dozen fires: just before take-off the plane had taken on thousands of litres of fuel. Naked apart from my trouser belt with a few scraps of cloth attached, I limped with difficulty towards the wreck. In my confused state, I didn't think of the danger of exploding fuel-tanks. I could see bodies lying around and hear the cries of the injured. In the dusk, with the background of leaping flames, it was like a scene from Hell. Some footballers ran towards me with flames shooting up from their heads: they had been drenched with petrol.

With my arm I tried to wipe away the blood that was streaming down from gashes on my brow and blurring my vision. From cuts on my lips and broken front teeth my mouth kept filling with blood, which I had to make a tremendous effort to spit out so as not to choke. Blood was flowing freely from other wounds, and my back started to hurt as badly as my knee. As I lost more blood and the pain grew worse, it became hard to move. I stood silent, helpless and unable to help, horrified by the sights around me. On the ground nearby lay the lifeless body of the steward, Tommy, who had asked me to change places with him. I

Wreckage of the plane carrying Manchester United FC from Belgrade to London which crashed at Munich Airport on 6th February 1958

recognised him only by his uniform. Some of the players with minor injuries ran past, shouting in panic for Matt Busby. By the light of the flames, I recognized Vera Lukić, wife of the Yugoslav air attaché in London, who was being given a lift from Belgrade to the UK. Out of her mind, covered in blood, she was running wildly around, screaming for her two-year-old daughter, Vesna. Before our third take-off attempt, I had noticed her sitting in the front of the plane, hugging the little girl tightly. A moment or two later, I saw Harry Gregg emerging from the wreck of the plane holding little Vesna in his arms.

Then salvation arrived in the form a vehicle that looked to me like an open truck. Dead and the injured were all put in together. I recognised Bobby

Charlton, Ray Wood, Harry Gregg and Dennis Viollet. Bobby and Ray didn't look to be hurt, but the other two had blood on their faces. All of them were extremely agitated and kept asking one another and me what had happened to other players, and particularly to Matt Busby.

When we arrived at Munich's renowned Rechts der Isar Hospital, a team of surgeons and other doctors, led by Professor Georg Maurer, was already waiting. We were rapidly taken inside and I found myself lying on a trolley in a large operating theatre. I gazed at the surgeons expertly wielding their scalpels as they cut the flesh of their unconscious patients. Other passengers, dead and alive, were laid out on trolleys in this big room.

A doctor came over to examine me. He didn't speak English and I knew just a word or two of German, but when he heard I was from

Yugoslavia he addressed me in Russian, which I had studied at school and at the faculty. In the midst of that nightmare scene, with the injured crying and groaning all around, as he worked on me he talked away calmly in Russian, recounting his experiences on the Eastern Front, his capture and time in a prison camp. Though I desperately wanted to ask about my injuries and whether I would survive, I didn't interrupt these reminiscences: I was stopped by the thought that he might interpret this as fear, which a Montenegrin must never show.

After a while, he reported on his findings:

"Your left knee is broken and right knee damaged. The cuts on your face, head and body are superficial. We'll get your front teeth fixed later. The pain in your back will be investigated tomorrow, but if you can move your limbs, it's not broken. That's enough for today. I have to move on to another patient. You'll live!"

Those last, magic words filled me with a glorious feeling of relief and happiness. Nurses pushed me into a corridor in which there were other injured passengers. They carefully lifted me from the trolley and put me into something like a metal trough under dozens of bare light bulbs – to counteract hypothermia and prevent pneumonia. All through that night spent lying naked in the corridor in the warmth generated by the light-bulbs, I couldn't stop congratulating myself on having cheated death once again. The problem that had sent me to Belgrade now seemed insignificant in comparison with the tragedies of the families who had that day lost their sons, husbands, fathers. That night, for the first time, I felt completely free, without the sense of obligation to society that had held me back. Munich had resolved my dilemma: as soon as I got to London I would get married, provided, of course, I was in fit shape and Madge would have me.

Next morning, after being thoroughly X-rayed, I was put in a room with less seriously injured players: Bobby Charlton, Ray Wood, Dennis Viollet and Albert Scanlon. So many journalists came to interview us, we hardly had a chance to talk among ourselves until late afternoon, when visitors were sent out. The players were shocked and saddened by the loss of many friends and team-mates, and very worried about those who were seriously injured, such as Matt Busby, who seemed like a father to them: "Is the old man going to pull through? Can we see

Manchester United manager Matt Busby and sportswriter Frank Taylor meeting with fellow crash survivor Bato Tomašević in Belgrade, c. 1960

him?" they kept asking. Naturally, they were also worried about their own future, whether their injuries would affect their careers. They were all fine, modest young men, still without much experience of life compared with myself, a twenty-eight-year-old war veteran. Dennis Viollet was the one I talked to most as he was interested in various subjects besides football on which I was well informed. He was keen to hear of my experiences in the Partisans and the part Munich played in Hitler's rise to power.

Every day we were taken for further examinations, fresh dressings and tests. The X-rays showed that my vertebrae had been compressed by the impact of landing: I was now two centimetres shorter than before the accident.

"When you get back to London you'll need physiotherapy. After that, walk a lot and never put on weight," my doctor advised.

Professor Maurer and the staff of Rechts der Isar, in addition to providing excellent treatment, did their utmost to meet our every wish. A dentist was brought to the hospital to make impressions for porcelain jackets, the last word in dental technology, for my two front teeth. The replacements, I decided, looked better than the originals. When I arrived at Victoria Station, though still walking with a stick, I at least had a nice smile. On the platform to greet me were most of the Embassy staff, including Ambassador Vejvoda, with Madge standing beside him. I was very touched by their concern. Shortly after, I informed them I was getting married.

Our wedding was arranged for Saturday, 19 April, in the registry office of Madge's home town, Newton Abbot in Devon. I invited my Embassy colleagues to attend and explained exactly how to get there. Besides our college and London friends, the guests included a few relatives and close local friends of Madge, her widowed mother, Hilda, and her Aunt Win and Uncle Ken, with whom she had spent most of her childhood. When her father, Edward Phillips, a London policeman, died of pneumonia at the age of thirty-six in 1939, Hilda sent the little girl, just five, to stay for a while with her aunt in Devon. Following the outbreak of war, when London children were in any case evacuated to the countryside to escape the bombing, Madge's mother returned to the nursing profession and this temporary arrangement became permanent.

It was a beautiful sunny day, and after the brief ceremony, we all walked to a local restaurant for the 'wedding breakfast'. The food was uninspiring, but there was plenty of the best Yugoslav wine, whisky and other drinks which I had bought through the Embassy at duty-free prices. All in all, it was a very happy occasion, though we were both a little disappointed that not one of our Yugoslav friends turned up, obviously afraid of incurring official disapproval.

The same evening we returned by train to London and our first home – a small rented flat. On our 'honeymoon' Sunday, we went for a walk in the local park. When I arrived at the Embassy next day, I was summoned by Ambassador Vejvoda. After congratulating me on my marriage and wishing us every happiness, he informed me, regretfully, that I would have to leave the Embassy within three days as my employment was automatically terminated by my action. This, of course, came as no surprise, but it was still a wrench. A diplomatic career, offering a secure and comfortable life, opportunities for travel and other privileges, was something that most young Yugoslavs could only dream of. What to do now was the big question. Fervent patriot that I was, I persuaded Madge that we should live in Belgrade, where the new Yugoslavia was being created. I very much wanted to be part of this and believed that Madge and I stood a good chance of getting employment where we could make use of our qualifications. A few weeks later, we took the train to Belgrade.

Motovun, Istria, which gave
its name to the Motovun
Group Association of
international publishers

The Tito Era

Yugoslavia in 1958, when we moved to live in Belgrade, was lacking a great many things: adequate housing was one of them, and all kinds of material goods. But not enthusiasm. The great majority of people, still with vivid memories of the hardships and terrors of wartime, looked forward with optimism to a better life, determined to build a new, more equitable society.

Many of the leaders of the Partisan movement had been young left-wing intellectuals, participants in the Spanish Civil War and anti-fascist movement of the Thirties, idealists who wanted to change the world overnight, put all injustices to right. They were without administrative experience and unaware of the cost of providing all they had proclaimed: free education and health care, jobs for all, pensions and other benefits. Putting all this into practice placed an enormous strain on the weak, underdeveloped economy and, subsequently, on the standard of living.

During my five years in England, my family had expanded and flourished. Ljuba and Vicko with their three daughters were living in Belgrade, where he had a senior post in the Ministry for Internal Affairs. Stana, still single, was Minister for Labour in the Federal Government. Before I left, Nada had married a Croatian youth leader, Jozo Bačić, who was now serving at our embassy in Warsaw. Mother had gone there to live with them and help Nada with her two small children. Aco, in the meantime, had married Nadja, a girl from a Sarajevo Moslem family. With their two little daughters they had moved into the flat overlooking Kalemegdan Fortress where Mother lived when she was in Belgrade. It was to one small room in this flat that I brought my bride in the summer of 1958.

Father was retired and living with his second wife in the Serbian spa town of Vrnjačka banja. So as not to be alone, he had persuaded his nephew Jovan, Luka's only son, to move there with his wife Danica. He had tried unsuccessfully to get other relatives in Kosovo to join him, but times had changed. He was no longer young and healthy with a promising career ahead, as he had been when he brought them to Kosovo. Besides, as a pensioner without influence in local government circles, he couldn't get them jobs and houses. Father and Jovan both lived on their small pensions in rented rooms in this pleasant, but run-down, little place. Before the war, well-to-do Serbian families had gone there to take the waters and had built themselves large villas, now mostly used as workers' holiday hostels.

Soon after our arrival in Belgrade, Madge and I decided to go to visit Father in our new little pale blue Ford, of which we were so proud. It was one of the few private cars at the time – the registration number, 2227, signified the number of cars in the whole of the Belgrade district, and more than half of these were state-owned. Still holding strong egalitarian views, I felt somewhat embarrassed to admit I was the owner of a private car, so I avoided mentioning this to my friends.

The only paved road in Serbia, built before the war, led south from Belgrade some eighty kilometres to the village of Oplenac, where the Karadjordjević family had raised their mausoleum, decorated with garish mosaic copies of medieval Serbian fresco paintings, after the assassination of King Alexander in Marseille in 1934. Luckily, as we thought, this road led in the direction of the spa. We had not expected it to be in such a terrible state of repair, and that the macadam continuation would be nothing but ruts and holes. Fearing for our cherished car, I drove extremely slowly, raising clouds of dust, and arrived in the late afternoon in a state of physical and nervous exhaustion.

I had not seen Father for over six years. He was delighted I had got married and with my choice, and kept asking me to translate for Madge his anecdotes of my childhood. Since the war had parted us when I was ten, there wasn't much else for him to recall.

"What a pity I didn't learn a few words from the English in Mitrovica," he lamented. "But who would have guessed that one day we would have family connections with England."

Next morning we visited Jovan and his wife Danica. I hadn't seen my cousin since leaving Mitrovica twenty years before. He was now nearing fifty, tall, thin, with the dark complexion of a sick man. I knew he had suffered from epilepsy since his years in a German prison camp.

"When I got back to Kosovo," he recalled, "it was changed from before the war. The new government passed a law saying the land belongs to those who work it. But most of us who returned were no longer fit enough to farm, so the Albanians kept the land and we were left to go out into the wide world like beggars. Look at Uncle Djuro, in some wretched home for old people. Your government proclaimed equality for all, but there are many more of them and now they're the rulers of Kosovo. They're taking our jobs away from us."

Talking about this brought on one of Jovan's epileptic fits. Danica, accustomed to them, for he had daily attacks, bent down and pushed a towel between his teeth, while he thrashed around on the floor. Madge and I stood by, shocked and unsure what to do, until it passed.

My relations with Father, whom we all adored as children, were now quite distant because of Mother, who had rallied all the family around her. We regarded his second marriage as an act of betrayal we could not forgive. For this reason, when Madge and I met his wife and she offered us something to eat and drink, I refused quite coldly and could hardly wait to leave. Father accompanied us to the car, and stood there, a lonely figure, waving until we turned the corner. Madge had noticed my reserved manner:

"You weren't very nice to your father," she remarked.

⁂

On the model of the BBC World Service, the Government had set up Radio Yugoslavia, which broadcast on short waves in a dozen languages. Its task was to explain to its few listeners around the globe Yugoslavia's independent 'third way', the system of local and worker self-management, Tito's policy of peaceful coexistence, and the role of the Ustashas, Chetniks and Partisans during the war. A Party congress held in Ljubljana not long before our return had adopted a new programme that heralded a greater degree of democracy in the country, which had been slowly opening towards the West since the Soviet economic blockade. It was important to tell the world that something new was happening here, something previously unknown in the international workers' movement, to which Yugoslavia was still ideologically bound. In the English Section of Radio Yugoslavia there was a pressing need for more 'native speakers' as announcers and language editors. Madge applied for one such job that was advertised and was immediately taken on.

Six months had gone by since my return and I still hadn't found a suitable job. People avoided employing anyone who had broken the rules, for fear they might have someone from UDBA on their backs or it would be a black mark against them in their own careers.

"Now you're on the list of unreliable people we in UDBA keep tabs on," Nikić confided when I met him in the street one day.

Not long after, our Macedonian concierge, who lived with her family in the basement flat, came knocking on our door one morning. As she was very friendly with Mother, she came to warn me, in the strictest secrecy, to be on my guard, as someone from UDBA had been enquiring what sort of company I kept, whether I brought any foreigners home. Usually, she said, they asked only about Doli, a good-looking, well-dressed blonde in her late thirties who lived above us. She was the daughter of the former owner of the whole building, which had been nationalised, like all big buildings, just after the war, leaving the owners one or two flats for their own use. She was said to have been the girlfriend of the young King Peter, but their romance was cut short in 1941 when the King with the Yugoslav Government fled the country. Gossip had it that after his marriage in London to the Greek Princess Alexandra, he didn't forget Doli and tried to arrange an exit visa for her. In any case, Doli was seen in the company of British diplomats and this had not escaped the attention of the police department that kept an eye on foreigners and locals who mixed with them. As in other countries, the concierge was often required to provide information for the police.

I contacted Nikić again about this.

"Take her advice. Be careful! Now you have a foreign wife, don't go round with foreigners or bring them home. Then you won't draw the attention of our service. But one thing I'll tell you, Bato. While I'm in the service and others who know you from the good old Partisan days, you're safe as houses. I'd strangle with my own hands anyone who tried to do you any harm. But we won't be there for ever: keep that in mind. You were always different from the rest, didn't stick to the rules. Remember the time you brought that unlucky capitalist from Kotor to sleep in our barracks in Nikšić? But you must meet the wife and children. She keeps saying: 'When are you going to bring home that Bato you talk so much about?' "

⁂

By a stroke of luck, one day I bumped into an acquaintance from London, Alija Vejzagić. In the latter half of the Fifties, when federal and republican institutions realised that expanding contacts with the West made it necessary for their personnel to speak English, Alija was one of several hundred younger people already in responsible jobs who were selected to go to language schools and stay with families in England. At the Embassy I came into contact with many of them and got friendly with some.

Alija, a likeable and dynamic person a few years my senior, came from a Moslem family in Livno, Western Bosnia. He had joined the Partisans in 1942, when not yet fifteen, and was wounded in a battle with Chetniks. During the war, his father and brother were shot by Ustashas. In London we immediately got on well and often used to meet up for a stroll and a drink in a pub. Once or twice Madge joined us. Now he greeted me warmly:

"I'm delighted to hear, Bato, you've married that wonderful, clever girl."

"Yes, but that's why I can't find a job!" I answered with a grin.

"Listen, I'm in the Federal Ministry for Information, in charge of the Foreign Department. If you'd like to work there, I'll have a word with the minister, Bogdan Osolnik," he said without hesitation. "Slovenes like him have freed themselves from much of the nonsense the rest of us are still slaves to. How could anyone possibly doubt your loyalty? Since '48 and the conflict with Stalin, UDBA's got out of hand. They behave as if we exist because of them, and not the other way round. Only don't repeat what I said!"

A few days later I was asked to come for an interview with Minister Osolnik and was offered a job in Alija's department. To start with, I was to act as interpreter for important English-speaking foreign guests and travel around the country with them. My brief interpreting career was not short of comic incident. The Ministry would draw up an itinerary and programme intended to suit specific interests, and present this to guests, usually not in great detail, for their approval, which was generally given. Thus it happened that I found myself conducting a high-ranking Indian politician to inspect a brand-new food processing factory in a town in Serbia. The idea was to show our distinguished guest the Government's efforts to improve the diet of the working people.

On our arrival, the manager delivered a short speech of welcome in the festively decorated reception room before we toured the plant, which turned out to be a broiler factory. He explained that before the war ordinary people prepared chicken only for special guests or when someone was ill. Now, they could afford to eat it every day, thanks to battery farming and automated broiler factories like this one, constructed entirely by our own engineers.

After this preliminary talk, we were taken into an extremely long hall. Moving towards us on a thick steel chain above our heads were a hundred identical white chickens, hanging head down in a perfect line. As each one came more or less level with us, a large pair of shears severed its neck and blood spurted out on all sides. The headless birds continued to flap their wings as they were conveyed further on this deadly carousel. The proud manager turned to see what impression this marvel of modern technology had made on our guest, only to find that he had fainted.

We carried him back into the reception room, laid him on a couch and sprinkled water on his face. To our relief, he quickly recovered, whereupon the manager proceeded to describe the next phases of the conveyor belt system – plucking, disembowelling and washing the chickens – which we had unfortunately missed seeing. He was rather put out when I refused to translate this. Later we learnt that our Hindu visitor was a strict vegetarian who would never deliberately step on an ant. No wonder he was overcome by the sight of this mass slaughter.

After several more trips, a highly critical report on my work arrived at the Ministry from Macedonia. I was accused of not translating accurately the speeches and replies in discussions of some local leaders while accompanying another Indian guest, Sadiq Ali, a prominent Moslem in Nehru's Congress Party. This was perfectly true. Out of embarrassment for my fellow countrymen, I refrained from translating some of their more bombastic statements suggesting that India, with an ancient culture and hundreds of millions of inhabitants, had a lot to learn from little Yugoslavia, with less than twenty million. Again I was in trouble for stepping out of line. Alija once more came to my aid and quickly transferred me to the sector for foreign-language publications, where I worked happily for the next couple of years.

In June 1960, we decided to go for a holiday to the picturesque old seaside town of Piran in Istria, close to the Italian border. Our journey by car was a long and difficult one, for there were only short stretches of paved road: work had hardly begun on the Brotherhood and Unity Highway that was to link up Belgrade, Zagreb and Ljubljana. While we were in Piran, Madge took a bus across the border to Trieste to buy a few things for the baby we were expecting in six months' time. Our shops still offered a very meagre choice of consumer goods, and a shopping trip to Trieste, to buy jeans and plastic raincoats, and have a pizza and a Coca Cola, was the dream of many Yugoslavs at the time.

When we were discussing who to send postcards to, Madge said we should certainly write one to my father and tell him about the baby.

Next day, a telegram arrived:

"This morning Father died in hospital. Funeral day after tomorrow at Belgrade New Cemetery. Love to you and Madge, Stana."

This news, so unexpected, released all the feelings for Father I had suppressed for so long, and I wept for the first time since that evening in Nikšić when I learnt of Duško's death. The telegram had been sent the previous day and now it was unlikely that I could reach Belgrade in time for the funeral. I didn't want to take Madge with me in the summer heat on that strenuous journey, whether by car or some combination of public transport, and I didn't want to leave her alone in her condition. Perhaps, though, this was really an excuse to avoid facing the reality of Father's death. I remembered how he had dashed off to Mitrovica from Cetinje when news of Grandpa Filip's death arrived. Ever after, when I thought of him, I felt a pang of guilt that I had not tried to make it to the funeral.

✳

In late summer 1960, Hugh Gaitskell and Denis Healey, then members of the British Shadow Cabinet, accepted Tito's invitation to pay a two-week visit to Yugoslavia with their wives and several trades union leaders. Relations between the British Labour Party and Yugoslav Party had been virtually frozen for some time because of the arrest and trial of Milovan Djilas, previously one of Tito's closest associates. Aneurin Bevan, the charismatic leader of Labour's left-wing, had been a friend of Djilas and was thought to have exerted a strong political influence on him. In any case, they were very similar in temperament, both impulsive, fiery and unswerving in their beliefs. Bevan had publicly condemned Djilas's imprisonment and called for his immediate release. Tito, much offended, had ignored this appeal. Recently, however, Bevan had died and Djilas had been let out, so that the obstacles to restoring relations between the two parties were for the most part removed.

After talks with Tito in Belgrade, according to the programme drawn up with great care by Tito's Office and the Ministry for Information, the guests were to tour all the Yugoslav republics and provinces. Though I was no longer working as an interpreter, on the insistence of Minister Osolnik, I was selected to accompany the group as their sole guide and companion.

"I'm very keen that you, Bato, should be with them from morning to night for these fifteen days," the Minister told me. " Nobody can do the job better. You know the British well, how to get on with them, what to say to them. This is a rare opportunity for our country, and we mustn't waste it. It's not just a matter of translating, but a chance to tell them the right things. Very soon they may be in power again, and both of us would like to see good relations with the British."

Photo of Bato Tomašević by Dennis Healey (Lord Healey), former British Chancellor of the Exchequer, taken on his visit to Yugoslavia with a Labour Party group headed by Hugh Gaitskell, August 1960

My nervousness at meeting the Labour leaders and the important task ahead of me vanished as soon as I shook hands with Denis Healey and he began presenting me to the others in a pleasant, informal manner:

"This is my wife Edna, this is our leader, Hugh Gaitskell and his wife…" and so on around the group.

"The two of us will discuss all the arrangements as we go along. What's important is that we have plenty of time to rest, talk and enjoy ourselves, and do as little work as possible," he joked.

"They told us your wife is English," Edna broke in. "Couldn't you bring her along?"

When I explained that this was not feasible, she at once turned to Denis and proposed that they should have dinner with us that very evening, before setting off, so they could meet Madge and apologise for making her a grass widow for two weeks. And so the four of us had a delightful meal together. As it progressed, the Healeys put us completely at our ease, enquiring about our lives and work, and I realised my apprehension had been groundless. Denis was particularly interested in the Munich crash and Edna in living conditions, the food, and other matters which Madge knew more about. When we set off home late that night, we both felt that we had made new and sincere friends.

Travelling around with the British visitors turned out to be an exceptionally enjoyable experience. Interpreting this time proved to be no problem as the hosts with which they had talks in the various republics were intelligent people with a modern outlook – probably specially chosen for that reason. Everywhere we stayed in the large villas in beautiful locations that were used by foreign guests and, more often, by republican leaders and their families for holidays. This was noted by Denis, who remarked to me:

"If we in Britain had anything like this, even one villa, let alone this many, we'd never get elected!"

The weather throughout was wonderfully warm and sunny. After talks and an official lunch or dinner with our republican hosts, the guests would sit together on a terrace, usually with a breathtaking view of the coast or mountains, and talk late into the night about the people they had met that day and the places they'd seen. Whenever I tried to leave them alone, someone would always stop me:

"Don't go! We need you to explain certain things. Nothing's being said that's not fit for your ears. Anyway, we already regard you as part British because of your wife!"

They asked a lot of questions about the war, the Chetniks and Ustashas, the differing views on the future course of Yugoslavia, the differences in level of economic development between the richer and poorer regions. I took the opportunity to ask them, in their talks with influential people, to stress their support for changes in the country towards greater democracy, human rights and personal freedom. This was particularly important, I said, when they had their farewell meeting with Tito, who could change everything, if he wanted to, get rid of the people who were obstructing progress and replace them with those with more democratic views.

The oldest among the guests was Sam Watson, a former miner and now a trades union leader. A short, soft-spoken man with lively eyes, he asked innumerable questions about living and working conditions, education and housing.

"There are two things that have completely won me over: Israel's kibbutzim and your worker management," he said to me. "You have already achieved something of my dream. I truly believe that, following your example, one day all over the world workers will win the right to decide on production and distribution, together with the owners, and so class conflicts will disappear and there will be a more equitable life for all."

After listening to Sam, Denis joked:

"I hope that the Russian idea of equality won't be part of your new order, Sam. I must tell Bato my experience in this respect.

"When we paid a visit to the Soviet Union, after the farewell dinner, Khrushchev lined us all up, not according to height, which wouldn't have been bad for me, but according to our rank, the position we occupied. Being the youngest and lowest in rank, I stood at the very end of the line, and our leader [he pointed to Hugh Gaitskell] at the head. Then Khrushchev went to the table where gifts were laid out. Mr

Gaitskell got the largest and most beautifully packed, after which the packages got smaller and plainer until finally it was my turn.

"Afterwards, when we compared our presents, it turned out that we had all received cameras, but each of us had a different model. Our leader had been given the latest and most expensive, produced in a limited number for high-ranking functionaries, and the rest of us had got cameras to suit our Party seniority. I got a mass-produced model that already hung round the neck of almost every Russian. Still, for a while I made use of it. After some jolly gathering of the kind where it was impossible to refuse a glass or two, I would take a few pictures. I never knew whether it was the camera or myself that was seeing double – perhaps both!"

As the days went by, I spent more and more time with Denis and Edna. They were always cheerful, pleasant and interested in everything. The least approachable in the group were the Gaitskells: polite and attentive, but reserved. They somehow kept a little apart from the rest, seemed less interested and rather tired.

In many places we visited, Hugh Gaitskell was met by British and other journalists who wanted to hear his views on current topics: relations between Tito and Khrushchev, the severe chill in East-West relations following the downing of the American U-2 spy plane, Yugoslavia's influence on East Europe and the African countries that were then gaining independence, John Kennedy's chances at the upcoming US presidential election, the successful return from Space of the Russian satellite with two dogs…

In Dubrovnik there were no official meetings, so the time was spent sightseeing in this beautiful Renaissance walled city. On departure day, the Montenegrin government sent several black limousines to drive us along the southern coast via Kotor and Budva to Titograd (Podgorica). I wondered why Cetinje was not included, and persuaded Denis that the route should be altered to include this historic town. From Kotor we would drive to the former capital up the famous serpentine road that had frightened the life out of George Bernard Shaw when he visited the area between the wars. While being driven down this road from Cetinje at great speed by a local driver keen to show his prowess, Shaw held tight, gritted his teeth and uttered not a word. When they reached Kotor at the bottom and he was asked if he'd enjoyed the trip, Shaw replied:

"It was very beautiful and exciting, but you're not taking me back to Cetinje!"

On our travels through Yugoslavia, I had talked about Cetinje and its famous medieval monastery, where the first books in the Cyrillic alphabet were printed: how it had been built by the ruling Crnojević family when they moved their court from Lake Skadar up into the mountains, away from the Turks. Not without a certain pride, I mentioned that as a boy I had sung in the choir of the great monastery church.

When we arrived in Cetinje around noon, the sun was beating down and the deserted streets were shimmering in the heat. It was one of the last days of an exceptionally hot summer. I was hopeful that it would be cool in the former palace of King Nikola, now a museum, but this turned out to be closed for repairs. I next led my perspiring group to the monastery church, where we were met at the entrance by several priests in their long black robes.

"Since we can't all get in at once," one of them said, "we'll wait for you outside."

To my astonishment, there was scarcely room for our group to squeeze in.

"Why don't we go into the main church?" I asked a priest who reminded me very much of Father Vukmanović.

"This is the biggest one we have, friend," he replied. "There's no other in this monastery."

"I mean the big one. My whole class and the teacher used to go in together for services."

He smiled: "A child's eyes sees everything bigger – people, houses, trees… When you grow up, it all comes to its proper size."

I felt acutely embarrassed in front of Denis and the others. I had altered the programme so they could see Cetinje, its handsome people – among the tallest in Europe – its palace and great monastery, and all they had seen were deserted sun-baked streets and a small church of no architectural distinction. I never mentioned Cetinje to them again.

To my grief over Father's death was added the worry of how we should cope living in one room with a baby. Fortunately, just then the Ministry was allocated a certain number of flats for its staff, and in October 1960, after more than two years of stumbling over trunks and unopened boxes, Madge and I moved out of our cramped room into what seemed to us a spacious flat – two larger rooms and one tiny one, with a kitchen and shower-room. At the time there was an acute housing shortage because of the wartime damage and post-war influx into the cities. Private home ownership was not encouraged, except in rural areas, and anyway was too expensive for most people, so they could do nothing but wait in rented rooms or shared flats for their turn to come on the housing list at their place of work.

We were among the pioneers in the new satellite town of high-rise apartment blocks being built on former marshland across the Sava river. Our part of Novi Beograd (New Belgrade) had only two completed blocks on a vast building site. We were deafened by pile-drivers and choked by all the sand blowing around, but we were deliriously happy to be in our first proper home, particularly as the baby was due in three months.

That same October Madge returned to teaching as a language in-structor (*lektor*) in the English Department of Belgrade University. Graduates of English Language and Literature were much in demand, so the Department was inundated by hundreds of would-be students, while the Russian Department had shrunk drastically.

The Head of Department was Mrs Mary Stansfield Popović, a lady of about sixty. She had met her husband, Vladeta, when they were both students at Cambridge, and together with him had pioneered the teaching of English at the University in the Twenties. During the war, he was sent to Dachau concentration camp and she was interned, hav-ing refused to leave the country. In poor health after his return home, Professor Popović died in the early Fifties and his wife took over as head of what was now a fully-fledged department until her most tal-ented students could complete their doctorates and a successor could be chosen.

A small, bespectacled, scholarly woman, her quiet, modest manner concealed great determination and courage. On her retirement she learnt to drive and bought a small Yugoslav-made Fiat car in which she motored, somewhat erratically, around the country and even abroad. After the demolition, because of urban redevelopment, of the modest house where she and her husband had held garden parties for generations of students and Anglophiles, she lived in a modest two-room apartment, the walls covered in books, which in her last years blindness prevented her re-reading. She was visited there by devoted former colleagues and students for afternoon tea, poured from a Georgian silver tea-pot, the water kept hot by a spirit burner. Her one luxury was to import tea specially blended in London to suit the chemical composition of Belgrade water. In socialist Yugoslavia, where she was widely respected, her book-lined sitting room was a sanctuary of learning and cultivated conversation from another age.

Not long before we moved, General Jovo Kapa came to the Ministry. A tall, handsome, broad-shouldered man with curly auburn hair and freckled complexion, he had ended the war a National Hero and a favourite of Tito, who often cited him as an example of a fearless commissar. He had been ambassador in Budapest during the turbulent events of 1956 and then in Stockholm. His father, a priest, had been my teacher of Religious Education at Cetinje *gimnazija*. A fervent supporter of King Nikola, he had accompanied him into exile in Italy after the king's abdication. Jovo was born there, in Gaetta, a place where many royalist Montenegrins took refuge and stayed for some years before returning home. Though we were both from Cetinje, I first got to know Jovo well in London, where he had come to improve his English before his diplomatic posting. We soon became friends, even though he was some ten years older and much above me in the hierarchy. This friendship was resumed when he came to the Ministry as my superior, for he never paid much attention to protocol.

Unlike many high-ranking people I knew, even war heroes, he was never afraid to speak his mind when he disagreed with official political stands. Jovo Kapa belonged to the group of people who wanted the country to shake off its Bolshevik legacy with all speed, open up to the world, and tread the path of Scandinavian social democracy. In the Party, now renamed the League of Yugoslav Communists, in the Government and the Army, there were 'hardliners' who couldn't accept or adapt to the demands of democracy, fearing for their positions and privileges, and there were others, more flexible, and often more educated and capable, who were for reform and democratisation.

※

After we settled into our new flat in Novi Beograd, a frequent visitor was Ilija, my best friend in the OZNA Escort Company, whom I had left behind in Cetinje at the end of 1944 when setting off for Albania. In the meantime, he had graduated from Belgrade Medical School, where he was now an assistant professor completing a doctorate in paediatrics. It was great to renew our friendship and comforting to have his advice after the birth of our daughter, Una, in January 1961.

Among the families that moved at the same time as we did into the two new multi-storey apartment blocks in Novi Beograd, there were several people I knew from various periods and places, even Cetinje. At one of the residents' meetings, held to discuss problems such as maintenance, cleaning and the functioning of lifts, I met Česo Ražnatović, an older friend of Duško's who used to come to our house in Cetinje. When I returned from work, Česo and I would sometimes go for a walk on the dunes. These had been created by pumping sand from the Sava riverbed to fill in the marshes, in preparation for the construction of dozens more high-rise blocks. Česo had been in the Partisans from the start and had stayed in the forces after the war, rising to the rank of air-force colonel. But when he was commander of Pula military airport, he was retired early, before he was forty. This he explained by a change in policy towards Montenegrins. Because they had provided more Partisan commanders than other nations, after the war there were more of them in the highest echelons of the armed forces. Now the policy was proportionate representation of all the nations, regardless of their wartime contribution, and this meant a drastic reduction in the number of Montenegrin senior officers.

Česo was divorced and lived alone. His son also lived in Belgrade, but with Česo's mother. I remembered her well from occupied Cetinje, where she and my mother used to help each other out and take food to the prison together. Because of his early retirement and divorce, Česo was lonely and disillusioned. He was also worried about the upbringing and education of his son, Željko, nicknamed Arkan, who was already in trouble with the law for stealing and unruly behaviour. On more than one occasion Česo asked me to get Stana to intervene to have Arkan released from reformatory, "which will only make him worse". Stana liked and respected Česo and always did what she could. "A lot of our comrades who were so brave in the war and suffered so much can't seem to make a success of marriage. Masses of them are divorcing, and this is bound to affect the children," she commented, trying to find some explanation for the delinquent behaviour of this lad from a highly respectable family.

The Sixties in Yugoslavia was a decade of growing prosperity and burgeoning democracy. We were still very poor by western standards, but there was a sense of collective pride in the visible progress we were making, a feeling of optimism. We attributed it all to the success of worker management, which certainly gave the economy a great boost, though western aid was also a very significant factor. Over the years, our life, like that of most people in the country, steadily improved in every way. There was a free health service, free education to university level, a very advanced social welfare and pension system, cultural events with highly subsidized tickets for the theatre, opera, concerts, to mention just a few of the benefits. There was a feeling of safety and security as law and order prevailed.

We used many opportunities to travel abroad and, naturally, in all parts of Yugoslavia. Like many foreigners, Madge was fascinated by the country's complex and stormy history and by the culture, customs and way of life of all the many nationalities who had settled in this region over the centuries. Within a year she learned the language well enough to be able to communicate and began to augment our income by translation work.

One day, Jovo Kapa called me into his office and offered me a job that was to set my career on a new course. The Government had decided it needed to boost foreign tourism by publishing, in a number of languages, an illustrated monthly magazine of the type put out by the United States, the Soviet Union and many other countries at that time. In format it was to be modelled on Time and Newsweek, with a lot of pictures and interesting articles on a wide range of subjects. But the first two issues, in English to start with, were overloaded with photographs of Tito shaking hands and boring reports on his various official meetings. Jovo decided it would be a good idea if I took over as editor and tried to liven it up and make it more attractive for foreign readers. The magazine, though subsidised by and under the auspices of the Ministry for Information, was part of the publishing house of the Borba daily newspaper. A move there would mean leaving the security of government employment and entering the world of journalism, which, as Stana pointed out, was still a fairly high-risk occupation if one stepped out of line. Madge was also dubious, but I couldn't resist the challenge: I knew I was not cut out to be a bureaucrat. My three years in the Ministry's publishing sector, many contacts with foreigners, and studies at the School of Journalism and Diplomacy would all help me, I hoped, to make a success of this challenging new job.

That Stana was right about the risk factor was proved after the very first issue I edited. The leading article was an illustrated reportage on the most famous bridges in the country, symbolic of its history and the links between its different peoples and faiths. On the cover we featured the lovely single-span bridge (*most*), built in 1566 in honour of Sultan Suleiman the Magnificent, that gave its name to the city of Mostar. The magazine, called Yugoslav Review in English, was printed in Italy on quality paper, well designed, and illustrated with good colour photography. It was, in fact, Yugoslavia's first glossy magazine, though aimed at foreign readers, and was soon to be emulated by many others for home consumption. Dispatched around the world to Yugoslav embassies, expatriate associations and others with an interest in the country, as well as to foreign embassies in Belgrade, it received high praise for its attractive appearance and interesting, well-translated articles, free from the usual political jargon and exaggerated glorification of the country's achievements.

However, soon after it appeared, a high-ranking comrade rang up Jovo Kapa to enquire why, in this latest number of the new magazine, unlike in the first two, there was not a single picture of President Tito. Who was this new editor who had taken it upon himself to ignore the head of state? He should be checked out, for he certainly had some ulterior motive. Jovo had staunchly defended me, but my editorial future hung in the balance until one day I received a call from Tito's press secretary:

"The President and Comrade Jovanka like your magazine very much and wish to receive it regularly."

Straight away I phoned Jovo Kapa with the good news and added:

"Please tell that over-zealous comrade that if he has any more complaints about the magazine, it would be best to talk to Tito personally."

"Don't worry, Bato, I'll do so with pleasure. I only wish I could see his face when he hears this!"

We tried to be scrupulously fair in allocating space to each republic and province. In time, we built up a wide readership abroad and our articles began to be reprinted in the western press. In consequence of this success, within a year French, German, Spanish and Russian editions were launched. The whole of the last, I suspected, was bought by the State and dumped somewhere, so that Soviet citizens would not get ideas from our articles on our system of worker management and the clear evidence of our artistic freedom from the dictates of socialist realism.

One day my secretary announced that the Soviet press attaché had come and would like to talk to me. Though I knew it was contrary to the established procedure – diplomats were supposed to visit only by appointment through the Foreign Ministry – I felt I couldn't be impolite and refuse to see him.

"I just happened to be passing your office, and wanted to make the acquaintance of the editor-in-chief," he greeted me with a smile.

I offered him the customary Turkish coffee, but he replied, in good Serbo-Croatian, that he would prefer a *loza*, to toast our meeting. This he did at some length, mentioning the age-old friendship between our countries, our wartime comradeship in arms, the closeness of our political views… Then he turned to the actual purpose of his visit:

"From our comrades in Moscow we have received comments on the first few issues of your magazine in Russian which you send to the Soviet Union and some other brotherly socialist countries. The general conclusion is that the content is not sufficiently adapted to suit the interests of our readers. We should be pleased to help you make the magazine more successful by collaborating with you on the choice and treatment of topics – as we have been doing for a long time with other socialist countries that publish similar magazines. The best way would be for you to send us a list of proposed subjects for several numbers in advance, and then we could meet to discuss them."

"If I've understood you properly," I replied to this uninvited guest, "you'd like me to accept your censorship and publish only what suits you and serves the purposes of Russian propaganda, like the countries in your bloc do. But we don't belong there, so why would we agree to this?"

Obviously dissatisfied with this forthright refusal of his 'fraternal help', the Soviet press attaché left abruptly, scarcely bothering to say goodbye.

Before a month had passed, a friend who worked in the Soviet Department of the Foreign Office phoned to tell me that our Moscow Embassy had received a sharp note of protest from the Soviet Foreign Ministry:

"They're threatening to ban the distribution of your Russian edition because of some articles they say are damaging to our State and Party relations. This is a very serious accusation we can't ignore. A commission of enquiry is being formed, made up of representatives of the Ministries for Foreign and Internal Affairs and Information. You'd better prepare yourself well for an interview!"

Again Jovo Kapa came to my aid.

"You just keep quiet, Bato," he said. "Don't let anyone provoke you. With an English wife you can't afford to quarrel with the Russians. Let me tell them what I think about this Russian habit of calling us to heel and threatening us. Don't forget there are plenty of people here who still think like the Russians and would be glad to see us back in their camp."

On Jovo's insistence, the commission met in his presence in the Ministry for Information. The Foreign Ministry took the view that there was no point in needlessly annoying the Russians since they would simply destroy the magazine and it would never reach any readers. Perhaps it would be better, it was suggested, to prepare a modified version for the Soviet Union, while the other language editions could continue as before.

The UDBA representative took a harder line:

"We think the editor-in-chief, whether intentionally or not, has damaged our good relations with the Russians and should be held accountable for this."

Having listened to the other commission members, Jovo spoke up:

"In answer to the colleague from the Foreign Office, I'd like to ask how long there have been two truths, one for the West and one for the Russians? Like it or not, for us there is only one truth, so we can't produce two magazines with different contents. We mustn't let every Russian note scare us out of our wits, so that we set up commissions and condemn people who are only doing their job properly. With their notes they want to intimidate us, make us toe the line and stop us following our own independent path. To our colleague from the Police, I would say that it would be better if his people stopped Russians sneaking into our offices and factories, wheedling information out of people, making notes of who is for or against them, instead of calling to account those who resist this Russian practice."

Thanks to Jovo, the disciplinary procedure against me was dropped and I remained editor-in-chief.

From the outset, Madge was kept busy in her free time from the University working on the English edition – she was by now much in demand as a translator and editor and earning considerably more than I was. Her extra work helped to finance our summer trips by car to stay with Aunt Win and Uncle Ken in Newton Abbot. With Una and our second daughter, Stella, born in December 1963, we would set out with great excitement, and some trepidation, for the long drive across Europe in our small, no longer new car, staying as cheaply as we could in interesting places along the way, and ever fearful we might break down and not have enough money for repairs.

Early in 1963, Stana called to say she would like to drop in on us in Novi Beograd that evening with some interesting news.

"Tito asked to see me yesterday. He was relaxed and in a very good mood. 'You know, Stana,' he said, 'the Norwegians are great friends of ours. We saw that during the war when they helped our people interned in the north of the country to survive the German camp, the cold and the hunger. When I go to Norway on an official visit, I should like you to be there as our ambassador. You were the first woman commissar in the war, so why shouldn't you be the first woman ambassador in peacetime? I think the Norwegians would like that.' "

When she arrived in Oslo, a tall, elegant, striking woman in her early forties, she was greeted warmly as an old acquaintance: it transpired that in 1944 British aircraft had dropped leaflets over Norway with the photograph of Stana in Partisan uniform taken by John Talbot, calling on young people to follow the example of Tito's youth.

The mid-Sixties brought radical changes that generally improved life for most people. The economic reform of 1965 was meant to develop a market economy in a non-capitalist society, and make Yugoslav goods more competitive abroad. At the same time, wider powers were transferred to the republics and local government.

More dramatic than this, though not unconnected, was the power struggle within the League of Communists between the reformers, such as the Croatian and Slovene leaders Vladimir Bakarić and Edvard Kardelj – the ideologist of worker management, and the conservatives, headed by Vice President Aleksandar Ranković, a Serb and former

Minister for Internal Affairs, who still pulled the strings in UDBA and appeared to be Tito's most likely successor. The reformers won over Tito's support. Ranković was accused, among other things, of bugging the President's homes and dismissed from his post, but otherwise came to no harm. This was probably because, personally, he was no Beria, but a pleasant, unpretentious man. He was certainly no Serb nationalist either – his wife was a Slovene economics professor – but simply believed, like many others, that centralised government was best for the country. With his fall, the struggle for greater decentralisation had been won.

Immediately after this, UDBA's power was drastically curbed. Its number of employees was halved, many being pensioned off overnight – among these was my old friend Rade Nikić. Steps were taken to destroy the network of police informers: all concierges in the country lost their jobs and UDBA's men who occupied posts in every enterprise

Stana Tomašević with President Tito before her departure for Norway to become Yugoslavia's first woman ambassador in 1963 were withdrawn. From now on people were much less cautious about speaking their minds.

What particularly pleased the general public was the opening up of the frontiers and the guaranteed right to be issued a passport within one week of applying. Instead of standing in line for hours at government offices, you could just hand over your documents to a travel agent. The Yugoslav delegate to the UN was warmly applauded by the General Assembly when he announced that his country, the first in the world, was abolishing visas for all foreigners. This encouraged some fifty states to end visas for Yugoslavs. We thus enjoyed complete freedom to travel that made us unique among the socialist states and much envied by their citizens. It also meant that the Yugoslav passport, which gave access to both East and West, was the most sought-after on the black market.

Several hundred thousand workers made redundant by the economic reforms got themselves passports and hurried off to find jobs in western Europe, the largest number to Germany, which was crying out for manual labour.

꓿

When Stana returned to Belgrade from Oslo in 1968, to everyone's astonishment she brought with her a husband, Eugen Arnesen, a tall, erect Norwegian a few years her senior. Hearing that he had fought in the Norwegian resistance, Mother welcomed him warmly – she had always worried that Stana would marry someone 'unworthy' of her.

"You see what happens when you send a woman as an ambassador," some people in government circles began saying. Stana might well have disappeared from the political stage if Tito hadn't heard of this, and invited her and Eugen to his Adriatic retreat in the Brioni Islands as personal guests of his wife Jovanka and himself – quite a rare honour. News of their four-day stay soon got round, and after that there was no more gossip and cold-shouldering because of her marriage.

꓿

The Soviet-bloc military intervention following the Prague Spring of 1968 aroused widespread anger and alarm in Yugoslavia. Crowds of people paraded through Belgrade shouting pro-Czech and anti-Soviet slogans. Emergency measures were taken throughout the country in case the Warsaw Pact forces should decide to 'help' Yugoslavia in the same way as Czechoslovakia. Soviet tanks were reported to be massing on our border with Hungary. The armed forces were placed on full alert; all citizens of military age were 'mobilised' for territorial defence and given weapons. Everyone knew what they were supposed to do and where to go in case of invasion or air attack.

When Madge and I went over to visit Stana and Eugen one day, we found our Norwegian brother-in-law sitting on the floor polishing a military carbine made in the Kragujevac arms factory. He was extraordinarily proud that he had been entrusted with this weapon, noted for its precision:

"I'm ready to fight for Yugoslavia, if need be. I told them I was a good marksman when I was in the army, so they gave me a really good weapon. They said, if we're invaded, everyone should fire out of his own window, without waiting for orders."

In a month or two, things calmed down, but for some time after we were required to attend lectures on 'nationwide defence' in our place of work or local community, and this was made an obligatory subject at secondary-school and college level, so that the whole population had a kind of military training.

The following year, Stana invited the family over one evening. Besides Mother, there were Ljuba and Vicko, Nada and Jozo, Nadja and Aco, Madge and myself, and all the children – getting on for twenty of us. Eugen seemed in a very cheerful mood, laughing and cracking jokes all evening. When it was time to leave, he raised a glass for a final toast:

"Excuse me for talking all evening, not letting anyone else get a word in. It's probably because I like to hear my own voice, and this evening is my last chance to do so, because I won't have a voice from tomorrow. I wanted to tell you how happy I've been among you. The warmth I've found in this family and throughout your lovely country has made up

Madge and Bato
with their daughters,
Una and Stella,
in Belgrade, 1966

for leaving my own. It was important for me to say this to you out loud this evening."

The following day Eugen entered hospital to be operated on for cancer of the throat. Ten days later he came home with no voice. But this drastic operation was too late. When it was clear that he was dying, he asked Stana to take him back to Norway. A month later she returned alone.

❧

Review had an enthusiastic and talented staff who, like myself, were always ready to try something new. Publishing an illustrated magazine meant that we soon accumulated a sizeable photographic archive which, it occurred to me, could be profitably used for coffee-table books. So Review took its first step into book publishing in 1964 with a volume entitled 'Cities of Yugoslavia'. Like the magazine, it was printed on glossy paper and much more modern in design than most other Yugoslav publications of that time. I was keen to expand and make money from book publishing, since a greater degree of financial independence would mean less Government interference.

Yugoslav Review had its cultural section, and in my search for local subjects I became fascinated by naive art, which was then flourishing in Yugoslavia, particularly in northern Croatia, where Ivan Generalić, Ivan Rabuzin and Ivan Lacković were its most famous exponents. There were, I discovered, many talented but unknown self-taught artists, mostly peasants, in other parts of the country as well, especially Vojvodina, Serbia proper and Slovenia. While this art owed much to folklore traditions, still very much alive in the region, it was also a consequence of the war and revolution. These had brought far-reaching changes to both town and countryside, releasing enormous human potential, particularly among the semi-literate peasants, who could best express themselves pictorially. Their paintings were often a response to the country's rapid industrialisation: an attempt to record for posterity the old customs and ways that were passing. For some who had left the land and moved to town, painting idealised pictures of country life was a means of expressing their nostalgia.

Going around visiting and interviewing them, hearing their stories and discussing their work, I developed a passionate interest in this art, which was both an aesthetic and a sociological phenomenon. In many cases I did not have far to travel: only an hour's drive from Belgrade into the Vojvodina plain and you come across dozens of villages populated by different ethnic minorities – Hungarian, Slovak, Romanian, Ukrainian, and many others – where naïve art flourished.

Review's offices were located on Terazije Square in the very centre of the city, so there was a constant stream of visitors. One day, a friend called in and asked for help:

"You've been to Istria, but maybe not to the little town of Motovun: it's on a hill twenty kilometres inland. My brother and I are from nearby and joined the Partisans from there. We Yugoslavs fought and died so Istria could belong to Yugoslavia, but when we got it, we just neglected all the small places the Italians left empty, let them fall to ruins. With every storm, more houses collapse. Even the massive walls of Motovun that have stood since Celtic and Roman times badly need repairing.

"The reason I've come is to ask whether you at Review could help. Your journalists might be interested in buying a holiday place for themselves – the houses are being sold cheaply at pubic auction – and maybe for your office you could take one of the bigger buildings, perhaps as a place to work with partners."

After several trips to Motovun, it was decided that Review should buy a large, dilapidated house on the top of the hill, facing on to the main square and with a spacious, though overgrown, garden, encircled by the town walls, behind it. In a few months it was completely renovated, with lavish use of the beautiful Istrian marble.

Review also launched a campaign throughout Yugoslavia for the revival of this historic and picturesque place, collecting contributions from companies and individuals. The local authorities gave us a long list of their needs, and we began financing some of the most pressing: street lighting and repairs, parking space, etc. One of the items which immediately attracted my attention was the most expensive project, which the local people thought would be a good way of attracting tourists and generating income. This was a plan to restore the narrow-gauge railway that had wound its way through the hilly landscapes between Trieste and Poreč. It had been built by the Austrians in 1903 and had remained in use until 1936, connecting and serving the needs of many small places like Motovun (Montona). According to the locals, the rails were torn up by soldiers, on the orders of Mussolini, shortly after the occupation of Abyssinia, in order to be used for the first railway in that country. They never reached their destination as the boat carrying them sank in a storm. And so the small steam locomotives no longer puffed and whistled their way through the many tunnels and the neat little station houses of Istrian stone stood empty or were turned into homes. Our finances did not permit us to undertake such an expensive project, so it was left for better times, and we did what we could for the everyday needs of the three hundred or so inhabitants of Motovun.

Among those who bought houses in Motovun, besides Madge and myself, was my sister Nada, the closest to me in age. On summer holidays there, we at last had time to reminisce about our childhood and life before we were separated by the war. Her experiences in the camps had left their mark: she was always terrified something was going to happen to her two children, never slept in the dark, and barricaded the doors and windows at bedtime. She had suffered a further trauma when her husband, Jozo, after two years as ambassador in Bolivia, had been recalled and dismissed from the diplomatic service because of some conflict in the Ministry. For some time after this he lived in South America, Colombia, helping his elder sister and her husband to run their hotel, hoping to earn enough money to keep his family at home in comfort, as Dalmatians like himself had been doing for generations.

Nada had literary talent and wrote short stories and articles for magazines, but she lacked the drive and persistence to make a real career as a writer. Mother, strong and dominating, ran the household, pleased to have a useful role in life, while Nada entertained her wide circle of devoted friends with her witty gossip over coffee.

One day, feeling unwell, she went to her doctor. Cancer was diagnosed, but, as with Eugen, the operation came too late. A few months later, in January 1973, she died at the age of forty-four, the fourth of Mother's children to die before her.

In 1974, Yugoslavia adopted a new constitution. Behind it lay the fear that, after Tito's death, Serbia, the most populous republic, might upset the country's delicate national balance. Serbia's two autonomous provinces, Vojvodina and Kosovo, were given virtually the same degree of autonomy as the six republics. Some people thought they should be granted republic status, on the grounds that all nations, big and small, should have equal rights in the multi-national community.

Bato with his mother and sisters Nada (above) and Stana in the early 1970s

"The nationalism of minority peoples, like us Albanians, can be harmful, but it can never endanger the whole community, as long as the majority nation behaves in a responsible manner," said Redžaj Suroj, a friend from the School of Journalism and Diplomacy, who was now Deputy Minister for Foreign Affairs and a member of Review's Editorial Board.

※

In 1976, I suggested to the Swiss publisher Jürgen Braunschweiger that we should celebrate the publication of our co-edition 'Islands of the Adriatic' in the most appropriate way: a cruise along the eastern Adriatic coast visiting some of those lovely islands. We hired an old wooden sailing boat, the 'Adria', which had been simply adapted for cruising, and together with another eleven publishers – business partners and friends – sailed among the islands, bathed, consumed quantities of Dalmatian fish and wine, and sat around on deck talking about books, while our wives got to know one another.

At the end of the ten-day cruise, the Norwegian publisher William Nygaard proposed we should sail again on the 'Adria' the following year. It turned out that besides enjoying ourselves, we had done some serious work discussing and planning other co-editions. Next year the number of publishers rose to twenty and the following year we had to find a bigger sailing boat to take all those eager to join us.

Reluctantly, we agreed that if the group continued to grow we should have to give up cruising every year and find a land base. The obvious place was Motovun in Istria, where Review's house was ideal for meetings, and people could stay across the square in the Hotel Kaštel, former residence of the Polesini family, owners of large chunks of Istria for several centuries.

Our growing number made some kind of organisational structure necessary, and so the Motovun Group Association (MGA) of international publishers was officially established. Our first chairman was Ed Booher, President of the Book Division of McGraw Hill, the biggest US and world publisher at that time, with a staff numbering eight thousand. With his wife, Agnes, he purchased and renovated a house in Motovun, where they spent several weeks each summer for nearly twenty years.

On the spacious terrace of Review's house and in its beautifully kept garden, backed by Motovun's medieval walls, members of the group could sit under sunshades sipping coffee or cold drinks and discussing their new projects. We received envious glances from the occasional tourist walking on the walls to view the breathtaking panorama of Istria's green hills and the Mirna river valley. In this Cold War era, besides co-productions of illustrated books we often discussed the political and ideological division of East and West and its impact on all fields of culture. Among other things, it had deprived readers in both blocs of full and free access to the other's achievements. As publishers we should do what we could, we agreed, to fill the gaps created by the long years of cold-war isolationism, and to serve as a bridge. For a start, we tried to attract a number of East European publishers, which was not easy as they were rarely allowed to travel to the West except in strictly supervised groups. Because of its more liberal type of socialism, Yugoslavia was treated in this respect like a western country, though certain exchange visits were permitted.

As editor-in-chief of Review, for instance, I was invited with Madge to visit my Romanian counterpart, the editor of the Bucharest publishing house Meridian. Most of the editors and writers we met there were cultivated people who spoke several languages and were extremely well-read. If they wanted to keep their jobs or even their families together, they were obliged to lead a double life. At work they paid lip-service to the Ceausescu regime; only in private, when together with like-minded friends, could they express their real views. Madge and I were privileged to visit the home of Riza, a likeable, lively, polyglot editor, who invited some colleagues to join us.

"You know, Bato," he confided, "while you're free to travel and work abroad, bring back foreign currency and spend it as you like, I'll tell you how we Romanians travel. The crowd of us you see here decide to drive to the airport – on the way, the police stop us a couple of times at least, to check our identity cards. Then we occupy a table in the restaurant, order coffee and some strong drinks, and listen to the announcements of the departure of planes for Paris, London and other cities in the West. That's how we travel the world!"

One of the Romanians at Riza's party asked me in confidence about the attitude of the Yugoslav police to the gatherings of foreigners in Motovun, which I had talked about. Had they given permission for this? I answered that I'd never asked for permission: I had simply exploited the decentralisation of authority in Yugoslavia, which extended to the police. In Motovun they thought Zagreb had approved the annual meeting; in Zagreb they believed it had the blessing of Belgrade, and vice versa. I was convinced that I was doing something useful for the country as well as for Review, since the Motovun meetings were in line with our policy of cultural exchange as a means of increasing international understanding between East and West. In fact, the Motovun Group soon drew the attention not only of publishers but of the governments of several countries, who offered to host the MGA's annual meeting.

After the Cultural Revolution, China's new leaders, wanting to open up to the world, invited the Motovun Group to visit the country. In Spring 1980, our party of over eighty people arrived in Beijing for a most memorable eighteen-day tour. Our Chinese hosts described it as an historic event: the first visit to the country of a large group of foreign publishers.

One morning when we came down to breakfast, we found about twenty Chinese officials and publishers waiting for us in the hotel lobby. Usually all smiles, that day they were standing in silence and looking very glum. One of them approached me, shook hands, took out a sheet of paper and began to read, while the interpreter beside him translated in solemn tones:

"On behalf of Comrade Deng Xiaoping, the Party leadership, state ministers and all the working people of China, we wish to express our profound sympathy on the death of the President of Yugoslavia, Comrade Josip Broz Tito."

The date was 4 May 1980.

We watched the funeral on television in Beijing, and again back in Belgrade, in one of the numerous repeats. It was an unforgettable sight as a great river of people from all parts of the country moved slowly from the Parliament, where Tito had been lying in state, towards his burial place, near his residence on Dedinje hill. Stana, as President of the Federal Assembly, had been on the Blue Train carrying Tito's body from the Ljubljana clinic where he died to Belgrade, and was among the Yugoslav leaders at the head of the funeral cortège. At that time she was the highest-ranking woman in public life.

The coffin was followed by 240 heads of state and government, royalty, foreign ministers, senior military figures and political representatives from one hundred and twenty countries: the largest number gathered together since the funeral of Winston Churchill. Britain was represented by Prime Minister Margaret Thatcher and Prince Philip. They had come to pay tribute to the last survivor of the allied leaders of World War II, a statesman who had given encouragement and hope to a third of mankind, the 'underdeveloped' world, a man who had rejected Stalin's domination and led his country along an independent path. The foreign press gave him credit for holding the country together, but again posed the question they had been raising periodically for the past ten years: what would happen to Yugoslavia after Tito.

To succeed him there was to be a collective body known as the Presidency, formed on Tito's initiative to safeguard his legacy and ensure there was no single heir. It was made up of one representative from each of the six republics and two autonomous provinces, who were to take it in turn to serve as official head of state for one year.

"My late father would never have believed that an Albanian could be president of the whole of Yugoslavia," an Albanian friend remarked when it was Sinan Hasani's turn to take over as head of state.

This rather cumbersome system seemed to work well enough for some years, since power was increasingly wielded by the constituent units of the Federation rather than the central government. Still, people were apprehensive, for throughout history, and not only in the turbulent Balkans, the passing of a strong and charismatic leader had often led to dissolution and chaos.

Yugoslavia: The Dream that Died

The early Eighties were overshadowed by illness, death and grief in my family. In 1982 it was discovered that Stana had cancer of the liver, the consequence, it was thought, of the blood transfusion infected with hepatitis she had received just after the war. That summer we went together to London so she could undergo further tests and possibly treatment.

"Both Father and Nada died of this disease; now it's my turn," she said calmly when we arrived at the small apartment near Hyde Park rented for a month. "But I'm very happy we shall finally spend some time together. My whole life I've missed not seeing more of the family."

Waiting for the doctor's findings, we went for daily walks in the park. The weather was warm and sunny, and we used to sit beside the Serpentine, talking about 'old times' and watching the ducks and geese. Towards dusk, huge flocks of them would take off noisily, reminding us, here in the heart of London, of the small Balkan places where we lived as children, of the wild goose Duško had once caught and brought home, of the time when it seemed that nothing could ever break up our close-knit, loving family.

When we arrived at the hospital on the appointed day, we were told that her cancer was inoperable.

"Where shall we go?" I asked when we got outside, not knowing what else to say.

"Hyde Park," Stana replied, "to feed the ducks."

We sat on a bench by the lake. She had brought along a bag of stale bread and began throwing crumbs into the water. We were soon surrounded by dozens of birds, among them a duckling that always lost out to the bigger ones in the scramble for food. Stana started throwing bits of bread straight to it, and was pleased when it succeeded in catching them. She was always one to help lame ducks, I thought, remembering how many people had come to her in some kind of trouble. Then a couple of swans glided near and she tossed them the last of the bread.

"Swan lake, swan song," she murmured.

She died soon after.

Only six months later my eldest sister, Ljuba, died. Vicko, a strong, healthy man, outwardly rather brusque and domineering, had cared for her devotedly with the help of their daughters during her long illness. He made all the funeral arrangements, saw to the flowers and transport to the cemetery, received mourners at home as is customary after the burial. When everyone had left, he suffered a stroke and died during the night.

Each time Mother followed the coffin in silence, not weeping, proud and upright. "I've cried all my tears long ago," she used to say. "God has punished me to die after my children."

Before Stana died, Mother had moved to live with Madge and me. Every week she visited the cemetery, placing flowers on the family graves: Nada buried with Father, Ljuba with Vicko, and Stana in the part of the cemetery reserved for heroes of the Partisan war. Madge and I were both working, Una and Stella were away studying in England, so she was quite often alone, though her passion for television made up for this. Four years later, when she was ninety and still very strong in body and mind, she fell and broke a hip.

"I don't know how I was so careless," she said, angry with herself. "I went to open the door and missed the handle, for the first time in my life!"

Aco and I, the two survivors of her eight children, were at her bedside when she died ten days later. She was laid to rest in the Avenue of National Heroes beside her beloved Stana.

❦

The latter half of the Eighties saw the rise of nationalism. This owed much to the country's economic difficulties (partly the consequence of EC tariffs on Yugoslav exports), high unemployment and inter-republican friction, with each republic blaming others for their problems.

A document known as the Memorandum issued in April 1986 by the Serbian Academy of Science and Art intensified the atmosphere of mistrust. It declared publicly, for the first time, that the creation of 'Tito's Yugoslavia' had been greatly to the detriment of the Serbian nation. By decisions of the provisional wartime parliament held in the temporarily liberated Bosnian town of Jajce in 1943, the post-war Yugoslav state was to be a federation of six equal republics and two autonomous provinces. According to the Memorandum, the decisions of this body were not lawful and had damaged the Serbs: the borders drawn between the republics were administrative, not the true national ones. Even at that time, it was claimed, there had been a Croat-Slovene alliance against the Serbs, which had been further strengthened by the long post-war co-operation of Tito and Kardelj. Croatia and Slovenia were directly blamed for Serbia's relative economic stagnation, the idea being that their industries had developed by exploiting Serbia's cheap raw materials. The Memorandum put forward the theory of historical injustice, first elaborated by the writer Dobrica Čosić, whereby the Serbs are victors in wars and losers in peace.

Serbian government circles immediately reacted to this provocative document, condemning its attempt to set the Serbs against the Croats and Slovenes, and to reopen the Serbian national question from the position of the Chetnik movement, with its goal of a Greater Serbia.

The Memorandum was particularly strongly criticised by the President of Serbia, Ivan Stambolić. Second in the hierarchy was his close personal friend, whose career he had done much to advance, Serbian Party Chairman Slobodan Milošević.

As it happened, around that time I often visited the Academy's handsome building in Prince Mihajlo Street to attend meetings chaired by one of its vice-presidents, the writer Antonije Isaković. The reason was the planned facsimile edition of the twelfth-century Prince Miroslav Gospels, the most important Serbian illuminated manuscript, which is kept in the National Museum in Belgrade. Review was supposed to be arranging for the printing in Milan of five hundred numbered facsimile copies, which would make this priceless early manuscript accessible to the public and scholars in libraries around the world.

Among those who attended the meetings was Professor Voja Djurić, an eminent authority on Byzantine art, whom I knew well: a few years earlier we had spent three weeks together in Chilandar on Mount Athos, during the preparation of the first serious, illustrated volume on this, the most important medieval Serbian monastery, which Review had published to great acclaim.

One day, when we'd stayed behind to have a chat, he brought up the subject of the Memorandum:

"I overheard Antonije Isaković speaking to Stambolić about it, and I was most surprised at the tone he adopted with the President of Serbia. He was furious because of the attack on the Academy, even swore at him. Isaković would never have dared do that unless he had the backing of someone just as powerful as Stambolić. I think it's Milošević. Something's brewing, but I don't know what. Could be the two friends have fallen out over that piece of paper."

If this was indeed the case, they were not the only ones. Now, whenever Madge and I met up in the evening with Serbian friends we had been close to for many years, people who shared our views on greater democracy and the hope that Yugoslavia would soon 'go into Europe', as we used to say, there were heated arguments as soon as the Memorandum was mentioned. Instead of a modern Yugoslavia, many of them now wanted a Greater Serbia. The issue divided not only friends but the Party – the Serbian League of Communists – which was still the dominant political force.

Passions were further enflamed by the arrival in Belgrade from Kosovo of delegations of angry Serbs seeking protection from ill-treatment by Albanians and the Albanian-dominated authorities in the Province. The Belgrade press took up their cause, every day reporting further details of persecution, rape, murder, desecration of graves, churches and monasteries…

In April 1987, Slobodan Milošević was dispatched from Belgrade to defuse a large protest meeting of Serbs gathered at Kosovo Polje. When things were getting out of hand, he adopted a different tack, saying what the crowd wanted to hear. After this, the Kosovo Serbs looked to him as their protector.

At the session of the Central Committee of the Serbian Party held in September of the same year, Milošević, supported by the conservative wing, emerged as the strong man of Serbia, having toppled his former friend and patron, Ivan Stambolić.

The crucial significance of this meeting was stressed by Ivan Djurić, a popular young professor of history at Belgrade University, when we met soon after to discuss the publication of a book he was writing. A supporter of democratic reform and a man with a modern, European outlook, he subsequently stood as a Serbian presidential candidate against Milošević and received a lot of votes in Belgrade.

"This session could easily destroy Yugoslavia," he said. "Serbian nationalists in the Party, for their own ends, supported Milošević, who will easily swap his communism for ultra-nationalism if it ensures him power, and put the whole of the Party apparatus at its service. There's a real danger that with all the outcry about the threat to Serbs living outside Serbia proper, he'll gradually win over the Yugoslav Army. As you well know, many senior officers are from the Serb-populated parts of Croatia and Bosnia. If this happens, every nation in Yugoslavia will look to that period in its history when it had the most extensive rights to its own and others' territory, and lay claim to everything that suits its leaders."

Most Serbian historians at that time were busy reminding people that the Serbs had contributed most to the liberation of the South Slavs from Turkish and Austro-Hungarian rule and to the creation of Yugoslavia in 1918. As the largest nation they had naturally taken the leading role until the communists with Tito had given all the others, even the Albanians, equal status. Now the time had come, they declared, to right this injustice…

Very quickly Milošević managed to get a firm grip on the Serbian press, radio and television and used the media to further the aims of the Serbian nationalists, who were beginning to talk openly about creating a Greater Serbia by redrawing the republican boundaries at the expense of Croatia and Bosnia-Herzegovina so as to incorporate all the Serb-populated regions.

Following well-orchestrated public demonstrations in October 1988, Milošević managed to oust the governments of Vojvodina and Montenegro with the aim of placing them entirely under Serbian control. But Kosovo continued to resist. To preserve the autonomy the province had enjoyed under Tito, the ethnic Albanian majority staged protests and strikes that ended with arrests and the trial of their legally-elected leaders. After this clamp-down, the small minority of Serbs, backed by large special police and military units, again controlled Kosovo. Albanians were sacked from their jobs and thrown out of Priština University, radio and television. The Albanian language was no longer in official use. The great majority of Kosovo's inhabitants found themselves deprived of their civil rights and in no better position than when my father served there in the inter-war years.

All this aroused alarm and concern throughout the country among non-Serbs and those Serbs and Montenegrins, like myself, who supported the equality of all the nations in the Federation. Public protests against what was happening in Serbia were loudest in Slovenia – the Croats were more restrained for they had their own problem with the Serbs in Croatia. Human rights in Kosovo were not an 'internal' matter of Serbia, the Slovenes insisted, but concerned the whole country, which was a signatory of the Helsinki Agreement. Milošević responded by launching a campaign against everything Slovenian, first encouraging people to boycott Slovenian goods and then closing the Serbian market to them. These and other measures were intended to show the Slovenes, and other nations in the Federation, who was really boss.

In March 1989, the problem with the provinces was 'solved' by an amendment to the Serbian Constitution that abolished their autonomy. Many saw it as a cause for rejoicing that Serbia was whole again!

The support of the Serbian Orthodox Church was now courted: high-up politicians were seen on television kissing the Patriarch's hand. Money was found to continue the building of St Sava's Shrine in Belgrade, begun before the war, which was to be the largest Orthodox church since the construction of Haghia Sophia in Constantinople. The six hundredth anniversary of the battle of Kosovo provided an ideal opportunity for whipping up patriotic sentiments. The relics of Tsar Lazar, slain in the battle, were taken from nearby Gračanica Monastery and for several months carried in processions headed by the clergy through villages and towns inhabited by Serbs, both in Serbia and outside it. Sermons dwelt on the "reawakening of the long-suffering Serbian nation".

Vidovdan, 28 June 1989, saw the culmination of all this: the arrival of Milošević by helicopter at Gazimestan on the plain of Kosovo to address a million cheering Serbs gathered from all parts of the country and abroad. He vowed that after this things would change; Serbs would be nobody's vassals. He did not exclude the possibility of fresh Serbian battles, if it proved necessary.

In Spring 1989, the Motovun Group paid its second visit to China for a three-week tour that included a cruise down the Yangtze with eighty Chinese publishers. In some of the cities we visited – Xian, Chengdu, Wuhan and Beijing – we ran into crowds of young people marching along, chanting and waving banners, or had our itinerary abruptly altered to avoid them. We were told in confidence by interpreters that demonstrations in favour of democratic changes in society were taking place in many towns.

It was mid May when we arrived back in Beijing for the last few days of our stay. As we made our way through crowds along the broad boulevard leading to Tienanmen Square, columns of young men and women were walking in the same direction and beside them a slowly-moving line of open military trucks carrying armed soldiers. The young people were waving cheerily to the troops, tossing flowers on them, offering them fizzy drinks. The soldiers, too, looked completely good-natured and relaxed. On the vast square, speakers were holding forth, groups of young people were dancing and singing, everyone seemed to be having a good time, like at some youth festival. Many of them wanted to talk to us foreigners, to explain why they were in the square.

Accompanying us throughout our trip was a team from Zagreb Television, headed by a well-known TV presenter and journalist, Silvija Luks, which was making a documentary on the Motovun Group in

China. Naturally, these latest events were a far more exciting subject for them.

"Just look at their demonstrations, without any violence or anger, any of the destructiveness you'd have back home," Silvija remarked.

A few days after we left China, Tienanmen Square was drenched with blood.

Not long after, I had a long phone call from Silvija in Zagreb:

"My colleagues who have looked at the material we shot in China and know about your activities, would like you to be the guest of TV Zagreb. The programme will be broadcast by all the republican TV centres, under the agreed exchange system, so it'll be seen all over the country. As you know, the occasional programme is all that's left of our joint broadcasting schedule now that every republic has its own service.

"What we have in mind is an hour-long interview, illustrated with appropriate filmed footage, in which you would talk about your Partisan past, your sister Stana and your various activities. I should particularly like to ask your views on the present situation in the country: how the problems can be overcome in order to save the Federation which you Partisans created."

This chance to put the arguments in favour of a united Yugoslavia to such a wide audience was something I couldn't refuse. A few days later I found myself sitting in a Zagreb TV studio being interviewed for a popular one-hour current affairs programme. It was very important to me to express emphatically my faith in the survival of Yugoslavia, whose nations had so much in common. Hadn't forty years of peace, harmony among all nationalities, progress and growing democracy been proof of that? Any other solution, I argued, was bound to lead to bloodshed far worse than on Tienanmen.

I was rather pleased with what I'd said, my message to viewers who were in general subjected to a great deal of inflammatory nationalistic rhetoric. The programme was pre-recorded and on the day when it was broadcast, Madge and I happened to be in Motovun. When it was over, eager to hear a reaction from Belgrade, I phoned a close friend.

"What happened to your programme?" he asked. "We were all waiting to see it at the time you said, but there was nothing of any interest on."

Next day I called Zagreb Television.

"The programme was very well received in Croatia by both Serbs and Croats," they reported. "People have been phoning in with congratulations from all over. But, unfortunately, Serbian TV refused to broadcast it. They got the recording in advance, of course, and didn't like it – you must judge for yourself why. This is the first time something like this has ever happened; I'm afraid it means the end of our joint programming."

When I got back to Belgrade, a friend in the Federal Government told me that Premier Marković had watched the programme in Zagreb:

"He said it was a pity there weren't more of that kind, that the common core of TV broadcasting had disappeared, and now every republic was blowing its own trumpet."

❧

Milošević's challenge had met with an immediate response from Croatia, under General Franjo Tudjman, where nationalism, fostered by the Catholic Church and the heirs of the Ustashas, had become the loudest political voice. There was no essential difference between the two leaders, both former communists who incited and exploited nationalism to gain personal power, except that Tudjman was far wiser, turning at once to the richer West, while Milošević looked to bankrupt Russia and the Orthodox Church for allies. Tudjman now sought independence for Croatia, which raised the question of the many Serbs in Croatia and the Croats in Bosnia-Herzegovina, and threatened to lead to Yugoslavia's disintegration, perhaps even war.

Early in 1990, Federal Premier Ante Marković asked me to come to see him. He had been thinking for some time about starting a federal television channel, he said. Every republic had its own press, radio and television, while the Federal Government, which was trying to reform the economy and take the country into Europe, had no way of presenting its policies and goals to viewers. To get these across, he wanted a federal TV channel to start operating as soon as possible. He believed that the Army, of which he was the official head, would make its wavelengths, transmitters and equipment available to the new channel, since it was the Army's duty to defend all the country's nations and its unity. It was considered that I would be a good choice to head this channel since my views on preserving Yugoslavia were well known.

"Our road must lead west, towards progress, and not east, back to the myths and darkness of the past," he said. "If we speak to them honestly, people will accept us, especially the several million in mixed marriages, and their children. Nobody mentions or cares about them. Then there are millions of others, like you and me, who love our own nation, but equally so all the other nations in our community, who think that Yugoslavia has a place in the civilised world. If we don't succeed, millions of people will become victims of poisonous nationalism."

Needless to say, I couldn't refuse this chance of doing my bit to hold Yugoslavia together and prevent a repetition of the bloodshed in the last war.

In the evening, Madge, Una and I were sitting at home watching the News on Belgrade Television. This consisted mainly of accusations directed at Slovenia and Croatia, which seemed to be responsible for all Serbia's economic and social ills and national problems. The grim-faced newsreaders warned the Serbian people in dramatic terms of the danger from Moslems in Bosnia, Albanians in Kosovo, Serbia's enemies within and without.

"What kind of news is this?" asked Madge. "Why are they stirring up so much hatred? If they want to save Yugoslavia, as they keep saying, they're going just the wrong way about it. I can't for the life of me see how the majority nation can be threatened by the smaller and weaker ones."

"Our TV channel will change all that," I assured her. "There will be no threats and accusations. We'll give every side a chance to put forward their views calmly and debate them in a civilised manner. Our programme will be based on what binds us together: free borders between the republics and provinces, the free flow of goods, people and ideas. All this functioned for almost half a century after the war with very few problems. Now, when the states of Europe want to achieve the same thing, some extreme and irresponsible nationalists in our country want to return us to the nineteenth century."

"Your new channel ought to have a short, snappy name, easy to remember. What about YUTEL?" Una proposed.

⅍

At the next meeting of the Federal Government, in March 1990, I was appointed Director General of Federal Television, to be known as Yutel. From that moment my troubles began. The Army at first promised its help, but soon reneged on this, as it departed ever further from the Partisan concept of unity and equality of all nations. I remembered Duško's words when Yugoslavia capitulated in April 1941: "The damned generals have betrayed us." But the weak Royal Army had faced Hitler's might. Now there was no foreign enemy: we were destroying our own country from within.

Yutel set up production studios in all the republican and provincial centres and planned to broadcast from Belgrade, but we did not get the necessary permission from the Serbian government. One by one, the other republican television centres also refused to transmit Yutel's programme, with the exception of Bosnia-Herzegovina, so our team of about fifty excellent journalists from all parts of the country moved to Sarajevo.

Yutel started broadcasting at 8 p.m. – prime time – on 23 October 1990 from one of Sarajevo TV's studios.

"Good evening, Yugoslavia!" Goran Milić, a Croat, Yutel's Main Editor, greeted viewers. He was a popular, highly talented and widely respected broadcaster; his decision to join Yutel did much to attract viewers and boost confidence in the channel. Then followed an hour of news, reports and comments from all parts of the country. Yutel's policy was to let the viewers reach their own conclusions after hearing both sides, instead of telling them what to think, as was the norm in the republican media.

From 9 p.m., when the first broadcast ended, until dawn the telephones never stopped ringing as viewers called in, enthusiastically praising a programme that offered hope that people of whatever nation and creed could continue to live peacefully side by side, as in Tito's time. The large hall of Sarajevo TV was bursting with local people who had watched the programme and rushed straight over to welcome this new messenger of peace and unity, without which multi-ethnic Bosnia had no future.

❦

The launching of Yutel as part of the Federal Government's efforts to preserve Yugoslavia did not pass unnoticed abroad. The world media were already full of the latest developments and the worrying news coming from all parts of the country, so that a new TV channel directed towards all Yugoslavs, not just the people of a particular republic, seemed like a welcome ray of hope. Yutel was besieged by foreign journalists. Besides talking to them, I also had long and exhaustive discussions with the ambassadors of the United States, Great Britain, Italy and Germany. Afterwards I would report their views and advice to Premier Marković. They all expressed the wish to do what they could to prevent the country's disintegration.

Naturally enough, there were others who were interested in Yutel from a commercial aspect. Since we were having problems financing this expensive station, we made it known that we would welcome partners who would buy shares in it. Soon after, I was telephoned from London by a director of the communications empire of Robert Maxwell, who was at that time planning to set up a pan-European television network to rival the giant North American systems CBS, NBC and ABC. The director assured me they were very interested in getting involved in Yutel.

"Why don't you come to London straight away for talks," he proposed. "If the Boss is here, he'd like to meet you too."

In fact, already I knew Robert Maxwell slightly from a few short meetings connected with publishing. Through his Pergamon Press, he wanted to establish himself in the book markets of Eastern Europe and extend his influence and activity into other important spheres as well. A few days later, at the London Head Office, we discussed various technical and costing questions and the possibilities of their participation. It was arranged that we should meet again shortly, this time in Belgrade.

But Maxwell was not the only media baron interested in Yutel. While I was in London, Berlusconi's TV group had been in contact with my office. Not long before I had been informed by Slovenian TV that he wanted to get involved in Radio Capodistria, located in the Slovenian port of Koper.

I discussed these propositions with the Italian ambassador, a very constructive, well-intentioned and pleasant person. A few days later he informed me that I had been invited, with my wife, to spend three days in Trieste as Berlusconi's guest, while I had talks with his associates.

Madge and I had often visited this city while holidaying each summer at our house in Motovun across the border in Istria. We would spend sweltering hours in the long lines of Yugoslav cars at the frontier crossings so that we could buy jeans, fashionable shoes and small luxuries not available in Belgrade at that time. Rushing around the shops with children in tow, we had never found time to explore properly this impressive city with its unique blend of Mediterranean and Central European. Now was our opportunity.

This time in Trieste we were accommodated in the elegant Hotel Duca d'Aosta on the magnificent waterfront Piazza de l'Unita d'Italia. Waiting for us we found a welcome message and two tickets for Verdi's Nabucco at the city's opera house. That cool, showery, out-of-season weekend, the city was quite Italian, without the crowds of Yugoslavs who packed the shops, restaurants and streets in summer. The Ponte Rosso area, no longer cluttered by market stalls and litter, revealed its true beauty. As we wandered the almost empty streets and squares admiring the imposing architecture, Madge and I for a while forgot Belgrade, all the tensions and disturbing events. We tried to picture Trieste as it had been in its heyday, the Trieste of Maximillian of Mexico, James Joyce, and other notable historical and literary figures.

"It was from here, before the First World War, that my uncles set out for America," I told Madge. "They hung around the port until they found a ship to take them from the poverty of their homeland to a better world, free from wars and bloodshed – or so they hoped."

In the evening, sitting in the splendidly ornate opera house built at the time when Trieste was at its zenith, we observed the elegantly dressed audience – smiling, relaxed people who were living a normal life. When the lights dimmed and the glorious Verdi chorus of Israelites filled the theatre, I felt an unutterable sadness, thinking of what awaited us on our return to Belgrade. Tears came to my eyes, just like all those years ago at the concert in Nikšić, except that then war was just ending, and now it was looming ahead.

We hurried back to Belgrade since the development of events demanded my urgent return. The talks in London and Trieste came to nothing: foreign investors were no longer interested for, unfortunately, Yutel's programme could be seen by only a quarter of Yugoslavia's TV viewers, those within the range of Sarajevo Television.

༉

To try to change this, Premier Marković thought I should spend the next month going around the republican television centres and ministries of information. I mostly managed to meet the presidents of republics when they came to Belgrade. Some were ready to listen and promised help, others were quite hostile. The pleasantest were Kiro Gligorov of Macedonia and Milan Kučan of Slovenia. It seemed that Yutel didn't bother them, and soon their republican televisions started transmitting our programme.

The meeting with President Tudjman took place in the Palace of the Federation in Belgrade. Thinking he would be pleased, I mentioned the gatherings of the Motovun Group of publishers that were held in Istria and how much we all loved the region. I added that many local people wanted to know when they would be able to receive Yutel's programme. Quite contrary to my intentions, he took my story as deliberate provocation and flew into a rage. His face contorted with anger, he declared that he knew why we met in Motovun and travelled around Istria: in order to raise support for Yugoslavia, although this was Croatian territory.

Despite this less than pleasant encounter, because of public interest and pressure from the West, Croatian Television did begin transmitting Yutel early in 1991. Soon after, Serbia and, finally, Montenegro followed suit. At last people in every part of Yugoslavia, except Kosovo, could receive our programme – provided they were prepared to sit up until two or three in the morning, which was the usual broadcasting slot allocated to us everywhere except in Bosnia. Many viewers did stay awake. But in mid May Croatian Television ceased transmitting Yutel, followed shortly after by the televisions of Serbia and Montenegro. In the end, all my efforts to get our programme into homes throughout the country had failed, and it was limited once more to the range of Sarajevo TV.

⚡

Despite the disturbing news of Yugoslavia's political troubles, many publishers set out for the 1991 summer meeting in Motovun, which was due to begin on 26 June and last a week. They had been coming to this peaceful little place for years and could not imagine they would encounter any difficulties. No-one, least of all myself, believed that Yugoslavia, for so long held up as an example of a successful multi-national state, could fall apart.

To save time, Madge and I travelled with our little Renault 4 on the overnight train from Belgrade to the Slovenian port of Koper, close to Trieste and less than an hour's drive from Motovun. At the time we didn't realise that this was an historic journey: we were on the last Yugoslav train to travel between Serbia and Slovenia.

The Motovun Group meeting could not have been timed for a more dramatic moment. While members were travelling from all over the globe, Slovenia and Croatia declared their independence and the Yugoslav Army intervened. Though the state borders were soon blockaded by tanks, some people who were driving – Chairman Karel Schuyt from the Netherlands, Secretary-Treasurer Jürgen Braunschweiger from Switzerland, and others – managed to get through before they were all closed. From the UK, France, Scandinavia and further afield, publishers arrived by plane at Ljubljana Airport before it, too, was closed and damaged by bombing the following day. Others flew to Trieste and in rented cars tried to find minor crossing points that were still open.

Blissfully unaware of the drama that was unfolding, in the early morning sunshine Madge and I drove southward into Istria. When we reached the little Dragonja stream, which we jokingly used to refer to as the 'frontier' between Slovenia and Croatia, we were surprised to see a group of Slovene police putting up some kind of hut and ramp, watched by two or three bemused-looking local people.

Throughout the day, people came trickling into Motovun, all with their own story to tell. Some were worried about how they would ever get out of the country; others were treating it as an exciting adventure. Though a dozen who had set out never managed to reach Motovun, we tried to carry on with our meeting as usual. Two days later, when we were dining al fresco, enjoying lamb roasted on the spit on a nearby hill, we could hardly believe our eyes: walking towards us through the vineyard were our Japanese member Hideo Aoki and his wife Sissi. With incredible persistence they had finally made it from Tokyo.

Returning from Motovun, we avoided Slovenia, taking the more difficult route via Rijeka to Zagreb. Driving along the highway towards Belgrade, usually so crowded with traffic, was an eerie and unnerving experience – Madge said it reminded her of scenes in 'On the Beach', a film about a few survivors after a world-wide nuclear disaster. Apart from occasional groups of police, armed with automatic rifles, standing around beside their cars at junctions, the highway was completely deserted.

※

Just a day or two after our ghostly drive, military skirmishes began in Croatia and in the course of the summer escalated into heavy fighting in Slavonia, the flat eastern region of Croatia bordering on Serbia. The town of Vukovar became a focus of the Serb-Croat conflict. With mounting anxiety, people throughout the country were glued to their television screens, incredulously watching the tragedy unfold.

At the suggestion of Lord Carrington, chairman of the EEC conference on Yugoslavia, Sir Fitzroy Maclean came to Belgrade in September.

"I'd like to come over and see you," he said, phoning from the residence of the British Ambassador, Andrew Wood, only five minutes' drive from our house.

In the years since our first meeting when I was a student in England, I'd seen Fitzroy from time to time on his visits to Yugoslavia, when he was always the guest of his war-time friend, President Tito. After our collaboration on several books on Yugoslavia, I felt he had become a family friend. Sitting on the terrace in the warm evening sunshine, sipping the Montenegrin *loza* he always enjoyed, we discussed the situation.

"It's very sad to see Yugoslavia falling apart," he said. "In Europe the borders between states that were enemies until yesterday are being removed, while in Yugoslavia they're being established. I've had long talks with General Kadijević and Admiral Brovet. Milošević didn't have time for me. War with Croatia is the worst thing that could have happened. What is tragic is that people in the Academy of Science and Milošević don't understand that, in Europe at least, the time has passed when war was the surest way of achieving national ambitions. The crazy idea that with the Army, by a blitzkrieg, you can move frontiers and keep all you capture is one that could only occur to unschooled politicians, of the kind that have regrettably gained the upper hand in Serbia.

"They say Yugoslavia can exist as long as it has at least two republics. But we think that without Slovenia and Croatia, or any other of its parts, Yugoslavia won't and can't exist. But anything is better than war. It could be something like the European Economic Community, if it can't go on as before. But in that case Montenegro, too, would have to be an independent sovereign state. That's the only way to re-establish co-operation on the former territory of Yugoslavia."

Yutel's journalists and cameramen in Belgrade and all the republics, except Bosnia, were finding it increasingly difficult to get access to the scene of important events, and the Army banned them completely. Members of the extreme Serbian nationalist group known as the White Eagles broke into the Belgrade studio from time to time, chased our people out and physically ill-treated them. One day when I returned from Sarajevo, Madge reported that a man kept telephoning and asking for me.

"He sounds strange, doesn't want to give his name or leave a message. He only wants to talk to you. I told him you'd be home this evening."

Less than an hour later the phone rang and Madge answered. Handing me the receiver, she murmured that it was the same man.

"Am I talking to Bato?" asked an unfamiliar voice.

"Yes. Who's speaking?"

"I daren't give you my name because of what I'm going to tell you. Let's say I'm a well-wisher. I admire what you're doing. I watch Yutel whenever I can. You're all good people, afraid of nobody. But not everyone likes Yutel. That's why I wanted to warn you, give you some advice. Don't go anywhere alone. Beware of dark places: the dark could swallow you up. I've heard that something's being planned for you, so I decided to call."

"Many thanks," I replied, touched by this friendly concern on the part of someone unknown to me.

I repeated the conversation to Madge and remarked that it was probably some well-meaning person close to the Serbian authorities who had got wind of their plans.

At Yutel we all stayed until late at night: there were too few of us to cope with all the work and problems. Around midnight, in a state of physical and nervous exhaustion, I got in the car and drove home. When I approached the garage, I put on the full headlights to check whether there was anyone standing in the dark. Previously I had never done so.

Next day I mentioned this to a friend at Yutel, more as a joke at my own expense.

"Well, they've succeeded!" he said.

"What do you mean?"

"They've managed to upset you, scare you a bit, make you think of yourself and not of Yutel."

One night after a late return home, I was getting ready for bed when the phone rang.

"Who can be calling so late?" Madge asked crossly. "Little Andrea will wake up."

Una, our son-in-law Vladan and their one-year-old daughter were living with us at the time. Again it was an unfamiliar male voice, but a quite different one, hoarse and much rougher.

I asked who he wanted, whether he'd got the wrong number.

"No mistake," he said. "I recognise your voice –" Then abruptly he started swearing crudely and violently at me. I swore back, which provoked more obscenities and threats:

"You'll pay for what you're doing, traitor. We'll get you."

"How do you mean to do that?" I asked to keep him talking, hoping to get a clue as to who was behind this.

"We can show you right away. Just come out of your house for a moment!"

For a long time I couldn't get to sleep.

Una told me that during the day there were some suspicious-looking types hanging around and watching the house. She was afraid for Andrea. When I mentioned this next day, Goran Milić said he, too, got threatening phone calls late at night.

"They've even drawn up a list of people condemned to death. About twenty of us in Yutel are on it, including you and me."

❧

Several days later, early in the morning the door-bell rang. Madge opened the door, then called me:

"Bato, the postman wants you to sign personally for a summons."

"What summons?" I asked, immediately alarmed.

"Court summons," said the man in uniform, who was not our regular postman but someone from the court.

"What have I done wrong now?" I asked myself aloud, but the man answered:

"Just you sign that I've delivered this, then read it. It's all nicely written down…"

'Nebojša-Bato Tomašević, General Director of Yutel, is summoned to appear before this court to answer the charge of damaging the Republic of Serbia…'

I read the tiny, almost illegible print of the lengthy charge against me. Serbian nationalists, it seemed, wanted to get rid of all those who in any way, however slight, obstructed the creation of their 'Greater Serbia'.

Why did we need a Greater Serbia when the whole of Yugoslavia was ours? I asked myself. What was the point of a free corridor to link up all the Serbs in one state when we'd always been free to travel to any part of the country where Serbs lived? How many of us here in Serbia in the forty-five years since the war ever visited Knin, centre of the Serbs in Croatia, or some Serbian place in Bosnia-Herzegovina? Nobody ever stopped us travelling there, or going there to live and work, if we wanted to, so why go to war over the drawing of imaginary borders? This terrible nationalism had destroyed the country, divided friends, brought racists to power; criminals were getting rich from profiteering and plunder. The state and socially-owned property was up for grabs.

That evening Madge and I discussed the situation until late at night. I turned on the television. Young men were being ordered to report immediately to their military units. The newsreader announced the

Three generations of the Tomašević family photographed in Kosovska Mitrovica in 1930

successes of the Yugoslav Army and Serbian volunteers in the battle for the town of Vukovar.

Why Vukovar, where Serbs and Croats had been living together for centuries? In whose interest was it to destroy that age-old harmony, kill women and children? For what insane reason was a fine city being razed to the ground while both sides were promising greater freedom, more democracy, a better life?

There was only a week to go before the court hearing. I was becoming more and more alarmed they would come and take away my passport to stop me leaving the country. It was obvious that the purpose of the trial was to try to discredit Yutel and put me in prison. We decided we should leave. The News said that the Belgrade-Zagreb highway was now closed because of fighting between Serbs and Croats around Okučani, one hundred kilometres east of Zagreb. The only way for us to get to Italy was to drive to Montenegro and try to get on the ferry, if it was still operating, between Bar and the Italian port of Bari.

We packed a few things. From the wall of my mother's bedroom I took down a faded family photograph and studied it for a while, as though for the first time. An inscription on the back recorded that it was from 1930. In front sat Grandpa Filip and Grandma Stana in Montenegrin costume. Behind stood my mother, in a combination of Montenegrin and city dress, beside her Aunt Mileva, then Father and all the children in descending height, except for Aco, not yet born.

"I'm glad the others in this picture are dead and gone," I said to Madge. "It would have been torture for them to watch the break-up of the country they loved and fought for. That little boy in the sailor suit gave his life for it."

The coming journey to Montenegro reminded me of my childhood, of Cetinje during the war. I thought of Olga, the source of the only pleasant memories from that terrible time. What had become of her? How had she spent the forty years since our last, sad meeting? Through my boyhood friend Rajko, who was still in Cetinje, I found out she had moved to Podgorica in 1953, soon after I'd gone off to study in

England. I managed to get her telephone number and started dialling, but stopped half way to think more clearly what I was going to say. How to explain why I was calling now, after so long, just before leaving for England, and why I hadn't done so when leaving the first time, almost forty years ago? Perhaps I could say that this new war had made me think of the last one…

I plucked up courage and dialled the whole number this time. The phone rang a long time before a pleasant, young-sounding woman's voice answered. It seemed somehow familiar. I gave my name and said I was a childhood friend of Olga's. The woman said her mother was at home and she would call her at once, adding: "I'm sure she'll be pleased."

Then silence. I waited a long time, an eternity. Finally the young woman was back on the line, sounding rather confused, apologetic.

"My mother doesn't remember you at all, doesn't recall ever hearing your name. She says there must be some mistake. I'm sorry, you're probably looking for someone else."

❧

The whole day as we travelled to Montenegro I was in a strange state of mind. It was like a dream journey through childhood as we passed through Nova Varoš, Kolašin, the Morača canyon, Podgorica…

When we reached Bar, to our great relief we found the ferry was still operating. At passport control, the policeman just glanced at Madge's British passport and handed it back. Mine he studied for a long time, compared the photograph and my face, then started paging through a thick, well-thumbed book, searching for my name. This could be the end of me, I thought. From his expression I saw that I was not yet on the list, and gave thanks, for the first time, for the slowness of Balkan bureaucracy.

As the ferry drew away from the shore, gliding across the smooth surface of the Adriatic, I took a last look at the bare, grey mountains of my childhood. Night fell. I was in a peculiar state of mind. In one way I was happy and relieved to be across the border, away from the threat of arrest, the horrors of war. For the first time in my life I had no obligations to society, no place or role, like a soldier just demobbed after doing his military service. It occurred to me that I was the last soldier of a long line in my family, stretching back many generations, who had defended this land, loved it passionately and served it faithfully… At the same time I was immeasurably sad about everything that had happened, was still happening, to shatter a great dream: that people of many different nations and faiths could live together in peace and harmony. I was also worried about our future, which we had believed was securely provided for. Now we were like an old tree that had been uprooted and had to be re-planted in another place. But where and how? On what soil could it flourish?

In the morning the piercing ship's siren announced our arrival in the port of Bari. As we waited to drive off the ferry, Madge said that now we should try to forget everything that was happening across the sea, relax and start to live a new life with the children and our friends, of which, thankfully, we had many abroad as well as at home.

Like regular tourists, we went into Bari Cathedral. Though not religious, when I visited churches I used to follow the practice of lighting candles for loved ones who were no more. On this occasion I bought a large number for the dead members of the family. As I lit them one by one, I could see each dear face in the flame. In my mind I said goodbye in turn to each of them, wherever their bones might lie: scattered on battlefields or buried in family graves. One candle was for Grandma Stana, born Francesca Papani, whose family had originally come from a village near Bari.

Studying the road map, my eye was caught by the name Colfiorito, a little place not far from Assisi in the province of Perugia.

"I know where we must get today and spend the night," I said to Madge. "It's high time I visited Colfiorito, almost fifty years after Duško."

It was in the winter of 1942 that my brother arrived there in chains with his comrades. One of them who had returned, Mošo, told us that during the crossing from Bar to Bari in the overcrowded hold of the vessel, Duško had felt ill and had a bad nose-bleed. The guards ordered him to be taken on deck, where he spent all night in a cold wind. After that he got pneumonia, but being strong and healthy until then, he had somehow survived. Weakened by hunger and this illness, however, he developed tuberculosis. When Italy capitulated and the prisoners got out of the camp, Duško was too ill to set off on the long walk to Yugoslavia. The camp doctor and his wife had taken him into their home to look after him.

As Duško had told Stana at their brief meeting in Drvar, this couple had hidden and cared for him for two months until he was well enough to leave. They had pressed him to stay until the war was over and offered to adopt him, as they were middle-aged and had no children of their own.

Now I felt I had to visit the place whatever happened. All these years since the war I had been wanting to do so, but my journeys had always taken me elsewhere. 'I know, Duško, that's a pathetic excuse.' I said to myself.

The road wound through the lovely landscapes of Perugia. It was late afternoon, the sun low in the sky, when we reached Colfiorito, a small place lying in a narrow valley. The road ran through the middle, becoming its main street. Halfway along there were a few little shops and a café. The dozen or so elderly men and women sitting at the tables on the pavement seemed untroubled by the stream of cars speeding past, some giving a blast on their horn. I parked and went across to speak to them.

"Excuse me, but was there a camp for Montenegrins here in the Second World War?"

They put down the playing cards they were holding and all turned at once to look curiously at this stranger asking such an unusual question.

"*Si, si!*" They answered in chorus, and told me that the camp had been set up in the nearby army barracks, now used as military stores. Why did I want to know, they asked. I told them about my brother and the kind couple who had hidden him from the Germans for two months. Now I had finally come to see where he was imprisoned. One of them promised to take us there next day.

"I can't forgive myself for not coming here after the war, to thank the doctor and his wife. They must have died years ago."

"No, no!" they all spoke together. "That would have been Dr Luigi, and he's alive!" To my astonishment, it turned out that the doctor was still hale and hearty in his nineties, but had moved to Rome after the death of his wife some years before. From time to time, he came to his house in Colfiorito, where a relative was now living with her family.

"Tomorrow you could go to see the house as well, if you like," someone suggested. "Perhaps they can show the room where your brother was hidden."

Through this chance meeting with a group of strangers, I was learning about that period in my brother's life that had remained a mystery all those years.

They directed us to a small hotel nearby and arranged to meet us at nine next morning at the same place. One of the elderly women added:

Military barracks at Colfiorito, central Italy. During the Second World War they served as an internment camp where Duško was incarcerated for nearly two years. Photo by Madge Tomašević, 1991

"It's Sunday tomorrow. I'd like you to see our church. But if you can't, no matter. I'll pray for the soul of your brother, and for your Montenegrin princess, our Queen Elena…"

The nearness of the camp, memories of my brother, the scene that last night when they came to take him away – all this kept me awake until dawn. When I finally fell asleep, once more I had that same dream that used to recur so often in the years following the war.

The war is over. I am at the railway station meeting trains bringing home former prisoners. I keep running up and down the platform, afraid I'll miss my brother. Suddenly I see his smiling face and feel a great surge of happiness. "At last you've come back!" I call out to him, and wake up.

When I opened my eyes, I consoled myself that I had seen him again, if only for a brief moment in a dream.

At nine Madge and I were in front of the café. Only one of last evening's group was waiting for us: Guido, a small, broad-faced man with white hair. All the rest were going to church, he told us.

"I was a guard in the camp during the war. I don't remember your brother, of course, but I do remember when all your countrymen arrived. Before that I was a policeman at the local station, but one day we were all taken off in a hurry to be guards in the camp. We were surprised at how young they all were, kids really, hardly any of them above twenty. When news of the capitulation got round, a group of them rushed at us guards and escaped. We didn't do anything to stop them. Within twenty-four hours the Germans were here and stopped the rest from getting away. They put them on a train and sent them off to Germany, together with us guards. So I ended up in a German prison camp with your Montenegrins!"

Listening to the elderly Guido's reminiscences, we walked to the camp.

"Here it is," he said. "Nothing much has changed since the time your brother escaped."

The high, wide gate stood ajar. Without waiting for him, I hurried inside. A dozen long, low huts were arranged in two rows with an empty space in between. At one end, a hill rising behind it, stood a large, three-storey stone building painted white, which had housed the camp administration and guards. I began running from hut to hut, seized by a burning desire to see and memorise everything, every inch of this camp, to experience it in the way Duško had done. A whole lifetime too late, I had come to meet my brother. How wonderful it would have been, I thought, if I could have waited for him there at the entrance in 1943. Maybe the two of us together would have made it.

We continued our journey to England. As we neared the Channel I remembered with emotion the many times we had crossed it with Una and Stella on the way to spend a summer holiday with Madge's Aunt Win and Uncle Ken. They would not be there to welcome us this time: they had died, within two weeks of each other, a year before. As we were leaving at the end of our holidays, we would always look back at the White Cliffs of Dover and vow that when we retired on our well-deserved pensions, we would spend half the year in England, half in Yugoslavia. Then, on our return to Belgrade, we would work even harder so we could make this dream come true.

Spring 1992. Still regarding my stay in London as temporary, I often phoned my lawyer in Belgrade, who was working in my absence to get the court case dismissed. When he succeeded and the danger had passed, I would return home. In the meantime, I was doing my best to keep in contact with Yutel. Every now and again I managed to get through to Sarajevo.

"Goran, is there any way I can help?" I asked.

"You could get statements from well-known people and telephone them to us. We could include them in the news. We're working in impossible conditions, Bato. After the broadcasts, we all stay in the studio till dawn – we daren't go out at night for fear of our lives. It's doubtful whether we can hold out much longer. Moslems and Serbs are already fighting up in the mountains of Bosnia-Herzegovina, not only armed units but also the local people, who until recently lived together in friendship. The Yugoslav Army is completely on the Serbian side. When they withdraw from their garrisons, they leave their arms and equipment to the Serbs. The Moslems and Croats want all army weapons placed under joint control, but the Serbs refuse. All the propaganda has made people believe that their freedom, homes and lives are in danger, so they're joining the various national military formations that are fighting one another. We in Yutel are the ones still calling on people to come to their senses and live together in peace. But now the Army's started targeting our transmitters. When these are destroyed, Yutel will be finished."

Against all reason, I clung to the belief that this 'family quarrel' could still be settled peacefully, especially as the United Nations had passed several resolutions on Yugoslavia, calling for the immediate cessation of hostilities and a negotiated resolution of our problems – we had always been great supporters of the UN and respected all its decisions.

The time was approaching for the publishers' meeting in Motovun, traditionally held at the end of June, and members began phoning me to ask whether it was safe to travel in view of the bad news coming out of Yugoslavia. I reassured them that there was no cause for concern – Istria, part of Croatia, was far from the fighting in the Bosnian highlands, the Army had withdrawn from the region without a single incident, and the troubles would not affect the work of our annual gathering, which was due to be opened by the Croatian Minister of Culture. By their presence in Yugoslavia, publishers from a score of countries would make their contribution, demonstrate their belief that people of different races and faiths could live and work together in harmony, which had always been the credo of our group. By this and much more besides, I did my best to encourage members to attend the 1992 Motovun meeting.

Some weeks before this gathering, I managed with difficulty to get a connection with Sarajevo and speak to Goran.

"Yutel is on its last legs, Bato. The Serbs have destroyed our main transmitter on Mount Vlasić in central Bosnia, so now only Sarajevo can see us. Our people no longer go home in case someone comes to murder them. I'm in hiding at a friend's house. Sarajevo is completely surrounded by Serbs. Their guns are firing down on the city from the hills. As I speak, planes are flying low over the studio. They want to hit the transmitter on the roof above our heads. I must break off now and go into the shelter – it's getting dangerous…"

The last surviving transmitter was bombed out of existence and Yutel ceased broadcasting on 11 May 1992.

Later I read with sadness the study on Yutel by the British writer and journalist Mark Thompson, published by the International Centre Against Censorship:

"Yutel was a federal television station which started its short troubled life in October 1990, amid high hopes. By contrast with *Tanjug* [Yugoslav news agency] and *Borba* [national newspaper], which were conceived to serve the information system in a one-party state, Yutel's political goal was to speed Yugoslavia's passage toward full democracy. By aspiring to the highest standards of journalism, Yutel would show all facets of the truth to all Yugoslavia's fractured and bewildered public. It would remind people, by force of objective programming, why Yugoslavia should stay together.

"The main figure behind Yutel was Ante Marković, the Federal Prime Minister. The director was Nebojša Bato Tomašević, a former diplomat turned emigré publisher (based in London), who was well connected among Belgrade political circles. The editor-in-chief was Goran Milić."

"Bosnia was the republic where Yutel was truly popular; its editorial balance appealed especially to Muslims, caught between Serb and Croat territorial ambitions, and to anyone who supported the sovereign integrity of the republic."

Oppressed by a sense of guilt and worried about the fate of the people I had persuaded to join Yutel, I set out for the sixteenth annual summer meeting of the Motovun Group. I felt extremely grateful to the members travelling from as far away as Japan, the United States and Canada, as well as from many European countries, who had decided to participate, this time less for business reasons than out of friendship and solidarity. By coming they would show that it was the pen and not the sword that could bring peoples together, put an end to prejudice, fear and distrust, oppose insane ideas about the superiority of one nation over another, the rule of lawlessness and violence.

When I arrived at Ljubljana Airport, a Slovenian official examined my passport at length, then asked me to step aside until the other passengers had gone through. It was necessary, he said, to fill out a form and pay for a visa. My first reaction was to protest, but as there were people waiting for me in Motovun I couldn't risk it. I felt utterly humiliated. Why, I asked myself, when this was my country? Until yesterday all our frontiers had been completely open for all Yugoslavs and foreigners.

From a Ljubljana hotel I phoned a Motovun member and old friend, Laki, in Zagreb. As previously agree, he would come by car to pick me up and we would drive together to Motovun.

"You won't get into Croatia without a visa," were his first words. "I've been trying all day to arrange one. I even got as high as the Minister of Internal Affairs. He'll have a fax sent to the frontier, telling them to let you in. Wait for me at the hotel. I'll get there as fast as I can."

I still hadn't grasped the seriousness of all this. There must be some mistake, I thought. Everything would be cleared up when we reached Istria, where they were always pleased to see the Motovun Group members.

As we drove south towards Motovun, Laki told me that Slovenia and Croatia had agreed between themselves on opening nearly thirty frontier crossing points. At each of these they had built ramps and barracks and posted military and border guards. I remembered seeing the first of these being hastily erected on the way to Motovun exactly one year before.

"On my way to Ljubljana," he told me, "after ten minutes' drive from Zagreb, as I was leaving Croatia I was stopped by our border guards. I had to show my passport, get out of the car, open up the boot. Then they started paging through the books I'm bringing to the meeting. All this was repeated on the Slovenian side of the frontier. The same thing will happen now when we leave Slovenia and go down into Istria. When I return to Zagreb from Motovun, both of them in Croatia, because I pass through Slovenia I'll have to stop four times, show my passport, get out of the car, lose time. The round trip with eight frontier stops will take me twice as long as before!"

A fax about my arrival had been sent to one particular frontier crossing, by which I would be allowed to enter and leave Croatia. After driving for an hour or so, we reached the border in the middle of woodland, marked by a ramp across the country road and a newly-built wooden hut. Luckily, they knew about me: the Minister had sent the promised fax. We reached Motovun in the early afternoon. By evening, the others would have arrived and we would all dine together.

Sitting in the sunshine on the terrace of the Hotel Kaštel, I gazed across the elongated piazza paved with pale, polished flag-stones at our beautiful white house at the far end. I remembered how I had bought it, half-derelict, many years before and persuaded Review's board to spend a fair amount of money renovating and equipping it for meetings with foreign publishers. After I left Review in the mid-Eighties and started working independently in publishing, the Motovun Group had taken a long lease on the building, which members could use at any time. Now I could see several policeman standing in front of the house and doing something to the front door. They must be checking it's secure, I thought; they were always keen to make sure nothing unpleasant happened to our publishers. Then one of the policemen, whom I knew well, left the others and strolled towards me across the square. Pleased to see him, I stood up to shake hands.

"Comrade Bato, we've had an order from Zagreb to seal up the building and forbid the holding of your meeting. As for you personally, we've been told to arrest you, but none of us wants to do it – we all know you well. The order came down from Zagreb, not from the commune, which used to be in charge of the police, but not any more."

In a state of shock, together with Laki I rushed to the telephone. We called Zagreb, first of all the Minister for Culture. A secretary asked who was speaking, then, after a perceptible pause, told us the Minister was out of town. This seemed good news: he must have already left for Motovun to stay overnight somewhere in the vicinity so he could open our gathering in the morning. To be on the safe side, we also called the Minister for Information. He would certainly be able to explain what was happening.

"Minister for Information of the Republic of Croatia speaking. Why do you want to speak to me?"

I begged him to hear me out. The Motovun Group meeting was about to begin, I said, people were arriving from all over the globe, but the police said they had an order to ban it and had sealed up our building. I spoke of all the expense and effort our members needed to reach Motovun. The Japanese, for instance, had to fly from Tokyo to Paris, change planes there for Milan, then travel by plane or train to Trieste, where they would hire a car to drive to Motovun. What was I to tell them when they arrived? For sixteen years they and the others had been coming regularly to Motovun. They had published books on Istria, Croatia and Yugoslavia… I deliberately didn't mention my own case: what was important now was to ensure the meeting could go ahead. I felt certain that when the Culture Minister arrived, my problem could be sorted out: why would anyone want to arrest me when I had demonstrated how much I loved Motovun, Istria and Croatia? Had I not put together and published the first comprehensive illustrated history of Croatian art and architecture, not to mention many other books on the republic and its historic cities?

The Information Minister was clearly embarrassed. No-one had told him the meeting had been banned, he said, and apologised for the awkward situation in which we found ourselves. We should phone back in two hours, by which time he would have found out how such a mistake could have occurred and had it rectified.

Our chairman, the Dutch publisher Karel Schuyt, and the group's secretary, Jürgen Braunschweiger from Switzerland, found us sitting nervously by the phone, waiting for the time to pass and wondering who else to call.

"What's happening, Bato?" asked Karel. "Our members are arriving, but at the bottom of the hill the police are stopping our cars, asking where we're going and why. I hardly managed to get past."

I explained our problem and that Laki and I were waiting to hear from the Croatian Minister for Information, who'd promised to correct this mistake, made, as he said, by some irresponsible person.

"We'll stay by the phone and telephone Zagreb for as long as is necessary," I said. "Please welcome the members, help them find their rooms, and do your best to calm everyone down. I'm sure this will be solved by dinnertime."

But when we contacted the Minister after two hours, he apologised profusely: he had not yet discovered who had given the order to stop the meeting and close the house. "Call me again around ten this evening," he ended.

During dinner in the hotel, instead of the usual cheerful atmosphere of our first evening together, with old friends noisily greeting one another, the mood was subdued. I blamed myself for encouraging people to come, putting them to trouble and expense for a meeting that might never take place.

"It's all my fault because I'm so fanatical about Yugoslavia," I said to Laki as we waited by the phone for ten o'clock. "It's a kind of blindness that comes from loving and believing in something too much. I can't accept the fact that my country no longer exists, that it's been destroyed."

Exactly at ten we called the Minister for Information.

"He's left. He had to go somewhere," the duty officer told us. "He said to give you the telephone number of General Tudjman's personal security advisor, Mr Erzegovac. He's informed about your case."

Until almost midnight, Laki and I took turns dialling the number. It kept ringing but no-one answered. We had almost given up hope when someone eventually lifted the receiver: it was Erzegovac himself.

Pleased at the chance to put matters right, I repeated my story, ending with the fact that the Croatian Minister for Culture was due to open our meeting next morning, that he was probably already on his way to Motovun.

"Now let me tell you something," Erzegovac replied in an unpleasant tone. "I personally gave the order for the ban and the sealing of the building. And no minister is going to open your Chetnik meeting while I have a say here. Any minister who dared to do it would be arrested by me personally."

He put down the receiver.

Although it was midnight, everybody was still in the hotel restaurant. Madge, who had arrived from London with the British group, asked me in Serbo-Croatian, so the rest wouldn't understand, what had been the outcome of our calls. But from my expression it must have been clear to all. I asked Madge to go around discreetly and invite the Executive Committee and several others to meet to discuss our predicament. Ten minutes later we were gathered on the beautiful terrace of the house belonging to committee-member Philip Wilson. The night was warm and clear, the sky studded with stars. There were jugs of wine on the tables, but no-one felt much like drinking.

Without beating around the bush, I repeated the message from Tudjman's advisor and my conversation with the local policeman. Everyone urged me to get out of Croatia at once.

"But how, is the big question," I said. "It would be pretty risky."

Some thought the whole group, myself included, should leave Croatia next day as a mark of protest. Laki suggested that early in the morning he should drive me back to Slovenia via the same crossing point. Since they'd received a fax allowing me to enter, there should be no problem in my getting out that way.

I realised that it was up to me to decide and that a wrong decision could have disastrous consequences. After so many years, I still vividly remembered the sad fate of the industrialist Vučković from Kotor.

"On consideration," I said, "I think if everybody left in protest, it might make my position worse. And I can't risk going back by the same crossing: the fax may say to let me in but arrest me when I try to leave! I'll have to try to get out at some other crossing, but I'm not sure what would be the safest way of going about it."

"Can we help?" asked John Clark, backed by his wife Thekla. They had US passports and were driving a car with foreign registration plates, so there was a good chance they would not be checked at the border. After thinking it over, I gratefully accepted their offer. There was some risk involved, but I could see no other solution. We drew up our plan of action, with everyone contributing suggestions. It was arranged that John would drive, I would sit in the back, and Thekla would sit beside him, waving their passports with mine sandwiched in the middle. We would cross early in the morning, when the guards were half asleep. The strategy was further refined: Madge and our secretary Maria Seed would drive a rented Renault 4 with Yugoslav plates just ahead of the Clarks' car. This would almost certainly be stopped at the border and the foreign car just behind would probably be waved through. If our plan failed and I was arrested, John and Thekla would drive on to Zagreb and with American diplomatic aid hopefully get me released. After all, General Tudjman was counting on the United States to defend, as he liked to say, "our young Croatian democracy".

The next few hours, when I tried to get some sleep, passed in the same sort of nightmare as before my abrupt departure from Belgrade. I was beginning to understand that what was happening in Yugoslavia was a continuation of what the Partisans had cut short by their victory in 1945. During the war, when the Partisans had been fighting for the ideal of brotherhood and unity, my brother Duško had somehow managed to sneak back into Yugoslavia, only to be murdered by Chetniks. Now, here was I, forty years later, trying to sneak out to avoid arrest, and maybe worse, by heirs of the Ustashas. The Partisans had now withdrawn before the onslaught of nationalism, and the resurrected Chetniks and Ustashas wanted to renew the war and, if possible, win the battles they had lost when fighting on the side of Hitler. They thought it was still not too late to achieve their goals of a greater Serbia and greater Croatia by means of violence and plunder, ethnic cleansing and concentration camps.

At dawn, we set off, making for the frontier crossing in the Mirna river valley. When the Croatian border guards saw the two cars slowly approaching their post, a couple of them came out towards us, scanning the registration plates. With his truncheon, one of them motioned the first car to stop. As the second car slowed down, Thekla leant out the open window, holding out our "American passports" and smiling sweetly, while John at the wheel gave a cheery wave. Touched by this greeting from friendly American tourists, the guards stepped aside and signalled us to pass without stopping.

When we were out of sight on the Slovenian side of the border, John pulled into a lay-by. Before long Madge and Maria joined us, grinning with delight. There was a great deal of hugging and back-slapping. John brought out a bottle of old Istrian *loza* and we all celebrated my latest escape.

It was decided that Madge and Maria should return to Motovun at once, and John and Thekla would drive me to a hotel in Ljubljana, where I would await developments for a day or two.

"Perhaps when I'm out of the way they'll open the house and allow the meeting to go ahead," I said to Madge before leaving. "If that happens, please do what you can to help everyone arrange the display of books and projects, so people can work normally."

"Tell me, Bato, what the Croatian authorities have against you," John asked as soon as we were on the road again.

"Nothing, except that I'm not a Croat. I belong to a different nation – that's my greatest sin. Laki says that on the territory of Croatia only a Croat could be president of the Motovun Group. But besides that, as director general of Yutel I fought for the survival of Yugoslavia and stressed the need for us all to live together."

From Ljubljana John and Thekla at once drove back to Motovun, while from my hotel room I carried on long conversations with Madge, Karel and Jürgen. I was told that, in protest, all the publishers wanted to hold the plenary meeting in the open air in a meadow on the Slovenian side, but I advised strongly against doing anything that would irritate the Croatian authorities. In the hope of salvaging something, I proposed resigning as executive president – the office could simply be abolished – if this meant that the house would be opened and the group could work normally. But the members present voted unanimously against remaining in Croatia under these conditions. It was agreed that the authorities in Zagreb should be contacted again in an attempt to clear up the matter, but on no account should they be allowed to interfere in the group's work and rules. Either all members, whatever their nationality, would be allowed to attend meetings, or the group would look for another, more democratic environment in which to meet. Unfortunately, no amount of persuasion or threats of international repercussions moved the Croatian authorities, and the Motovun House was still sealed when members dispersed five days later.

Getting on a flight to London proved difficult. Ljubljana was crowded with Moslem refugees, driven out of Bosnian towns and villages in areas which Serbian forces wanted to join to Serbia. On the plane I got into conversation with the passenger sitting beside me, an attractive young Moslem woman named Nermina Kamber, until recently president of the district court in the town of Bijelina, close to the Serbian border. To my astonishment, it turned out that her husband was a nephew of Alija Vejzagić, the friend who had come to my aid when I was searching for a job thirty-five years before.

On the flight to London, where her husband and two school-age children had already sought asylum, Nermina described growing up in Bijelina, going to school, playing with Serbian children. Afterwards, at university, her best friends were Serbs, but, in the whole post-war period, few people made any distinction between Moslem and Orthodox.

After graduating in law, she got a job at the court and in time became a judge. Eventually she was made president of the court, ahead of her male colleagues, both Serbs and Moslems. Through her work she got to know a rising young lawyer, Rusmir Kamber, and before long they fell in love. After their wedding before a registrar, the many Moslem and Serb guests celebrated together. Successful in their careers, comfortably off and with two lovely children, their happiness seemed assured until dark clouds of intolerance and hatred began to gather.

One day, when Nermina was alone in their large, beautifully furnished flat overlooking Bijelina's main street, she heard the sound of shooting outside. She ran to the window in time to see men in strange uniforms chasing and seizing a neighbour and then shooting him in cold blood. Horrified by the scene and terrified for her husband and children, she stayed by the window and saw another neighbour suffer the same fate. Soon after Rusmir hurried in with the children and told her the unbelievable news: Moslems were being slaughtered in the town. Arkan had arrived from Belgrade with his *Delije* ('Heroes'). Miloševic and the Army had given them uniforms and weapons and sent them to clear Bijelina of Moslems. They had lists of names and addresses and were going from house to house, liquidating people. All they could do, she said, was to stay locked up in the flat and wait for the orgy of killing to pass.

With curtains drawn and lights off, the Kamber family spent six days in hiding.

By listening to the local radio station, they learnt that Bijelina was now Serbian, and that a Chetnik formation known as the White Eagles was patrolling the town. After six days, when all the Moslem names had been crossed off their lengthy list, Arkan and his 'Heroes' moved on, to clear, in the same way, the corridor towards predominantly Serb-populated Banja Luka. Then, somehow, the Kambers had managed to get out of Bijelina. Nermina didn't know how Rusmir had been overlooked – probably a clerical error on the part of by the new Serbian authorities…

Then I told Nermina what I knew about Arkan and his 'Heroes': how I had been a friend of his fine father, Česo, and the whole Ražnjatović family from Cetinje; how Česo had several times asked Stana to get Arkan out of reformatory, afraid that it would do him more harm than good. Nothing, however, had stopped Arkan from following a life of crime. Not long before all the troubles began, he had been involved in organising a group of supporters of Belgrade's Red Star Football Club to cheer their team on during matches. These self-styled 'Heroes', mostly uneducated and unemployed youths whose main interest in life was their team, were easily manipulated. At Arkan's bidding, their football fanaticism was soon channelled into hatred, plunder and murder in the name of the new Serbian patriotism, with its subculture based on ignorance and vulgarity.

❧

Soon after my return to London, the Croatian state began a war against the Moslems in Bosnia-Herzegovina. In exactly the same way as the Serbs, its troops and paramilitary units cleared towns and villages of their Moslem inhabitants. Now columns of refugees, mainly women and children, were fleeing before Croatian soldiers. Heads of families were separated, taken off to camps, tortured and killed; women and girls in the camps were raped. General Tudjman, like Slobodan Milošević, laid all the blame for this genocide of Moslems on local paramilitary units, unconnected with the government, that had sprung up spontaneously and were out of control. In fact, it was generally believed that long before this Milošević and Tudjman had got together and reached a secret agreement, at the expense of the Moslems, to split Bosnia-Herzegovina between them. Now worried that the Serbs, backed by the Yugoslav Army, would seize more than their agreed share of the territory, Tudjman had decided that he, too, would secure part of Bosnia-Herzegovina by military means. Neither of them, however, counted on the Moslems' readiness to defend their hearths.

Boxing Day 1992. Some twenty people, brought to England by the war in Yugoslavia, have gathered in our home in north London. Among them are Nermina, Rusmir and their children, friends from Croatia, Macedonia, Serbia, Slovenia, Montenegro. We didn't plan it that way, but looking around I realise that every one of the former republics is represented. Seeing them all chatting and joking with one another, I remark sadly to Boris Marelić from Croatia:

"It's hard to imagine, my dear Boris, that for a long time to come so many different nations will get together for a party anywhere in our former homeland. Yet once upon a time this was perfectly normal, so normal you never even noticed the fact."

Through the big bay window I can see dark rain clouds scudding across the sky, driven by the wind from the Atlantic Ocean. One of our Jewish neighbours passes, dressed, as always, in black and wearing a broad, flat fur hat. Two curly locks of hair frame his pale face with its long auburn beard. Beside him walks his wife with the youngest of their six children in a push-chair. The other children, the girls identically dressed, follow close behind. One of the smaller boys wears a sailor suit. They are taking a stroll on the holiday. In a flash I am back in my childhood, walking with my own family on Kosovo Polje, the 'holy land' of the Serbs.

Building of the
headquarters
of Milošević's
party and of his
daughter's radio
station in Belgrade,
after a direct
hit by a NATO
rocket, 1999.
Photo by Dragoljub
Zamurović

Beginning of the End

When Milošević made his fatal decision to ethnically cleanse Kosovo of Albanians with the use of the army, police and paramilitary formations, I decided to return to Belgrade to follow more closely the events that were already greatly alarming people at home and abroad. There was no longer any danger for me personally: eight years had passed and the charges against me were out of date. Yutel was already forgotten and I was not of any interest. All that Yutel had struggled to preserve had been swept away by extreme nationalism.

In Belgrade I spent my time with the same circle of about thirty relatives and friends, all that were left after nearly half a century of life in the capital of the former Yugoslavia. Every day around noon, a number of them would drop in for a coffee or drink and a chat. Some were retired, some were on 'compulsory holiday', others were looking for a job, but with no hope of finding one.

Unlike in the 'old days', when we used to talk about where we were going on holiday, the latest film, play or opera production, the conversation was now mostly about basics: food, heating, transport. The pensioners discussed whether they were getting a full pension this month, or only half, and what date it would be paid. If they got it at all, it would be the one that was due four or five months before. Those who'd been told to stay home on half pay, wondered if they'd receive even this. The ones without a job, scraping by on minimal social assistance with the help of family and friends, felt that they were worse off than either. They were already in their thirties, but none of them were married: they couldn't afford to start a family.

Belgrade, 24 March 1999. The Kosovo crisis was nearing its climax. My visitors anxiously questioned me as someone who was supposed to know about the West's intentions towards Serbia.

"What do you think, Bato, is NATO really going to bomb us because of Kosovo?" asked Pavle, a retired diplomat and a friend since university days.

"If they do," answered my niece Sonja, a bank manager, "our people are ready to hit back. For months now, in complete secrecy they've been moving army installations, military stores and vital institutions, in order to trick NATO in the event of war."

"It's all just empty threats," someone declared. "They daren't attack us. We're stronger than all of them put together."

"That's what they said in Montenegro back in 1941," I added. "Then German tanks overran the whole of Yugoslavia in a week."

"We have to accept, once and for all, that Kosovo belongs to the people who live there, whatever their race or religion," Pavle went on. "The best solution would be to make it a UN protectorate and free Serbia from responsibility for the situation there. Don't you agree, Bato? You were born in Kosovo and you still have relatives there."

"By this evening we'll know for certain whether we're going to be bombed or not," said a friend who had a relative working in the US Embassy.

"I hope NATO know that, if they attack us, in no time the Serbs will start slaughtering and expelling the Albanians, and not a single one will ever return. Kosovo will then be purely Serbian. That's what they've been saying everywhere: in the press, on radio and television," said my niece's husband.

"Well, see you tomorrow!" One of my visitors, an eternal optimist, rose to leave.

"As an experienced soldier, to be on the safe side I'll check my line of retreat," I said jokingly. "I'll find out if there are any planes out of Belgrade this evening, so you may not see me tomorrow."

"Really it would be better if you left," Sonja advised. "You've only just got over a serious operation. If you're stuck here without proper medical care, it'll be the end of you."

When I was left alone, I phoned the owner of a small travel agency I happened to know, who now made a living by selling tickets since there was no longer any tourism in Serbia.

"There are no more flights out of Belgrade," he told me. "All the airlines have suddenly cancelled them."

"How can I leave Belgrade this evening, if I need to?" I asked, trying to sound calm.

"You're in luck, Bato. Our mini-bus is taking some Montenegrin boxers to Budapest Airport. They're supposed to fly to Germany tomorrow for a match. The bus is leaving around six this evening, when they get here from Podgorica. You can go along with them."

"Could the bus leave a bit later, say, eight o'clock in front of my house? By then we'll know the outcome of the talks. If the danger has passed, I'd rather stay here a few days longer, as I originally planned."

"Alright, I'll fix that," my travel agent friend promised. "But be ready to leave from home at eight o'clock sharp. If you decide to stay, they'll just drive straight on – your house is more or less on the way."

Feeling better now I could count on this, I had a rest, not sure I would get to bed that night. Then I started phoning round to relatives and friends to tell them of my plan, but every number was engaged. As soon as I put the receiver down, my phone rang.

"I've been trying to get through for the past fifteen minutes," said my friend with the relative in the US Embassy. "Turn on the television and radio and keep them on. They're already broadcasting warnings to the nation. The Serbian Parliament has voted almost unanimously to reject the demands regarding Kosovo. The Opposition voted with Milošević. The Government has proclaimed the highest state of emergency. When I hear more, I'll call you again."

Time passed slowly for me, alone in the large house. Suddenly it began to get cold. The heating, supplied by a central plant for the whole area, had gone off. I put on the thickest jumper I could find. I turned on both the radio and television and could hardly believe my ears: citizens were being instructed to fill up their baths and all available containers with water; collect together matches, candles and torches in one place; stick adhesive tape across all windows and keep them open; close shutters; keep all first-aid material close at hand; find a safe place for themselves and the children to shelter in the home, and stay indoors. The announcers went on to explain the reasons: the water mains might be damaged, the electricity cut off, windows broken by blast, causing injuries from flying glass…

The telephone rang. It was my niece again, to find out whether I'd heard the warnings:

"Please do as they say, so you're not left without water. Have you taped the windows?"

"How can I tape the windows when I have nine big ones? Anyway, I haven't any Sellotape."

"Let's hope the mini-bus comes, but I'm afraid it may be too late to leave. There are crowds of police in the streets, stopping cars."

Time crawled by. I looked at my watch. It was only just seven. Whatever happened at those talks, I decided, I would leave at eight o'clock. I regretted delaying my departure: by now I could have been well on the way to the border. For the next hour I tried to phone, but every number seemed to be engaged. I packed my medicaments, some food and a bottle of water in my hold-all and waited impatiently for the mini-bus.

Just before eight the same friend phoned again:

"Thank goodness I've got through. The news from the Embassy is bad. Planes are already in the air, heading for Belgrade. Find a safe place in the house to shelter. Perhaps the basement…"

At that point the line went dead. "Hello! Hello!" I shouted, but there was no response or signal. Then the television screen went blank. Only the radio continued to give warnings and instructions.

At the sound of a wailing siren I suddenly felt weak, shivers ran down my spine: I was back in 1941, but then the whole family – Father, Mother and six brothers and sisters – were alive, and now I was alone. In an agitated voice, the newsreader announced that NATO aircraft had begun their "cowardly attack on sovereign, independent Yugoslavia".

At that very moment, I heard explosions. Shocked and scared by this sudden turn of events and the thought of what might follow, I went down into the basement, full of old furniture and books. It was very cold and dark down there. After a while, when I recovered my nerve, I went back upstairs and then outside to see if the mini-bus had arrived. Even if it came now, I doubted if we would be able to get past the airport, let alone reach Novi Sad and Subotica, without being turned back by the police or stopped by the army and the tanks I could hear at that very moment rumbling along the main road a hundred metres away.

From time to time the TV, now working again, showed pictures of huge fires resulting from rocket attacks on Belgrade, Priština, Novi Sad, Subotica, and Podgorica. I had expected Montenegro to be spared in view of its strong opposition to Milošević.

Around ten thirty, when my nerves were near breaking point from the waiting, I at last heard a vehicle stopping and hurried outside. The driver, a young man of about twenty, was getting out of the mini-bus.

"It took us two hours to get through town. I had the radio on. All the time they were telling motorists to leave their cars and take shelter."

Beside the driver sat a man of massive proportions, and behind him a tiny fellow who kept coughing and sneezing.

The big man at once swore at me for stopping them getting away earlier:

"We must get to Budapest Airport by morning, even if we have to walk. We can't miss our match – it was fixed up a month ago. They'd have to give back the ticket money and there'd be no more matches for us. I'm the manager of this bloke here. He's got 'flu, but he'll have to get himself fit by the day after tomorrow."

I said I was all for going, whatever the radio said, but first we needed to agree on a couple of things.

"Have you got enough petrol?" I asked the driver. He said he had a full tank.

"Well, if the police try to stop us, don't slow down, but drive as fast as you can, double flash your long headlights and sound your horn. That's what the police do when they're in a hurry. We'll have to bypass places that are being attacked, and take country roads. In particular we must avoid Subotica; being on the border, it'll be full of police and soldiers."

"That we can't do, pal. We have to stop in Subotica to collect a heavyweight who's coming with us. He's a border cop, but he'll be waiting for us at home."

As soon as we got outside Belgrade, near the airport, a group of police, seeing us coming on the straight road, signalled us to stop.

"What'll I do?" asked the driver in a panic.

"Step on it! Speed up! Headlights and horn!" we all three shouted.

The police stepped aside to let us pass.

"That's the way, my lad!" said the big man, slapping the driver on the back, then turning to me: "You must be from the police if you know their signal."

I said I wasn't.

"Well, then, if you're that clever, you must be a Montenegrin."

"Yes, I am a Montenegrin," I replied.

He leant towards me, put a huge hand around my neck, pulled me towards him and gave me a smacking kiss on the cheek.

"Our Montenegro's small, but we can beat the whole world!" he said with a broad grin. "You with your brains and us with our fists. If you'd been with us today coming from Podgorica, we'd have got to Belgrade much quicker. The Serbian Army was on all the roads. This is a good excuse for them to lean on Montenegro, because we want to break away. We must do that, or the Serbs will always be pushing us around."

"Are you a boxer?" I asked

"I used to be, one of the best. There was nobody could stop me in Germany before I put on weight from that beer of theirs. Just look at me! Like a pig! So now I manage our boxers, like Smajo here, and the cop you're going to see, I hope."

Smajo, sitting behind me on the back seat, was still coughing and sneezing – I could feel the spray on the back of my neck.

"How are you going to fight in that state, Smajo?" I asked, offering him a packet of paper handkerchieves.

"It won't bother me. I've been fighting in Germany for twenty years, and earned good money at it. I can make as much as two thousand marks sometimes."

"That policeman, how can he leave his post on the frontier and go to Germany?" I asked the manager.

"Nothing easier! He goes to the doctor and says he's feeling out of sorts, gets a few days' sick-leave, and goes off to box."

The road to Novi Sad, due north of Belgrade, was empty until we got near the town and saw a convoy of army trucks led by a police escort coming towards us. Behind them, in the distance, tall red flames were licking at the night sky.

"Get off the road quick, and wait for them to pass," I said to the driver, who already had the same idea. "That must be the oil refinery burning."

For almost an hour we waited out of sight of traffic, watching the bright trails of anti-aircraft fire, until the road cleared and we set off again. On the way we left the main road from time to time, drove through villages, and after fully three hours reached Subotica, only about a hundred kilometres north of Novi Sad. Luckily, the boxer lived on the northern outskirts of town, towards the border. It was already four in the morning when we reached his small house and the manager banged on the door. A light went on and a large man appeared in his underwear.

"I'll be right with you, just to get dressed. I thought you'd given up the idea, so I went to bed."

Soon after, wearing a track suit, he climbed in beside me.

"Everything arranged for the match?" he asked. "The Germans haven't cancelled?" The manager reassured him that all was well.

"Now, driver, for the next twenty kilometres to the border, you just keep going and I'll give you directions. We have to go by a roundabout country road. Otherwise we'd never get through. Hundreds of buses, cars and trucks have been waiting to cross for two days."

We drove through the dark along a muddy track, from time to time glimpsing in the distance the lights of an endless column of vehicles motionless on the main road. Finally we emerged right on the border. Behind us stood waiting buses, their lights on, with mothers covering the faces of their sleeping children.

"They're not likely to let that poor crowd into Hungary," said our policeman-boxer. "The big shots left for Budapest in their Mercs a week ago and filled up all the five-star hotels."

He took our passports to his colleagues at the border crossing, shook hands with them, got the passports stamped, then walked across the space to the Hungarian guards. We waited a long time for him to come back, fearful that the Hungarians might have just decided to close the frontier.

"The sods take hours over it," he complained, "look at every page ten times, then type on the computer. They're in no hurry, unlike us."

On the way to Budapest we were stopped twice and had our passports examined. At seven, when we arrived at the airport, we praised our driver and congratulated one another on our safe arrival.

"Good luck in your fights. I hope you win. And you get well by tomorrow, Smajo," I wished them as we parted.

"Don't worry, we will. Montenegrins have always won their battles."

I hurried to the British Airways counter: it was closed. Then I ran from one counter to another. Malev, the Hungarian airline, was the only one with a flight to London.

"We have a plane boarding in half an hour, but it's full, unless someone cancels at the last minute. If you have only hand luggage, you can wait a little, till we find out," the girl at the Malev check-in told me.

The sleepless night with all its alarms and uncertainty had left me completely exhausted, hardly able to stay on my feet. The minutes ticked by. After what seemed an age, the check-in girl beckoned me over:

"Give me your passport. You're very lucky. There's one empty seat."

Sitting in the plane, I began to think back over the past of my country and my family, the two so closely intertwined, and remembered the words spoken by my grandfather many years ago: "Damned Kosovo, how many more times will the Serbs conquer and lose you?"

A year and a half after the NATO bombing, the presidential election was held on 24 September 2000. It was finally clear to all that Milošević had suffered the worst defeat of his despotic reign. For the first time since he came to power in 1987, the people of the rump Yugoslavia (Serbia and Montenegro) had shattered the image of his invincibility. The man who defeated him, Vojin Koštunica, was a little-known constitutional lawyer with nationalist views, leader of the tiny Democratic Party of Serbia. He was chosen as a compromise candidate by eighteen opposition parties, who had at last stopped their squabbles and joined forces to overthrow the common enemy. As he had done in the past, Milošević attempted to falsify the electoral results, demanding a second round of voting. The United Opposition refused, despite a ruling of the pro-Milošević Constitutional Court, which with comic haste changed its decision when it realised the strength of popular revolt.

And, finally, the hopes and prayers of people scattered around the world – refugees from his persecution or the wars he had instigated – and of the great majority of the inhabitants of what was left of Tito's Yugoslavia, were suddenly and unexpectedly answered. Contrary to general belief at home and abroad, this time no amount of Balkan intrigue could save Milošević from the day of reckoning. The Devil had come for his own, as the saying goes.

On 5 October 2000, around one million people, many of them armed, converged on Belgrade from all over Serbia, storming the barricades raised in their way and taking over the Federal Parliament and television. The thirteen years of the most shameful period of Serbian history were over. The dramatic turn of events was welcomed by people not only in Yugoslavia but all over the world.

But the will and resolution of the people alone would not have been enough to achieve this. As the failure of innumerable protest meetings and marches in the past had clearly shown, it was of paramount importance to neutralize the Army and Special Police. For as long as these two pillars of Milošević's regime remained loyal to him, there was no hope of victory. At the crucial moment, some members of the opposition parties managed to strike a secret deal with sections of both the police and the army, securing this neutrality. But their compliance, as it turned out, had a price: protection from the vengeance of the angry crowds for themselves and even for their leader. So, contrary to the general wishes and expectations, Milošević, his police and army chiefs, and other indicted war criminals were not immediately brought to justice, tried at home or handed over to the court in The Hague. They continued for a while to live in government villas, under the protection of their bodyguards and special units.

The Serbs and other peoples of former Yugoslavia were now left to ponder on the rise and fall of Milošević and the tragic consequences of his rule. Unfortunately, he was allowed to wreak destruction for far too long. Behind him he left a terrible legacy: two hundred thousand people dead in a succession of aggressive wars, two million people uprooted by ethnic cleansing, heinous crimes committed inside and outside Serbia, most recently in Kosovo, an economy in ruins, personal savings plundered, wages and pensions slashed, and an area that was among the most prosperous in Eastern Europe turned into a centre of poverty and degradation, complete humiliation and isolation from the civilised world…

But Milošević alone could not have committed all the evils, just as Hitler could not have led Germany into war without the support of the people. For, in the beginning, millions of Serbs, in a fervour of nationalism, voted him into power, enthusiastically embracing the concept of a Greater Serbia – all Serbs living in one state – which could not be realised except by changing existing republican borders and waging war. The fall of the dictator, unfortunately, did not mean the end of nationalism. The Serbian nation, together with its leaders, still had not freed itself of delusions of grandeur, the myth embodied in national folklore, with very little historical basis, that it was a chosen people destined to rule its neighbours. Still, there were many Serbs who realised that the final catharsis would come about when people stopped blaming Milošević for losing the wars and condemned him for starting them: only then would they be able to live in peace with themselves and the world.

The new government ushered in some positive changes, the most important of all being freedom of speech, for so long curbed by Milošević. People now felt free to express their views and opinions without fear of being picked up in the street and disappearing, like Ivan Stambolić, the former Serbian President, and many other less prominent persons who dared to stand in the dictator's way.

On a more personal note: in the intervening decade, ten hard and painful years, among other things I was diagnosed with cancer and underwent an operation to remove my stomach and spleen. With my immune system greatly weakened, I caught, and barely survived, the dreaded 'hospital bug', MRSA, a bacterium resistant to most antibiotics that causes the death of thousands of patients in British hospitals.

After two months in hospital and facing an uncertain future, I found great comfort in recalling my childhood and remembering my large family, now, sadly, no more. I thought of my own and earlier generations of children whose tender years had been spent in wars – those Balkan warrior children. I began to write down my own experiences and the stories recounted so often by my father and grandfathers, first of all so they would not be forgotten and my daughters would know more about my family. Eventually, these writings grew into a book, but it was possible to publish it in Belgrade only after the removal of Milošević.

As the date of publication approached, I grew more and more excited; I couldn't wait to get to Belgrade and Cetinje, where there were to be separate book launches. I was particularly anxious to have this event first in Cetinje: after all, the greater part of the book dealt with my family and childhood in Montenegro.

As we drove from Podgorica towards Cetinje my thoughts returned to 1939 and the old London taxi that had transported my numerous family on this same journey. I thought about my grandfather Filip, dead over sixty years but still vivid in my mind, and the many earlier generations of the Tomašević clan who had fought and died in defence of Montenegro's independence. What would they have thought about its present position? Milošević and the Serbian nationalists had turned it into little more than a province of Serbia. It must throw off this domination and become a sovereign state once again, I was now convinced. Since Yugoslavia was no more, I wanted to be the citizen of a free and independent Montenegro.

Back in the old capital, nearly sixty years since that wintry day when I parted with Olga, I hurried to see our house and the apartment building opposite where she had lived with her parents. The windows were shuttered, just as they had been on that distant day when I returned with my unit from Nikšić. As then, I rushed off to look for Rajko. In the doorway of the modest stone dwelling appeared a shortish, grey-haired man with a neat moustache. Rajko's lively black eyes sparkled as brightly as before. We hugged warmly, gazed at each other for a long time, joked about our changed appearance and exchanged news about our families. After a while, I asked:

"What happened to Olga? Have you ever seen her or heard anything about her?"

"All I know, Bato, is that she's still living in Podgorica. She never comes to Cetinje. I was told she married some Partisan invalid with one leg who was very jealous, mistreated her and made her life miserable. Fortune never smiled on her, poor girl!"

He already knew about the book launch, like many other Cetinje people who listened to the local radio.

"You know, Bato, a lot of our friends have passed away: some from illness, some from idleness and boredom. You remember Pušo – the son of your high-school headmaster who was shot for collaboration? Well, he's dead. And a relative of Raco Vuković told me he also died recently. After he left your house and escaped abroad, he went to Canada and worked all his life in a factory. But I didn't do any better myself. I never got an education: I worked for thirty odd years as a compositor in the local printing house – except for the one year I spent in gaol for being too fond of Stalin!"

Rajko then told me what others of our generation had done in life.

"Some were bus or lorry drivers, some were pen-pushers in the local government offices. Pule, who studied with you in Belgrade, is the only one who's done well. He was an ambassador until he retired. All of them will be in the theatre tomorrow night, and can hardly wait to see you again."

Madge and I took our places at the table on the stage when everyone was seated and the book presentation was about to start. I looked around the auditorium and the balconies. The theatre was packed, every seat filled, as though the people of Cetinje wished in this way to revive their memories of the distant years of war and occupation.

To celebrate our triumphant arrival in Cetinje in 1939, my father had bought front-row seats in this same theatre for himself, my mother and us six brothers and sisters. It was a performance of the historical drama *Balkan Empress* by King Nikola, which in 1888 had opened the Montenegrin National Theatre, built in the ornate style of European theatres of that time. Now, a lifetime later, I was back amidst its red velvet, chandeliers and gilded ornamentation.

The audience were all in their best dresses and the dark suits they kept for special occasions. Recognising childhood friends from Cetinje and my Partisan days, I was deeply moved. The festive atmosphere, speeches and general excitement proved too much for my fragile state of health and I suffered heart failure. Next day Madge and I had to fly back to Belgrade, where I was sent straight to the intensive care ward of the Cardiology Clinic.

As it happened, my admission to hospital occurred two weeks before the US-imposed deadline, 31 March 2001, by which the hesitant Serbian government was to imprison Milošević. Failure to comply would mean that the US Congress would cancel vital aid and block the country's access to important economic and financial organisations. For several weeks already, a group of Milošević's supporters, vowing to prevent his arrest by force if necessary, had been standing guard day and night in front of the presidential residence, which he and his family had still not vacated.

After ten days of treatment in hospital, it was decided I would need a minor operation to slow down and regulate my heart-beat. Before this, I was allowed home for a few days to rest and also to attend the Belgrade launch of my book. Our house was only ten minutes' walk from the large villa protected by high walls where Milošević had gone to ground with several dozen hired bodyguards. Television cameras focused on the fortress-like main gateway through which passed the occasional limousine with tinted glass. The whole surrounding area was overrun with police, who had followed their chiefs in switching allegiance to the new government and were now awaiting the order to arrest the former president.

Tension was high as 31 March dawned. It was a bright, sunny day, ideal for a stroll through this leafy suburb set in parkland. Eager to be involved in some way in this momentous event, albeit only as a witness, I set off along the fashionable residential street towards the villa, avoiding groups of helmeted police armed with automatic rifles and wearing battle fatigues and bullet-proof vests. Somehow I managed to get through unchecked to the first group, perhaps two hundred people, confronting the police. Several older men came over to ask suspiciously where I thought I was going. Taught by Partisan experience never to give anything away, I craftily replied that I had come to see how 'our people' were doing, how many we were, whether we had managed to break through the police cordon around the villa… Assuming, naturally, that I was a hard-core Milošević supporter like himself, one of them put me in the picture:

"All last night we stayed on guard in front of his house, but early this morning a strong police force pushed us back. We broke through their cordon several times, but they managed to push us back again and split us into two groups, to weaken us. But we'll never surrender our president," he confidently assured me.

I next set off to look for this second group, having been advised to make my way through a patch of woodland and so avoid the police. Eventually I came upon a crowd of about the same size which was also being stopped by rows of police from approaching the Milošević villa from the other side. Formulating my question in the same way, I asked a middle-aged man whether 'our people' had broken though the police cordon.

"Not yet," he replied, "but our numbers are growing all the time. The police are keeping us away from that crowd over there. This new government's no better than the old one – the bastards haven't arrested him yet. They ought to leave it to us. We'll string him up on the nearest tree for all he's done to us!"

Then I realised I was not among the second group of Milošević supporters but with a crowd of like-minded citizens. Pleased to hear that their number was rapidly swelling, I set off homeward, quite exhausted from all the excitement. That night, before dawn, Milošević, who had sworn to shoot his family and then himself rather than surrender, gave himself up, reportedly drunk and distraught, and was driven off to gaol.

In the newspapers I was avidly reading on my return to hospital a day or two later, I saw pictures of his infamous wife, Mira Marković, bringing food to her husband in prison. When Madge appeared, as she did daily, carrying lunch for me to supplement the meagre hospital fare, I could not but ponder on life's little ironies.

Appendix
A brief outline of Yugoslav history 1945-2006

The fall of the Berlin Wall on 9 November 1989 and disintegration of the East European system inevitably had far-reaching repercussions in Yugoslavia. Ideologically, the country still belonged to some extent to that system: the League of Communists remained the main cohesive force and sole political party. In many other respects, however, it had deviated from that rigid and oppressive form of government. After the conflict with Stalin in 1948, Yugoslavia gradually adopted the norms of the democratic West with regard to individual freedoms and civil rights. Freedom to travel, for example, which citizens of Eastern Europe gained in the 1990s, was something Yugoslavs had already enjoyed for over a quarter of a century. Visas had been abolished with most countries, and Yugoslavia's frontiers were among the most open in Europe. Relations with Italy, for example, were so good that many millions of Yugoslavs and Italians crossed the border annually.

Throughout the cold war years, the country served as a bridge between East and West. Along with Premier Nehru of India and President Nasser of Egypt, Tito was one of the founders of the non-aligned movement, an alliance of newly independent colonies and other countries that preferred to stay outside military-political blocs. The first conference of the non-aligned, attended by twenty-five heads of state or government, was held in Belgrade in 1961. Yugoslavia was hailed as a country that had successfully solved its 'national question' and served as a model of national and religious equality – the first such example in the war-torn history of the Balkans. It was a state that appeared capable of further reform and democratization that would bring it closer to the West.

Josip Broz Tito led his Partisans and Party to victory in the Second World War primarily because he offered the South Slav peoples and other ethnic groups – regardless of size, race or religion – the prospect of living together at the end of the war as equal partners, unlike in the former Kingdom of Yugoslavia, where the Serbs were the dominant nation.

The wartime promise was fulfilled. The constitution proclaimed in November 1945 made Yugoslavia a federal state in which each of the six republics: Bosnia-Herzegovina, Croatia, Macedonia, Montenegro, Slovenia and Serbia, and the two autonomous provinces within the republic of Serbia (Kosovo and Vojvodina), had its own parliament and government. Their representatives were elected to the Federal Assembly and formed the Federal Government. Josip Broz Tito subsequently became president of Yugoslavia and held that office until his death in 1980. From then on, until the disintegration of Yugoslavia, the country was headed by a collective body, known as the Presidency, composed of one representative of each republic and autonomous province, who took it in turn to serve as head of state for one year.

The republics and provinces enjoyed a high level of autonomy, legislating on all fields of public life except defence, foreign policy and overall economic affairs, which they controlled indirectly, through their representatives in the Federal Assembly, Presidency and Government.

Yugoslavia's 24 million inhabitants were mostly South Slavs speaking closely related languages, all in official use: Serbo-Croatian (since the break-up of Yugoslavia, called Bosnian, Croatian, Montenegrin and Serbian), Slovenian and Macedonian. The Cyrillic script is mostly used in the eastern, Orthodox regions, and the Latin script in the western, Catholic parts of the former Yugoslavia.

Besides the Christian South Slavs, there were some two million Moslems, the majority in Bosnia-Herzegovina, who enjoyed the status of a separate nation. The multi-national mosaic also included nearly two million Moslem Albanians (mostly living in Kosovo), four hundred thousand Hungarians (in Vojvodina) and many other smaller ethnic groups that had settled in the region in various periods: Italians, Turks, Gypsies, Slovaks, Czechs, Romanians, Ruthenians (Ukrainians), Bulgarians… Wherever there was a sizeable population of these minorities, eight-year primary schooling was provided in their languages. The Albanians, Hungarians and Italians also had higher education, up to and including university level, in their own languages, as well as their own press, radio and television stations. In the areas where they were spoken, the minority languages were used in courts, the administration and all forms of communication.

Endeavouring to put an end, once and for all, to centuries of national and religious intolerance, oppression by the stronger of the weaker, pogroms, ethnic cleansing and violence of all kinds, the post-war government adopted an entirely different approach to multi-nationalism. The wealth and beauty of the Yugoslavia Federation, it was constantly asserted, lay precisely in its diversity of peoples, languages, faiths and cultures. In post-war Yugoslavia, any expression of national intolerance was severely punished by law.

It looked as if this historic experiment had succeeded, that the stability of Yugoslavia would ensure lasting peace in the Balkans. But the death of Tito, a strong, charismatic leader, and the subsequent dissolution of the Party resulted in a power vacuum that had to be filled. Nationalism, incited by religious leaders and irresponsible, power-hungry individuals, again reared its ugly head, particularly among the Orthodox Serbs and Catholic Croats, the most numerous of the South Slav nations. To consolidate or increase their power, two former communists, Slobodan Milošević and Franjo Tudjman, took up the Chetnik cause of Greater Serbia and Ustasha cause of Greater Croatia respectively, each aiming to expand their territory at the expense of other Yugoslav nations. The division of Bosnia-Herzegovina, lying between these republics, seemed to offer the easiest option. They did not count on the resistance of the Bosnian Moslems, who saw such a division as a disaster for themselves.

Originally keen to preserve Yugoslavia, the western powers, in the euphoria that followed the fall of the Berlin Wall and collapse of the eastern bloc, threw out the Yugoslav baby together with the bath water. Yugoslavia was consigned to the same heap as the states of the Soviet bloc, to which it did not belong. Germany rushed to recognize the proclaimed secession of Slovenia and Croatia, a move that was soon followed, under German pressure, by other western states.

Using the Army, where ethnic Serbs predominated in the upper echelons, Slobodan Milošević first encouraged the Serbian population in Croatia to rebel, then fought a war with Croatia to secure a corridor linking Serbia with the territory populated by the rebellious Croatian Serbs. To achieve this it was deemed necessary to destroy the attractive baroque town of Vukovar on the Danube, inhabited by equal numbers of Serbs and Croats.

The international recognition of Bosnia-Herzegovina triggered off a fresh conflict begun by Bosnian Serbs urged on by Belgrade. Milošević dispatched 'volunteers' from Serbia who were formed into paramilitary units. Together with the Army they began a campaign of ethnic cleansing, plunder and slaughter of the civilian population. For all this Milošević placed the blame on Moslems, Croats, and paramilitary and army units over which he had no control. The long and bloody war involving Serbs, Moslems and Croats in Bosnia-Herzegovina and Croatia ended with some 250,000 Serbs being driven from the areas of Croatia in which their forebears had lived for centuries by General Tudjman and his army in 'Operation Storm' in August 1995. Most of these are still living as refugees in Serbia. Overt hostilities were concluded by the Dayton Accord signed at the end of 1995. In Milošević, who had made certain concessions at Dayton, the West saw someone who could help to calm the situation in former Yugoslavia, someone it could 'do business with'.

After Dayton, many western envoys journeyed to Belgrade seeking advice and support from Milošević, whose mediation and influence on the Bosnian Serbs was expected to ensure the implementation of the accord, of which he was a signatory. In fact, the West had little choice but to rely on him since the opposition leaders, with very few exceptions, were themselves supporters of a Greater Serbia, fragments of the same nationalism. They, like the majority of the Serbian people, blamed Milošević much more for losing the wars than for starting them.

Freed to a great extent from western pressure after Dayton, Milošević, aiming to boost his rapidly waning popularity, turned his attention again to the situation of the Serb minority in Kosovo, which he had exploited to gain power ten years earlier. The Albanian majority in the province, having been deprived by the Milošević regime of all their former rights, had continued to resist Belgrade. To an increasing extent they fell under the influence and control of extreme nationalists, who saw a chance of creating a Greater Albania comprised of Albania, Kosovo and other predominantly Albanian-populated areas of Serbia, Macedonia and Montenegro. Milošević's efforts to counter this movement and 'cleanse' Kosovo of its ethnic Albanian inhabitants led to the military intervention of NATO, the bombing of Serbia, and the subsequent expulsion of the majority of Kosovan Serbs from the province.

Following his indictment for war crimes by the International Tribunal in The Hague, Milošević's only hope was to hold on to power by whatever means, for without it he faced imprisonment or sudden death. There were plenty of precedents for the latter: 'Black George' Petrović, leader of the 1804 uprising against the Turks was slain by a rival in 1818; King Mihailo Obrenović of Serbia was killed in Belgrade in 1868; King Alexander Obrenović with his wife in 1903; King Alexander Karadjordjević of Yugoslavia in Marseilles in 1934. The Balkans have never been short of conspirators. [In 2003, the energetic and reforming Serbian Prime Minister Zoran Djindjić, who had pledged to combat organised crime, was shot dead while entering his office in Belgrade.]

The chances of Milošević being ousted by democratic elections looked slim, thanks to his control of the Army, the Police, the media and the electoral machinery, as well as his skill in manipulating the ineffectual opposition: some of its leaders were bought, some intimidated, while the rest for a long time seemed incapable of joining forces out of personal vanity or animosity. The former President of Serbia, his one-time friend and patron Ivan Stambolić, was murdered when he was becoming a political threat.

But by the year 2000, so widespread was the discontent with his failures and the country's impoverished, lawless condition, Milošević was finally defeated at the ballot box. His attempt to falsify the election results brought out over a million people in protest and he was finally deposed, eventually arrested and then deported to The Hague.

Following a referendum in 2006, Montenegro severed its union with Serbia and like all the other former republics of Yugoslavia became a sovereign state.

Chronology

6-7th c.	South Slav (Yugoslav) tribes (later differentiated as Serbs, Montenegrins, Croats, Slovenes and Macedonians) settle in the Balkans.
1331-55	Reign of Tsar Dušan the Mighty, when the Serbian empire covers most of the Balkans, from the Danube to the gates of Constantinople.
1389	Defeat in the Battle of Kosovo by the Ottoman Turks, signalling the end of the medieval Serbian empire.
1482	Montenegrin ruler Ivan Crnojević moves his capital from Lake Skadar to the mountain fastness of Cetinje to avoid capture by the Turks. For 500 years Montenegro was the only free land in the Balkans, fighting continuously to maintain its independence.
1804	Serbia, under Karadjordje (Black George) Petrović, rises against the Turks and eventually gains autonomy within the Ottoman Empire as a principality ruled by Miloš Obrenović.
1878	The Congress of Berlin recognises Serbia and Montenegro as sovereign states. Montenegro is ruled by Prince Nikola Petrović (proclaimed king in 1910).
1912	First Balkan War, started by Montenegro and joined by Serbia, Greece and Bulgaria, drives Turkey out of Europe.
1913	Second Balkan War: Serbia, Greece and Montenegro fight and defeat their former ally, Bulgaria, over the division of Macedonia.
1914	Archduke Franz Ferdinand, heir to the Austro-Hungarian throne, is assassinated in Sarajevo by Gavrilo Princip, a Bosnian Serb, an act that triggers off the First World War.

1915	After protracted heroic resistance, the Serbian army withdraws through Montenegro and Albania to the island of Corfu, its rear guarded by the Montenegrin army.
1916	Montenegro capitulates for the first time in its history and is occupied by Austria-Hungary.
1916-18	The Serbian army, together with the western allies, fights on the Salonika front and eventually liberates the country.
1918	The new Kingdom of Serbs, Croats and Slovenes (later renamed Yugoslavia) is created under the crown of Serbia, the largest South Slav nation, from the kingdoms of Serbia and Montenegro and the former Balkan territories of the Austro-Hungarian Empire. King Nikola of Montenegro abdicates.
1934	King Alexander Karadjordjević assassinated in Marseille. His cousin, Prince Paul, becomes regent during the minority of the young King Petar II.
1941	April: Yugoslavia occupied and divided among Germany, Italy and their Hungarian, Bulgarian and Albanian allies. The King and royal government flee the country. July: start of the Partisan guerrilla war against the occupiers under the leadership of Josip Broz Tito.
1945	The Partisan army, with Allied help in the final phase, liberates the country. The monarchy is abolished and replaced by a federal republic comprised of six republics (Bosnia-Herzegovina, Croatia, Macedonia, Montenegro, Serbia, Slovenia) and two autonomous provinces within Serbia (Kosovo and Vojvodina). Josip Broz Tito becomes Prime Minister, later President.
1980	Death of President Tito, followed by the re-emergence of ethnic and religious conflicts.
1991	Slovenia and Croatia secede from the Federal Socialist Republic of Yugoslavia, followed later by Macedonia. Serbs in Bosnia-Herzegovina and Croatia are encouraged by Serbian President Milošević to start a war and ethnic cleansing that results in years of bloodshed and destruction.

1999	NATO bombing of Serbia in response to Milošević's policy towards the ethnic Albanians in Kosovo Province.
2000	24 September, fall of Milošević following electoral defeat.
2001	31 March, Milošević imprisoned in Belgrade; 29 June, extradited to War Crimes Tribunal in The Hague.
2003	The name 'Yugoslavia' is abolished and a loose union named; Serbia and Montenegro is created; Prime Minister Zoran Djindjić assassinated in Belgrade.
2005	Slobodan Milošević dies while on trial in The Hague.
2006	Montenegro becomes a sovereign state following a referendum.
2008	Kosovo proclaims independence from Serbia.

Index